Rousseau and Liberty

In memory of Ralph Alexander Leigh

Rousseau and liberty

edited by
Robert Wokler

Manchester University Press
Manchester and New York
Distributed exclusively in the USA and Canada by St Martin's Press

Copyright © Manchester University Press 1995

While copyright in the volume as a whole is vested in Manchester University Press, copyright in individual chapters belongs to their respective authors, and no chapter may be reproduced wholly or in part without the express permission in writing of both author and publisher.

Published by Manchester University Press
Oxford Road, Manchester M13 9NR, UK
and Room 400, 175 Fifth Avenue,
New York, NY 10010, USA

British Library Cataloguing-in-Publication Data
A catalogue record for this book is available from the British Library

Library of Congress Cataloguing-in-Publication Data
Rousseau and liberty /
    edited by Robert Wokler.
        p. cm.
    Papers originally presented at a colloquium at Trinity College, Cambridge, Sept. 28–30, 1988.
    Includes bibliographical references and index.
    ISBN 0 7190 3510 4 (hbk) — 0 7190 4721 8 (pbk)
    1. Rousseau, Jean-Jacques, 1712–1778 – Contributions in political science.
    2. Liberty.
    I. Wokler, Robert. II. Trinity College (University of Cambridge).

ISBN 0 7190 3510 4 *hardback*
ISBN 0 7190 4721 8 *paperback*

Typeset in Great Britain
by Carnegie Publishing Ltd, Preston

Printed in Great Britain
by Bell and Bain Ltd, Glasgow

Contents

Notes on contributors		vii
Preface		ix
Acknowledgements		xiv
List of abbreviations		xv

Part I Reading Rousseau contextually

1. Rousseau's general will: freedom of a particular kind
   Patrick Riley — 1
2. Hume, Smith and Rousseau on freedom
   Norman Barry — 29
3. Human nature, liberty and progress: Rousseau's dialogue with the critics of the *Discours sur l'inégalité*
   Christopher Kelly and Roger Masters — 53
4. Rousseau and Tocqueville on democratic legitimacy and illegitimacy
   Melvin Richter — 70

Part II Interpreting the *Social Contract*

5. Thinking one's own thoughts: autonomy and the citizen
   Geraint Parry — 99
6. 'Forced to be free'
   John Hope Mason — 121
7. Rousseau, the problem of sovereignty and the limits of political obligation
   John Charvet — 139
8. Eternal vigilance: Rousseau's death penalty
   Felicity Baker — 152

Part III	Locating Rousseau's meanings and significance	
9	Rousseau and his critics on the fanciful liberties we have lost *Robert Wokler*	189
10	'But in a republic, men are needed': guarding the boundaries of liberty *Ursula Vogel*	213
11	Rousseau's theory of liberty † *Maurice Cranston*	231
12	Rousseau's *soi-disant* liberty *Lester G. Crocker*	244
13	Rousseau and totalitarianism – with hindsight? *Iain Hampsher-Monk*	267
	Index	289

† deceased

Notes on contributors

Felicity Baker is a Reader in French in the University of London whose publications include articles on Rousseau and Revolutionary fraternity, and on Lorenzo Da Ponte's libretto for Mozart's *Don Giovanni*. She is currently preparing a monograph on the category of the sacred in the *Social Contract*, and a book, *Don Giovanni's Reasons*.

Norman Barry is Professor of Politics at the University of Buckingham. His books include *Hayek's Social and Economic Philosophy*, *An Introduction to Modern Political Theory* and *Welfare*.

John Charvet is Reader in Political Science at the London School of Economics. He is the author of *The Social Problem in the Philosophy of Rousseau* (1974), *A Critique of Freedom and Equality* (1981), and *Feminism* (1982). A new work is about to be published entitled *The Idea of an Ethical Community* (1995).

Maurice Cranston, who died in November 1993, was Professor of Political Science both at the London School of Economics (1969–85) and at the European University Institute in Florence (1978–81). His many publications include *John Locke: A Biography* (1957), *What are Human Rights?* (1963, 2nd ed. 1973) and two volumes (of a planned three) of a biography of Rousseau (1983, 1991).

Lester G. Crocker, Wm R. Kenan Professor Emeritus, the University of Virginia, has written extensively on Diderot, Rousseau and the Enlightenment. His most recent publication is the Introduction to Blackwell's *Companion to the Enlightenment*.

Iain Hampsher-Monk is Professor of Political Theory at the University of Exeter, and currently (1994–95) Fellow at the National Institute for Advanced Study at the Hague. He is joint founder and editor of the journal *History of Political Thought*. He recently edited and contributed to *Defending Politics: Essays presented to Bernard Crick* (1993) and his *History of Modern Political Thought* (1992) won the Political Studies Association 1994 MacKenzie Book Prize.

John Hope Mason is Senior Lecturer in European Intellectual History at Middlesex University. His publications include books and articles on Rousseau and Diderot; he is currently completing a study of the emergence of the modern value of creativity.

Christopher Kelly is Associate Professor of Political Science at the University of Maryland Baltimore County. He is the author of *Rousseau's Exemplary Life: The 'Confessions' as Political Philosophy* and is co-editor of *The Collected Writings of Rousseau*.

Roger D. Masters is Professor of Government at Dartmouth College. His most recent book is *Beyond Relativism: Science and Human Values*. He is also co-editor of *The Collected Writings of Rousseau*.

Geraint Parry is W. J. M. MacKenzie Professor of Government in the University of Manchester. His most recent publications are *Political Participation and Democracy in Britain* (joint author), *Democracy and Democratization* (joint editor), and he is currently working on a study of educational and political thought.

Melvin Richter, Professor of Political Science, Graduate School and Hunter College, City University of New York, is the author of *The History of Political and Social Concepts. A Critical Introduction* (1995).

Patrick Riley is Professor of Philosophy and Politics at the University of Wisconsin. He is the author of *The General Will Before Rousseau* (1986), of which the Italian edition appeared in 1994. A new work to be published in 1995 is *The Political Philosophy of Leibniz*.

Ursula Vogel is Senior Lecturer in the Department of Government, University of Manchester. She has research interests and publications in the history of political thought with special emphasis on gender and citizenship.

Robert Wokler is Reader in the History of Political Thought in the University of Manchester. He is joint editor of *Diderot's Political Writings*, a three-volume revised edition of John Plamenatz's *Man and Society, Rousseau and the Eighteenth Century* (all 1992) and the forthcoming *Cambridge History of Eighteenth-Century Political Thought*, and author of *Rousseau on Society, Politics, Music and Language* (1987) and *Rousseau* (1995).

Preface

As a major contributor to the *Encyclopédie* and one of the principal victims of official censorship in eighteenth-century Europe, Rousseau was a central figure of the Enlightenment, who espoused liberal and humanitarian principles in confronting the sinister forces of both political and religious despotism. At the same time he was fiercely critical of those institutions and tendencies in modern civilisation which progressive philosophers of his day characteristically applauded, such as the development of the arts and sciences, the growth of commercial society and the establishment of representative government. Perhaps the most radical major political thinker of his century, he at once belonged to the Enlightenment and opposed it, speaking in an idiom which post-modern critics of contemporary culture have sometimes found congenial, even though he was himself drawn to a remote and partly mythical domain of ancient liberty and would have shunned much of the nihilism of post-modernism today. Hostile to all forms of political violence and suspicious of revolutionary fervour, he nevertheless became a patron saint of many of the most militant leaders of the French Revolution, who shared his visceral contempt for the *ancien régime* and were inspired by what they took to be his vision of an alternative world, built afresh from new first principles, cleansed from the ashes of morally corrupt states. No one so appalled by political conspiracies, and so anxious to be untouched by them in his own lifetime, ever exercised so genuine and substantial an influence upon them after his death. If a zealous commitment to first principles can be a real spur to reform, if political ideals can actually give rise to comprehensive social upheaval, the career of Rousseauism, or what was taken to be Rousseauism, in the course of the French Revolution, points the clearest way to the unity of theory and practice in the modern world.

The attachment to Rousseau's ideals of liberty shown by modern romantics and revolutionaries alike has been profound, and at the same time matched by the contempt in which his doctrines are held by conservatives and by liberals of a different denomination, convinced that no one ever subjected freedom to greater abuse. Whatever else may divide them, few of Rousseau's readers have found it possible to remain indifferent to his principles. In this collection, Patrick Riley locates the love of freedom which lies at the heart of Rousseau's political philosophy around his doctrine of the general will above all, which Riley traces to its essentially theological roots in Augustinian and then Jansenist sources. Elucidating the meaning of Rousseau's theory of the general will both with respect to his own notions of autonomy and citizenship and in terms of its connections with and differences from Kant's and Hegel's conceptions of a moral will, Riley concludes that Rousseau's idea of liberty requires that human nature be fundamentally recast along lines made explicit in his theory of education. Norman Barry, by contrast, situates that notion of liberty mainly with reference to Rousseau's pre-eminent contemporaries among philosophers in the English-speaking world, David Hume and Adam Smith. The uncompromising hostility to all forms of personal dependence which Rousseau displayed contrasts with the more empiricist perspectives of these proponents of commercial society, argues Barry, for they recognised, as he did not, that social interdependence might be compatible with freedom, a point made all the more stark by the fundamentally communitarian perspectives embraced in Rousseau's own notion of unconstrained individual preferences.

Christopher Kelly and Roger Masters concentrate instead upon the gestation of Rousseau's idea of freedom in his earlier political writings, particularly in his controversy with the critics of his *Discourse on the Arts and Sciences*, which was to give rise to some of the main themes of his second *Discourse on Inequality*. Addressing themselves principally to Rousseau's exchanges with Voltaire, Charles Bonnet and Georges Leroy, they contend that Rousseau's opposition to dogmatic denunciations of Providence and his adoption of an alternative stance of optimism lent special weight to his notions of human freedom and responsibility. In focusing upon the similarities and contrasts between Rousseau's and Tocqueville's accounts of legitimacy in democracies, Melvin Richter considers Rousseau's conception of egalitarian freedom by way of its institutional abuse under illegitimate government, as perceived by France's most illustrious political thinker of the post-revolutionary era. Remarking upon Rousseau's contempt for Cromwell, whose authority had relied on force, and upon his definitions of tyranny and despotism, which would have embraced the regime of Napoleon, Richter argues that, for all their striking differences, Rousseau and Tocqueville were largely agreed about the nature of despotism; and he suggests that, according to his own strictures, Rousseau would have decried Napoleon's regime, notwithstanding the defence of it which was sometimes offered in terms of a Rousseauist doctrine of popular sovereignty. The general will did not give rise to the general's will.

At the heart of Rousseau's conception of freedom lie two ideals which are essentially at odds, observes Geraint Parry – a commitment to individual autonomy and an equally strong attraction to communitarianism. That tension is evident not only in Rousseau's *Social Contract* but also in his theory of education, which portrays individual self-reliance as conflicting with the requirements of citizenship, and Parry considers how far Rousseau's contrasting objectives can be reconciled, such that a community comprised of citizens who share a common experience can nevertheless encourage creative impulses of exceptional originality. John Hope Mason considers much the same themes in Rousseau's political philosophy with respect to a passage in Book I, chapter 7 of the *Social Contract*, whose apparent confusion of freedom with compulsion has alarmed many of his liberal interpreters. On Hope Mason's reading of the expression 'forced to be free' in the light of related passages elsewhere in the corpus of Rousseau's works, the remark is essentially an inescapable implication of the rule of law, and what appears novel in Rousseau's conception of obedience to law is not that it should make men free but that fully socialised citizens must all be obliged to take part in establishing the rules that bind them.

John Charvet pursues this theme principally in terms of another passage in Book I, chapter 6 of the *Social Contract*, in which Rousseau remarks that subjection to communal law must leave citizens as free as they were before, obedient to themselves alone. According to Charvet, Rousseau ultimately fails in his various attempts to reconcile the supremacy of community principles with the unassailable integrity of individual judgements, for he is required by his own arguments to accept an essentially Hobbesian 'surrender of each person's private judgement to the collective authority of the state', giving rise to a theory of justice best superseded not by Rousseau's strictures but by certain aspects of modern contractarian political philosophy, in the manner of John Rawls and Thomas Scanlon. Felicity Baker addresses the tension between force and freedom in Rousseau's political philosophy with special reference to its rhetoric in the penultimate chapter of the *Social Contract* on the civil religion. Noting other passages in the text in which Rousseau remarks upon Caligula's perception of his own nature, she places Rousseau's treatment of political evil at the heart of his account of a free community and contends that the invocation of the death penalty figures in a people's consciousness of its own identity through its legitimate response to the abuse of its authority by a persecutory prince or leader.

Several of these essays give prominence to the contrast between negative and positive liberty as expounded most particularly by Isaiah Berlin, and that theme is taken up by Robert Wokler mainly in the light of criticism of Rousseau's political philosophy since the French Revolution. Remarking upon commentators who have supposed that Rousseau confused liberty with sovereignty, Wokler argues that moral and civil liberty, as defined in the *Social Contract*, exclude the tyrannies of public opinion and political repression frequently but wrongly ascribed to Rousseau, and he contends that the account of natural liberty so central to his philosophy of history turned his interests largely away from the state and society and drew him instead towards a romantically individualist world of reverie and solitude. With reference above all to the *Letter to d'Alembert on the Theatre* and *Emile*, Ursula Vogel pursues Rousseau's notions of liberty in the light of his views of sexual difference and attraction. The ideals of civic liberty and fraternity which Rousseau espoused in his republican conception of the state depend upon women's exclusion from the public sphere, she argues, while his emphasis upon the complementary nature of man and woman brought together by love establishes an hierarchical relationship of authority which achieves liberty for one sexual partner only at the cost of the subordination of the other. Maurice Cranston addresses his attention to sexual freedom as well, here mainly with reference to the *New Héloïse* and most particularly the *Discourse on Inequality*, where Rousseau notes that the fierce ardour of sexual love in our societies has rendered 'dominant the sex that ought to obey'. In distinguishing various forms of 'freedom lost' from 'freedom acquired' in Rousseau's writings across different disciplines, Cranston shows how his philosophy of history articulates the manifold forms of human servitude which he perceived, although Cranston concludes that economic freedom, about which so much has come to be written after Rousseau's day, was seldom considered by him except with reference to other sorts of freedom.

Inviting readers to consider the institutional framework in which Rousseau's ideals might be exercised, Lester Crocker identifies power rather than liberty as his most pressing concern. Such power was always entrusted to an elite, often of a charismatic kind, Crocker argues, and its purpose, as evidenced in Rousseau's chapter on the legislator in the *Social Contract*, for instance, was to denature man, to regiment behaviour, to form citizens subject to continual surveillance by recasting the pliant clay of human nature. Iain Hampsher-Monk traces contemporary readings of Rousseau's putative collectivism to the epilogue of Vaughan's edition of *The Political Writings of Rousseau*, published at the dawn of English Idealism, when such a doctrine of community could still be deemed more liberal, in a higher sense, than self-interested individualist ideals of natural right. But at least since the end of the First World War, collectivism has come to be discredited as fundamentally illiberal, and Hampsher-Monk explains how Rousseau's doctrines came to be interpreted in terms of current totalitarian regimes, only to acquire fresh topicality in the light of recent attempts to conflate the distinction between negative and positive liberty.

Consensus with respect to either the meaning or significance of Rousseau's reflections on liberty has never been achieved, and we do not aspire to it here. But if we have not settled long-standing disputes about the place of freedom in his political doctrines, we trust that we have at least shed light upon some of their real or apparent obscurities and in certain instances turned them in more pertinent and more profitable directions. A collection of essays marked by its authors' fundamental disagreements with one another may at least express a unanimously shared belief in the importance of our subject and our common conviction that the pursuit and protection of freedom in the modern state and in contemporary civilisation is as pressing a problem for us as it was for Rousseau.

RW

Acknowledgements

This work began as a collection of papers for a colloquium on the subject of 'Rousseau and the Cause of Liberty' held at Trinity College, Cambridge, from 28 to 30 September 1988. To the Liberty Fund Inc., which sponsored that meeting and bore all its expenses, and to Charles King, then its Vice-President and now President, who attended it, our greatest thanks are due. The colloquium was conceived in part to mark the culmination of the fifty-volume set of the *Correspondance complète de Rousseau* by its editor, R. A. Leigh, a Fellow of Trinity College, who was chiefly responsible for the agenda of our programme and for domestic arrangements with his College Council. Together with Peter Jones, Director of the Institute for Advanced Studies in the Humanities at the University of Edinburgh, Leigh was also due to have presided over our meeting. But he died suddenly in December 1987, and his responsibilities accordingly fell in part to me and, within the College, to Peter Laslett, who acted both as our host and as a participant. To Dr Laslett and the Master and Fellows of Trinity College, Cambridge, we owe a debt of gratitude. To Professor Jones, whose industry on behalf of us all proved boundless, our special thanks are due. In other circumstances, if his diverse commitments permitted it, he would have been joint editor of this volume. Not all the participants of our colloquium were able to complete texts for publication, but those that could not – including John Gray, Ronald Hamowy, Terence Marshall and Yves Michaud – may be persuaded that certain themes in some of these papers have been designed to meet provocative points which they raised, so that the vigorous oral exchanges of our meeting still inform our printed words. For retyping so much of the material in the format and language required, and for her painstaking efforts on our behalf in so many unforeseen ways, we are grateful to Marilyn Dunn. For steering this volume through its stages of production, our thanks are also due to Richard Purslow, Celia Ashcroft and Rebecca Crum at the Manchester University Press.

List of abbreviations

Leigh   *Correspondance complète de Jean-Jacques Rousseau,* édition critique, établie et annotée par R. A. Leigh, Geneva and Oxford (The Voltaire Foundation), 1965–

Pléiade   *Oeuvres complètes de Jean-Jacques Rousseau,* ed. Bernard Gagnebin, Marcel Raymond *et al.*, Paris (Bibliothèque de la Pléiade), 1959–

Vaughan   *The Political Writings of Jean-Jacques Rousseau,* ed. C. E. Vaughan, Cambridge (Cambridge University Press), 1915, reprinted Oxford (Blackwell), 1962

Part I

Reading Rousseau contextually

1 Patrick Riley

Rousseau's general will: freedom of a particular kind

I

Had Rousseau not been centrally concerned with freedom – above all with the voluntariness of morally legitimate human actions – some of the structural features of his political thought would be (literally) unaccountable. Above all, the notion of *general will* would not have become the core idea of his political philosophy: he would just have spoken, *à la* Plato, of achieving perfect *généralité* through civic education, as in *Republic* 462b ('do we know of any greater evil for a state than the thing that distracts it and makes it many instead of one, or a greater good than that which binds it together and makes it one?'),[1] or would have settled for Montesquieu's republican *esprit général*;[2] he would never have spoken of generalizing the *will* as something central but as difficult as squaring the circle – difficult because one must 'denature' particularistic beings without destroying their (ultimate) autonomy. But one must (for Rousseau) have *volonté générale*, not a mere *esprit général*: for 'to deprive your will of all freedom is to deprive your actions of all morality,' and 'civil association is the most voluntary act in the world.'[3] That voluntarist side of Rousseau is brought out best by Judith Shklar, who has argued persuasively that the notion of general will 'conveys everything he most wanted to say' precisely because it is 'a transposition of the most essential individual moral faculty [volition] to the realm of public experience.'[4] (By contrast Bronislaw Baczko, in his mainly splendid essay, 'Moïse, législateur . . .,' over-stresses *généralité* at the expense of *volonté*: 'The highest political achievement [on the part of Moses or Numa or Lycurgus] is that of attaching the citizen to his state by indissoluble bonds, such that love of his country shapes his whole existence.'[5] In Rousseau one needs not just *amour*, but *volonté*; it is not just a matter of quasi-Platonic erotic *ascent*, in the manner of Phaedrus.[6])

Moreover: were not generalized will – a will of a very particular kind – essential in Rousseau, the Great Legislator would not have to achieve his civic results (in *Du contrat social* II, 7) by such tortured means – such as 'compelling without violence' and 'persuading without convincing'.⁷ Plato (again) didn't worry about this kind of difficulty because the philosopher-king simply knew the eternal verities such as 'absolute goodness' (*Phaedo* 75d) which even the gods know and love (*Euthyphro* 10d–e) and therefore deserved to educate and rule (*Republic* IV); for Rousseau what is needed for perfect politics (*Du contrat social* II, 6) is 'a union of will and understanding',⁸ so that the Great Legislator's civic knowledge is finally, at the end of civic time, *absorbed* into an (originally ignorant) popular general will which is ultimately as 'enlightened' as it was always 'right'.⁹ (If Aristotle's critique of *Protagoras* is correct, Plato lacked any adequate notion of volition;¹⁰ but one can only generalize a 'will' that actually exists.)

Here the history of 'the general will' before Rousseau is illuminating. In Rousseau, the general will is non-natural: it is artificially produced (over time) through the 'denaturing', counter-egoistic educative ministrations of Lycurgus or Moses – though at the end of education informed, independent choice must finally be possible (as Emile ultimately says, 'I have decided to be what you made me').¹¹ But in the seventeenth century inventors of *volonté générale* – Arnauld, Pascal, Malebranche, Fénelon, Bayle, Leibniz – the general will of God (to 'save all men' after the Fall)¹² is *naturally* general: how could one 'denature' or transform the will of a perfect being, make him 'become' over time what he 'naturally' was not? (For Malebranche, e.g. the 'generality', uniformity and simplicity of God's [Cartesian] operation expresses his perfection: 'God acts by *volontés générales* . . . in order to construct or to preserve his work by the simplest means, by an action that is always uniform, constant, perfectly worthy of an infinite wisdom and of a universal cause . . . to act by *volontés particulières* shows a limited intelligence . . . little penetration and breadth of mind.'¹³) Rousseau – who knew intimately the entire seventeenth-century controversy over 'general will'¹⁴ – knew too that a non-divinity must be (to revise a phrase) 'forced to be general'. But that non-divinity's freedom must finally arrive, as a child (in *Emile*) finally becomes what it was not. Indeed the central problem of all Rousseau's thought is to find a form of non-authoritarian educative authority which will 'make men what they ought to be' (*Economie politique*)¹⁵ without (permanently) depriving them of the freedom without which 'neither virtues, nor vices, nor merit, nor demerit, nor morality in human actions' is conceivable (*Lettre à M. de Franquières*, 1769).[16]

None the less, even if Rousseau's aim is to 'generalize' will over time without destroying freedom – which makes it crucial that he find a non-authoritarian authority that can 'compel without violence' – one can say that Rousseau has a more difficult time in *reconciling* freedom and 'what men ought to be' than (most notably) Kant; and here a comparison with Hegel will also be helpful. Rousseau, Kant and Hegel – separated by whole universes as they are – are all *voluntarists* who make 'will' ethically weighty (in the shape of 'general will', 'good will', and [so-called] 'real will'[17]). All three are in search of a non-willful will; all are in full flight from capricious *volonté particulière*, from what Shakespeare calls 'hydra-headed willfulness' (*Henry V*, I, i).[18] But for Rousseau the flight from egoism and *amour propre* ends at the border of Sparta (with the 'Spartan mother' on the opening page of *Emile*), while for Kant one 'ought' to move on to a universal Kingdom of Ends or (failing that) at least to universal republicanism and eternal peace.[19] But Kant more easily preserves freedom/autonomy than Rousseau – or Hegel, who wants our 'real' will to be 'recognition' of the state as rational freedom concretely *realized*[20] – because what 'generalizes' (or rather universalizes) will is reason-ordained 'objective ends', not Lycurgus (or *Bildung*). What moves us away from 'pathological' self-love, for Kant, is not a denaturing civic education within Spartan or Roman borders, but simply 'seeing' – at the 'age of reason' – a moral law which (as a 'fact of reason'[21]) is just *there*. It is no accident that education (domestic and civic) is everything in Rousseau (and nearly everything in Hegel),[22] and (nearly) nothing in Kant: if 'ought' is a fact of reason, Moses' heroic efforts are superfluous (and possibly autonomy-endangering). Rousseau, of course, doubted that there could be a reason-ordained *morale universelle*; for him the crucial line should be drawn *between* the 'general' and the 'universal', the *polis* and the *cosmopolis*. Doubting (in advance of Kant) that a 'Kantian' *kind* of autonomy was possible, Rousseau set himself the daunting task of generalizing will without recourse to 'objective ends' – but *with* recourse to educative authority whose highest ambition is to wither away after injecting its (civic, 'politan') knowledge into beings who become free in the course of time.

In what follows there will be, first, an examination of the (particular) way in which Rousseau generalizes *volonté* – leaving it (he hopes) free but not willful; and second, a fuller comparison of Rousseau and Kant (and also Hegel) which will try to determine which of these three great modern voluntarists does best in 'canceling and preserving'[23] the will.

II

Rousseau's reasons for using 'general will' as his central political concept were essentially philosophical – however read-made for his purposes the seventeenth-century theological notion may have been. (Does not the Spartan mother have a *volonté générale* to 'save' the city, as God has a general will to save 'all men'?) After all, the two terms of *volonté générale* – 'will' and 'generality' – represent two main strands in Rousseau's thought. 'Generality' stands, *inter alia*, for the rule of law, for civic education that draws us out of ourselves and toward the general (or common) good, for the non-particularist citizen-virtues of Sparta and republican Rome.[24] 'Will' stands for Rousseau's conviction that civil association is 'the most voluntary act in the world', that 'to deprive your will of all freedom is to deprive your actions of all morality.'[25] And if one could 'generalize' the will, so that it 'elects' only law, citizenship, and the common good, and avoids 'willful' self-love, then one would have a general will in Rousseau's particular sense. The (originally divine) *volonté générale* of Pascal, Malebranche, Fénelon and Leibniz corresponded closely to these moral aims: hence why not employ a term already rendered politically usable by Bayle in the *Pensées diverses sur la comète*?[26]

It is scarcely open to doubt, indeed, that the notions of *will* and *generality* are equally essential in Rousseau's moral and political philosophy. Without will there is no freedom, no self-determination, no 'moral causality' (*Première version du contrat social*),[27] no obligation; without generality the will may be capricious, egoistic, self-obsessed, willful.

Rousseau shared with modern individualist thinkers (notably Hobbes and Locke) the conviction that all political life is conventional, that it can be made obligatory only through voluntary, individual consent. Despite the fact that he sometimes treats moral ideas as if they simply 'arise' in a developmental process, in the course of socialization (*Lettre à M. de Beaumont*),[28] he often – particularly in his contractarian vein – falls back on the view that the wills of free men are the 'causes' of duties and of legitimate authority. Thus in an argument against slavery in *Du Contrat social*, Rousseau urges that 'to deprive your will of all freedom' is to deprive your actions of 'all morality', that the reason one can derive no notion of right or morality from mere force is that 'to yield to force is an act of necessity, not of will.[29] (This shows in advance how carefully one must interpret the *deliberately* paradoxical phrase, 'forced to be free'.) In *Inégalité*, in a passage that almost prefigures Kant, he insists on the importance of free agency, arguing that while 'physics' (natural science) might explain the 'mechanism of the senses', it could never make intelligible 'the power of willing or rather of choosing' – a power in which 'nothing is to be found but acts which are purely spiritual and wholly inexplicable by the laws of mechanism.'[30] It is this power of freely willing, rather than reason, which distinguishes men from beasts. In the (unpublished) *Première version du contrat social* he had even said that 'every free action has two causes which concur to produce it: the first a moral cause, namely the will which determines the act; the other physical, namely the power which executes it.'[31] Rousseau, then, not only requires the Kant-anticipating idea of will as 'moral causality'; he actually uses that term.

All of this is confirmed by what Rousseau says about will in *Emile*, in which he argues (through a speech put into the mouth of the Savoyard Vicar) that 'the motive power of all action is in the will of a free creature', that 'it is not the word freedom that is meaningless, but the word necessity'. The will is 'independent of my senses': I 'consent or resist, I yield or I win the victory, and I know very well in myself when I have done what I wanted and when I have merely given way to my passions.' Man, he concludes, is 'free to act', and he 'acts of his own accord'.[32] Moreover, human free will does not derogate from Providence, but magnifies it, since God has 'made man of so excellent a nature, that he has endowed his actions with that morality by which they are ennobled.' Rousseau cannot agree with those theologians (for example, Hobbes) who argue that human freedom would diminish God by robbing him of his omnipotence: 'Providence has made man free that he may choose the good and refuse the evil . . . what more could divine power itself have done on our behalf? Could it have made our nature a contradiction and have given the prize of well-doing to one who was incapable of evil? To prevent a man from wickedness, should Providence have restricted him to instinct and made him a fool?'[33]

To be sure, the pre-Kantian voluntarism of *Emile* and of *Inégalité* is not the whole story; even in the *Lettres morales* (1757), which were used as a quarry in writing *Emile*, the relation of free will to morality is complicated and problematical. The opening of the fifth *Lettre* – 'the whole morality of human life is in the intention of man'[34] – seems at first to be a voluntarist claim, almost prefiguring Kant's notion in the *Grundlegung* that a 'good will' is the only 'unqualifiedly' good thing on earth.[35] But this *intention* refers not to the 'will' of *Emile*, but rather to 'conscience' – which is a 'divine instinct' and an 'immortal and heavenly voice'. Rousseau, after a striking passage on moral feelings ('if one sees ... some act of violence or injustice, a movement of anger and indignation arises at once in our heart'), goes on to speak of feelings of 'remorse' which 'punish hidden crimes in secret'; and this 'importunate voice' he calls an involuntary feeling (*sentiment involontaire*) which 'torments' us. That the phrase *sentiment involontaire* is not a mere slip of the pen (or of the mind) is proven by Rousseau's deliberate repetition of 'involuntary': 'Thus there is, at the bottom of all souls, an innate principle of justice and of moral truth [which is] prior to all national prejudices, to all maxims of education. This principle is the involuntary rule [*la règle involontaire*] by which, despite our own maxims, we judge our actions, and those of others, as good or bad; and it is to this principle that I give the name conscience.' Conscience, then, is an involuntary moral feeling – not surprisingly, given Rousseau's view that 'our feeling is incontestably prior to our reason itself.'[36] And so, while the fifth *Lettre morale* opens with an apparent anticipation of *Emile*'s voluntarism, this is only an appearance which proves that it is not straightforwardly right to 'find' in Rousseau a predecessor of Kant. Rousseau's *morale sensitive* (one strand of his thought) is not easy to reconcile with rational self-determination (another, equally authentic, strand) – for if Rousseau says that 'to deprive your will of all freedom is to deprive your actions of all morality', he also says that conscience is a *sentiment* which is *involontaire*.

The fact remains, however, that while *Emile* was published, the *Lettres morales* were held back. (Perhaps Rousseau anticipated the judgement of Bertrand de Jouvenel that 'nothing is more dangerous' than the sovereignty of a conscience which can lead to 'the open door to subjectivism'[37] – a judgement no less effective for being borrowed from Hegel's attack on Lutheran 'conscience' in the *Phenomenology*.[38]) And in *Emile* Rousseau insists on the moral centrality of free will: so much for the supposed 'Calvinism' of one who was (often) closer to being a Pelagian – as Pascal would have pointed out.[39] Hence Rousseau can understand 'will' as an independent moral causality with the power to produce moral effects. He definitely thought that he had derived political obligation and rightful political authority from this 'power' of willing: 'Civil association is the most voluntary act in the world; since every individual is born free and his own master, no one is able, on any pretext whatsoever, to subject him without his consent.' Indeed, the first four chapters of *Du contrat social* are devoted to refutations of erroneous theories of obligation and right – paternal authority, the 'right of the strongest' (*à la* Thrasymachus), and obligations derived from slavery. 'Since no man', Rousseau concludes, 'has natural authority over his fellow men, and since might in no sense makes right, [voluntary] convention remains as the basis of legitimate authority among men.'[40]

Even if 'will' is plainly a central moral, political and theological notion in Rousseau, this does not mean that he was willing to settle for just any will – such as a particular will or a 'willful' will. His constant aim, indeed, is to 'generalize' will[41] – either through civic education, as in the *Gouvernement de Pologne*, or through private education, as in *Emile*. In his view, ancient societies such as Sparta and Rome had been particularly adept at generalizing human will: through their simplicity, their morality of the common good, their civic religion, their moral use of fine and military arts, and their lack of extreme individualism and private interest, the city-states of antiquity had been political societies in the proper sense. In them man had been part of a greater whole from which he 'in a sense receives his life and being';[42] on the other hand, modern 'prejudices', 'base philosophy' and 'passions of petty self-interest' assure that 'we moderns can no longer find in ourselves anything of that spiritual vigor which was inspired in the ancients by everything they did' (*Pologne*).[43] And that 'spiritual vigor' may be taken to mean the avoidance – through identity with a greater whole – of 'that dangerous disposition which gives rise to all our vices', self-love. Political education in an extremely unified ('generalized') state will 'lead us out of ourselves' and provide us with a general will before the human ego 'has acquired that contemptible activity which absorbs all virtue and constitutes the life and being of little minds (*Economie politique*).[44] It follows that the best social institutions 'are those best able to denature man, to take away his absolute existence and to give him a relative one, and to carry the *moi* into the common unity' (*Emile*).[45]

If these reflections on the pernicious character of self-love and particularism are reminiscent of Malebranche – who had urged that 'to act by *volontés particulières* shows a limited intelligence',⁴⁶ and whose love for divine *généralité* had led Rousseau to rank the great Oratorian Father with Plato and Locke⁴⁷ – it is in contrasting Rousseau with Malebranche that an important difficulty arises. In Malebranche, God's will is essentially and naturally general; in Rousseau, men's will must be *made* general – a problem which he likens (in the correspondence with Malesherbes) to that of squaring the circle.⁴⁸ But one can reasonably ask: is will still 'will' (*qua* independent 'moral cause') if it must be denatured, transformed? Do Rousseau's notions of education – private and civic – leave will as the autonomous producer of moral 'effects' that he seems to want? One is tempted to say that this is *the* question for one who wants *volonté* and *généralité* to fuse – so that (at the end of time) a perfect '*union* of will and understanding' will synthesize (Lockean) 'voluntary agreement' and (Platonic) generalizing education, will blend antiquity ('Sparta') and modernity ('contract') in this 'modern who has an ancient soul.'⁴⁹

To retain the moral attributes of free will while doing away with will's particularity and selfishness and 'willfulness' – to generalize this moral 'cause' without causing its destruction – is perhaps the central problem in Rousseau's political, moral and educational thought, and one which reflects the difficulty Rousseau found in making free will and rational, educative authority coexist in his practical thought. Freedom of the will is as important to the morality of actions for Rousseau as for any voluntarist coming after Augustine's insistence (*De Libero Arbitrio*) that *bona voluntas* alone is good;⁵⁰ but Rousseau was suspicious of the very 'faculty' – the only faculty – that could moralize. Thus he urges in the *Economie politique* that 'the most absolute authority is that which penetrates into a man's inmost being, and concerns itself with his will no less than with his actions.'⁵¹ Can the will be both an autonomous 'moral cause' and subject to the rationalizing, generalizing effect of educative authority? This is Rousseau's constant difficulty. Even Emile, the best-educated of men, chooses to continue to accept the guidance of his teacher: 'Advise and control us; we shall be easily led; as long as I live I shall need you.'⁵² How much more, then, do ordinary men need the guidance of a 'great legislator' – the Numa or Moses or Lycurgus of whom Rousseau speaks so often⁵³ – when they embark on the setting up of a system which will not only aid and defend but also moralize them! The relation of will to authority – of autonomy to educative 'shaping' – is one of the most difficult problems in Rousseau. The general will is dependent on 'a union of understanding and will within the social body':[54] but that understanding, which is provided (at least initially) by educative authority – rather than by a Kantian 'fact of reason' giving 'objective ends' – is difficult to make perfectly congruent with 'will' as an autonomous 'moral cause'.

This notion of the relation of educative authority to will appears not just in Rousseau's theories of public or civic education (particularly in the *Economie politique* and the *Gouvernement de Pologne*[55]), but also in his theory of private education in *Emile*. In educating a child, Rousseau advises the tutor, 'let him think he is master while you are really master.' And then: 'there is no subjection so complete as that which preserves the forms of freedom; it is thus that the will itself is taken captive.'[56] One can hardly help asking what has become of 'will' when it has been 'taken captive', and whether it is enough to preserve the mere 'forms' of freedom. On this point Rousseau appears to have been of two minds: the poor who 'agree' to a social contract that merely legitimizes the holdings of the rich 'preserve the forms of freedom', but Rousseau (in *Inégalité*) dismisses this contract as a fraud.[57] Thus it cannot be straightforwardly the case – as John Charvet argues in his remarkable Rousseau study – that the *citoyen de Génève* simply was not 'worried by the gap which opens up between the appearance and the reality of freedom.'[58] And yet Charvet has something of a point, since will is 'taken captive' in *Emile* and 'penetrated' by authority in the *Economie politique*; and neither that captivity nor that penetration is criticized by Rousseau – despite his *dictum* about depriving one's actions of all morality if one deprives his will of 'freedom'. So one sees again why a general will would appeal to him: capricious willfulness would be 'canceled', will rationalized by authority, 'preserved'.[59]

If will in Rousseau is generalized primarily through an educative authority, so that volition as 'moral cause' is not quite so free as he would sometimes prefer, it is at least arguable that any tension between 'will' and the authority that 'generalizes' it is only a *provisional* problem. Rousseau seems to have hoped that at the end of political time (so to speak) men would finally be citizens and would will only the common good in virtue of what they had learned over time; at the end of civic time, they might actually be free, and not just 'forced to be free'.[60] At the end of its political education – no *more* 'denaturing' than any education – political society would finally be in a position to say what Emile says at the end of his 'domestic' education: 'I have decided to be what you made me.'⁶¹ At this point (of 'decision') there would be a 'union of understanding and will' in politics, but one in which 'understanding' is no longer the private possession of a Numa or a Lycurgus. At this point, too, 'agreement' and 'contract' would finally have real meanings: the 'general will', which is 'always right', would be enlightened as well, and contract would go beyond being the mere rich man's confidence-trick (legalizing unequal property) that it is in *Inégalité*. At the end of political time, the 'general will one has as a citizen' would have become a kind of second nature, approaching the true naturalness of *volonté générale* in Malebranche's version of the divine *modus operandi*. 'Approaching', however, is the strongest term one can use, and the relation of will to the educative authority that generalizes it remains a problem in Rousseau – the more so because he often denied (in his more Lockean moods) that there is any natural authority on earth.⁶²

One can still ask: how can one reconcile Rousseau's insistence on an all-shaping educative authority with his equal insistence on free choice and personal autonomy ('civil association is the most voluntary act in the world')? A possible answer is: *through* his theory of education, which is the heart of his thought – the one thing which can make Rousseauianism 'work'. At the end of civic time, when men have been denatured and transformed into citizens, they will finally have civic knowledge and a general will – just as adults finally have the moral knowledge and the independence that they (necessarily) lacked as children. For Rousseau there are unavoidable stages in all education, whether private or public: the child, he says in *Emile*, must first be taught necessity, then utility, and finally morality, in that inescapable order; and if one says 'ought' to an infant he simply reveals his own ignorance and folly. This notion of necessary educational time, of *becoming* what one is not – Aristotelian potentiality-becoming-actuality, transferred from *physis* to the *polis* – is revealed perfectly in Emile's utterance, 'I have decided to be what you made me.'⁶³ That is deliberately paradoxical (as many of Rousseau's central moral-political beliefs are cast in the form of paradoxes); but it shows that the capacity to 'decide' is indeed 'made'. (It is education that 'forces one to be free' – by slowly 'generalizing' the will.) Similarly, Rousseau's 'nations' are at first ignorant: 'There is with nations, as with men, a time of youth, or, if you prefer, of maturity, for which we must *wait* before subjecting them to laws.'⁶⁴ Waiting, however, requires time; autonomy arrives at the end of a process, and the general will is *at last* as enlightened as it was (always) right. On the most favorable reasonable reading, then, Rousseau does not, as some critics allege, vibrate incoherently between Platonic education and Lockean voluntariness;[65] if his notion of becoming-in-time works, then the *généralité* of antiquity and the *volonté* of modernity are truly fused by this 'modern who has an ancient soul'.

III

In the end, the 'generality' cherished (variously) by Pascal, Malebranche, Fénelon, Bayle and Rousseau turns out to occupy a place midway between *particularity* and *universality*; and that *recherche de la généralité* is something distinctively French. This becomes visible if one contrasts French moral-political *généralisme* with the thought of Kant, viewed as the perfect representative of German rationalistic universalism ('I am never to act otherwise than so that I could also will that my maxim should become a universal law . . . reason extorts from me immediate respect for such [universal] legislation'[66]), and with that of William Blake, seen as a typical representative of English ethical 'empiricism':

> He who would do good to another
> must do it in Minute Particulars,
> General Good is the plea
> of the scoundrel, hypocrite and flatterer.[67]

The discovery of an *ethos* that rises above 'minute particulars', that moves toward universality but has its reasons (*le coeur a ses raisons*) for not building on reason, and for drawing up short at a more modest *généralité* – the advocacy of a kind of (free) willing that is more than egoistic and self-loving and *particulière* but less than a Kantian, universal, 'higher' will[68] – that is the distinctively French contribution to practical thought worked out by Rousseau, who socialized the 'general will' bequeathed to him by his greatest French predecessors. The genesis of 'general will' is in God; the creation of the political concept – yielding a covenant and a law that is a mosaic of the Mosaic, the Spartan, the Roman, and the Lockean – is the testament of Rousseau.

But why should Rousseau – unlike Kant – have drawn the dividing line between *généralité* and *universalité*, between the *polis* and the *cosmopolis*, between the 'citizen' and the 'person'? And why does this particular 'placing' of the line make it visibly easier for Kant to *reconcile* freedom with 'what men ought to be' than for Rousseau? Here a fuller Rousseau-Kant comparison will be helpful; and after that a contrasting of Rousseau and Kant with Hegel may be illuminating.

No one has ever doubted that Kant begins his moral philosophy with an insistence on 'good will'[69] – that is, with the idea of a 'moral causality' (owed to Rousseau), itself independent of natural causality, which is the foundation of man's freedom and responsibility. That good will is crucial to Kant's understanding of politics is quite clear: 'public legal justice' is necessitated by the partial or total absence of a good will that would yield, if it could, a non-coercive, universal 'ethical commonwealth' (or 'kingdom of ends') under laws of virtue. Good will's absence necessitates politics' presence. And the *idea* of an ethical commonwealth generated by good will serves as a kind of utopia that earthly politics can 'legally' approximate through eternal peacefulness, both internal and international.[70]

Kant was by no means the first moral philosopher to insist that a good will is the only unqualifiedly good thing on earth; on this point he simply reflects and repeats St Augustine's *De Libero Arbitrio* I, 12, which argues that a *bona voluntas* is 'a will by which we seek to live a good and upright life' and that 'when anyone has a good will he really possesses something which ought to be esteemed far above all earthly kingdoms and all delights of the body.'[71] (This is remarkably 'pre-Kantian': indeed one can wonder whether Kant's kingdom of ends was not suggested by Augustine's denigration of earthly kingdoms.) But Kant, given his radical distinction between 'pathology' and morality, could not have accepted Augustine's further notion of moral 'delectation', could never have said, with Augustine, that the 'man of good will' will 'embrace' rightness as the 'object of his joy and delight'.[72] The Augustinian notion of opposing higher 'delectations' to lower ones, so that 'concupiscence' is replaced by the love of temperance, prudence, justice, ultimately *God* – by quasi-Platonic sublimated (made-sublime) erotism (as in the *Phaedrus*[73]) – is alien to Kant (though not always to the Rousseau who could speak of *morale sensitive*). If, then, Kantian good will is not an Augustinian *delectio*, or 'higher' love, what is it? If it is not to be 'pathological', it must surely be the capacity to determine oneself to action through what ought to be, so that 'ought' is the complete and sufficient incentive. And if what ought to be is defined as respect for persons as members of a kingdom of ends, then Kantian good will will mean 'determining oneself to act from respect for persons.'[74] Surely this is a reasonable way to read

Kant's moral philosophy; for at the outset one cannot know exactly what post-Augustinian *bona voluntas* actually involves.

If, however, good will begins in Augustinianism, Kant, in insisting on will as a kind of undetermined 'moral causality' is still more closely related to Rousseau – who, as was seen, had actually urged (in the *Première version du Contrat social*) that 'every free action has . . . a moral cause, namely the will which determines the act.'[75] And Rousseau had also insisted – in an already-examined passage from *Inégalité* – that while 'physics' might explain the senses and empirical ideas, it could never explain 'acts which are purely spiritual and wholly inexplicable by the laws of mechanism': above all 'the power of willing or rather of choosing', and 'the feeling of this power'.[76] All of this – will as free 'moral cause', as something spiritual and not mechanically determined – Kant could and did applaud. But then Rousseau had gone on to say (in *Inégalité*) that one must draw a line between 'free agency' and 'understanding'; that 'if I am bound to do no injury to my fellow-creatures, this is less because they are rational than because they are sentient beings.'[77] And this Kant could not accept at all. In Kant's view, if the duty not to injure others rests on 'sentience', then one can have duties only if one feels (and sympathizes with) the pains and pleasures of sentient beings. For Kant this is a calamitous view of morality: it makes duty a mere reflection of psychological facts (feelings) that change from moment to moment.[78] Rousseau, in Kant's view, cannot have it both ways: it cannot be the case that 'will' is an independent 'moral cause' that freely determines moral acts, and the mere tip of an iceberg of feelings. For in the second case 'good will' would once again become a quasi-Augustinian *delectio*; it would not be self-determination through a rational concept (e.g. 'ought').

Indeed, had not Kant been so boundlessly devoted to the 'Newton of the moral world' as the moralist who had 'set him straight' and taught him to 'honor' mankind[79] – had Rousseau's thought been a mere *objet trouvé* that Kant stumbled across – he would have dealt more harshly with Rousseau. He might easily have said that Rousseau gets the concept of 'negative freedom' – not being determined by mechanism – right, but without knowing why. To use the arguments from the *Critique of Pure Reason*, negative freedom in Rousseau is not 'critically' established by showing that while *phenomena* must be understood as caused, *noumena* or 'things in themselves' are undetermined.[80] At best, from a Kantian perspective, Rousseau can offer an intuitive account of the *feeling* of freedom, as in *La Nouvelle Héloïse*:

'A reasoner proves to me in vain that I am not free, [for] inner feeling [*le sentiment intérieur*], stronger than all his arguments, refutes them ceaselessly.'[81] For Kant this anti-Spinozist feeling, however eloquently expressed, must yield to the 'Transcendental Deduction's' proof in *Pure Reason* that being an undetermined 'moral cause' is conceivable.[82]

But in the treatment of 'positive freedom', Rousseau is still more problematical from a Kantian point of view. For positive freedom in Kant means self-determination through an objective moral law ('ought') enjoining respect for persons-as-ends. But Rousseau (a strict Kant would say) is wholly sound neither on self-determination nor on 'ought'. He frequently undercuts real self-determination – true spontaneity or 'autonomy' – by reducing morality to a natural, 'pathological' feeling (such as sympathy), or by saying, as in the *Lettres morales*, that 'conscience' is a *sentiment involontaire* which precedes both reason and will.[83] As for 'ought', that shifts from work to work: in *Du contrat social* it is *généralité* and the avoidance of 'particularism' in one's willing;[84] in the *Profession de foi du Vicaire Savoyard* it is an 'order' that reflects the divine world order, making morality nature's 'analogue';[85] in the earlier books of *Emile* it is Stoicism or limiting one's desires to match one's powers.[86] Only in the eighth of the *Lettres écrites de la montagne* (1764) does Rousseau get both negative and positive freedom nearly right from a Kantian perspective; there he speaks of not being determined and of not determining others:

> It is vain to confuse independence and liberty. These two things are so different that they even mutually exclude each other. When each does what pleases him, he often does something displeasing to others; and that cannot be called a free condition. Liberty consists less in doing one's will than in not being subject to that of another; it consists again in not submitting the will of another to our own. Whoever is master cannot be free; to rule is to obey.[87]

(This is one reason why the 'great legislator' does not *rule*, but only helps a people to 'find' the general will it is 'seeking' – or would seek, if it 'knew'. If the legislator were a 'master', he would not have to bend backwards to 'persuade without convincing' – so that freedom can *finally* arrive.)

One wonders whether Kant did not have this passage from the *Lettres écrites de la montagne* in mind when he said that 'Rousseau set me straight . . . I learned to honor mankind.' Rousseau's notion in *Montagne* that one should neither be subjected, nor subject others, comes closest to a Kantian 'negative' freedom which allows one 'positively' to respect persons as objective ends.

But if this is Rousseau's closest approach to Kant, Kant still wanted to turn back Rousseau's claim that 'free agency' is separated from understanding or reason. Against that, Kant wanted to show that a truly free will – finally *good*, not merely *general* – would be determined by 'practical reason' itself. That is why Kant insisted in the *Grundlegung* that

> Everything in nature works according to law. Rational beings alone have the faculty of acting according to the conception of laws, that is according to principles, i.e. have a will. Since the deduction of actions from principles requires reason, the will is nothing but practical reason. The will is a faculty to choose that only which reason independent of inclination recognizes as practically necessary, i.e. good.[88]

Had Rousseau (consistently) risen to this view of rational self-determination, in Kant's opinion, he would not (occasionally) have undermined his own distinction between 'physics' and free agency by reducing good will to non-rational sympathy for sentient beings. For Kant sympathy and sentience are, equally, 'pathological' feelings caused by nature;[89] that being so, one does not escape from the very 'laws of mechanism' which Rousseau himself rejected by placing a gulf (unreasonably) between reason and freedom. All of this suggests what Kant actually believed: that one cannot find a real duty *in* sympathy, feelings of pleasure and pain, or happiness, simply because the concept 'ought' cannot be extracted from these facts of pathology. The concept of moral necessity cannot be derived from the bare *data* of psychology.[90] Why Kant thought that 'ought' cannot be extracted from nature – even human 'nature' or psychology – he made especially clear in a quasi-Platonic passage from *Pure Reason* that is the foundation of his whole practical philosophy:

> That our reason has causality, or that we at least represent it to ourselves as having causality, is evident from the *imperatives* which in all matters of conduct we impose as rules upon our active powers. 'Ought' expresses a kind of necessity . . . which is found nowhere else in the whole of nature. The understanding can know in nature only what is, what has been, or what will be . . . When we have the course of nature alone in view, 'ought' has no meaning whatsoever.[91]

Precisely here – and equally in *Practical Reason*'s insistence that the moral law is just there as a 'fact of reason', underivable from *anything* else (nature, custom, God)[92] – lies the gulf that separates Rousseau and Kant (anti-willful voluntarists though they both are). If, for Rousseau, reason had 'causality', we would not stand in need of Moses' or Lycurgus' *educative* 'causality': the will would be generalized (or rather universalized) by a Kantian 'objective end' (respect for persons as members of a kingdom of ends) which is *unproblematical* for freedom because all rational beings simply 'see' that end (at the age of reason). The whole Kantian 'universalizing' operation is completely impersonal: there is no person (Lycurgus) bending backwards to be impersonal, non-authoritarian, persuading without convincing. In Kant one is not made free (in time): one simply knows 'ought' and takes oneself to be free (able to perform ought's commands) *ab initio*[93] – much as Meno's slave just 'has' astonishing geometrical knowledge.[94] Of course – and Rousseau would (reasonably) insist on this – Kantianism works only if there are universal, reason-ordained 'objective ends' which we 'ought to have' (*Religion*[95]); and Rousseau would have worried about every term in that sentence: whether we can know a *morale universelle* which is 'beyond' the *générale*, whether 'reason' ordains anything (morally), whether there are 'ends' that all rational beings 'see' (as facts of reason). Negatively, Kant and Rousseau are companions-in-flight from self-loving *volonté particulière*; positively, they offer the still-viable *contrasting* possibilities once that flight is over – rational, universal, cosmopolitan morality valid for *persons*, vs. educator-shaped, general, politan *civisme* valid for a *citoyen de Génève* or *de Sparte*. (Try to imagine Kant as *citoyen de Königsberg*: that will measure very precisely the distance from Switzerland to Prussia.)

Without 'waiting' (as it were) for the actual Kant, Rousseau treated 'Kantian' moral universalism and rationalism in his great attack on Diderot, the *Première version du contrat social* – a work in which Rousseau says, in effect: *of course* one can readily make freedom and 'what men ought to be' congruent if autonomous rational agents just 'see' the right and the good for themselves. But what if a moral or general standpoint has to be *attained*, over time, through a denaturing anti-egoism which will none the less finally *cause* autonomy? That is the permanent 'Rousseau-question' which 'Kantians' *ought* (suitably enough) to keep in mind – as Kant himself certainly did.

Rousseau's radical doubts about the real existence of any universal, reason-ordained morality come out most plainly and brilliantly in the *Première version* – that remarkable refutation of Diderot's

Encyclopédie article, 'Droit naturel', arguing that there is a universal *volonté générale* of and for the entire *genre humain*, a rational *morale universelle*.

In 'Droit naturel', Diderot had argued that 'if we deprive the individual of the right to decide about the nature of the just and the unjust', we must then 'take this great question . . . before the human race', for the 'good of all' is the 'sole passion' that this most-inclusive group has. Paralleling Rousseau (initially), Diderot goes on to say that '*volontés particulières* are suspect', for they can be indifferently good or wicked, but that 'the general will is always good', since it has never 'deceived' and never will. It is to this always-good, never-deceiving *volonté générale* 'that the individual must address himself', Diderot insists, 'in order to know how far he must be a citizen, a subject, a father, a child, and when it is suitable for him to live or to die.'[96]

So far, no great gap has opened up between Diderot and Rousseau. But when Diderot begins to indicate where the general will is *deposited*, he moves in the direction of a proto-Kantian universalism which is (usually) foreign to the citizen of Geneva. The general will can be 'consulted', he urges, 'in the principles of the written law of all civilized nations; in the social actions of primitive and barbarous peoples; in the tacit conventions of the enemies of the human race between themselves; and even in indignation and resentment, those two passions that nature seems to have placed even in animals, to supply the defect of social laws and public vengeance.' Diderot's nominal *généralité* is in fact a *morale universelle* (to use his own term); it relates to the whole *genre humain*, and seems to extend even to 'honor among thieves'.[97] Rousseau's *volonté générale* – of Rome, of Sparta, of Geneva – is a great deal more *particulière*; indeed in the *Gouvernement de Pologne* Rousseau insists on the importance of national peculiarities and particularities that should not be submerged in a cosmopolitan universalism.[98] For Diderot, then – as Robert Wokler has elegantly put it – the general will is to be found almost everywhere, whereas Rousseau doubts that it has ever been fully realized anywhere.[99]

In the next section of 'Droit naturel', Diderot goes on to urge – after repeating that 'the man who listens only to his *volonté particulière* is the enemy of the human race'[100] – that 'the general will is, in each individual, a pure act of the understanding which reasons in the silence of the passions about what a man can demand of his fellow-man and about what his fellow-man has the right to demand of him.'[101] And it is at this very point that Diderot begins to be separated from Rousseau:

the *citoyen de Génève*, as he styled himself, would have stressed precisely 'citizenship' and 'Geneva', and would never have urged that *volonté générale* is immediately dictated by understanding or reason (as distinguished from will-generalizing civic education). Had Rousseau thought that, the passions being 'silent' (a phrase Diderot borrows from Malebranche[102]), understanding and reason could alone dictate what is right, he would never have made his famous claim that 'the general will is always right' but 'the judgment which guides it is not always enlightened'. If reason alone dictated right (as in Kant it furnishes 'ought'), Rousseauian men would have no need of a Numa or a Moses to help effect 'a union of understanding and will'.[103]

Book 1, chapter 2 of Rousseau's *Première version* is a refutation of Diderot's rationalism and universalism; but it also provides more than a hint of what Rousseau *would* have said about Kant's distinctive way of combining 'ought' and freedom. At one time, to be sure, Rousseau had himself stressed a roughly comparable *morale universelle*; in an early, unpublished fragment called *Chronologie universelle* (*c*. 1737) he had appealed to Fénelon's notion of a universal Christian republic:

> We are all brothers; our neighbors ought to be as dear to us as ourselves. 'I love the human race more than my country,' said the illustrious M. de Fénelon, 'my country more than my family and my family more than myself.' Sentiments so full of humanity ought to be shared by all men . . . The universe is a great family of which we are all members . . . However extensive may be the power of an individual, he is always in a position to make himself useful . . . to the great body of which he is a part. If he can [do this], he indispensably ought to.[104]

Later, of course – most clearly of all in the *Première version* – Rousseau would abandon the *universelle* in favor of the *générale* and exchange the *respublica christiana* for more modest republics: Sparta, Rome, Geneva. Indeed his great difference from Diderot – and, 'in advance', from Kant – rests precisely in the difference between the *universelle* (known to all by reason alone, in the 'silence of the passions') and the *générale* (known to citizens of a particular republic through a civic education supplied by Numa or Moses or Lycurgus). Hence Rousseau's problem with freedom: he must find an authoritative person who is neither authoritarian nor personal, who generalizes the will while leaving it voluntary. Diderot and Kant, different as they are, do not have this difficulty.

That Rousseau is not going to argue for a reason-ordained *morale universelle* valid for the entire human race – whether in a late-Stoic,

Diderotian, or Kantian shape – is evident in the opening sentence of the *Première version*: 'Let us begin by inquiring why the necessity for political institutions arises.'[105] If a passion-silencing reason spoke to and governed all men, no mere particular political institutions would arise at all (as Locke had already shown in section 128 of the *Second Treatise*, saying that only a 'corrupt' rejection of reason keeps a unitary, unified mankind from being perfectly governed by natural law[106]). Rousseau is struck by the beauty of Diderot's *morale universelle*: 'No one will *deny* that the general will in each individual is a pure act of the understanding, which reasons in the silence of the passions about what man can demand of his fellow-man and what his fellow-man has the right to demand of him.' But where, Rousseau immediately and characteristically asks, 'is the man who can be so objective about himself, and if concern for his self-preservation is nature's first precept, can he be forced to look in this manner at the species *en général* in order to impose on himself duties whose connection with his particular constitution is not evident to him?' If reason is not directly morally efficacious (as it cannot be, if great legislators are to have the important formative function that is assigned to them in *Du contrat social*), and if 'natural law' is scarcely natural (as *Inégalité* tries to prove), then the natural man who fails to find his particular good in the general good will instead become the enemy of the *genre humain*, allying himself with the strong and the unjust to despoil the weak. 'It is false', Rousseau insists, 'that in the state of independence, reason leads us to cooperate from the common good.'[107]

So strongly does this current of thought sweep Rousseau along that he mounts a brief assault on *généralité* that would be fatal not just to Diderot, but to his own political aims as well: 'If the general society [of the human race] did exist somewhere other than in the systems of philosophers, it would be ... a moral being with qualities separate and distinct from those of the particular beings constituting it, somewhat like chemical compounds which have properties that do not belong to any of the elements composing them.' In such a *société générale* 'there would be a universal language which nature would teach all men and which would be their first means of communication'; there would also be a 'kind of central nervous system which would connect all the parts.' Finally, 'the public good or ill would not be merely the sum of private goods and ills as in a simple aggregation, but would lie in the liaison uniting them. It would be greater than this sum, and public felicity, far from being based on the happiness of private individuals [*des particuliers*], would itself be the source of this happiness.'[108]

Plainly this argument goes too far, since Rousseau himself wants to argue for a general good that is more than a mere sum or aggregation of private goods and ills; it is no wonder that he suppressed the *Première version*. Nevertheless the dilemma remains that a general society cannot be produced by passion-silencing 'reason' alone.[109] The only way out of the dilemma, *selon* Rousseau, is through denatured, non-natural 'new associations' (Sparta, Rome, Geneva) that take the place of well-meant but imaginary reason-governed *sociétés générales* and which, through rigorous civic education, draw natural beings out of their (equally natural) egocentrism, bringing them to think of themselves (finally) as 'parts of a greater whole' – a whole less extensive, but more realizable, than a *respublica christiana* or a kingdom of ends. The particular social remedies designed to overcome *particularité* and self-preference at the end of the *Première version* are rather abstractly, even vaguely, characterized ('new associations', 'new insights', 'perfected art'[110]); but one knows from other works such as the *Economie politique* and the *Gouvernement de Pologne* how Rousseau proposes to produce, through an educative shaping which finally yields 'enlightened' free choice, a civic *volonté générale* which is certainly no cosmopolitan *esprit universel*.[111]

In the end, for Rousseau, no *morale universelle* – not a Christian one based on universal charity, not a Diderotian one grounded in passion-silencing reason, not a Kantian one resting on reason-ordained 'objective ends' – can help in the transformation of natural men into denatured citizens. The *générale* must be (somewhat) *particulière*. This explains the weight which Rousseau gives to education. For him, men do not naturally think of themselves as parts of a greater whole[112] – a *genre humain* or a *Reich der Zwecke* – and must therefore be *brought* to a non-natural civic belief. But at the end of civic time – if *volonté* is to be equal to *généralité* – they must finally see the force of Emile's 'I have decided to be what you made me.'

IV

If Rousseau's 'generalism' can be illuminated by contrasting it with Kant's 'universalism' – and this makes it plain that for Rousseau freedom must be made congruent with *shaping* and *becoming*, while for Kant ought is just 'there' and does not endanger autonomy – one can throw some further light on Rousseau's effort to find a generalized *volonté* which will be voluntary but not 'willful' by contrasting the Rousseauian operation with that of Hegel.

Here the first thing to be said is that Hegel strives to place more distance between himself and the citizen of Geneva than is really warranted. After all, Rousseau would agree with Hegel's assertion, in the Preface to the *Philosophy of Right*, that human thought is 'perverted into wrong' if it 'knows itself to be free only when it diverges from what is generally recognized and valid [*Allgemein-Anerkannten*], and when it has discovered how to invent for itself some particular character.'[113] That sounds like, and is, a Teutonic echo of the *Economie politique*. Rousseau, moreover, would find little to reject – though much to re-word – in Hegel's further claim that in the 'ethical substantial order . . . the self-will of the individual has vanished together with his private conscience which had claimed independence and opposed itself to the ethical substance', so that there is finally an 'identity of the general will with the particular will [*Identität des allgemeinen und besonderen Willens*].'[114] And Rousseau would surely approve Hegel's definition of hypocrisy as 'knowledge of the true general' coupled with 'volition of the particular which conflicts with this generality' – a particular willing which is 'evil in character'.[115]

But if Hegel praises Rousseau for correctly 'adducing the will as the principle of the state' (rather than falling back on 'gregarious instinct' or 'divine authority'), if he congratulates him for seeing that 'the will's activity consists in annulling the contradiction between subjectivity and objectivity and giving its aims an objective instead of a subjective character, while at the same time remaining by itself even in objectivity', he also, quite surprisingly, accuses Rousseau of deifying 'the will of a single person in his own private self-will, not the absolute or rational will.'[116] This seems unjust, even perverse, if it is true that Rousseauian *volonté générale* is neither merely 'private' nor simply 'rational' – that it is general rather than universal, Lycurgus-shaped rather than reason-ordained. Hegel speaks as if there were nothing between the private and 'capricious' on the one hand, and the rational and the universal on the other; but that simply rules out Rousseau's distinctive mediation between subjective egoism and objective 'higher' will. Thus when Hegel says in section 258 of the *Philosophy of Right* that Rousseau's '"general will" reduces the union of individuals in the state to a contract and therefore to something based on their arbitrary wills', he neglects (generally, willfully) Rousseau's heroic effort to transform traditional Lockean contractarianism into a notion of educated, no-longer-fraudulent consent at the end of civic time, after the general will is finally as 'enlightened' (and free) as it was always 'right'. He does injustice to Rousseau's valiant striving to transcend arbitrariness by bringing each denatured citizen to think of himself as 'part of a greater whole'. To be sure, Hegel thought he saw in Rousseau the embryo of Robespierre, the germ of the Terror: 'The phenomena which [Rousseauianism] has produced both in men's heads and in the world are of a frightfulness parallel only to the superficiality of the thoughts on which they are based.'[117] Despite the incomparable brilliance of Hegel's reading of the unfolding of Western *Geist* – one thinks of his definitive interpretations of 'Antigone' and 'Hamlet' – this reading of Rousseau is itself 'superficial': Rousseau, not unlike Hegel, wanted citizens to embrace a 'concrete' universal (the polity), not mere Kantian universalizing of maxims through non-political 'good will'.[118] In short, Hegel ought to have understood Rousseau better, but he (in Shklar's words) 'refused to honor his debt to Rousseau'.[119] (May it be the very fact that Rousseau, Kant and Hegel are 'anti-willful voluntarists' that leads Hegel to accuse Rousseau of 'superficiality' and Kant of being an 'arid formalist' who tries to torture substantive ethics out of bare logic ['universality']? May the fact that Rousseau and Kant were half right – in opposing *volonté particulière* – have distressed Hegel, who wanted will to be 'satisfied' with the modern state *qua* rational freedom concretely 'realized'? Were Rousseau and Kant too close for comfort, but not *quite* right enough?)

V

Following these Kantian and Hegelian critiques of the precise way in which Rousseau balances freedom and 'what men ought to be' – and what Rousseau always wants is a generalized *volonté* which is finally free because it finally 'sees' ('I have decided to be') – one can give the final word to Rousseau himself.

Rousseau not only wanted to 'secularize' the general will – to turn it (mainly) away from theology (and God's will to save 'all men'); he wanted to endow human beings with a will, a really efficacious 'power' of choosing, which can then be subjected to the generalizing influence of civic education – a republican education which Montesquieu eloquently described but took to have vanished from the modern (monarchical) world. First *real* will, then *general* will; that is what Rousseau would say to his great French predecessors. This is not to say that Rousseau thought he knew perfectly what *la volonté* is: but in his most extensive and important treatment of volition (*Emile*, Book 4) Rousseau never allowed (unavoidably incomplete) knowledge of will to cast doubt on either the real existence or the moral necessity of this 'faculty'. And so he has the Savoyard Vicar ask:

> How does a will produce a physical and corporeal action? I know nothing about that, but I experience in myself [the fact] that it produces it. I will to act, and I act; I will to move my body, and it moves; but that an inanimate body at rest should begin to move itself by itself, or produce movement – that is incomprehensible and unexampled. The will is known to me by its acts, not by its nature. I know this will as motor cause, but to conceive matter as the producer of movement is clearly to conceive an effect without a cause, which is to conceive absolutely nothing.[120]

This doctrine, Rousseau has the Vicar say, is admittedly 'obscure'; but it 'makes sense' and contains nothing repugnant to either reason or observation. 'Can one say as much of materialism?' the Vicar finally asks.[121]

The answer is clearly, 'no'. And that answer remained constant, seven years after *Emile*, when Rousseau wrote his magnificent *Lettre à M. de Franquières* – in which he urges his correspondent to abandon a materialism and a determinism which are fatal to freedom and morality:

> Why do you not appreciate that the same law of necessity which, according to you, rules the working of the world, and all events, also rules all the actions of men, every thought in their heads, all the feelings of their hearts, that nothing is free, that all is forced, necessary, inevitable, that all the movements of man which are directed by blind matter, depend on his will only because his will itself depends on necessity; that there are in consequence neither virtues, nor vices, nor merit, nor demerit, nor morality in human actions, and that the words 'honorable man' or 'villain' must be, for you, totally devoid of sense . . .
> Your honest heart, despite your arguments, declaims against your sad philosophy. The feeling of liberty, the charm of virtue, are felt in you despite you.[122]

Here, more than anywhere else in Rousseau, *le coeur a ses raisons que la raison ne connaît point*. But this Pascalian 'heart' is used to defend a freedom of willing that Pascal himself would certainly have called 'Pelagian'. And if that will can be generalized by a non-authoritarian educative authority, the final product will be the realization of Rousseau's highest civic ideal: the *volonté générale* one has 'as a citizen'.

Had Rousseau not been centrally concerned with freedom – above all with the voluntariness of morally legitimate human actions – he would never have made 'the general will' the core idea of his political philosophy.

Notes

1 Plato, *Republic*, 462a–e. Cf. the astonishingly 'parallel' passage in I *Corinthians* xii – which makes one wonder how completely St Paul was rejecting 'the wisdom of the Greeks'.

2 Montesquieu, *Mes Pensées*, in *Oeuvres complètes de Montesquieu*, ed. R. Caizzois (Paris: Gallimard, Bibliothèque de la Pléiade, 1949–51), vol. 1, p. 1434: 'It is essential in republics that there be an *esprit général* which dominates. In proportion as luxury is established, the spirit of particularism is established as well.' Here one has *généralité* – but not yet *volonté*.

3 Rousseau, *Du contrat social*, in Vaughan, vol. 2, pp. 105, 28.

4 Judith N. Shklar, *Men and Citizens: A Study of Rousseau's Social Theory* (Cambridge: Cambridge University Press, 1969), p. 184. See also J. N. Shklar, 'General Will', in *Dictionary of the History of Ideas*, ed. P. Wiener (New York: Scribner's, 1973), vol. 2, pp. 275 ff.

5 Bronislaw Baczko, 'Moïse, législateur . . .', essay in the collection, *Rousseau* (Manchester: Manchester University Press, 1982), pp. 88–90.

6 Cf. Plato, *Phaedrus*, 252b ff.

7 Rousseau, *Du contrat social*, Vaughan, vol. 2, 7.

8 *Ibid.*, vol. 2, 6.

9 *Ibid.*

10 See A. W. Adkins, *Merit and Responsibility* (Oxford: Oxford University Press, 1960).

11 Rousseau, *Emile*, trans. Foxley (London: Dent, 1910), p. 435.

12 See the author's *The General Will before Rousseau* (Princeton: Princeton University Press, 1986), pp. 4 ff.

13 Malebranche, *Traité de la nature et de la grâce*, in *Oeuvres complètes* (Paris: Vrin, 1958), vol. 5, pp. 147–8, 166.

14 See the author's *The General Will*, op. cit., ch. 5.

15 Rousseau, *Economie politique*, in *The Social Contract and Discourses*, trans. G. D. H. Cole (New York: Everyman, 1950), p. 297.

16 Rousseau, *Lettre à M. de Franquières* (1769), in *Lettres philosophiques*, ed. Henri Gouhier (Paris: Vrin, 1974), pp. 180–1.

17 See the author's *Will and Political Legitimacy: A Critical Exposition of Social Contract Theory in Hobbes, Locke, Rousseau, Kant and Hegel*

(Cambridge, Mass.: Harvard University Press, 1982), *passim*, for a full account of 'voluntarism' in Rousseau, Kant and Hegel.

18 Shakespeare, *Henry V*, Act I, scene i. Since the phrase refers to the King's previous incarnation as Prince Hal, the word 'wilfulness' is most apt. Certainly in the final scene of *2 Henry IV* the new king subordinates a *volonté* which had been *particulière* on a Falstaffian scale to the *bien général* of the English state:

> Presume not that I am the thing I was,
> For God doth know, so shall the world perceive,
> That I have turn'd away from my former self.

This 'turn' is precisely from radical *particularisme* to civic *volonté générale*.

19 Kant, *Rechtslehre*, in *Immanuel Kants Werke*, ed. E. Cassirer (Berlin: Bruno Cassirer Verlag, 1922), vol. 7, pp. 161–2. See also the author's *Kant's Political Philosophy* (Totowa: Rowman & Littlefield, 1983), pp. 167 ff.

20 Hegel, *Philosophy of Right*, trans. T. M. Knox (Oxford: Clarendon Press, 1942), p. 105: 'Ethical life [in modernity the state] is the Idea of freedom . . . the good endowed in self-consciousness with knowing and willing and actualized by self-conscious action.' For splendid appreciations of Hegel's version of voluntarism, see George A. Kelly, *Hegel's Retreat from Eleusis* (Princeton: Princeton University Press, 1978), pp. 113–14, and Michael Oakeshott, *On Human Conduct* (Oxford: Clarendon Press, 1975), p. 160: 'The only conditions of conduct which do not compromise the inherent integrity of a Subject are those which reach him in his understanding of them, which he is free to subscribe to or not, and which can be subscribed to only in an intelligent act of Will.'

21 Kant, *Critique of Practical Reason*, trans. L. W. Beck (Indianapolis: Library of Liberal Arts, 1970), p. 48: 'The moral law is given, as an apodictically certain fact, as it were, of pure reason.'

22 Hegel, *Phenomenology of Mind*, trans. W. Baillie (New York: Harper & Row, 1967), p. 89, where Hegel urges that each individual must 'go through the stages through which the general mind has passed.'

23 *Ibid.*, p. 234.

24 See above all Rousseau, *Gouvernement de Pologne*, in Vaughan, vol. 2, pp. 424 ff.

25 Rousseau, *Du contrat social*, in Vaughan, vol. 2, pp. 105, 28.

26 Bayle, *Pensées diverses. Ecrites à un docteur de Sorbonne*, 4th ed. (Rotterdam: Chez Reinier Leers, 1704), vol. 2, pp. 452 ff. For Bayle's political-moral argument that *généralité* is good, *particularité* evil, see the author's *The General Will before Rousseau*, *op. cit.*, pp. 79 ff.

27 Rousseau, *Première version du Contrat social*, in Vaughan, vol. 1, p. 499.

28 Rousseau, *Lettre à M. de Beaumont*, in *Oeuvres Complètes* (Paris: Editions du Seuil, 1971), vol. 3, pp. 340 ff.

29 Rousseau, *Du contrat social*, in Vaughan, vol. 1, p. 26.

30 Rousseau, *Discourse on Inequality*, in *The Social Contract and Discourses*, trans. Cole, *op. cit.*, p. 208.
31 Rousseau, *Première version, op. cit.*, p. 499.
32 Rousseau, *Emile*, trans. Foxley, *op. cit.*, pp. 243–4.
33 *Ibid.*
34 Rousseau, *Lettres morales*, in Pléiade, vol. 4, pp. 1106 ff. For the importance of the *Lettres*, see Shklar, *Men and Citizens, op. cit.*, pp. 229–30.
35 Kant, *Grundlegung*, trans. T. K. Abbott as *Fundamental Principles* (Indianapolis: Library of Liberal Arts, 1949), p. 11.
36 Rousseau, *Lettres morales, op. cit.*, pp. 1111, 1107, 1108, 1109.
37 Bertrand de Jouvenel, 'Essai sur la politique de Rousseau', in *Du contrat social* (Geneva: Editions du Cheval Aile, 1947), p. 78.
38 Hegel, *Phenomenology, op. cit.*, pp. 660–2.
39 Pascal, *Ecrits sur la grâce*, in *Oeuvres de Blaise Pascal*, ed. Brunschvicg (Paris: Librairie Hachette, 1914), vol. 11, p. 134.
40 Rousseau, *Du contrat social*, in Vaughan, vol. 2, pp. 105, 27.
41 Rousseau, *Première version, op. cit.*, pp. 472–3, in which he urges that every authentic 'act of sovereignty' involves 'an agreement between the body politic and each of its members' which is 'equitable because it is voluntary and general'. Here *volonté* and *généralité* are of equal weight.
42 Rousseau, *Du contrat social, op. cit.*, p. 52.
43 Rousseau, *Gouvernement de Pologne*, ed. Vaughan, *op. cit.*, vol. 2, p. 430.
44 Rousseau, *Economie politique*, trans. Cole, *op. cit.*, p. 308.
45 Rousseau, *Emile*, excerpt in Vaughan, vol. 2, p. 145.
46 Malebranche, *Nature et grâce, op. cit.*, pp. 147–66.
47 Rousseau, 'Le Persifleur', in *Les Confessions*, Pléiade, vol. 1, p. 1111, where Rousseau urges that *la plus profonde métaphysique* is that of 'Plato, Locke or Malebranche'.
48 Rousseau, letter to Mirabeau, in *Lettres philosophiques*, ed. Gouhier, *op. cit.*
49 Rousseau, *Jugement sur la Polysynodie*, in Vaughan, vol. 1, p. 421.
50 St Augustine, *De Libero arbitrio*, Book I, ch. 12.
51 Rousseau, *Economie politique*, trans. Cole, *op. cit.*, p. 297.
52 Rousseau, *Emile*, trans. Foxley, *op. cit.*, p. 444.
53 Rousseau, *Gouvernement de Pologne*, in Vaughan, vol. 2, pp. 427–30. See also Rousseau's early prize-essay, *Discours sur la vertu du heros*, in *Oeuvres complètes*, du Seuil ed., *op. cit.*, vol. 2, pp. 118–20.
54 Rousseau, *Du contrat social*, in Vaughan, p. 51.
55 Rousseau, *Gouvernement de Pologne*, in Vaughan, vol. 2, pp. 437–43.
56 Rousseau, *Emile*, trans. Foxley, *op. cit.*, p. 84.
57 Rousseau, *Discourse on Inequality*, trans. Cole, *op. cit.*, pp. 180–2.
58 John Charvet, *The Social Problem in the Philosophy of Rousseau* (Cambridge: Cambridge University Press, 1974), p. 58.

59 Hegel, *Phenomenology, op. cit.*, p. 234.
60 Rousseau, *Du contrat social, op. cit.*, p. 36.
61 Rousseau, *Emile*, trans. Foxley, *op. cit.*, p. 435.
62 Rousseau, *Du contrat social, op. cit.*, p. 27.
63 See note 60.
64 Rousseau, *Du contrat social, op. cit.*, p. 56.
65 Particularly Vaughan, in his 'Introduction' to Rousseau's *Political Writings*, vol. 1, pp. 35 ff.
66 Kant, *Grundlegung*, trans. Abbott, *op. cit.*, pp. 19–21.
67 Blake's lines are quoted by A. J. Ayer in *Part of my Life* (New York: Oxford University Press, 1977), p. 176.
68 Shklar's phrase in 'General Will', *op. cit.*, p. 279.
69 Kant, *Grundlegung*, trans. Abbot, *op. cit.*, pp. 11–12.
70 The notion that the 'ethical commonwealth' of *Religion within the Limits* should be viewed as Kant's 'utopia' was suggested (*en passant*) by Judith Shklar.
71 St Augustine, *De Libero Arbitrio*, trans. Russell (Washington: Catholic University of America Press, 1968), pp. 95–6.
72 *Ibid.*, p. 97.
73 Plato, *Phaedrus*, 253b–257b.
74 Kant, *Grundlegung*, trans. Abbott, *op. cit.*, pp. 55–6.
75 Rousseau, *Première version, op. cit.*, p. 499.
76 Rousseau, *Inequality*, trans. Cole, *op. cit.*, p. 208.
77 *Ibid.*, pp. 208, 194.
78 Kant, *Grundlegung*, trans. Abbott, *op. cit.*, p. 29: 'all moral conceptions have their seat and origin completely *à priori* in the reason.'
79 Cited by Ernst Cassirer in *Rousseau, Kant and Goethe*, trans. Gutmann et al. (New York: Harper, 1963), pp. 1–2.
80 Kant, *Critique of Pure Reason*, trans. N. K. Smith (London: Macmillan, 1962), pp. 464–5 (A 533/B 561).
81 Rousseau, *La Nouvelle Héloïse*, Pléiade, vol. 2, p. 683.
82 See note 79.
83 Rousseau, *Lettres morales, op. cit.*, p. 1107.
84 Rousseau, *Du contrat social*, in Vaughan, pp. 42–50.
85 Rousseau, *Emile*, Pléiade, vol. 4, p. 588: 'Le mal général ne peut être que dans le desordre, et je vois dans le système du monde un ordre qui ne se dement point.' See also André Robinet, 'A propos d'Ordre dans la Profession de Foi du Vicaire Savoyard', in *Studi Filosofici*, I, Naples, 1978, pp. 39–76.
86 Rousseau, *Emile*, trans. Foxley, *op. cit.*, pp. 303–6.
87 Rousseau, *Lettres écrites de la montagne*, Pléiade, vol. 3, pp. 841–2.
88 Kant, *Grundlegung*, trans. Abbott, *op. cit.*, p. 30.
89 *Ibid.*, pp. 17, 58–9.
90 *Ibid.*, p. 29.
91 Kant, *Pure Reason, op. cit.*, A 547/B 575.

92 Kant, *Practical Reason*, trans. Beck, *op. cit.*, p. 48.
93 *Ibid.*, p. 29. For Kant we *think* freedom because we *know* 'ought'.
94 Plato, *Meno*, 82b ff.
95 Kant, *Religion within the Limits of Reason Alone*, trans. T. M. Greene and Hoyt Hudson (New York: Harper & Row, 1960), p. 6n.
96 Diderot, 'Droit naturel', in *Rousseau: Political Writings*, in Vaughan, vol. 1, p. 431.
97 *Ibid.*, pp. 431–2.
98 Rousseau, *Gouvernement de Pologne*, *op. cit.*, chs. 1–4.
99 Robert Wokler, 'The Influence of Diderot on Rousseau', in *Studies on Voltaire and the 18th Century* (Banbury: Voltaire Foundation, 1975), vol. 132.
100 Diderot, 'Droit naturel', *op. cit.*, p. 432.
101 *Ibid.*
102 Malebranche, *Recherche de la vérité*, in *Oeuvres complètes*, *op. cit.*, vol. 2, p. 490.
103 Rousseau, *Du contrat social*, *op. cit.*, vol. 2, 6.
104 Rousseau, *Chronologie universelle*, in *Annales de la Société Jean-Jacques Rousseau* (Geneva: Jullien, 1905), vol. 1, pp. 213 ff.
105 Rousseau, *Première version*, in *On the Social Contract*, trans. Masters (New York: St Martin's Press, 1978), p. 157.
106 Locke, *Two Treatises*, 'Second Treatise', sec. 128.
107 Rousseau, *Première version*, Masters ed., pp. 159–60.
108 *Ibid.*
109 Rousseau, *Du contrat social*, p. 48. Cf. George A. Kelly, 'Rousseau, Kant and History', in *Journal of the History of Ideas*, vol. XXIX, no. 3, 1968, p. 353: 'Rousseau is not an irrationalist. But . . . reason is highly corruptible; the passions distort it into self-serving "raisonnements". Though reason enables us to know the truth, only conscience can make us *love* it.'
110 Rousseau, *Première version*, Masters ed., pp. 162–3.
111 Rousseau, *Gouvernement de Pologne*, in Vaughan, p. 437: 'Tout vrai republicain . . . ne voit que la patrie, il ne vit que pour elle . . .'
112 Rousseau, *Du contrat social*, *op. cit*, p. 52.
113 Hegel, *Philosophy of Right*, *op. cit.*, Preface, p. 4.
114 *Ibid.*, p. 142.
115 *Ibid.*, sec. 140.
116 *Ibid.*, pp. 156, 32–3.
117 *Ibid.*, pp. 157, 33.
118 See Kelly, *Hegel's Retreat from Eleusis*, *op. cit.*, pp. 55 ff.
119 Judith N. Shklar, *Freedom and Independence* (Cambridge: Cambridge University Press, 1976), p. 207.
120 Rousseau, *Emile*, Pléiade, vol. 4, p. 576.
121 *Ibid.*, pp. 576–7.
122 See note 16 above.

2 Norman Barry

Hume, Smith and Rousseau on freedom

For certain very obvious reasons, the moral and political thought of Jean-Jacques Rousseau seems to belong to a different world from that of David Hume and Adam Smith.[1] Rousseau's work is thought to be backward-looking, belonging perhaps to the classical era where political order and social stability were functions of participation by the citizens (albeit a narrowly confined group) and where the public good was discernible to each person and made the object of his rational activity. The private world was of significantly less value and the pursuit of commerce was not an activity that contributed to a person's proper goals (Aristotle made a nice distinction between true 'friendship' and the mere 'advantage relationship' that characterised trade). Hume and Smith, however, celebrated the commercial order, the largely anonymous world of abstract agents held together by rules and conventions that did not have their origins in the direct wills of the citizens but which emerged spontaneously as mere devices to enable persons to pursue their essentially private projects in circumstances of some predictability. In this vision, the public good was not a discernible collective goal for a community but the unplanned outcome of individual striving. In Smith's (1976a: 456) famous phrase, the individual: 'By pursuing his own interest frequently promotes that of society more effectually than when he really intends to promote it. I have never known much good done by those who affected to trade for the public good.' In contrast, Rousseau (1913: 77) argued that it was because of the 'hustle of commerce and the arts, through the greedy self-interest of profit' that personal service to the community is undermined and voluntary contributions are replaced by money payment (taxes). Thus the link between the individual and the collective is severed, and the political liberty of the public world is lost to the bogus liberty revealed in private gratification.

No doubt the contrast presented here is something of a caricature that fails to capture the nuances of the respective positions, but it does describe some competing views of morality and politics that have survived into the late twentieth century. More specifically, it generates starkly different concepts of freedom. One that views liberty almost instrumentally, as in Smith's notion of 'natural liberty' (1976a: 37–8) which fundamentally describes those human actions which, if left more or less undisturbed, can be relied upon to generate social utility, or Hume's similar celebration of economic liberty in his essay, 'Of Commerce' (1987: 253–67), and one which sees freedom as essentially moral, a form of self-control in which the immediate urgency of ephemeral desire is subordinated to the striving for a form of perfectionism. Rousseau's commitment to the latter view is captured in his claim that: 'To renounce liberty is to renounce being a man, to surrender the rights of humanity and even its duties . . . to remove all liberty from his will is to remove all morality from his acts' (1913: 8). For Hume and Smith, then, freedom is little more than physical movement; for Rousseau it is inextricably bound up with the will: indeed, life is a constant struggle within each individual between the prompting of the self-destructive momentary will and the moral demand of the social, sanitised will in which true individual freedom is realised.

This is not a simple conflict between negative and positive liberty. After all, both Hume and Smith, unlike Bentham, recognised that not every law is a restraint on liberty and argued that freedom is actually advanced by predictable rules. Furthermore, though Rousseau is often interpreted as a positive theorist of liberty he is, on occasions, anxious to stress freedom as security from external threats and, in *The Social Contract* at least, he talked of a person's freedom as 'civil liberty and the proprietorship of all he possesses': terms which would not have been too distressing for J. S. Mill. Still, the connection between liberty and law obsessed him, not the dry definition of liberty, and it is because liberty is indissolubly bound up with freedom of the will that Rousseau was led to the quest to discover

> a form of association which will defend and protect with the whole common force the person and goods of each associate, and in which each, while uniting himself with all, may still obey himself alone, and remain as free as before (1913: 12).

It was this search that led him towards the positive liberty camp. His claim (1913: 3) that 'Man is born free and everywhere in chains' indicates dramatically his desire for a conception of law that bound the individual in freedom to the community rather than one which saw it as a necessary restraint for fractious individuals.

For Hume and Smith, because they were uninterested in the freedom of the will, the existence of law, as a protective device for individual interaction, simply produced a net benefit to society in liberty terms, not a solution to the moral problem of political obligation. Questions of legitimate authority were turned into enquiries into expediency and convenience. The moral value of the community was inextricably bound up with the opportunities that it offered for private satisfaction. Although Smith had serious doubts about the possible long-run implications for social cohesion if individualism were pressed too far, they never drove him to the wholesale criticism of commercial society that Rousseau indulged in.

It was not that Rousseau saw a potential conflict between justice and utility, in which justice must always prevail, but rather that in the ideal form of association the 'right the social compact gives the sovereign does not . . . exceed the limits of public expediency' (1913: 113). For Hume (1972: 227–9) justice could sometimes prescribe a different rule of conduct from that decreed by utility-maximisation. For although rules of justice are adopted precisely because they produce long-run benefit (and acquire a certain kind of *moral* gloss for this reason) their immediate enforcement may be inconsistent with utility. The conflict is perhaps unsatisfactorily resolved by complex redefinitions of utility. But for Rousseau there is no conflict because there is no distinction between the long run and the short: political obligation to a political system is owed by a moralised individual, and, if properly constituted, the sovereign always acts in his interest, although he may not always see it.

Yet those fundamentally contrasting metaphysical presuppositions should not distract us from the fact that Rousseau shares with both Hume and Smith a distrust of reason in political affairs. This obviously manifested itself in wildly different ways (indeed, Rousseau's contempt for existing forms of political association may have produced, ironically, a perverse rationalistic alternative) but the starting point for them is a rejection of the idea that an abstract reason can be a source for political values. There is no natural law that transcends human experience and dictates our duties; instead it is the opinions, attitudes and volitions of human beings that provide the materials out of which legitimate political orders are formed. It is *nature*, not reason, to which we must look if we are to discover appropriate forms of conduct, both moral and political. The trouble is that the very promiscuity of the concept of nature permits dramatically different systems of values to claim validation by its tenets. The phenomena that Hume and Smith thought of as natural would be regarded by Rousseau as the products of a will that has been detached, by art and design, from its proper end. They would be the outcome of a morally illegitimate social order.

Nature

Rousseau argues that as long as we are ignorant of natural man it is 'in vain for us to attempt to determine either the law originally prescribed for him, or that which is best adapted to his constitution' (1913: 157). The progress of reason has had disastrous results for mankind precisely because it has distorted our true nature. The arts and sciences have not been beneficial because they have distracted the individual from the pursuit of virtue, which can only be found in concert with others, and encouraged him to seek only the admiration of others. The natural liberty of a state of nature which, for all its moral inadequacies, at least guaranteed man's independence, has been exchanged for an ersatz liberty of civil society. The security individuals have achieved has been bought at the cost of a genuine civil liberty: a liberty which would only be possible in that institutional framework that unites the individual will with the collective endeavour. The freedom of contemporary society consists only in the satisfaction of egoistic desire, and that itself constitutes a new form of constraint. In fact, liberty is achieved by the suppression of desire since the lust for commodities and the ephemera of civilised life produces a dependency not on the community (which is perfectly proper) but on *others*. It is not self-love (*amour de soi*) which is destructive of a liberty that finds its highest expression in the community, but our seeking the opinions of others (*amour propre*). This threatens liberty precisely because it drains relationships of their social content and turns them into arrangements for egoistic gratification.

Rousseau's concept of nature is perhaps best understood in comparison with its great rival in eighteenth-century thought – empiricism. This latter approach starts from supposed indubitable, and more or less permanent, features of the human condition, and then works out, with the use of a modest concept of reason, what are the most appropriate rules and institutions for coping with these unalterable facts. In this analysis, experience is the pre-eminent source of moral knowledge and it also sets the limits to the possible improvements that can be made on social rules and practices. Hume argues in the *Treatise of*

Human Nature that: 'As it is impossible to change or correct anything material in our nature, the utmost we can do is to change our circumstances and situation, and render the observance of the laws of justice our nearest interest, and their violation our utmost remote' (1972: 262). This does not prevent laws and practices, for example, the rules of justice, being fully universalisable, for the human charactcristics to which they are a response are themselves thought to be pretty much unalterable and common to humanity. It does, however, tell us that we should not go against the grain of what is believed to be an accurate account of human nature.

For Rousseau, however, we find an idealised concept of nature, described in *The Discourse on the Origins of Inequality*, in which on the one hand, certain features of the human condition are assumed to be universal – one being a concern for our own welfare, and the other, perhaps more significant socially, a 'natural repugnance at seeing any other sensible being, and particularly any of our own species, suffer pain or death' (1913: 157) – but on the other hand some attributes, greed, envy and social inequality, are understood to be *merely* contingent and hence alterable. The picture of human nature so described is not one, then, that is formed out of natural social experience but one that seeks to capture the essence of man, unsullied by what Rousseau regards as the unnecessary ephemera of civil society. Indeed, he accuses other writers (and he has Hobbes particularly in mind), who similarly write of a natural man, of merely reading back into a state of nature these very social contingencies. They claim a universality for what are, in effect, conventional, hence alterable phenomena.

Rousseau is able to attribute to natural man, and make it the basis of his radical social philosophy, the idea of perfectibility, 'the faculty of self-improvement, which by the help of circumstances, gradually develops all the rest of our faculties' (1913: 170). The specific institutional programme outlined in *The Social Contract* has to be understood as a response then to Rousseau's peculiar view of nature. Man, indeed, can change but the transformation is only possible in this social framework: all preceding forms of order are founded upon the temporary not the permanent interests of man.

This approach has great significance for the understanding of freedom, for if laws can be designed for Rousseau's 'natural' persons, i.e. pre-social individuals, then they can be plausibly said not to restrict their liberty. For Hume, the necessities of the human condition dictate that legal institutions restrict liberty because he uses this concept in an entirely empirical sense; there is no specific morality of social freedom, there are only those ethical rules which are the necessary constraints on what otherwise would be a socially destructive liberty. For him, Rousseau's concept of natural man is simply man not yet civilised by general rules.

Smith, however, is a little different. For without in any way adopting a Rousseauistic naturalism he does, by way of some obscure observations, concede that there is something more in the connection between liberty and law than mere utility. For example, of apprenticeship laws, he writes that apart from their disruptive effect on price signals in the labour market they are a 'manifest encroachment upon the just liberty both of the workman, and of those who might be disposed to employ him' (1976a: 138). There is in Smith's ethics a notion of nature which suggests the impropriety of certain forms of conduct, especially breaches of the rules of justice, that is apparent to us in advance of any utilitarian considerations that might condemn them. Our sympathy with the victims of injustice, and our resentment at its occurrence precedes any calculation of malign consequences. He does maintain that justice is a natural, not an artificial virtue, precisely because it accords with certain natural predispositions, the moral force of which obtains independently of the existence of formal rules.

Yet whatever minor modifications Smith may have made to Hume's utilitarianism, the nature described and celebrated by these two writers would be anathema to Rousseau. The rules and practices that had evolved naturally to cope with more or less unalterable circumstances were in fact destructive of that natural potential for goodness that he had detected; and so far from encouraging a natural sociability they had produced irreconcilable divisions. Those Humean 'conventions' which had developed to protect property and contract had merely reinforced those institutions that had deceived natural individuals. Man's liberty was not to be found in the predictability that law provided but in a form of moral community in which human behaviour has not taken an individualistic, competitive form. Conventional law provides mere security, not liberty.

The social distortion of nature

For Rousseau natural man, and his innate perfectibility, is destroyed by a number of interrelated factors which featured in the transition from the natural state to civil society. This is not a description of a particular moment in history but a hypothetical reconstruction of the growth of civilisation. These factors are dependency, vanity, inequality and conventional property. It is not that man's natural wickedness makes law necessary. This is an arbitrary supposition of Hobbes and his followers rather than a true description of natural motivations. Rousseau maintained that in the natural state the presence of compassion makes the Hobbesian description a caricature of humanity.[2] It is a description, Rousseau argues, which is not adhered to consistently by these writers, all of whom are compelled to make some reference to sociability in their explanation of order. In an obscure reference to Bernard Mandeville (1913: 183) he even detected in that arch-egoist an acknowledgement of the pity that we all feel for the sufferings of others. Rousseau's claim is, rather, that the perverse development of social institutions had created *artificially* those desires which made coercive law necessary. Rousseau's argument seems to be that if a theorist starts from a mistaken view of human nature, then he is bound to produce the justification for a social order that unnecessarily reduces our liberty.

In his description of the state of nature individuals are free because they do not depend on each other: liberty is in fact self-sufficiency, where that means independence of the dehumanising desires brought about by the constant interaction with others, and freedom from that striving for material advantage, which he associates with civilisation (he normally means here, commercial society). Civilised man 'is always moving, sweating, toiling and racking his brains to find still more laborious occupations' (1913: 220) and in so doing he loses his strength and individuality. This natural liberty may be incomplete because it lacks a morally necessary social dimension, but for Rousseau it is infinitely preferable to the, in his view, bogus freedom brought about by, in Smith's words, the desire to 'better ourselves'. The only acceptable form of dependence exists in his ideal republic where we need each other as citizens in a common enterprise, not as traders in essentially private relationships. It is in this form of dependency only in which liberty and law can be in harmony.[3]

This really is an odd account of dependency. As Hume and Smith were anxious to stress, our liberty is actually advanced by the constant interaction brought about by the rise of commerce. Montesquieu was, in fact, the first major theorist to point out the advantages for liberty that commerce introduced, and he contrasted it nicely with the bellicosity that arises whenever the public and the political is made the exclusive concern of man. But Rousseau is oblivious of the pacificity that is a feature of commercial dealings conducted under general rules of law. This is perhaps a consequence of his insistence, in *The Social Contract* especially, that proper law must proceed from the will, expressed through an arcane, crypto-democratic deliberative procedure. He was unaware of the fact men could live harmoniously under laws which were not directly of their own making. For Hume and Smith, freedom under the law was possible to the extent that a general system of rules increased opportunities for mutually beneficial interactions. It was not the source or origin of law that was dependency-producing but its range and extent. Hume (1987: 87–96) could even consider the possibility that absolute monarchy was more protective of liberty than a republic. He would have regarded the participatory methods of law-making recommended by Rousseau as likely to produce an abject form of dependency.

Freedom and interdependence

Rousseau sets himself an insuperable problem because he presents a stark dichotomy between independence and dependence and fails to appreciate that *interdependence* is the crucial feature of all societies. It merely becomes more sharply focused, not qualitatively different, with the rise of commercial society. When people make mutually beneficial exchanges the fact that they depend on each other for the fulfilment of the contract does not produce a kind of enslavement, as Rousseau seems to imply, but rather a recognition of the possibility of the satisfaction of a potentially infinite range of desires. A Rousseauistic world of self-sufficiency is a world without significant desires, except the desire for the public good in a well-ordered republic. The coincidence between public and private desire that he yearns for is only possible by narrowly confining human wants.

What Rousseau is implicitly objecting to is the division of labour which, as Marx was to claim later, apparently destroys self-sufficiency. But this somewhat specialised form of self-sufficiency (which would exclude the more advanced forms of exchange) makes not only progress impossible; it would also stultify the development of a certain kind of morality: the ethics of social cooperation under general rules. Rousseau cannot plausibly argue here that the theorists of the division of labour were rationalists anxious to destroy the freedom and spontaneity of the individual by entrapping him in liberty-reducing schemes designed to subordinate his interests to some centrally-ordered productive plan. The division of labour is not a product of reason, or of the devious arts of a decadent civilisation, but is, in Smith's famous words, the 'necessary, though very slow and gradual consequence of a certain propensity in human nature . . . the propensity to truck, barter and exchange one thing for another' (1976a: 25) To what extent can this plausibly be said to involve a loss of liberty? Indeed, the whole market system was already in existence before Hume and Smith arrived to describe it. If freedom consists in self-sufficiency it is a confined kind of liberty, the liberty that is a feature of a society which is content to satisfy only the most basic of human needs.

The eighteenth-century writers on commerce were not unaware of the fact that market relationships produced a kind of dependency but insisted that it was not something which was malign. Neither was a change in human nature required for the alleviation of such dependency that might be *potentially* harmful. As Smith commented: 'man has almost constant occasion for the help of his brethren, and it is vain to expect it from their benevolence alone' (1976a: 432). For him, self-interest is the driving force of social cooperation and hence a diminution of it would actually reduce individual autonomy. For a person to rely upon the weak force of benevolence, charity, or what Rousseau would call compassion, would be the ultimate sign of a baleful dependency. What Rousseau would call egoism, Smith would call simple prudence. He was able to distinguish between selfishness, a wilful failure to have a regard for the interests of others, and self-interest which, if exercised under rules, especially the rules of justice, could benefit all. Rousseau's concept of *amour de soi*, the natural affection for the self, seems to have none of the important social implications that self-interest has, for it would appear to apply only to the condition of self-sufficiency, i.e. the absence of those interactions or interdependencies characteristic of commercial society.

That Rousseau simply could not see that the public good emerges from self-interest is apparent from a revealing passage in *The Discourse on the Origins of Inequality*, where he claims that 'we find our advantage in the misfortunes of our fellow creatures, and that the loss of one man almost always constitutes the prosperity of another' (1913: 273). Now in a trivial sense the first part of this proposition is true. There are occasions when not only the misfortunes of some benefit others but, more importantly, there are clear cases where selfish individuals use the public for their own advantage. Hume and Smith were obsessively concerned to show how the rules of justice had to be enforced, precisely because the exploitation of goodwill leads inevitably to the drying up of the supply of that goodwill. However, since the quoted passage occurs in the context of a general critique of money and commerce, the only conclusion we can draw is that Rousseau felt that this was the defining characteristic of that society: it must be transcended through a change in character. The occasional aberrations of the parts of a civil order were interpreted as ineradicable features of the whole.

For Rousseau similar considerations apply to the notion of *vanity*. Natural man had been deceived not by the gentle passion of self-love but by the constant desire to seek the approval of others; a corrosive desire that produces dependency and saps our morality. Not only that, but vanity produces distinctions that undermine our communal moral instincts. The desire to be the best at any activity was the 'first step towards inequality, and at the same time towards vice' (1913: 197). Man is distracted from his essence and governed by the appearance he presents to others. But again we have to ask, why is this unnatural? It is, of course, unnatural only by the tenets of Rousseau's concepts of freedom and independence; for these would seem to dictate that any attempt to increase our material well-being beyond the requirement of self-sufficiency would be simply pride, and hence likely to produce an anti-social resentment.

Not surprisingly, Hume and Smith (to a lesser extent) took a different view. It was not just that vanity actually provoked human activity to labour and industry for the ultimate benefit of all but that, so far from being divisive, it actually promoted a certain amount of social concord. Hume argued that the desire to be esteemed was a social passion and that the rich and the powerful actually provoked a certain kind of satisfaction in people (1972: 107). Hume had good reason for saying this. Morals had to be internalised, and this meant that a variety of devices were appropriate for their transmission and sustainability in a sociological sense. Esteem was particularly important because it inspired *sympathy*, our ability to share in the satisfaction of others, which is the fundamental source of approbation and disapprobation.

Smith, in *The Theory of Moral Sentiments*, whilst holding that vanity and the desire for personal success were inevitable and not undesirable features of commercial society, added a moral component that Rousseau would not have found entirely objectionable. He

(Smith) pointed out that the individual desires not only praise but *praiseworthiness*. The moral agent wants to be the object of praise or blame even if these are not accorded to him by others (1976b: 166). The person is a moral agent because he has the right and natural motivation even if he happened to be evaluated only with reference to external signs of achievement. And again, despite his recognition of the social value of the 'toil and bustle of this world' he, nevertheless, showed a disdain for work-obsessed individuals who find 'wealth and greatness in mere trinkets of frivolous folly' (1976b: 261).

Still, we are in two different moral worlds, one (Smith's) in which society is a kind of 'mirror' of an individual's actions, a device through which he could assess his own moral progress and the other (Rousseau's) in which a perverse social development (commercial society) has stunted and distorted the morality of natural man. And this has great implications for freedom because for Rousseau the transition from natural liberty to social liberty required a reversal of those institutions and practices that, in his opinion, had diverted man from his proper end.

Equality and property

The most obvious sources of this diversion, and indeed cause of the resulting moral disorder, are property and inequality. The civilisation that Rousseau abhorred is founded upon a bogus contract that sanctified an originally illegitimate transfer (or, more exactly, creation) of right. But it was a process which, because it was not in accordance with the moral demands of our true nature, must be destructive of our liberty. Rousseau writes that: 'The first man who, having enclosed a piece of ground, bethought himself of saying "this is mine", and found people simple enough to believe him, was the real founder of civil society' (1913: 192). The introduction of property, probably via the establishment of distinctive families, was the 'source of a thousand quarrels and conflicts' (1913: 195). It was because of the unequal possession of property that there arose the constant comparing of one with another which Rousseau found so harmful to the creation and maintenance of true communities. Property divides people; it leads to rivalry and competitiveness.

However, despite what Rousseau often implies, it is not property itself that is objectionable but rather the rules that have developed to validate it. His ideal community would be a small, self-contained rural society of self-sufficient property-holders. But in those circumstances their possessions would not be a cause of quarrels: first, because their ownership rights would be legitimated by a sovereign (of which each individual would be equally a part) and second, because the approximate equality of those possessions could not give one person, or group of persons, *power* over others. However, in his hypothetical reconstruction of civil society described in *The Origins of Inequality*, the fractiousness and disorder produced by unrestrained property accumulation had driven people, in need of security, to the establishment, by contract, of a legal order which simply preserved the pre-existing anti-social and immoral inequality. It bound 'new fetters on the poor', destroyed natural liberty and 'converted clever usurpation into unalterable right' (1913: 205). Thus, though Rousseau may occasionally talk of his ideal republic as if it united utility and justice, this could never be a moral formula that permitted inequality. The incentives that commercial society provided may have advanced aggregate well-being (as many of the early apologists for capitalism maintained), but the inequality that it produced was itself immoral. For Rousseau there could be no social harmony without justice and equality, and their demands precluded what he would regard as mindless accumulation. Equally important, there could be no liberty in a world of gratification but only that dependency which is generated by ceaseless exchange.

Indeed, perhaps the first obligation of political authority in a well-ordered republic is to prevent actively the spread of inequality. There is a suggestion that there is something almost inexorable about this. In *The Social Contract*, he writes that 'force of circumstances tends continually to destroy equality' (1913: 42). One might well ask, as Hume and Smith did, why not accept this as natural and legitimate if it is subject to rules which ensure a predictable allocation of property titles? Now it is true that Rousseau is concerned with these rules in *The Social Contract*, but whatever legitimates individual ownership is immediately attenuated by communal needs. In fact, the individual claim to property derives from society, from laws and institutions. These rules are not there (as in Locke) to protect property validated by pre-legal moral criteria but to give it a social authorisation. Thus, in a somewhat ambiguous statement in *The Discourse on Political Economy*, Rousseau maintains that it is 'one of the most important functions of government to prevent extreme inequality of fortunes; not by taking wealth from its possessors, but by depriving all men of means to accumulate it' (1913: 250). There is, then, rightful possession but only a strictly limited right of acquisition.

It is, of course, tempting to dismiss Rousseau's concerns as the plaintive yearnings of a romantic for a past that never existed, the hopeless bleatings of a rural utopian who cannot come to terms with a modern world whose conditions have just as much a claim to be 'natural' as has his own somewhat eccentric version of nature. From a more sympathetic modern perspective, he might be regarded as the original author of the doctrine that law and government are simply devices through which the rich maintain their domination over the poor. They are not (at least in their present form) institutional arrangements to promote the interests we have as citizens, but they merely provide a fraudulent authorisation of the possessions of the deceitful few. There is much textual evidence to suggest that Rousseau does not wish to eliminate natural inequalities, but only those brought about by artifice, cunning and force.

Intriguingly, Smith himself suggests, in his posthumous *Lectures on Jurisprudence*, a similar process. He postulated that: 'Till there be property there can be no government, the very end of which is to secure wealth and to defend the rich from the poor . . . This inequality of fortune, making a distinction between the rich and poor, gave the former much influence over the latter . . .' (1978: 404–5). Of course, Smith had other reasons to accept existing forms of government, primarily for the security that they give to transactors and for their repair of the damage to civil society that an unrestrained market might produce. He wanted government not only to provide the familiar public goods but also to maintain a commitment to basic moral rules through education. However, the comment he makes in that work is nevertheless an example of the doubt that some eighteenth-century protagonists of commercial society had about the propriety of original property holdings and the exact rationale of government.

Since the anti-rationalism of Hume and Smith prevented them from adopting any Lockean natural law foundation for property (or government) they had no alternative but to rely on conventions (in fact, for Hume, if not Smith, all morality is a matter of conventions). Their conservatism, in a philosophical sense, arises almost inevitably from their acceptance of received social practices, which it would be folly to reject merely from the perspective of an abstract reason. It is true that Rousseau founds political institutions on a kind of convention, and he similarly rejects the notion of natural right (1913: 3–4), but it is very different from the conventions that Hume had in mind. For him conventions were accepted in the context of all those inequalities that Rousseau found so objectionable.

The plain fact is that for Hume the conventions that reinforced these inequalities were necessarily liberty-reducing. In his conception of natural man restraints were a universal necessity, for the permanence of scarcity and the assumed limitless nature of desire made some technical delineation of property titles imperative. We need to know what is mine and yours by convention since 'uninstructed nature never made any such distinction' (1975: 195). The rules of justice that governed, amongst other things, property were features of artificial virtue but their conformity to unalterable facts of the human condition made it not inappropriate to call them natural. For Rousseau, property holdings were alterable, and such alteration would increase liberty because it would eliminate unnatural desires.

Civil liberty

Rousseau finds, then, the existing form of civil society morally repugnant because its institutional structure is based on an alterable inequality, and the motivational framework which it presents to individuals encourages *amour propre* and a selfish, competitive individualism. It drains them of their genuine communal feelings. True freedom is found in a liberation from these artificially imposed constraints on the development of sociability. The key to moral *character* is the argument that a person's fulfilment lies in deliberate, cooperative activity; not in productive activity, as in, say, a collectivist or private enterprise economy, but in the making of the laws that should govern a social life which had little concern with production. The good does not emerge unintentionally, as in Hume and Smith (and for them laws and morals are as much matters of spontaneity as is economic well-being), but from deliberate acts of the will.

Thus *The Social Contract* is the solution to the moral problems posed by contemporary society. They require a transformation of character, a change that produces an active will, the exercise of which generates civic virtue. Law is necessarily involved in this transformation for the exchange of natural liberty for civil liberty, which heralds the birth of civil society proper and substitutes morality for instinct, necessitates that the individual puts himself under authority. Hence the importance of Rousseau's claim that the Legislator must somehow bring about the transformation: 'men would have to be before law what they should become by means of law' (1913: 34). The role of the Legislator is often claimed to be a totalitarian implication of Rousseau's thought but a more charitable interpretation of it might be to say that it is a somewhat melodramatic example of a familiar problem in social theory: how can legal institutions be so designed that they will not become a prey to selfish exploitation by private groups. Only the *experience* of the benefits of just laws can provide the conditions for individuals to sustain them. If people do not know the advantages that come from living under general rules, predatory action will continue. Rousseau's failure was his inability to understand that the requisite knowledge could be acquired spontaneously.

It might well be asked, though, what is the point of the social contract if Rousseau's ideal republic depends exclusively on a change in human nature? If the person has been cleansed of anti-social motivations then the will to the common good will emerge through the continual law-making process, without the creation of moral and political obligation by some specific act. Of course, previous contract theorists, notably Hobbes and Locke, do not suppose that human nature is changed through contracting: in their very differing ways they show how liberty is necessarily limited, and indeed exchanged, for something else (security for Hobbes, property rights protection for Locke). But for Rousseau the exchange of natural liberty for civic liberty does not involve the contraction of freedom but its expansion. Indeed, one could dispense with the notion of contract altogether and still examine whether he has succeeded in his primary aim of trying to explain how those things which we do have in common can be promoted over private and socially destructive interests. The problem about the change in human nature can be made more plausible if it is translated into a problem about motivation. For Rousseau, the presence of inequality is the major reason why general interests are not promoted. What makes his argument so implausible from the perspective of conservatism or liberal individualism is his assertion that inequality is unnatural, and somehow eliminable.

That Hume and Smith thought that inequalities were perfectly natural should not be interpreted to mean that they were not aware of the moral requirement that law should be perfectly general and not a product of particular interests. Hume (1972: 206) remarked that: 'It is only when a character is considered in general, without reference to particular interest, that it causes such a feeling or sentiment as denominates it morally good or evil.' And Smith believed that justice, no matter how limited in application it might be, still constitutes those general rules of society without which commerce would be impossible (1976b: 157–63). The difference from Rousseau, however, was that these moral demands were consistent with a conception of human nature as we commonly experience it, and their formalised expression in laws, rules, customs and practices necessarily involved reductions in liberty (in a straightforward empirical sense). Hume and Smith also believed that the coincidence between public and private interests would be brought about by conformity to those rules that had developed spontaneously in response to man's more or less universal needs rather than through the creation of law by deliberate acts of will. This would be regarded as a rationalistic folly and likely to be destructive of liberty because of the surrender of the individual to the collective which it implies.

Political legitimacy

However, even if we regard Rousseau's hopes for a change in human nature as somewhat fanciful, it cannot be denied that he located one very important problem in social theory: the creation and maintenance of general rules of just conduct. If he was optimistic about these being generated by a transformation of character, then Hume and Smith were equally sanguine in their faith in the benign forces of spontaneous social evolution. In Hume's case, of course, we find an ultra-conservative (almost Hobbesian) contention that there was an obligation to obey received law and government since it was better to have some rules rather than none at all: 'Time and custom give authority to all forms of government . . . and that power which at first was founded only on injustice and violence, becomes in time legal and obligatory' (1972: 288). This gives the impression that the connection between law and liberty is almost serendipitous.

Rousseau is much more ambitious. He hopes to show, in *The Social Contract*, that liberty and law are consistent through a form of collective endeavour: 'each man, in giving himself to all, gives himself to nobody' (1913: 12). It is through his personal involvement in decision-making or, at least law-making,[4] that provides the generality which just law requires and preserves that liberty which is the object of civil society. This is specifically not a natural rights argument (which would authorise government to act in certain areas, and hence reduce the liberty of the individual) but a communitarian argument that legitimates collective action precisely because it is expressive of the real will of each individual. Indeed, in Rousseau's contract there is a 'total alienation of each associate, together with all his rights, to the whole community' (1913: 12). To hold back rights, in a Lockean manner, would apparently be to retain the means by which dissent and quarrels are produced, and by which the separateness between the person and the community is maintained. The exchange of natural liberty for civic liberty is, in fact, a Hobbesian surrender of rights to the sovereign, with the proviso that the sovereignty so created is one in which each individual somehow remains a part. Also it is not a once and for all action, for the morality of sovereignty has to be replenished by constant participation. The common good is clearly not the unintended outcome of a myriad of private actions but is the deliberate result of active citizenship. Freedom does not consist in the protection of the law (guaranteeing a private sphere) but in the opportunities the social contract allows for participation in the making of the law. The alleged dependency produced, for example, by market relationships is replaced by a dependence of the person on the city.

This brief description of Rousseau's conditions of political legitimacy seems not to have a lot to do with liberty, certainly not in the way that Hume and Smith understood the concept. It would only make sense if the criterion of unanimity were to govern all decision-making. It is true that the original contract (convention) is subject to unanimity (1913: 11), but Rousseau does not want this to constrain all decision-making and he rejects the idea that one person should be able to veto proposed legislation. The point of the original contract is to describe the conditions under which less than unanimity prevails while legitimacy is still preserved. This is not merely for convenience – though for practical affairs Rousseau says (1913: 89) that the voting rule should be less stringent than for 'grave and important questions' – but to claim a justification in morality for those occasions when the individual's *apparent* will is overridden. Majority rule is then specifically authorised by the contract (1913: 11).

Rousseau provides this moral framework by distinguishing between the general will, the corporate will and the particular will. The morality of perfect freedom is achieved only when the general will is in harmony with the particular will. But, of course, in any society this harmony is likely to be disturbed by the superficial attractions of group or corporate interests: 'Men always love what is good . . . it is in judging what is good that they go wrong' (1913: 105). The corporate will is more powerful a motivation than the desire for the general will – especially in circumstances of deception and inequality. In effect, conditions must be designed so that the general will prevails.

It really is a question of motivation, for all liberal theorists believe that there is a public realm and are worried by the fact that the individualistic incentives provided by commercial society will undermine it. Smith was obsessively concerned about the decline of the 'martial spirit' (the absence of love for a liberal society in general would leave it vulnerable to aggressors) and feared that the relentless progress of the division of labour would render the people too stupid and alienated (1976a: 788) even to understand the basic moral rules on which commercial life depends. Paradoxical though it may sound, the search for the common good that Rousseau engaged in for his backward-looking rural society was repeated, though somewhat more modestly, by the advocates of progressive, forward-looking commercial orders.

Rousseau's struggles here are not without interest, for all liberal theorists (apart from individualistic anarchists) are concerned to make a case for the public good. The key to his explanation is the distinction he makes between the 'will of all' (1913: 23) and the general will (see Barry, 1967: 112–26). If there is a general will it can often exist independently of individuals expressing a want for it; their particular wills may be too powerful. This is exactly like the problem of the production of public goods in liberal political economy: the familiar free rider problem means that they will not be produced privately, even though their non-provision leaves everybody worse off. Non-market arrangements, such as social contracts or voting procedures, have to be used to provide the force which is necessary for the provision of what individuals really want. Rousseau refers obliquely to this problem when he says that a person may wish to enjoy the rights of citizenship without fulfilling his duties as a subject: 'The continuance of such an injustice could not but prove the undoing of the body politic' (1913: 15).

What is more interesting is that people could actually agree voluntarily to the continuation of this socially destructive process: the will of all consists of the sum of all the particular wills, each of which is sufficiently powerful to distract individuals from the general will. But there is, of course, a general will which is revealed in Rousseau's mysterious sentence: 'take away these same wills the pluses and minuses that cancel one another, and the general will remains as the sum of the differences' (1913: 23). This means that within each person there will be a multiplicity of wills, all of which are mutually incompatible *except for the one that they share* (of course, it is logically possible, in a bitterly divided society that there is no one common interest). Under certain (alterable) conditions, however, the competing wills may not cancel each other out but lead to pointless quarrels from which no one benefits. Inequality is the most damaging of these conditions. But if, in Rousseau's republic, substantial equality is achieved, then the incentive for the particular will to predominate is reduced. Of course, there are solutions to these dilemmas that do not require substantive equality, but that is the only circumstance that interested Rousseau.

To take a more modern example – free international trade. For Hume and Smith this was for the common good, even though it might not seem to be in the interests of each transactor considered separately (the fact that Rousseau has other reasons for objecting to free trade does not affect the logic of this particular argument). Each producer may be seen to have three policy options: a policy in which his particular product is protected from foreign competition but every other item can be imported freely, a policy that protects all producers and, finally, one that allows unrestricted trade in all goods. The first is simply inconceivable since the traders are never going to let one of their number reap the advantages of protection for himself alone, the third would be in their general interest but no one trader has an immediate interest in promoting it unless he has the assurance that others will be so well-disposed (he might fear that a coalition may form which subjected him alone to the rigours of competition). It is quite likely that in a voting assembly composed of individuals driven by their more powerful particular interests, everyone would vote for all-round protection. This, then, would be a classic example of the will of all. A collective decision-making procedure has to be found which gets round this problem.

The will of all does emanate apparently from the voluntary choices of individuals, but this voluntariness is illusory because it results from the domination of a selfish impulse. In Rousseau's world it cannot represent true liberty since that must encompass a recognition of other purposes than the mere promptings of desire. In my example of free international trade, the collective decision to promote it is in a sense necessary only for the satisfaction of purely subjective wants, whereas for Rousseau one suspects that there are communal affiliations that cannot always be translated into mechanisms for the more efficient satisfaction of mere preferences (especially for commercial gain). Still, one must concede that the collective choice problem that he highlighted is a feature of a liberal social theory that is founded on a quite different metaphysics. Certainly, it seems to be the only way in which much sense can be made of Rousseau's infamous claim that a person may be 'forced to be free' (1913: 15), i.e. they may need some *method* which allows for their long-term interests to be promoted. An institutional arrangement could be imagined which provided for this without at the same time telling people what their long-term 'objective' interests really are.

It is true that most critics of Rousseau presuppose that some collective will, irreducible to individual choice, may impose a conception of the good on a society whose members are incapable of seeing it themselves. The language he uses suggests this, as well as the distaste he seemed to have for some fairly ordinary aspects of life, e.g. commerce. These were unaccountably deemed to be unnatural. Nevertheless, as noted earlier, his ultimate aim is to unite justice and *utility* in an order of freedom. No doubt his conception of utility would be an over-moralised one for Hume and Smith, but his inchoate suggestions as to how individual purposes may be made harmonious with the pursuit of necessary collective ends cannot, in principle, be excluded from the agenda of even economic liberalism.

Similar problems can also be seen in the struggles that Rousseau has in his discussion of the claims of unanimity and majoritarianism in the determination of the legitimacy of law (as distinct from the role of government). It seems clear that the will of all, though it comes from the voluntary choices of each individual taken separately, is not actually a case of unanimity: it is simply the malign arithmetic of an unfettered individualism. Presumably, when people are deliberating in the assembly as to whether or not a particular proposal is consistent with the general will, they will need some decision rule, no matter how public-spirited they may be, so that a final verdict can be obtained. For suitably moralised people, Rousseau has an *a priori* preference for unanimity: 'the nearer opinion approaches unanimity, the greater the dominance of the general will' (1913: 87). Of course, only at the contractual stage is unanimity *specifically* required; elsewhere 'the majority always binds the rest' (1913: 88). Still, the imposition of majority rule does not reduce a person's liberty for Rousseau; it merely indicates those communal interests which may not be visible to him.

However, he is concerned (1913: 88–9) about the liberty of individuals outvoted under majority rule procedures (just as he is vexed by the hold-out tactics that might be employed by a single individual under unanimity). His answer seems to be that majority rule would not be harmful to minorities if certain conditions are met. These are the well-known ones of approximate equality and the institution of a *non-representative* assembly (1913: 78–9). The latter is important because, according to Rousseau, if people deliberate as individuals they are less prone to the promptings of the corporate will and more likely to have, therefore, a greater incentive to will what is common to them as citizens. There is not a lot of difference between this proposition and the claim of modern public choice economists that self-interest, when expressed by groups, is destructive of the public interest which anonymous individuals share. And, of course, Adam Smith himself had many critical things to say about the anti-social activities of the merchant *class*, despite his general admiration for the ethics of commerce.

A more controversial claim that Rousseau makes is that the general will is likely to emerge in a voting procedure in which citizens do not communicate with each other (1913: 23). The claim is rather obliquely put but Rousseau presumably means that in conditions of anonymity coalitions cannot form which distract citizens from the public interest. One can imagine this to be a plausible argument if an assembly were to be set up in a rationalistic manner in which the designers were determined to engineer away any possible cause of factionalism. However, a liberal conservative, like Hume, would take the opposite view. He might be just as anxious to promote the public over private interests but could well argue that people would *learn* the advantages of cooperative action through the very act of communication. Hume's explanation of the spontaneous evolution of rules and practices, which are assumed to be antithetical to an uninstructed nature, depends surely for its validity on people learning through experience. Legitimacy is not the product of a once and for all act by anonymous individuals but emerges gradually as people come to realise the benefits of common rules. The social dilemma that Rousseau correctly identifies in fact can only be overcome by communication.

Conclusion

Despite the connection that Rousseau tries to make between individual liberty and the common good – a connection that, if successful, would end the perennial debate between individualism and collectivism – the ultimate conclusion must be that he is communitarian in inspiration. The intriguing suggestions he makes for the promotion of common interests and the attempt to derive these from individual preferences, should not distract us from the fact that his whole endeavour is to suppress certain preferences. This would be less alarming if he were concerned only with those preferences that were destructive of genuine public and shared interests. Hume and Smith could, with modifications, have agreed with this. But the impression he gives is that he wishes to eliminate certain preferences because they are purely private. It is these that divert individuals from their communal responsibilities. And Rousseau understands freedom as essentially a feature of public, communal and political action. Furthermore, Hume and Smith would not regard a system as liberty-preserving which binds individuals to a sovereign unconstrained by law. The fact that citizens are supposed to be contained within the sovereign, and hence the authors of law, would be a woefully inadequate safeguard.

This can be seen in Rousseau's obsession with public service. Individuals were led away from this by the lure of commerce and were prepared to pay others to perform their duties of citizenship. His objection to taxation was not that he wanted citizens to retain as much of their income as possible but because it relieved them of their social obligations. In one disturbing sentence he said: 'I hold enforced labour to be less opposed to liberty than taxes' (1913: 77). In direct contrast, Hume, in his essay, 'Of Commerce' (1987: 253–67) argued that the growth of an exchange economy actually strengthened the state. It made it possible for public defence to be taken care of by professional armies and its creation of luxury goods provided an additional source of taxation. In such circumstances, individuals would be left free to get on with their private lives. Whatever their morality, Hume's prognostications were more accurate with regard to the future development of Western societies. Rousseau's affections were for the classical world and the concept of freedom associated with it.

However, there is one aspect of Rousseau's thought that would find favour with non-communitarian liberals. This is his theory of law: especially the features of generality, equality and impersonality that define it. His demand that law should name no one, be blind to the differences in people and non-arbitrary in application (1913: 30) anticipates the Kantian conception of freedom under law and modern liberal theories of the rule of law. As he correctly argues, it is government that particularises, not the law. It is true that the creation of privileges (1913: 31) is possible with his idea of legality, but at least the beneficiaries of them cannot be named in advance. Even modern, individualistic jurisprudence has found it impossible to make the requirement of generality in law stringent enough to exclude any possibility of arbitrariness. A great deal of oppression can take place under perfectly abstract laws.

Even this gesture towards formalism that Rousseau makes tends to be submerged beneath a social philosophy that is suffused with a certain kind of activism. Law is the product of will, not evolution, and that in itself poses a threat to individuals and minorities who might find themselves at odds with that will. Ultimately, modern liberalism developed in a way which did not conceive of constant participation by concerned citizens as a reliable protector of liberty. The retreat into a private world protected by a carapace of general rules became a more attractive solution to the problems of politics.

Notes

1 All three writers lived at roughly the same period and were very much aware of each other's work. In fact, Hume befriended Rousseau briefly but the friendship ended in a bitter quarrel. They were poles apart intellectually and temperamentally. Smith clearly has Rousseau's *Discourse on the Origins of Inequality* (1755) in mind in parts of his own *Theory of Moral Sentiments* (1759).

2 Rousseau had other reasons for objecting to Hobbesian explanations of order, notably the physical impossibility of a tyrant establishing permanent control (1913: 6).

3 Rousseau had a non-social method for ensuring non-dependency, the educational programme described in *Emile*. For a discussion of this, see Charvet (1974: ch. 3).

4 In Rousseau's system citizens only participate in the making of general laws. It is governments that make particular decisions.

References

Barry, B. (1967), 'The Public Interest', in ed. A. Quinton, *Political Philosophy*, London, Oxford University Press.

Charvet, J. (1974), *The Social Problem in the Philosophy of Rousseau*, Cambridge, Cambridge University Press.

Hume, D. (1972), *A Treatise of Human Nature*, ed. P. S. Ardal, London, Fontana. First published 1739.

— (1975), *Enquiries Concerning Human Understanding and Concerning the Principles of Morals*, ed. P. H. Nidditch, Oxford, Clarendon Press. First published 1751.

— (1987), *Essays: Moral, Political and Literary*, ed. Eugene F. Miller, Indianapolis, Liberty Classics. First published 1777.

Rousseau, J. J. (1913), *The Social Contract and Discourses*, ed. G. D. H. Cole, London, Everyman. *The Social Contract* was first published in 1762 and *The Discourse on the Origins of Inequality* in 1755, on the *Arts and Sciences* in 1750 and on *Political Economy* (abstracted from the *Encyclopédie*) in 1758.

Smith, A. (1976a), *An Enquiry into the Nature and Causes of the Wealth of Nations*, eds R. H. Campbell and A. S. Skinner, Oxford, Clarendon Press. First published 1776.

— (1976b), *The Theory of Moral Sentiments*, eds D. D. Raphael and A. Macfie, Oxford, Clarendon Press. First published 1759.

— (1978), *Lectures on Jurisprudence*, eds R. L. Meek, D. D. Raphael and P. G. Stein, Oxford, Clarendon Press. First published 1896.

3   Christopher Kelly and Roger D. Masters

Human nature, liberty and progress: Rousseau's dialogue with the critics of the Discours sur l'inégalité[1]

Although the relationship between 'freedom' in its political sense and 'free will' as a metaphysical or theological concept is often ignored or misunderstood, the possible distinction between these two aspects of *liberty* is ultimately of immense theoretical importance. For no major thinker is a clear understanding of this relationship more important than Rousseau, yet contemporary commentators have often failed to address it.

In the *Discours sur l'origine de l'inégalité*, Rousseau for the first time explicitly addressed the metaphysical and moral dimension of human free will, and did so in the context of discussing the freedom he saw constituting the life of humans in the state of nature. In providing this context he indicated that the two fundamental dimensions of freedom can be understood only in the context of an analysis of the nature and history of our species. But given the immense controversies that have surrounded the interpretation of the *Discours*, what lessons are we to draw from that text?

We suggest a relatively unusual approach. The issues raised by scholars today are not new ones: from the outset Rousseau was subject to criticisms that foreshadowed some of the continuous and current debates about his meaning. By analyzing carefully Rousseau's replies to the critics of the *Discours sur l'inégalité*, we can shed new light on the articulation of his extremely complex view of human liberty in its different forms. In fact, although these debates cover a bewildering array of issues, underlying Rousseau's various replies is a concern for liberty of a very practical sort. At the very least the examination of Rousseau's dialogues with his critics allows us to sketch the context within which these issues emerge in his thought.

Rousseau and the critics of the *Discours*

Rousseau's life contains many valuable lessons about the practical disadvantages of making too many enemies. Nevertheless, it also illustrates the intellectual advantage that can be drawn from being attacked by a great number of people representing a wide range of points of view. The deluge of criticism that frequently greeted his work – coming as it did from Jesuits and anti-clerical intellectuals, a king and numerous academicians, defenders of tradition and proponents of innovation – allowed Rousseau to pick and choose which attacks he would answer. His selections show his effort to elaborate a consistent position that could transcend the differences that divided his opponents.

The storm aroused by the *Discours sur les sciences et les arts* was so great that it would have taken a life's work to answer all of its critics. In his 'Final Reply' Rousseau clearly expresses his view of this multitude of adversaries by declaring, 'I dare say that they have never raised a reasonable objection that I did not anticipate and to which I did not reply in advance.'[2] In spite of this disdain he spent a good part of two years writing responses to five of these opponents.[3] These responses to a wide range of attacks solidified the reputation that Rousseau had acquired with the *Discours*. More importantly, they allowed him to begin to show that the work that had catapulted him to fame was more than a clever paradox and that a consistent set of principles underlay his assertions.[4]

The flurry of controversy that greeted the publication of the *Discours sur l'inégalité* in 1755 was also significant even if it did not match the sensation caused by the earlier work. Although inequality did not find quite as many vehement defenders as the sciences and arts had, those who wrote about the second work were equally unanimous in their disagreement with it. On the whole, Rousseau seems to have found these critics to be inferior to those who attacked the *Discours sur les sciences at les arts*. In the *Confessions* he implicitly dismisses those who published attacks by saying that the work 'found in all of Europe only a few readers who understood it, and none of those who wanted to speak about it.'[5] Nevertheless, what changed most in the several years that separated the publication of the two *Discours* was less the quality of the criticisms than Rousseau's strategy for responding to them.

Rousseau did not publish a set of letters, observations, or replies to the critics of the *Discours sur l'inégalité*. Although he avoided public controversy, during the twelve months beginning in October of 1755 he could not resist composing answers to three of the most distinguished of his critics. The first of these was the Genevan naturalist Charles Bonnet, who argued for the natural basis of civil society in his 'Letter from M. Philopolis'. The second was the botanist Charles-Georges Le Roy, who relayed what were apparently Buffon's objections to some of the observations on animal behavior in the *Discours*. The third critic was Voltaire. Of Rousseau's answers, only the letter to Voltaire of 18 August 1756 was actually sent, and it was not published until 1760 when it was published without his permission. When they are considered in relation to each other these answers provide a striking example of Rousseau's effort to transcend the disputes of the day. They also show the extent to which a concern for liberty in a practical, but non-metaphysical, sense guided his responses.

The letter to Voltaire is the most remarkable of these responses for a number of reasons. In spite of the fact that it concludes with an invitation to Voltaire to join Rousseau in the project of fostering a genuinely tolerant civil religion, the letter is an important step in Rousseau's rupture with the literary society of which Voltaire was, in Rousseau's view, the leader.[6] This step is all the more striking in that it appears quite gratuitous. Unlike Bonnet and Le Roy, Voltaire had not yet made either a public or private attack on the *Discours* beyond a few reasonably good-natured jokes in his letter of acknowledgement for the copy Rousseau had had presented to him. In fact, there is little in the letter indicating that Voltaire had taken more than a cursory glance at the *Discours* by the time he wrote it. Aside from the opening lines, the letter discusses the themes of the *Discours sur les sciences et les arts*. In what may be an indirect comment on Rousseau's suggestion that Voltaire's talents had been wasted because he lived in a corrupt age, the older man presents an assortment of complaints about his ill-treatment from publishers, the public, and plagiarists. Rousseau quickly responded to Voltaire's remarks with a gracious good humor. It was only upon his reading of the *Poème sur le Désastre de Lisbonne* and *Poème sur la Loi naturelle* in 1756 that Rousseau decided to regard Voltaire as an opponent of his own thought.

At first glance this must seem surprising to any reader of the *Discours* and the poems because the latter works contain no references to the former. There is in fact little reason to believe that in these poems, in attacking providence and the optimism of Leibniz and Pope, Voltaire had Rousseau in mind, since the *Discours sur l'inégalité* contains no explicit discussion of optimism and Voltair probably did not even read the *Discours* carefully until several years later.[7] Moreover he had copies of the poems sent to Rousseau with the evident expectation that the younger man would be a sympathetic and intelligent reader. None the less, Rousseau reacted so strongly against the poems that he attempted to refute Voltaire's position in his letter of acknowledgement.

In the *Confessions* Rousseau indicates that the root of his disagreement centered on the issue of where to locate responsibility for evil or the ills of mankind. This issue shows the particular way in which liberty is a central issue for Rousseau. In his view the claim that the source of human ills resides either in human nature or in some outside agency such as providence entails a denial of human liberty in the sense of control over and responsibility for one's own destiny. Rousseau insisted, against Voltaire's attack on providence, that the source of ills resided 'in the abuse that man has made of his faculties more than in nature itself.'[8] The contention that the ills of human life are not intrinsic to human nature, but are the result of a combination of extrinsic accidental causes and wicked or foolish human decisions is one of the central theses of the *Discours* and, indeed, of Rousseau's thought as a whole. Accordingly, whether or not Voltaire had read the *Discours* by 1756 or was even conscious of his disagreement with Rousseau, the latter had good reason to regard Voltaire as one of his opponents.

Optimism and liberty

In fact, the issue of optimism and the source of human ills had already been raised in connection with the *Discours* by Charles Bonnet who read Rousseau's work as an attack on this doctrine. Under the guise of Philopolis, Bonnet explicitly presents himself as the ally of the 'sublime geniuses' Leibniz and Pope.[9] He accuses Rousseau of being the enemy of their doctrine. In his 'Letter to M. Philopolis' Rousseau directly criticizes the version of optimism defended by Bonnet. Less than a year later, however, in the letter to Voltaire, he reverses his approach. His expression of dissatisfaction with Voltaire's poems focuses on their attack on optimism. In the midst of his discussion Rousseau contrasts the *Discours sur l'inégalité* with Voltaire's bitter denunciation of providence. Having allied himself with Pope and Leibniz, Rousseau turns to a critical examination of the details of

Voltaire's attack before concluding the letter with the effort at reconciliation. That Rousseau deliberately portrayed himself as a member of the optimist camp is confirmed by his remark in the *Confessions* that Voltaire's ultimate response to the letter was *Candide*, his most biting satire on the defining optimist principle that this is the best of all possible worlds.[10] Thus in a rather short period of time Rousseau appears as both the defender and the opponent of optimism. This apparent contradiction suggests that Rousseau's defense of and attack on optimism warrant a closer look.

Rousseau's first important declaration on the subject of optimism appeared long before he achieved fame, in his letter of 17 January 1742 to François-Joseph Conzié. Rousseau says that it was his friendship with Conzié that began the development of his literary and philosophic taste. The letter was in response to the loan of a copy of a translation of and commentary on Pope's *Essay on Man*. At this period, not long before he attempted to break into Parisian intellectual life with his new system of musical notation, Rousseau described Pope's version of optimism as 'a very absurd, but very well-linked System',[11] a phrase that would be echoed later in his descriptions of his own thought. In other words he treats optimism as one contending philosophic doctrine among others. The most substantial part of his criticism of Pope concerns the famous 'great chain of being' extending from the lowest of creatures to God. Rousseau's objection is that this version of the chain establishes an untenable link between the finite and the infinite. While he could have saved the chain of being by making God stand apart from the succession of links – a correction which he later applauded Voltaire for making[12] – Rousseau is more concerned with defending a refined version of Epicureanism from the attacks launched by Pope and by theologians. In short, in this earliest expression of his opinion Rousseau stands as an opponent of optimism on purely philosophic grounds and an ally if not outright supporter of the dangerously unorthodox Epicureanism.

Coming as it does several years before the 'illumination' on the road to Vincennes, this letter cannot be assumed to represent Rousseau's mature opinion. Nevertheless, it is our contention that the movement from this early attack on optimism to the defense of this doctrine in the letter to Voltaire is less a mark of a greater appreciation of the intrinsic philosophic merits of the arguments of Pope and Leibniz than it is a sign of a recognition of optimism's possible utility in the support of Rousseau's particular concern for liberty. In fact, a significant part of the 'illumination' is the awareness that philosophically unprovable doctrines and even prejudices may be necessary supports for morality. The common thread in Rousseau's later attacks on and defenses of optimism is a concern for the extent to which the consequences of the doctrine are passivity or a spirited assertion of liberty.

Most of the complexity of Rousseau's position on optimism emerges in the brief discussion in the 'Letter to Philopolis'. His quarrel is less with optimism as such than it is with Philopolis's revision of Leibniz and Pope. In this case, as well as in the attack on Voltaire, Rousseau's response shows his concern for liberty in the sense of control and responsibility. In particular Rousseau claims that Philopolis's revision is subject to a crucial objection that could not be directed against Leibniz. Philopolis fails to distinguish between general and particular evil and therefore is forced to deny that a particular evil, such as Philopolis suffering a stroke, is a real evil.[13] Philopolis's advice, to which Rousseau objects most vehemently, is that we 'let the world go on as it does, and be certain that it is going as well as it could go.'[14] The consequence of Philopolis's position is the abandonment of any assertion of human liberty to overcome particular evils. Whatever might be said about free will, Philopolis's version of optimism deprives us of its use by endorsing anything that has occurred and forbidding any effort to change the current state of affairs.

Rousseau sees no such fatalism in the more sensible optimism of Leibniz and Pope, which relies on the crucial distinction between general and particular evils. This defensible optimism admits that particular evils are in fact evils, but merely claims that they make a contribution to, or do not detract from, the good of the whole. Philopolis misses the point of intelligent optimism which is intended to provide a justification of providence in the face of the existence of evil. Such optimism does not need to reject efforts to eliminate particular evils and does not lead to passivity and the abandonment of a human sense of liberty and responsibility. Rousseau's attack is directed only against a passive complacency which he regards as incompatible with the *Discours sur l'inégalité* and unnecessary to optimism. While Rousseau presents a view of human history that offers little hope for a comprehensive remedy for the human situation, his insistence that his account of human nature and evil is specifically intended to bring about a sense of responsibility suggests that he wished to avoid a passive fatalism that would undermine a sense of liberty.[15] In short, Rousseau's argument implies that the version of optimism offered by

Philopolis is opposed to the sort of spirited opposition to injustice that is necessary to political freedom. In spite of any theoretical objections he has against optimism in general, he spares Leibniz and Pope on this occasion because their doctrine is not hostile to liberty.

While Rousseau argues that the doctrine of Pope and Leibniz is immune to the objection he raises against Philopolis, he does not go so far as to endorse their position. In particular he denies – against both Pope and Leibniz as well as Philopolis – that providence needs justification from any system of philosophy. Optimism attempts a project that is both beyond its grasp and unnecessary. Finally he argues that, whatever strengths or weaknesses optimism might have, it has no bearing on his own position. He says that 'it is clear that properly understood optimism has no effect either for or against me.'[16] In effect, the argument of the *Discours sur l'inégalité* neither embraces nor rejects intelligent optimism; it is quite neutral with regard to the issues raised by Leibniz and Pope, although it is inconsistent with the form optimism takes under the pen of Philopolis.

Rousseau's neutrality on these issues does not commit him to a policy of avoiding all alliances with Leibniz and Pope, however, when the occasion calls for it. Even though he may not regard optimism as indispensable to the defense of liberty, it is no contradiction for him to defend the sensible version against Voltaire's attacks on providence. In fact, Rousseau argues that, for all his opposition to optimism, Voltaire ends by inspiring something that in practice cannot be distinguished from the complacent fatalism supported by Philopolis. In fact, far from contradicting himself, Rousseau uses some of the same arguments against Voltaire that he used against Philopolis.

In particular, Rousseau insists that Voltaire, like Philopolis, has missed the crucial distinction between particular and general evil. Philopolis and Voltaire make opposite versions of the same error of making the case for providence depend on their own personal comfort. While Philopolis's effort to defend providence forces him to deny that his having a stroke would be an evil, Voltaire's effort to attack providence forces him to insist that his having a toothache would be proof of the absence of providence. By presenting the existence of any suffering as refuting the possibility of providence Voltaire deprives those who suffer of any consolation and of any belief that there is an ultimate support for justice in the world. In place of the passive complacency offered by Philopolis he can offer only an equally passive complacency for the comfortable coupled with useless despair for the suffering.

While Voltaire's position does not follow Philopolis in depriving humans of the use of whatever freedom they might have, it does little to encourage them to use that freedom in a productive way.

Both Voltaire and Philopolis encourage men to feel that they are not free, that they are not responsible for their own fate. As Rousseau says, 'Thus, whatever part nature might have taken, Providence is always right among the Devout and always wrong among the Philosophers.'[17] It seems reasonable to regard Bonnet as a spokesman for 'the Devout' on this question. In the *Confessions*, Rousseau says that Bonnet was in fact a materialist but that he adopted 'a very intolerant orthodoxy' in matters that had anything to do with Rousseau.[18] In spite of the stark opposition of their positions, Voltaire and Philopolis meet each other on the same ground, but they do not share this ground with either Leibniz or Rousseau. In fact, Rousseau's argument agrees with Voltaire in implying that there is no personal providence, but disagrees in claiming that the issue of personal providence is of central importance.

A proper judgement of Rousseau's position depends on an assessment of the neutrality he adopts between the 'Devout' and the 'Philosophers'. As we have seen, in the letter to Conzié Rousseau spoke from a philosophic perspective. R. A. Leigh has pointed out that in an early draft of the letter to Voltaire he spoke about his skeptical friends with a degree of approval that cannot be found in later drafts, including the one sent to Voltaire.[19] Leigh concludes from this that the successive drafts of the letter form parts of a series of steps away from the *coterie holbachique* which Rousseau became more willing to take once he had left Paris. It is surely correct to say as Leigh does that it was 'neither easy nor politic' for Rousseau to express his differences with philosophic opinion while he was in daily association with Paris intellectuals.[20] It should also be noted, however, that for even more compelling reasons it was difficult and dangerous for him to express opposition to the devout both before and after he left Paris. In fact, as Leigh notes in a different context, even Rousseau's position in the published version of the letter to Voltaire (from which the favorable references to skeptical friends had been removed) seemed too tolerant of atheism to suit some of his more pious readers.[21] Such readers had cause for their uneasiness because Rousseau's statements distancing himself from his former associates do not move him particularly closer to the orthodox side. Instead they reinforce the distinctiveness of his own position.

This can be seen in the rest of Rousseau's arguments against Voltaire which – while they are very different from those in the 'Letter to Philopolis' – are comparable in one respect. Just as he had accused Philopolis of having a poor understanding of the position he is adopting, he accuses Voltaire, the French popularizer of Newton, of having a poor understanding of modern science. To Voltaire's claim that, far from being perfect as optimism required, nature is always imprecise and irregular, Rousseau responds that only nature is precise and regular and that its apparent irregularity is only a consequence of our ignorance of its laws. In effect Voltaire denies that nature follows regular laws, which Rousseau argues amounts to asserting 'that there are some actions without a principle and some effects without a cause; which is repugnant to all philosophy.'[22] It is in the name of philosophy, not religious orthodoxy or unorthodoxy, that Rousseau rejects Voltaire's arguments. Even when Voltaire is being a better physicist, as in his denial of a universal fluid in space, he is unnecessarily dogmatic. He refuses to acknowledge that even the most persuasive scientific theories are subject to revision in the face of new discoveries. Although elsewhere Voltaire showed that he was fully aware of the sorts of concerns raised by Rousseau, in this context his adherence to science betrays an unscientific dogmatism that rivals that of his devout targets.[23] It is Rousseau who maintains the undogmatic stance.

Given the reasonable objections that could be raised even to the most sophisticated versions of optimism – such as the objections he himself raised in his letter to Conzié – Rousseau is perfectly aware that it would be unwise to give more than qualified support to this doctrine. One of the responses to Le Roy shows the extent to which his own philosophic position can be considered as a more defensible substitute for optimism which steers clear of these objections. Le Roy objected to Rousseau's assertion that carnivores have an advantage over frugivores in finding food and had accused him of the sort of naive optimism defended by Bonnet. The supervisor of the gardens at Versailles denied that 'everything is well regulated in nature'.[24] After defending his position on carnivores, Rousseau responded that his general conclusion about nature was not dependent on this particular issue. He continues, 'Besides, whatever can be observed about particular facts, the proof that all is well organized is taken from a general and incontestable fact, which is that all the species continue to exist.' Rousseau appeals, not to a metaphysical doctrine, but to a hypothesis that can be tested. This claim that nature follows general rules, resulting in the continued existence of species despite individual death and harm, is a much weaker and easily testable version of the optimist claim that the whole is good, as is evident from the fact that it is broadly compatible with recent neo-Darwinian theories of evolution. Although the phenomenon of extinction, central to Darwin's theory of evolution, contradicts this point, Rousseau himself seems primarily concerned with the demonstration that natural variability is the result of rules or regularities. For example, Rousseau's specific point about the natural rules for foraging among different species parallels contemporary studies in the field of behavioral ecology.[25]

The consistency of Rousseau's position in his responses to Le Roy, Voltaire, and Philopolis is shown best by his attacks against dogmatism whether it comes from the side of the devout or that of the philosophers. His expressions of approval toward optimism are based on its compatibility with his goal of instilling a sense of freedom and responsibility rather than on any claim it makes to being unarguably true. As he says with regard to the question of whether the whole is good, 'Then it is quite evident that no man would know how to give direct proof either for or against; for these proofs depend on a perfect knowledge of the constitution of the world and of the purpose of its Author, and this knowledge is incontestably above human intelligence.'[26] Even when he expresses a preference for one of the competing views, this preference is based on a skepticism or neutrality about the philosophic merits of the alternatives as they are asserted by the dogmatists on either side.

Another way of putting this, which Rousseau also uses in one of the versions of the letter to Voltaire, is that on matters in which reason provides no grounds for being convinced, one chooses what is most persuasive.[27] In these terms being convinced of the truth of something means having compelling reasons for believing it to be true. It is quite possible for a conclusion to be convincing without being persuasive if the recipients of the argument find something unacceptable in it in spite of its truth because to accept it would be contrary to their self-interest.[28] Rousseau consistently pointed out that his critics appealed to the self-interest of literary men more than to the truth in the debate over the sciences and the arts. In Rousseau's moral vocabulary, something is persuasive if it is consoling, is appealing to the moral sense, or is in some other way psychologically satisfying.[29] Persuasion, in its most favorable sense, works in the absence of compelling reasons but it is not so much a guess about the way things are as it is an image about the way they ought to be. Thus the reason the most defensible form of optimism may be supportable is not because it demonstrates that this is the best of all possible worlds but because it gives a morally and psychologically satisfying view of the world.

In particular, this form of optimism is worth defending against friends like Bonnet and enemies like Voltaire because it supports a sense of human freedom and responsibility. In spite of Rousseau's persisting reservations about the ultimate truth of optimism there are very strong moral reasons for attacking Voltaire's attack on optimism and allowing people a consoling view of the world as long as this view does not lead to the passivity Rousseau condemned in Philopolis's doctrine. Therefore, while Rousseau's youthful rejection of Pope's optimism was based on conviction or philosophic argument, his later defense of a variant of this optimism is based on considerations of what will best support the sort of liberty that most concerns Rousseau.

Rousseau's discussion of civil religion at the end of the letter to Voltaire is an invitation to join him in the support of liberty. Rousseau expresses his preference for Voltaire's religious views over those of orthodox Catholicism and urges the poet to turn his artistic gifts to the political purpose of writing a compelling profession of faith for citizens. It is perhaps not fanciful to see the variant of optimism defended in the letter as Rousseau's theoretical contribution to this new profession of faith. This suggestion is supported by Rousseau's emphasis on the importance of the distinction between general providence and particular evil. A religion that teaches this distinction would be quite suitable for citizens who must learn to distinguish between their particular interests and the general will of the community. In the end perhaps Rousseau's sympathy for optimism stems from its potential to serve as an intellectually respectable support for civil religion rather than from a genuine theoretical commitment to the doctrine. To serve this purpose the doctrine must be presented through the poetic gifts of Voltaire.

The complexity of Rousseau's discussions of optimism helps to explain his political theory which was elaborated at the same time and in the context of these rejoinders to more metaphysical criticisms. Patrick Riley has ably demonstrated the theological origin of the term 'general will' in debates centering around the thought of Malebranche.[30] The importance of Malebranche's thought for Rousseau should certainly be attended to more than it usually is, but the argument made above suggests Rousseau elaborated his understanding of the underlying distinction between the general and the particular in defending his explanation of human evil in the context of the debate over optimism.

Natural goodness, perfectibility and political freedom

This account of Rousseau's neutrality between the friends and opponents of optimism sheds light on the central terms of the *Discours sur l'inégalité*, natural goodness and perfectibility. The doctrine of natural goodness could be considered as a metaphysically neutral replacement for optimism. It does not make the strongest of the claims on behalf of providence made by Leibniz and Pope; nor is it subject to the objections made by opponents like Voltaire. Its neutrality on the issues of providence, the existence of God, and whether this is the best of all possible worlds makes it more rationally defensible and potentially acceptable to parties at odds on these other issues. Finally, the term has connotations that make it serve rhetorically to support liberty against passivity or resignation.

Using skepticism, or constructive neutrality between competing doctrines, to give support to a morally salutary, but non-provable, doctrine, is one of the distinctive characteristics of Rousseau's writings. The claims raised more broadly in this essay concern Rousseau's adoption of a stance of neutrality for rhetorical and practical purposes even when he had fairly clear speculative opinions on these issues. Staking out a position that is both morally salutary and neutral to the dogmatic alternatives is a major part of his effort to change the terms of debate between the enlightenment and its opponents. At the outset of the *Discours sur les sciences et les arts*, he made clear his opposition to both the dogmatic faith of the fanatics and the dogmatic skepticism of the *philosophes*: 'At all times there will be men destined to be subjugated by the opinions of their century, their Country, their Society. A man who plays the free Thinker and Philosopher today would, for the same reason, have been only a fanatic at the time of the League.'[31] Furthermore, in defending the *Discours*, he conceded that he considered it a duty 'to depict virtue as beautifully as possible',[32] rather than state the strict truth in order to combat modern doctrines that undermined morality. Throughout his career, he sought a form of philosophic enquiry that could challenge convention in the name of nature without thereby undermining sound morals.

The prime example of this characteristic within the *Discours sur l'inégalité* itself once again shows the way the concern to defend a particular sense of liberty and responsibility guides Rousseau through a minefield of metaphysical complexity. Rousseau introduces the question of what characteristic distinguishes humans from other species with a resounding praise of freedom of will. In spite of this apparent endorsement of an anti-materialist and anti-fatalist position, he quickly drops free will from his discussion because of 'the difficulties surrounding all these questions'.[33] In place of free will he introduces the newly invented term, 'perfectibility' as his candidate for the distinctive human characteristic. Perfectibility has the dual advantage of being neutral in the metaphysical dispute over free will and of appearing to support liberty against fatalism.[34]

In fact, Rousseau's doctrine of perfectibility allows him to combine apparently opposing characteristics of the two alternatives to which he remains neutral. As is the case for the issue of optimism, Rousseau's neutrality or skepticism about the reasonableness of arguments against and for free will gives him the ability to stake out a position immune to criticisms from either side, while lending rhetorical support to the more salutary of the opposing positions. On the one hand, perfectibility is close enough to materialism to allow him to claim that the ways humans live are profoundly affected by the external environment in which they live. Thus he can respond to Philopolis's claim that society is the natural result of the development of human faculties by saying that the state of society 'is derived from the nature of the human race, not immediately as you say but only, as I have proved, with the help of certain external circumstances that may or may not happen.'[35] On the other hand, perfectibility is close enough to free will to allow Rousseau to insist that the particular form of unnatural human development triggered by changes in the external environment is subject to a degree of human control and, therefore, that humanity has only itself (i.e. neither nature nor God) to blame for its vices. Thus he can respond to Voltaire's barb that the *Discours sur l'inégalité* is a 'book against the human race' by saying that 'in depicting human miseries, my purpose was excusable, and even praiseworthy, as I believe, for I showed men how they caused their miseries themselves, and consequently how they might avoid them'.[36] This explanation consists in tracing all evil beyond purely physical ills to humans as a species that is 'free, perfected, thereby corrupted'. It is because humans are free (although not necessarily in the sense required by metaphysical doctrines of freedom of will) that they are responsible for the greatest part of even the physical evils accompanying the Lisbon earthquake. These ills were caused, and could have been prevented, by human choices about where and how to live.

The coherence of Rousseau's system

By not publishing (or at least delaying the publication of) his responses to the critics of the *Deuxième Discours*, Rousseau took the advice he offered Voltaire during this period, 'Scorn vain rumors whose intention is less to harm you than to distract you from doing good. The more you are criticized, the more you should make yourself admired. A good book is a devastating reply to printed insults.'[37] Thus, instead of engaging in a pamphlet war with people like his former confidant Père Castel (author of a critique of the *Discours* entitled *L'Homme moral opposé à l'homme physique*), Rousseau settled into the Hermitage and labored on his many literary projects, ultimately producing *Julie*, *Emile*, and the *Contrat social*. These works must ultimately be regarded as the best defenses of the practical and non-metaphysical defense of human liberty in the *Discours sur l'inégalité*.[38]

One example will suffice to illustrate the way Rousseau continued the strategy we have called constructive neutrality in these later works. Rousseau began contemplating *Julie* at approximately the same time he was writing the letter to Voltaire on optimism. When he tells the story of the composition of this work in the *Confessions*, Rousseau indicates that he decided to give his novel the political purpose of softening the mutual hatred of the devout and the Encyclopedists by destroying their prejudices against each other.[39] In the same context he indicates the dangers of this tactic. Rather than simply avoiding the disputes between the opposing parties or even bringing about their reconciliation, Rousseau's new system caused them to unite in opposition to him. The neutral who offered advice to both sides became their mutual enemy and ultimately suffered the consequences. He did, however, have considerable success at persuading a new generation of readers that the old disputes were irrelevant and that they should conceive of their problems in new terms.

In sum, an analysis of Rousseau's responses to the critics of the *Discours sur l'inégalité* reveals a systematic strategy of constructive neutrality on the issues that most divided his contemporaries, a strategy that guided Rousseau throughout his literary career and which to a large degree succeeded in reshaping intellectual debate in the Enlightenment. His tactic is to redirect rather than resolve old disputes. His insistence that his own doctrine neither required optimism nor was refuted by it amounted to the claim that disputes over optimism were simply irrelevant to the most important questions. His doctrine of perfectibility amounted to the claim that disputes over free will were similarly unnecessary for the effort to identify the source of human ills. In both these instances Rousseau adopted a philosophic stance of neutrality in his effort to aid his moral goal of instilling a sense of responsibility and practical liberty in his readers.

Notes

1 A shorter version of this essay was presented at the meeting of the North American Association for the Study of Jean-Jacques Rousseau, Trent University, Peterborough, Ontario, May 1993.

2 'Final Reply', in *Collected Writings of Rousseau*, edited by Roger D. Masters and Christopher Kelly (Hanover, New Hampshire: University Press of New England, 1989–), volume II, p. 110. This edition will be cited as *Collected Writings*. The French text can be found in Pléiade, vol. III, p. 72. In the following citations this edition will be cited as Pléiade with volume number in parentheses after the citation of the *Collected Writings*. A discussion of the controversy over the *Discours sur les sciences et les arts* can be found in the introduction to *Collected Writings*, vol. II. For a somewhat different view of the controversy see Robert Wokler, 'The Discours sur les sciences et les arts and its Offspring: Rousseau in Reply to his Critics', in *Reappraisals of Rousseau: Studies in Honour of R. A. Leigh*, ed. Simon Harvey *et al.* (Manchester: Manchester University Press, 1980), pp. 250–78.

3 Rousseau discusses the way the reception of the *Discours* absorbed his time in the *Confessions*, Book VIII (Pléiade, vol. I, p. 389).

4 On this point, see in particular, *Confessions*, Book VIII (Pléiade, vol. I, p. 388).

5 *Confessions*, Book VIII (Pléiade, vol. I, p. 389).

6 Letter to Voltaire, 10 September 1755 in *Collected Writings*, vol. III, p. 105 (Pléiade, vol. III, p. 226).

7 R. A. Leigh has made the case that Rousseau and Voltaire engaged in a 'desultory dialogue' over optimism in a series of works beginning with the *Discours sur l'inégalité* and ending with *Candide*. See, 'From the *Inégalité* to *Candide*: notes on a desultory dialogue between Voltaire and Rousseau', in *The Age of the Enlightenment: Studies Presented to Theodore Besterman*, ed. W. H. Barber *et al.* (Edinburgh: Oliver and Boyd, 1967), pp. 66–92. Leigh suggests that the *Discours sur l'inégalité* really entered this dialogue only after Voltaire read it carefully, probably in 1758. Our claim is that Rousseau took

Voltaire's poems as a challenge to the thesis of the *Discours* (if not to the work itself) much earlier.

8 *Confessions*, Book IX (Pléiade, vol. I, p. 429).
9 *Collected Writings*, vol. III, p. 124 (Pléiade, vol. III, p. 1384).
10 *Confessions*, Book IX (Pléiade, vol. I, p. 430).
11 Letter to Conzié, 17 January 1742 in *Correspondance complète de Jean Jacques Rousseau*, ed. R. A. Leigh, Tome I (Geneva: Institut et Musée Voltaire, 1965), p. 132.
12 See *Collected Writings*, vol. III, p. 114 (Pléiade, vol. IV, p. 1067).
13 *Collected Writings*, vol. III, p. 130 (Pléiade, vol. III, p. 233).
14 'Letter from Philopolis', *Collected Writings*, vol. III, p. 124 (Pléiade, vol. III, p. 1384).
15 It has been argued that the narrative structure of the *Discours sur l'inégalité* induces a satisfied passivity in the reader. See Dena Goodman, *Criticism in Action: Enlightenment Experiments in Political Writing* (Ithaca, New York: Cornell University Press, 1989), p. 226. There is certainly evidence that readers of the *Discours*, including those who disagreed with it, have been roused to activity by their reading.
16 'Letter to Philopolis', *Collected Writings*, vol. III, p. 129 (Pléiade, vol. III, p. 233).
17 Letter to Voltaire, 18 August 1756, *Collected Writings*, vol. III, p. 116 (Pléiade, vol. IV, p. 1069).
18 See *Confessions*, Book XII (Pléiade, vol. I, p. 632).
19 R. A. Leigh, 'Rousseau's Letter to Voltaire on Optimism (18 August 1756)', *Studies on Voltaire and the Eighteenth Century*, vol. LXXXIX (1972), pp. 299–305.
20 *Ibid.*, p. 299.
21 See *ibid.*, p. 266.
22 Letter to Voltaire, *Collected Writings*, vol. III, pp. 112–13 (Pléiade, vol. IV, p. 1065).
23 For a discussion of Voltaire's position on the generality of the laws of nature as examples of God's actions see Patrick Riley, *The General Will Before Rousseau: The Transformation of the Divine into the Civic* (Princeton, New Jersey: Princeton University Press, 1986), pp. 228–31.
24 'Observations of Charles-Georges Le Roy, with Rousseau's Replies', *Collected Writings*, vol. III, p. 134 (Pléiade, vol. III, p. 237). See also Letter to Voltaire, *Collected Writings*, vol. III, p. 115 (Pléiade, vol. IV, p. 1068).
25 See *Collected Writings*, ed. Masters and Kelly, vol. III, p. 199, note 5 to p. 134. For a recent neo-Darwinian account of such rules, see Robert Trivers, *Social Evolution* (Menlo Park, California: Benjamin/Cummings, 1985) and – for human applications – Eric Alden Smith and Bruce Winterhalder (eds), *Evolutionary Ecology and Human Behavior* (New York: Aldine de Gruyter, 1992).

26 Letter to Voltaire, *Collected Writings*, vol. III, p. 115 (Pléiade, vol. IV, p. 1068).

27 *Ibid.*, p. 118 (Pléiade, vol. IV, p. 1071).

28 On this point consider Rousseau's concluding word in the disputes over the *Premier discours*, 'I sense very well that the weapons will not be evenly matched, because I will be attacked with jokes and I will defend myself with nothing but reasoning: but as long as I convince my adversaries, I care very little about persuading them' ('Preface to Narcissus', *Collected Writings*, vol. II, p. 186 (Pléiade, vol. II, p. 959)).

29 See *Contrat social*, Book II, ch. VII (Pléiade, vol. III, pp. 381–4). For a more complete account of Rousseau's distinction between persuasion and conviction, see Christopher Kelly, '"To Persuade without Convincing": The Language of Rousseau's Legislator', *American Journal of Political Science*, 31 (May 1987), pp. 321–35.

30 See Riley., *op. cit.* Riley briefly discusses the relation between Leibniz and Malebranche, see pp. 59–63.

31 *Collected Writings*, vol. II, p. 3 (Pléiade, vol. III, p. 4).

32 'Final Reply', *Collected Writings*, vol. II, p. 121 (Pléiade, vol. III, p. 86).

33 *Discours sur l'origine de l'inégalité*, *Collected Writings*, vol. III, p. 26 (Pléiade, vol. III, p. 142).

34 On Rousseau's metaphysical neutrality, or 'detachable metaphysics', see Leo Strauss, *Natural Right and History* (Chicago: University of Chicago Press, 1953), pp. 265–6 and especially Roger D. Masters, *The Political Philosophy of Rousseau* (Princeton, New Jersey: Princeton University Press, 1968), pp. 66–74. For an argument in favor of the position that Rousseau presents humans as purely physical beings in the *Discours sur l'inégalité* see John T. Scott, 'The Theodicy of the *Second Discourse*: The "Pure State of Nature" and Rousseau's Political Thought', *American Political Science Review*, 86, 2 (September 1992), pp. 696–711.

35 Letter to Philopolis, *Collected Writings*, vol. III, p. 128 (Pléiade, vol. III, p. 232).

36 Letter to Voltaire, *Collected Writings*, vol. III, p. 109 (Pléiade, vol. IV, p. 1061).

37 Letter to Voltaire, 10 September 1755, *Collected Writings*, vol. III, p. 107 (Pléiade, vol. III, p. 228). Not long afterwards he offered the same advice to Diderot. See *Confessions*, Book IX (Pléiade, vol. I, p. 460).

38 The 'Geneva Manuscript' of the *Contrat social* in particular contains an important direct response to Diderot's *Encyclopedia* article, 'Droit naturel' which disagrees with important parts of the argument of the *Deuxième Discours*. An examination of the disagreement between Diderot and Rousseau is beyond the scope of this essay. For a brief discussion see *Collected Writings*, ed. Masters and Kelly, vol. III, pp. xxii–xxiii.

39 *Confessions*, Book IX (Pléiade, vol. I, p. 436).

Rousseau and Tocqueville on democratic legitimacy and illegitimacy

I

Although this paper treats the relationship between Rousseau and Tocqueville, its emphasis is upon their respective concepts of political legitimacy and illegitimacy in democracies. But is this a defensible comparison? Rousseau's conception of democracy was in part prescriptive, a deduction from the principles of political right he understood himself to have formulated for the first time. To the extent that Rousseau claimed that actual cases of democracy, as he understood it, had existed or did exist, his was a deliberately circumscribed and archaic model that served as part of his critique of politics, society, and economy in the pre-revolutionary Europe he knew. For Rousseau did not live to see the establishment of the United States, the French Revolution, and the great transformations that emerged from them.

Himself a political theorist, historian, and political actor, Tocqueville was well aware of the gap separating the France of the *ancien régime* from what it had subsequently become. On occasion, Tocqueville wrote as though these differences were of so great an order of magnitude that it was scarcely worth reading those theorists who had been formed by periods prior to the French and American Revolutions. If so, then what could Rousseau or Montesquieu tell a theorist of the modern age? A good deal, it turned out. A recent study by James Schleifer of the working manuscript and discarded materials for the *Démocratie en Amérique* has revealed 'a wonderful dialogue between Tocqueville and Montesquieu'.[1] Was there an analogous exchange with Rousseau? What were the uses of Rousseau made by Tocqueville when he considered legitimacy and illegitimacy in large modern representative and commercial democracies?

Tocqueville's primary concern as a theorist was to deal with the nature and implications of such states and societies. Modern democracy meant for him a political and social system based on equality among citizens. He tended to contrast two versions of democracy. One was the United States in the age of Jackson. After its one largely political revolution, the United States, in Tocqueville's view, had succeeded on the whole in combining liberty with equality: economic individualism with active citizenship in a large country where power was effectively divided by the federal system. Another form of democracy existed in his own country. France, although irreversibly democratic in the sense of having abolished pre-revolutionary distinctions based on ascribed status, was subject to both administrative centralization and an apparently permanent revolutionary process which produced indifference towards individual rights and constitutional procedures. Twice the ongoing Revolution had produced plebiscitary dictatorships in the form of Bonapartist emperors. Tocqueville was born during the First Empire and died under the Second.

Rousseau, of course, had known only the *ancien régime* in France and the repertoire of other pre-revolutionary political forms he treated in his own work. Yet he was among the few thinkers of his time to come out against monarchy and to make popular sovereignty into the criterion for legitimate political regimes. A contemporary Jesuit critic, Père Berthier, was not far off the mark in identifying Rousseau as the first theorist to hold that sovereignty cannot legitimately be exercised by monarchs, and that only democracies can claim political legitimacy.[2]

Although ostensibly placing monarchy among the legitimate forms of government, Rousseau did so in a way that excluded the usual understanding of monarchy as combining sovereignty and government. In its place he put his own assertion that the monarch is only the minister of the sovereign. In this case, 'the monarchy itself is a republic' (p. 212).* It has often been remarked that Rousseau's description of Machiavelli's *Prince* as 'the book of Republicans' applies equally well to the *Contrat social* (p. 224). There, however, the meaning of 'democracy' was confined to direct government by the people. It was not until the *Lettre à d'Alembert* that Rousseau defined democracy in the full sense as a state 'in which the subjects and the sovereign are only the same men considered in different relations.'[3]

---

* Whenever page references appear in the text, they refer to the *Everyman Rousseau* used in the seminar: Jean-Jacques Rousseau, *The Social Contract and Discourses*, tr. G. D. H. Cole (rev. ed., London, 1973). Derathé's analysis is in Pléiade, III, cvi–cvii.

My analysis of Rousseau will center on his uses of the terms 'legitimate' (*légitime*) and 'illegitimate' (*illégitime*) political authority in the *Contrat social*, the *Discours sur l'origine et les fondemens de l'inégalité parmi les hommes*, and the *Manuscrit de Génève*.[4] Rousseau's use of the term 'illegitimate' forces us to consider the part played by negative concepts in his theories of liberty and equality. As J. Starobinski remarks about the *Second Discourse*, '*Dans la discussion des notions fondamentales, la polémique joue une rôle considérable*'.[5]

It is my view, recently stated elsewhere, that Tocqueville regarded Bonapartism as a new and illegitimate form of rule. However, the rationalizations by which both Bonapartes sought to justify their mode of coming to power and their denials of political liberty rested, in Tocqueville's view, upon a perversion of democratic theory.[6] I have been concerned to identify the part played in Tocqueville's thought of his conceptualization of the phenomenon then called 'Bonapartism', 'Caesarism', 'Imperialism', or, in the language of our own time, plebiscitary dictatorship. The nineteenth-century neologisms were coined after Louis Napoleon's successful *coup d'état* in 1851. Theorists with different interests, and writing from discrepant political perspectives sought to describe and explain this striking event and its aftermath, the creation of the Second Empire, ratified by a plebiscite represented as democratic. The impact of this sequence of events upon observant contemporaries has been largely forgotten. The significance of Bonapartism as a concept closely linked to democratic theory has been eclipsed in our own time by recent and more thoroughgoing assaults upon political liberty, individual rights, and representative government.

The need to conceptualize and explain such events in France arose after the second time that a major European revolution, begun in Paris, ended with *coups d'état*, and plebiscites ratifying Empires more repressive than the monarchy in power when the revolution began. Thus those who coined or put to new uses such terms as 'Bonapartism' or 'Caesarism' were trying to encapsulate what was perceived as a related sequence: to designate as a recognizable pattern, the unanticipated outcomes of two revolutions made in the name of liberty and equality.

One diagnosis emphasized the pseudo- or post-democratic claim to legitimacy made by a leader, who after seizing power by force, then asserted that he ruled by right. This assertion of legitimate title derived from the subsequent approval by the people through a plebiscite. Both Napoleon and Louis Bonaparte claimed to incarnate the sovereignty of the people, to embody their general will, and to serve the general interest directly. This, they asserted, representative institutions had not and could not do. Speaking to the *Corps Législatif* in 1814, Napoleon claimed to be the elect of the sovereign people:

> Are you representatives of the people? I am: four times I have been called by the nation and four times I have received the votes of five million citizens. I have a title and you do not.[7]

During the Empire, Restoration, and July Monarchy, French liberals argued that Napoleon's justification of his legitimacy derived from Rousseau's political philosophy, the central elements of which they held to be the dogma of unlimited popular sovereignty, the surrender of individual rights to the general will of the community, and the denial of representative government. Thus Guizot:

> 'The elect of the sovereign': such was the declaration both of the Convention and of Napoleon; hence the destruction of all responsibility in power, and of all the rights belonging to citizens.[8]
> ... we have seen the sovereignty transferred from the people to that of a single individual: this was the history of Napoleon. He also was a personification of the sovereignty of the people ... 'Who has been elected,' he said, 'like me, by eighteen millions of men? Who is, like me, the representative of the people?'[9]

This was but one part of the liberal indictment of Rousseau, whom they held responsible for a number of further errors which produced violent consequences in the course of the French Revolution and the Empire.

Other points in the early French liberal case against Rousseau are well known: 1) Rousseau's conception of politics was based on ancient models, and so hostile to the tendencies of modern life that terror had to be introduced into the Revolution to overcome the society's resistance to this impossible political ideal; 2) individual rights were sacrificed to the general will; 3) the concept of freedom was turned into its opposite by the notion of forcing men to be free; 4) individual rights and interests were subordinated to the general interest, loosely or formally defined; 5) Rousseau's theory of civil religion would destroy individual freedom of worship and the autonomy of religious organizations; 6) his refusal to recognize representation in politics and the rights of intermediate and interest groups in politics led to centralization of state power.

These claims have reappeared in twentieth-century interpretations of Rousseau. J. L. Talmon's indictment of Rousseau as a totalitarian thinker were joined by those of Crocker, and, perhaps most subtle and influential of all, that of Isaiah Berlin.[10] But Talmon's book has in turn elicited powerful rejoinders. Among the most effective was that of R. A. Leigh, whose loss we all so much regret.[11] Robert Wokler has made a cogent reply to Isaiah Berlin's description of Rousseau's theory as based upon a concept of positive liberty.[12] Relatively little noted, however, has been the critique of Rousseau as creating the legitimation for plebiscitary dictatorship. Talmon mentions Napoleon only three times, and does little with this charge against Rousseau. Crocker, who identifies Rousseau's view of voting with the plebiscites held in modern totalitarian states, says nothing about their Bonapartist origins.[13]

My own interest in this question derives from my interpretation of the role played in Tocqueville's thought by his treatment of the two Napoleons and Bonapartism. I have been drawn to investigate Rousseau by Tocqueville's preoccupation with legitimate and illegitimate forms of democratic government. This very concern, I believe, was one source of his interest in Rousseau, who made equality among citizens into a prerequisite of legitimacy for political regimes. Another crucial point was Rousseau's insistence upon the moral and political benefits that derive from active political participation by citizens. This Tocqueville incorporated into his summary of what was to be learned from democracy in its American form. But it was the distinction between legitimate and illegitimate forms of democratic theory which informed Tocqueville's analysis of the Bonapartes' regimes. This question was central to Tocqueville's enquiries about what constituted legitimate rule in the age of democratic revolutions, and the proper relationship between liberty and equality. His own historical horizon was not that of Rousseau, who knew neither revolution in France nor democracy in America.

In many but not all respects, Tocqueville followed earlier French liberal thinkers who denounced the radical periods of the French Revolution, especially the Convention and the Terror. He did not attack democracy as thoroughly as they. Nor did Tocqueville believe the Revolution had ended in 1799. His own periodization of the Revolution included the Consulate and the Empire. But, like his liberal predecessors, Tocqueville believed that the theory of popular sovereignty developed by Rousseau had been pernicious in its revolutionary applications. However much Rousseau had qualified its abstract statement, in practice the theory was easily appropriated by the enemies of liberty. Popular sovereignty had been indispensable to Napoleon

Bonaparte's attempt to legitimate his use of force to violate the existing constitution. On other points as well, Tocqueville may have read Rousseau so as to discover how some forms of democratic theory may endanger liberty. For theorists may also be studied in order to discover the intellectual origins of condemned practices.

There are good reasons to believe that Tocqueville was deeply ambivalent about Rousseau. Depending on the subject, Tocqueville seems to have criticized, modified, and sometimes applied Rousseau's political thought. This Tocqueville seems to have read for the first time at the age of sixteen when going through an edition of Rousseau's *Oeuvres complètes* in his father's library.[14] Fifteen years later in 1836, while Tocqueville was working on the second part of *Democracy in America*, he wrote to his friend Kergolay that he was reading three authors every day: Pascal, Montesquieu and Rousseau.[15] In 1852, speaking as President of the *Académie des sciences morales et politiques*, Tocqueville included Montesquieu and Rousseau in his list of the six most significant theorists (*publicistes*) to have treated the general principles of politics and government.[16] Such abstract works were, in his eyes, far from unimportant. Indeed Tocqueville went on to attribute the origins of the French Revolution to those eighteenth-century theorists who had taken no part in the public affairs of their time:

> it was political science, often on the most abstract level, which planted in the minds of our fathers the seeds of those novelties which were to grow into so many previously unknown political institutions and civil laws.[17]

Along with others, I have tried to perceive how and why Tocqueville read Montesquieu, and to what uses the older theorist was put by the younger after the French and American Revolutions.[18] Rather less work has been done on the relationship between Rousseau and Tocqueville.[19] And much of what has been written assumes that any acknowledgement of Rousseau's influence upon Tocqueville entails playing down what Tocqueville owed to Montesquieu. This is a dubious assumption. For Rousseau fully acknowledged his own considerable debt to Montesquieu. Derathé has documented Rousseau's great admiration for Montesquieu, whom he never attacked with the acerbic tone found in his polemics against other theorists such as Grotius, Pufendorf, Hobbes and, after their break, Voltaire.[20] Indeed, in the *Emile*, when Rousseau summarized the principles of both the *Contrat social* and his never completed *Institutions politiques*, he concluded that Montesquieu was the master theorist of the positive right of established governments. This left for Rousseau the task, as he saw it, of establishing the principles of political right:

> One must construct a standard to which measurements one makes can be related. Our principles of political right are that standard. Our measurements are the political laws of each country.[21]

Of course, it may be, and has been, argued that Tocqueville was in fact little affected by Rousseau, or any other of the three theorists he reported himself as reading. This is the thesis of Robert Nisbet, whose interpretation of Rousseau is close to those of Talmon and Crocker:

> A belief has grown up that Tocqueville was a lifelong student of Pascal, Montesquieu, and Rousseau . . . But it stretches the evidence considerably to argue any persisting, serious intellectual influence of their works on Tocqueville's mind. Particularly is this the case when it is suggested that Tocqueville derived major ideas in his classic *Democracy in America* from Rousseau. The ideal society Rousseau dreamed of in his *Social Contract* and his *Discourse on Political Economy*, a society saturated with the application of power to human nature as the means of ensuring that the individual 'will be forced to be free' is very close to a Tocquevillian nightmare.
>
> A mind that did influence Tocqueville seriously . . . was Edmund Burke's.[22]

Nisbet, in his rush to claim Tocqueville as a conservative follower of Burke, has ignored how much Tocqueville owed to those earlier French theorists, whose liberalism had not kept them from condemning Rousseau. Certainly Tocqueville believed, as did Constant and Guizot, that 'no authority on earth is unlimited, not that of the people, those who claim to be its representatives, nor that of kings, by whatever title they rule.'[23] Tocqueville also held, with Constant, that citizens possess individual rights that may not be violated. Any government that does so is illegitimate (*illégitime*).[24] Constant and other French liberals believed Rousseau to hold a contrary position, which led in the Convention, the Terror, and the Empire to a new form of total domination. This Constant chose to call 'usurpation', an ancient term, which went back at least as far as St Thomas Aquinas's distinction between the two types of tyranny.[25] How Rousseau actually treated legitimate and illegitimate forms of political authority will be the subject of what follows.

II

In this part of my paper, I shall attempt to see in what contexts, and with which meanings Rousseau used the terms: *légitime, illégitime, légitimer*.[26] I am primarily interested to identify the semantic or linguistic fields within which these terms were employed by Rousseau. I have established that Rousseau used the term, *illégitime* primarily, although not exclusively, with *usurpateur, usurpation, usurper; despotique, despote, despotisme; tyran, tyranniquement, tyrannie; maître, esclave, esclavage*. A secondary semantic field for *illégitime* was created by Rousseau to apply to violations of property law and rights as he conceived them. But his characterizations of this set of property relationships as illegitimate are for the most part in works other than those I am analyzing, such as the *Discourse on Political Economy*, the *Project of a Constitution for Corsica, Considerations on the Government of Poland*, and *Emile*.[27] In addition, I shall consider the question of how Rousseau handled theories which sought to legitimate the alienation of the people's sovereignty to a single military person, whose position had been gained by force, thus violating the existing constitutional order.

So far as I know Rousseau did not use the abstract noun, *légitimité*. This form we habitually use without hesitating, as does Cole in rendering *l'institution légitime* as 'legitimacy' (p. 215).[28] Yet even the verb *légitimer* is used only once in the works I shall be surveying, and this negatively, in what may be a reply to Hume's 'On the Original Contract': 'As for tacit consent, by which it is sought to legitimate tyranny' (*A l'égard du consentement tacite par lequel on veut légitimer la Tyrannie*).[29]

Of course Rousseau himself theorized much about language, and the key to his use of the adjectives légitime and *illégitime* may be in his remark in the *Second Discourse* (p. 177) that 'the very idea of adjectives must have been developed with great difficulty; for every adjective is an abstract idea, and abstractions are painful and unnatural operations (*operations pénibles et peu naturelles*).' This did not keep Rousseau from making much use of them.

Even the most casual readers of Rousseau's political theory can scarcely miss his emphasis on legitimate rule in the *Contrat social*, although not all pick up the reference in its first sentence: 'I mean to inquire if, in the civil order, there can be any sure and legitimate (*légitime*) rule of administration, men being taken as they are, and laws as they may be' (p. 3). However, those who know no other paragraph of this book, encounter the term in Rousseau's familiar formulation of its central point:

> Man is born free; and everywhere he is in chains . . . How did this change come about? I do not know. What can make it legitimate (*légitime*)? That question I think I can answer (p. 3).

Rousseau's purposes, as he summarized them at the end of the *Contrat social*, were to lay 'down the true principles of political right' (*droit politique*), 'to give the State a basis of its own to rest on' (*de fonder l'Etat sur sa base*). As has been remarked, the subtitle of the *Du Contrat social, ou Principes du Droit Politique* may provide a better guide to Rousseau's intentions than the title.[30] Thus it is scarcely surprising that occurrences of *légitime* and *légitimement* far outnumber those of *illégitime* and *illégitimement*.

Let us examine first the positive uses of *légitime*. In Book I, chapter VII, *légitime* figures prominently in the famous passage stating that whoever refuses to obey the general will, shall be compelled to do so by the whole body, that is, forced to be free:

> In this lies the key to the working of the political machine; this alone legitimizes civil undertakings (*qui seule rend légitimes les engagements civiles*), which without it would be absurd, tyrannical (*tyranniques*), and liable to the most frightful abuses (p. 15).

Thus the social compact (*pacte social*) is said to guarantee the independence of each citizen, this engagement is legitimate, and contrasted to those in existing societies, which are tyrannical, that is illegitimate.

Book I ends as it began, with a discussion of what can make 'the whole social system' (*tout le sistême social*) legitimate. Rousseau's answer (p. 19) is the fundamental pact that substitutes for the physical inequality among men set up by nature, 'an equality that is moral and legitimate' (*une égalité morale et légitime*).

Book II continues to invoke the term *légitime* in a number of climactic definitions summarizing the main points of the argument. In Rousseau's definition of an act of sovereignty, its first characteristic is that it is legitimate:

> What, then, strictly speaking, is an act of Sovereignty? It is not a convention between a superior and an inferior, but a convention between the body and each of its members. It is legitimate (*légitime*), because based on the social contract (p. 26).

The same precedence is found in Chapter VI on law, where Rousseau appropriates the term 'republic' to designate any and every legitimate government. Only a government ruled by laws is 'legitimate':

> I therefore give the name 'Republic' to every state that is governed by laws, no matter what the form of its administration may be: for only in such a case does the public interest govern . . . Every legitimate government (*Gouvernement légitime*) is republican (pp. 30–1).

> I understand by this word, not merely an aristocracy or a democracy, but generally any government directed by the general will, which is the law. To be legitimate (*légitime*), the government must be one, not with the Sovereign, but its minister. In such a case, even a monarchy is a Republic (p. 31, n. 1).[31]

Book III begins with a definition of government, a crucial element of which is the legitimate exercise of executive power. This is distinguished sharply from the sovereign. Government is defined as an intermediate body, charged with executing the laws and the maintenance of civil and political liberty. It is set between the sovereign and its subjects. The act that put a people under a prince (the government) is not a contract. 'I call then Government, or supreme administration, the legitimate exercise (*exercise légitime*) of the executive power, and prince or magistrate, the man or body entrusted with that administration' (p. 47).

The last use of *légitime* in the *Contrat social* comes in the final chapter of Book III when Rousseau considers 'How to check the usurpations of government'. He states that this can be prevented only by having regular periodical assemblies of all the people. At these assemblies, whose sole purpose is to maintain the social treaty, two questions must be voted: 1) Does the Sovereign wish to preserve the present form of government? and 2) Does it please the people to leave its administration in the hands of those actually in charge of it? If the whole people decides to change either the form of government or those administering it, this is a regular and legitimate act, provided that all procedural formalities are followed. In such an assembly every fundamental law may be revoked, including even the social compact (pp. 83–4). It was this chapter that caused the *Contrat social* to be condemned in Geneva.[32]

This was the closest Rousseau came to acknowledging the claim later made by Napoleon: provided that regular voting procedures are complied with, the people may justifiably change both the form of government, and place it in the hands of anyone it pleases. But even here Rousseau insists that such changes must take place within a regular constitutional setting, rather than by the seizure of power by force. Hence a transfer of power along the lines of the Bonapartist case is, according to Rousseau, illegitimate. This judgement has been prepared earlier in the *Contrat social*, as well as in the *Second Discourse*.

What is said in chapter XVIII must be treated in connection with Rousseau's preceding arguments in chapter XVI of the same Book III. There Rousseau repeats that the institution of a government is not a contract. It does not oblige the sovereign people to obey. From this he draws two conclusions. The first is that the supreme authority cannot be alienated by the sovereign people:

> It is absurd and contradictory for the Sovereign to set a superior over it; to bind itself to obey a master (*un maître*) would be to return to absolute liberty (p. 81).[33]

The second conclusion is that any such contract would be illegitimate:

> Moreover, it is clear that this contract between the people and such and such persons would be a particular act; and from this it follows that it can be neither a law nor an act of Sovereignty, and that consequently it would be illegitimate (*illégitime*) (p. 81).

These two positions would seem to rule out any textual basis in Rousseau for justifying the transfer of sovereignty to a person such as Napoleon after an unconstitutional seizure of power. On this point, the text cannot be said to be ambiguous. When French liberal theorists accused Rousseau of having provided the grounds for Napoleon's claim to incarnate the national sovereignty, they must have had in mind, not Rousseau's texts, but the uses made of them in the tumultuous world of revolutionary politics.

Where in the *Contrat social* is *illégitime* first used? To which theories and which situations is it subsequently applied? In Book I of the *Contrat social*, *illégitime* is used only twice, but in crucial places. In chapter IV, Rousseau deals with consent theories justifying slavery. Suddenly he creates a whole semantic field of illegitimate domination: the despot and despotism, the master of slaves, slavery as an institution. And these relationships are tied to the political arrangements of absolute monarchies in societies that are decadent and luxurious at the top, while abject poverty and degradation are the lot of subjects below.

The *Second Discourse* also stresses the concept of legitimacy in order to point up the illegitimacy of states built upon inequality, civil and political. Rule by the strongest or by the richest, slavery justified by whatever pretext, are alike illegitimate. Arbitrary power is the depravation, the extreme phase of government. Such power is illegitimate (p. 212). In the *Second Discourse*, Rousseau distinguishes three stages of inequality: the establishment of laws and of the right of property; the institution of magistracy; and, finally, the conversion of legitimate to arbitrary power. In this last phase, the relationship of master and slave is dominant. At this point, either the government is dissolved by new changes, or else is brought back to *l'institution légitime* (rendered in the Cole translation as 'legitimacy').

Thus this period is characterized by great inequality of riches and statuses, vain sciences and arts, an infinite variety of luxuries and poverty. Rulers promote dissension among the different ranks, seeking to set the interests of one against another. Rousseau here develops his own image of despotism:

> despotism gradually raising up its hideous head and devouring everything that remained sound and untainted in any part of the State, would at length trample on both the laws and the people, and establish itself on the ruins of the republic . . . the monster would swallow up everything, and the people would no longer have chiefs or laws, but only tyrants . . . blind obedience is the only virtue which slaves can still practice (pp. 218–19).

Book III of the *Contrat social* deals again with 'The Abuse of Government and its Tendency to Degenerate'. Let me note here the close connection between this chapter, and the discussion of the last stage of inequality, 'despotism', in the *Second Discourse* (p. 218 *et seq.*). In the *Contrat social*, III, X, 'despotism', 'tyranny' and 'usurpation' are all compared, and declared illegitimate because of arguments made in Book I, chapter IV (p. 10). Why and how were these terms treated together? What lay behind Rousseau's reasoning and his repertoire of concepts?

With Book I, chapter IV, we are back with Rousseau's search for those principles of political right that can make a political order legitimate. In order to clear the way for his own theory, Rousseau systematically attacks alternative theories. In chapter IV, on slavery, Rousseau identifies and seeks to eliminate other theories of convention based on consent, theories he identifies with Grotius, Pufendorf and Barbeyrac. This trio appears together as Rousseau's principal targets of criticism in the *Second Discourse*, in the *Manuscrit de Gèneve*, and elsewhere in his work. He identifies them as the friends of despotism (p. 10). He declares illegitimate the grounds they provide for the obligations to obey (p. 10). For we are morally obliged to obey only legitimate powers (p. 6).

The positions Rousseau attacks are based on conventions made among men. Grotius and Pufendorf hold: 1) that an individual may for rational and moral reasons alienate his liberty, become a slave, that is, in order to save his life; and 2) that a whole people may be rightly enslaved, for two reasons: (a) by the law of nature it is free to exchange its liberty for subsistence or security, and (b) by the law of nations, conquerors in a just war may grant life to a defeated people in exchange for their perpetual enslavement. The defeated, on this view, may freely consent to become subjects of an absolute ruler. Rousseau here put to effective use in his philosophy of political right, those arguments first developed by Montesquieu.[34] At the end of chapter IV, Rousseau concludes that agreements to become the slave of a master, or the passive subject of a conqueror – these cannot ever become principles of right. 'The words *slave* and *right* contradict each other, and are mutually exclusive. They are based upon force only. Any such conventions are null and void. They are *illégitime*.'

This is a powerful case, a demolition of prestigious views that had long compelled agreement. We begin to see why the *Contrat social* has been said to have originated in Rousseau's wish to refute Pufendorf's *De officio hominis et civis* (1673), the highly abstract digest of his longer writings. This was put into French by Jean Barbeyrac, also Grotius's translator. In this French form, these works became among the most widely read books of political and legal theory in eighteenth-century Europe.

But why did Rousseau identify these theories with 'despotism', 'tyranny' and 'usurpation'? And why did he treat them both in the *Second Discourse* and the *Contrat social* as characteristic of the most corrupt stage of human political arrangements? In short, why did Rousseau make the institution of chattel slavery into the precise equivalent of three political regime types: despotism, tyranny and usurpation?

One answer derives from the history of terms used to translate the concept of despotism in Aristotle's *Politics*. William of Moerberke had translated the Greek *despotes* by *despotia*, and *principatus despoticus*. Leonardo Bruni scorned what he regarded as medieval barbarism, and replaced them by Latin words based on *dominus* and *dominatio*. For these usages, later scholars substituted the Latin words *erus* and *erilis* (*herus, herilis*), which referred to a master of slaves and his relationship to them.

Both Grotius and Pufendorf knew the concept of despotism as formulated by classical writers, and each developed his own formulation. Grotius designated despotism by the word *herilis*, as in *imperium herile*, the title of a chapter in *Du iure belli ac pacis*. In his *De iure naturae et gentium libri octi* (1673), Pufendorf included a chapter called *De potestate herili*. Jean Barbeyrac rendered *herilis* as *despotique*. This was a fateful step. It enabled Rousseau, like Montesquieu, to equate chattel slavery with the type of domination also found in despotisms. Although Rousseau read Barbeyrac in order to refute him and those he translated, Rousseau thus became a major figure in turning an argument against slavery into a condemnation of absolute monarchies as despotic.[35]

The climax of this argument in the *Contrat social* comes in Book III, chapter X. Rousseau's argument is that states degenerate in two ways: by becoming smaller, or by the dissolution of the state. Governments become smaller when they pass from the many to the few, that is, from democracy to aristocracy, and from aristocracy to royalty. In this form of degeneration, the state is reduced to the members of the government who become masters and tyrants over the people. This is to usurp Sovereignty. Now citizens obey because of force, not because of obligation. Here Rousseau's analysis brings in the concepts of illegitimate 'usurpation', 'despotism' and 'tyranny' earlier developed.

The second form of degeneration in government comes when the members of the government usurp for each of them the power they should exert only as a body. Then the state is dissolved. If democratic, it becomes an 'ochlocracy'; if an aristocracy, an oligarchy; if a monarchy, the degeneration is into tyranny. Rousseau, conscious that his terminology is conflating usurpation, tyranny and despotism, establishes a set of stipulative definitions to fit this older set of terms into the structure of his own argument. None of these governments is 'legitimate'. Thus each of these terms takes on a powerful negative charge:

> a tyrant is an individual who arrogates to himself the royal authority without having a right to it. This is how the Greeks understood the word 'tyrant'; they applied it indifferently to good and bad princes whose authority was not legitimate (*dont l'autorité n'étoit pas légitime*). *Tyrant* and usurper are thus perfectly synonymous terms (p. 72).

In order that I may give different things different names, I call him who usurps the royal authority a *tyrant*, and him who usurps the sovereign power a *despot*. The tyrant is he who thrusts himself in contrary to the laws to govern in accordance with the laws: the despot is he who sets himself above the laws themselves. Thus the tyrant cannot be a despot, but the despot is always a tyrant (p. 72).

It is perhaps worth noting that Napoleon, who was called a usurper by Constant, would have fallen into the categories of both tyrant and despot if classified according to the categories of Rousseau. Indeed all three terms would have made him an illegitimate ruler for Rousseau. Tocqueville also had problems with the nomenclature of regime types. Writing after the French Revolution, the Empire, and the beginning of an age of equality, Tocqueville wrote, in a different context, that the old words 'tyranny' and 'despotism' were no longer appropriate to express the type of oppression by which democratic nations were menaced.[36] But as we shall see, when Tocqueville came to consider the Bonapartist phenomenon, he too made use of the concept of legitimate and illegitimate regimes, of which Rousseau was the modern founder. In Tocqueville's hands, as in those of Rousseau, the concept of legitimacy was a moral term, related to the condition or stage of society and politics.

Finally, something ought to be said about Rousseau's treatment of dictatorship in Book IV, chapter VI. There he does not go beyond the legal conception of that institution in classical Republican Rome. Although he saw how the dictatorship had been abused towards the end of the Republic, Rousseau's praise of the office was conventional. How would he have viewed Napoleon?

As a good republican, Rousseau detested Cromwell for having used force against the Rump Parliament, and denounced him as a hypocrite.[37] Despite his admiration of Julius Caesar's prose style, Rousseau passed severe judgement on him for using his troops to dominate the Roman Republic, and thus creating general attitudes more appropriate to a military than to a republican government. Roman military conquests contributed greatly to the decline of the Republic.[38] 'Whoever wishes to remain free should not wish to be a conqueror.'[39] Soldiers come to define themselves as apart from the citizens, a point Tocqueville would develop in the *Democracy*, but in the light of Napoleon's coup.[40]

Rousseau declared that large standing armies were good only for conquering neighbors and enslaving citizens. Tyrants pretend to create standing armies to protect against attacks from abroad, but in fact such armies serve as instruments of oppression at home (p. 228).

As for Napoleon Bonaparte himself, apparently when young he much admired Rousseau, in part because of the Constitution Rousseau drew up for Corsica, but also because of Rousseau's statement that Corsica was among the few countries capable of sustaining legislation derived from a properly constituted set of principles.[41] Later Napoleon became as cynical about Rousseau as he was about other intellectuals, or those he called ideologues. However, during the Empire, Rousseau was often praised for his prophecy in the *Social Contract*: 'I have the feeling that some day that little island will astonish Europe' (p. 41).

III

Tocqueville's view of Napoleon and the Empire must be set within an altogether altered scene. Tocqueville regarded as unprecedented the revolutionary period through which France had passed since 1789, and which in his lifetime, he was continuing to experience. Revolution, counterrevolution, restoration, and imperial foundation – all occurred more than once during the period from 1789 to Tocqueville's death in 1859. Himself a political theorist, historian and political actor, Tocqueville was well aware of the gap separating the France of the *ancien régime* from what it had subsequently become.

Tocqueville saw the uniqueness of his age in the victory of equality over the society of orders, classes and statuses that had prevailed in Europe before the French Revolution. Now the political and social orders must be democratic in several different senses: that its citizens were regarded as equal before the law, equal in their civil rights, equally eligible for office, property, wealth and status. Along with equality, the French Revolution had enshrined liberty. But just what did equality and liberty entail? Were they compatible and necessary to one another, as Rousseau had argued? Or did they conflict? If so, did the claims of equality override those of liberty, or vice versa? Or could the nature and value of both be recognized and reconciled, provided that they were properly distinguished and their claims balanced? This was Tocqueville's position.

Equality could mean that all enjoyed rights, or that they were equally deprived of them. Such a society could be governed in very different ways. Was it not plausible, particularly for a reader of Rousseau, to consider whether in this new age, political democracy might take legitimate or illegitimate forms? This it seems to me is what Tocqueville was doing when he contrasted the democracy he saw in America to the political practices developed during the Terror, Consulate and Empire. In my view, when Tocqueville described Americans as self-limiting citizens who acknowledged the law to which they had consented and helped frame, he was applying what he had learned from Rousseau. And the same was true when Tocqueville considered the bracing effects of political participation upon citizens who understood and valued liberty because they themselves enjoyed it.

These were mutually reinforcing benefits of liberty and equality. Rousseau had had to break new ground when he argued the case for equality positively in the *Social Contract*, and negatively in the *Discourse on Inequality*. Tocqueville showed how political language registered the novel state of affairs in America and post-revolutionary France:

> I have frequently used the word *equality* in an absolute sense; nay, I have personified equality in several places; thus I have said that equality does such and such things or refrains from doing others. It may be affirmed that the writers of the age of Louis XIV would not have spoken in this manner; they never would have thought of using the word *equality* without applying it to some particular thing.[42]

My final contention is that despite all that separated Tocqueville from Rousseau, the analysis of Bonapartism we are about to consider owes much to the analysis of legitimacy and illegitimacy central to Rousseau's thought. Tocqueville read Rousseau and Montesquieu much as Rousseau had made use of Montesquieu. All were theorists and not historians of political thought. They read, criticized, and took what they could use in constructing their own theory. This is what they understood to be their task.

IV

Tocqueville very early took an important step in his use of the concept of Bonapartism. French liberals had from the beginning linked Napoleon Bonaparte to the Revolution. Madame de Staël, Benjamin Constant, Guizot, Royer-Collard had all asserted that because Napoleon came to power in the wake of the Revolution, this proved that democracy and equality were incompatible with an ordered liberty guaranteeing individual political and civil rights. Tocqueville was the first French liberal to argue that the only alternative to Bonapartism was an ordered, constitutional and self-limiting democracy along the lines of the United States as he described it.[43]

Yet Tocqueville did not abandon his distrust of the theory of unlimited popular sovereignty:

> I regard it as an impious and detestable maxim that in matters of government, the majority of a people has the right to do everything, and nevertheless I place the origin of all powers in the will of the majority. Am I in contradiction with myself?[44]

Tocqueville's answer resembles that given by Constant, who denied that supreme, unchecked power, whether in the hands of an individual or those of a whole people, could ever be legitimate. Tocqueville, however, diverged from French liberals of his time when he argued that there was no alternative to endowing everyone with the peaceful exercise of rights, including citizenship. Only in a democracy can modern men learn to respect the rights of others and for the rule of law that limits their own passions and interests. In the United States, he argued, ordinary men had been educated to respect rights by possessing and exercising them. They obey laws because of their part in making them. Only by participating in government can men identify with it and accept it as just.

To his French readers, Tocqueville wrote that he was not proposing that America could or should become a literal model for imitation elsewhere:

> The mores (*moeurs*) and laws of the Americans are not the only ones which may suit a democratic people, but the Americans have shown that it is not necessary to despair of regulating democracy by the aid of *moeurs* and laws.[45]

Tocqueville was not proposing that everything be done at a single stroke. But he argued that the alternative to establishing a legitimate form of democracy was an illegitimate Bonapartist dictatorship. This was a stark choice, but the question was which type of democratic equality would there be. For equality could also be achieved by denying rights to everyone:

> But I am of the opinion that if we do not succeed in gradually introducing democratic institutions into France, if we despair of imparting to all the citizens those ideas and sentiments which first prepare them for freedom and afterwards allow them to enjoy it, there will be no independence for anyone, neither for the bourgeois, nor for the noble; neither for the poor nor for the rich, but an equal tyranny for all; and I foresee

that if in time we do not succeed in establishing the peaceful rule of the greatest number, we shall sooner or later end up under the *unlimited* power of a single person.[46]

This passage contained a point dear to Rousseau: that citizens must be prepared, educated, that is, for freedom by teaching ideas and sentiments, and then allowed to participate as citizens. But the principal argument would lead to a consideration of how and why Napoleon was able to come to power, how he had used and betrayed democratic legitimacy, and how his rule had degraded those he had governed because of the new standards created by the Enlightenment (for which Rousseau had not much to say), and by the contributions made to liberty, equality and human dignity by the French Revolution (which Rousseau never experienced).

Tocqueville wished to describe, explain, 'to narrate and judge at the same time' the long-term effects of Bonapartism upon French political life. In what sense were Bonapartist regimes democratic? How did they affect democracy in France? In Tocqueville's view, the French Revolution had left an ambiguous heritage, two traditions of democracy. One was compatible with citizens ruling themselves, while enjoying liberty, civil equality, the rule of law and individual rights. Under the other, there was rule in the name of the people by individuals, groups, or parties openly contemptuous of any limitations on popular sovereignty, the ostensible source of the power they exercised. Prominent among the characteristics of the Revolution's illiberal legacy were those Tocqueville attributed to Napoleon: the perfection of a centralized administrative machinery; the codification of a civil law which encouraged individualist self-enrichment, but limited freedoms of the press and association; the launching of theoretical justifications and actual precedents for seizing power by force from constitutional governments; the invention of plebiscitary dictatorship as a pseudo-democratic alternative to representative government; the creation, among those who regarded themselves as friends of the Revolution, a tradition of disregarding individual rights and constitutional government.

In 1842 Tocqueville was inducted into the French Academy. Its protocol called for the new member to deliver a eulogy of his predecessor's life and work. Tocqueville's address was thus bound to address the career of a M. de Cessac, who had contributed to the *l'Encyclopédie méthodique*, served the monarchy, the Revolution, and held high administrative office under the Empire. Tocqueville chose to spend three-quarters of his address on Napoleon and the Empire. Although the address as given was printed in about twenty pages, more than a hundred pages of drafts have survived.

In this highly polished address, Tocqueville treated Napoleon Bonaparte's performances in the Directory, Consulate and Empire as among those phases of the Revolution which had contributed most to consolidating a despotic tendency in the French political tradition. Tocqueville then used the language of Rousseau to analyze what, once the *ancien régime* had been destroyed, had been the practical effects of the theory of the general will:

> Once the powers of directing and administering the nation were no longer considered the privileges of certain men or families, such powers began to appear as the product and agent of the will of all (*la volonté de tous*). It was then generally recognized that this will ought to be subject to no other limits than those it imposed upon itself. After the destruction of classes, corporations, and castes, this will appeared to be the necessary and natural heir of all secondary powers. Nothing was left so great that it was inaccessible; nothing so small that it could not be reached. The ideas of centralization and popular sovereignty were born on the same day.
>
> Although these ideas originated in (demands for) liberty, they could easily lead to servitude.
>
> Those unlimited powers that had been rightly refused to a king (*prince*) . . . now were conceded to an individual ostensibly representing the nation's sovereignty. Thus Napoleon could say, without much offending public opinion, that he had the right of command over everything because he alone spoke in the name of the people.[47]

What Tocqueville again stressed in this passage are the dangers to liberty from a leader who uses pseudo-democratic theories to legitimate the seizure and exercise of power in an egalitarian or democratic society. Such an abuse of democratic theory Tocqueville for the first time explicitly attributed to Napoleon, who had not been identified by name in the *Démocratie*. There Tocqueville had written about the strange discovery by modern demagogues that there can be legitimate tyrannies, provided only that they are exercised in the people's name.[48]

Tocqueville may have been pointing out how Napoleon's power had been served by the theory of the general will, although Rousseau, of course, could not have foreseen the new situation created by the liquidation of the monarchy. Tocqueville seems to be assessing the long-term effects of Rousseau's theories. For the first time Tocqueville links centralization to that of popular sovereignty. Yet he did not renounce Rousseau's faith in popular participation. Only political activity by citizens can serve as an antidote for those dispositions of democratic society he had identified as peculiarly dangerous to liberty. These dangers included individualism, as well as the preferences for equality over liberty, for centralization over local self-government, as well as the passion for material well-being. All these points occur in Rousseau. Some of them Tocqueville praises and adapts; others he condemns for their long-term effects. Points made in Rousseau's *Second Discourse* are linked to the theory of citizenship in the *Social Contract*:

> The diffusion of knowledge (*des lumières*) and the division of property has made each of us independent and isolated from the rest. Only interest in public affairs can temporarily unite our minds, and on occasion, our wills. But absolute power would deprive us of this unique setting for deliberating together and acting in common. It chooses to enclose us in that narrow individualism, to which we are already over inclined.[49]

Like Rousseau himself, Tocqueville was a theorist primarily concerned to think for himself about the questions he had identified as crucial in his own time and context. Such a theorist cares little about fidelity to a predecessor, however much admired. Although a predecessor may be carefully considered, he is always subject to criticism. What he has said may be substantially altered because of the later theorist's judgement that the circumstances of politics have been radically transformed. Although an earlier view may on occasion recommend itself, it is seldom followed in such a way as to violate the framework of a thinker concerned to put on record and maintain his own organized responses to the practical situations of his time. Perhaps the most remarkable use of Rousseau's category of legitimacy and illegitimacy by Tocqueville is precisely one that Rousseau himself would have neither understood nor found congenial. For it represents Tocqueville's view of the moral consequences of the Enlightenment (which Rousseau condemned) and of the French Revolution's first and most generous phase (which he never knew). Here Tocqueville condemns the French for having accepted Napoleon's illegitimate and usurped power.

On this point opposed to Rousseau, Tocqueville favorably contrasts the stage of modern morality to those of earlier ages or stages of civilization. From this analysis he concludes that modern men are degraded by obedience to absolute power. They have an obligation to disobey and resist it. This his countrymen had not done:

> In societies that either possess faith, or else possess little knowledge, absolute power often constrains men's souls, but without in the least degrading them. This is because such power is acknowledged as a legitimate state of affairs (*comme un fait légitime*). Then the rigors of absolute power are suffered unnoticed; endured, with no consciousness of its exercise. In our time, this cannot be the case. The eighteenth century and the French Revolution have not left us with any moral or honorable ways of submitting to despotism. Human beings have become too independent, too disrespectful, too sceptical to believe sincerely in the rights of absolute power. This they perceive only as a dishonorable escape from that anarchy they themselves were not brave enough to oppose, as a shameful protection necessitated by the vices and weakness of their own time. Thus they judge absolute power as at once necessary and illegitimate (*illégitime*), and when they submit to its laws, they can only despise it and themselves.[50]

Tocqueville is often placed among the enemies of the Enlightenment by those who judge him by his attack upon French eighteenth-century political thought in the *Ancien régime*, which appeared fifteen years after his induction into the *Académie française*.[51] Yet in his notable statement above, Tocqueville bases the obligation to resist absolute power upon the precepts of the Enlightenment and the early phase of the Revolution, the principles of 1789. Was this a youthful idealism Tocqueville abandoned after later disillusionments with the permanent French Revolution? Passages in his *Souvenirs* suggest as much. But there is a note written for his uncompleted history, which presents a position more in keeping with his earlier view: 'I find the absolute and systematic denigration in our time of what is called eighteenth-century philosophy to be as blind and foolish as the infatuation it once produced among its admirers.'[52]

There are good reasons for believing that at the end of Tocqueville's life he still believed in applying the distinction between legitimate and illegitimate forms of democracy originally suggested to him by Rousseau. There can be no doubt that both condemned military leaders who, like Julius Caesar, Cromwell and Napoleon Bonaparte, destroyed the power of popular assemblies and republican constitutions. Tocqueville's achievement was to perceive the Bonapartist phenomenon, whatever its analogies to the past, as a democratic and post-revolutionary phenomenon, a lasting threat to the liberty he wished to combine with equality.

Notes

1 James T. Schleifer, 'Tocqueville as Historian: Philosophy and Methodology in the *Democracy*', in *Reconsidering Tocqueville's 'Democracy in America'*, ed. Abraham S. Eisenstadt (New Brunswick and London, 1988), 161–4.

2 This paragraph is based upon Robert Derathé's introduction to the *Contrat social* in Pléiade, vol. IV. Unless otherwise indicated, all references to Pléiade are to tome III of that edition.

3 *Jean-Jacques Rousseau, Politics and the Arts. Letter to M. D'Alembert on the Theatre*, tr. Allan Bloom (Ithaca, NY, 1960), 115.

4 Pléiade has the additional merit of serving as the basis for a concordance by page and line to Rousseau's texts. A complete set of references to the concepts and terms I shall be analyzing may be found in Michel Launay and Gunnar von Proschwitz, *Index du 'Contrat social' (texte de 1762 et Manuscrit de Genève)* (Geneva, 1977), and Leo and Michel Launay, *Index-Concordance . . . et du 'Discours sur les origines de l'inégalité* (Geneva and Paris, 1981).

5 The citation from Jean Starobinski comes from Pléiade, III, lxvi.

6 Melvin Richter, 'Tocqueville, Napoleon, and Bonapartism', in *Reconsidering Tocqueville's 'Democracy in America'*, ed. A. S. Eisenstadt (New Brunswick and London, 1988), 110–45. This extends and modifies an earlier article closely related to the concerns of this paper: 'Toward a Concept of Political Illegitimacy: Bonapartist Dictatorship and Democratic Legitimacy', in *Political Theory*, 10 (1982), 185–214.

7 Cited in Guy Dodge, *Benjamin Constant's Philosophy of Liberalism* (Chapel Hill, 1980), 19–20.

8 References to the French text are from F. P. G. Guizot, *Histoire de la Civilisation en Europe depuis la Chute de l'Empire Romain* (8 vols; Paris, 1882); English translations follow those of William Hazlitt in F. Guizot, *The History of Civilization from the Fall of the Roman Empire to the French Revolution* (2 vols; New York, 1892). Guizot, *Histoire des origines du Gouvernement Représentatif* (2 vols; Paris, 1855), [F. Guizot, *History of the Origin of Representative Government*, tr. A. R. Scobie (London, 1852), 139–40]. F. Guizot, *Histoire de la Civilisation*, I, 261.

9 *Ibid.*

10 J. L. Talmon, *The Origins of Totalitarian Democracy* (Boston, 1952); Isaiah Berlin, 'Two Concepts of Liberty', in *Four Essays on Liberty* (Oxford, 1969), 118–72.

11 R. A. Leigh, 'Liberté et autorité dans le "*Contrat social*"', in *Jean-Jacques Rousseau et son oeuvre* (Paris, 1964). An abridged English translation by Alan Ritter is in *Rousseau's Political Writings*, ed. A. Ritter and J. C. Bondanella (New York, 1988), 232–44.

12 Robert Wokler, 'Rousseau's Two Concepts of Liberty', in *Lives, Liberties and the Public Good*, ed. G. Feaver and F. Rosen (London, 1987), 61–100.

13 L. G. Crocker, 'Rousseau et la voie du totalitarisme', in *Rousseau et la philosophie politique* (Paris, 1965), 109–10. See also Crocker's *Nature and Culture* (Baltimore, 1966), ch. VII.

14 The fullest account by Tocqueville himself is in *Oeuvres* (Mayer ed.), 15:2, 315. M. Jardin reports that the collection included the *Oeuvres complètes* of Voltaire, Rousseau, Montesquieu, Buffon, Mably, Raynal. André Jardin, *Alexis de Tocqueville, 1805–59*, 62–4. See also 15:2, 56, 82, where Tocqueville tells of losing his faith as the result of reading Voltaire and Rousseau.

15 Alexis de Tocqueville, in *Correspondence d'Alexis de Tocqueville et de Louis de Kergolay*, in *Oeuvres complètes*, ed. J. P. Mayer, 18 vols (Paris, 1949–), 13:1, 418. Henceforth this edition will be cited as Tocqueville, *Oeuvres* (Mayer ed.) to distinguish it from the older *Oeuvres complètes*, ed. Gustave de Beaumont, 9 vols (Paris, 1861–3), henceforth cited as Tocqueville, *Oeuvres* (Beaumont ed.).

16 The others were Plato, Aristotle and Machiavelli. Tocqueville, *Oeuvres* (Beaumont ed.), 9, 120.

17 Tocqueville, *Oeuvres* (Beaumont ed.), 9, 122–3.

18 Melvin Richter, 'Comparative Political Analysis in Montesquieu and Tocqueville', *Comparative Politics* 1 (1969), 129–60; 'The Uses of Theory: Tocqueville's Adaptation of Montesquieu', in M. Richter, ed., *Essays in Theory and History* (Cambridge, MA, 1970), 71–102; 'Modernity and its Distinctive Threats to Liberty: Montesquieu and Tocqueville on New Forms of Illegitimate Domination', in Michael Hereth and Jutta Höffgen, eds, *Alexis de Tocqueville – Zur Politik in der Demokratie* (Baden-Baden, 1981), 61–80.

19 Allan Bloom has twice dealt with the relationship between Tocqueville and Rousseau. In the Introduction to his translation of *Emile* (New York, 1979), Bloom asserts that the scheme of *Democracy in America* is adopted from Rousseau. Both Tocqueville and Rousseau are dedicated 'to the formation of free men and free communities founded on egalitarian principles' (p. 5). A somewhat longer discussion occurs in Bloom's 'The Study of Texts', in Melvin Richter, ed., *Political Theory and Political Education* (Princeton, 1980), 135–7.

Perhaps the longest article yet written on the Tocqueville–Rousseau relationship is by Wilhelm Hennis, 'Tocquevilles "Neue Politische Wissenschaft"', in Justin Stagl, ed., *Aspekte der Kultursoziologie* (Berlin, 1982), 385–407. This amplifies his 'Wider den Hund in der Sonne – Anmerkungen zu Tocqueville', in Michael Hereth and Jutta Höffgen, eds, *Alexis de Tocqueville – Zur Politik in der Demokratie* (Baden-Baden, 1981), 81–9. Hennis is among those who assume that interpreters of Tocqueville must choose between Montesquieu and Tocqueville. There can be one and only one correct path to understanding Tocqueville properly. In neither paper does Hennis address the crucial question of Rousseau's own complex relationship to Montesquieu.

20 Robert Derathé, *Jean-Jacques Rousseau et la science politique de son temps* (Paris, 1950), 53, 54, 281, 300. See also Derathé's introduction to the

Contrat social in Pléiade, III, civ, where Rousseau's representation of Montesquieu is corrected.

21 Rousseau, *Emile*, tr. Allan Bloom (New York, 1979), 458.
22 Robert Nisbet, in *Reconsidering Tocqueville's 'Democracy in America'*, ed. A. S. Eisenstadt (New Brunswick and London, 1988), 176–7.
23 Benjamin Constant, *Principes de Politique*, ch. I, in Constant, *Oeuvres*, ed. A. Roulin (Paris, 1957), 1004–5.
24 *Ibid.*
25 Aquinas distinguished two types of tyranny: usurpation (*tyrannus absque titulo*), the lack of proper title to authority; and that arising from conduct, that is, the abuse of power properly acquired (*tyrannus exercitio*). For an extended discussion, see Oscar Jászi and John D. Lewis, *Against the Tyrant* (Glencoe, IL, 1957), 26 *et seq*.
26 I have discussed the notion of a semantic or linguistic field, and how concepts can be treated synchronically or diachronically. Melvin Richter, 'Pocock, Skinner, and the *Geschichtliche Grundbegriffe*', *History and Theory*, forthcoming; '*Begriffsgeschichte* and the History of Ideas', *Journal of the History of Ideas*, 48 (1987), 247–63; 'Conceptual History (*Begriffsgeschichte*) and Political Theory', *Political Theory*, 14 (1986), 604–37.
27 On taxes, legitimate and illegitimate, see *Sur l'Economie politique*, 264, 270. Rousseau also used *illégitimement* to designate the conduct of a citizen who has violated a law limiting any future acquisition beyond what he already has. *Constitution pour la Corse*, Pléiade, III, 936. Rousseau described Solon's abolition of debts as an illegitimate act (*un acte illégitime*) in *Emile*, Pléiade, IV, 841; tr. Bloom, 462.
28 The most complete recent treatment of the concept of legitimacy is *Legitimität, Legalität* by Thomas Würtenberger, in *Geschichtliche Grundbegriffe. Historisches Lexikon zur Politisch-sozialen Sprache in Deutschland* [*Basic Concepts in History. A Dictionary on Historical Principles of Political and Social Language in Germany*], eds Otto Brunner, Werner Conze and Reinhart Koselleck (5 vols to date; Stuttgart, 1972–), 3, 677–740.
29 Rousseau, *Du Contrat Social (première version, Manuscrit de Gèneve)*, Pléiade, III, 304.
30 Derathé, Pléiade, III, civ.
31 Rousseau's use of the term 'Republic' here is, according to Derathé (Pléiade, III, cvii) disingenuous.
32 Pléiade, III, pp. 435–6 (text), 1490–1 (notes).
33 The editor of the definitive edition (Pléiade, III, 1489, n. 3) explicates this sentence by referring to Book II, ch. I: 'If then the people promises simply to obey, by that very act it dissolves itself and loses what makes it a people; the moment a master (*un maître*) exists, there is no longer a Sovereign, and from that moment the body politic has ceased to exist' (p. 20).
34 Montesquieu, *De l'Esprit des loix*, ch. XV.
35 Melvin Richter, 'Despotism', *Dictionary of the History of Ideas*.

36 Tocqueville, *De la Démocratie en Amérique*, *Oeuvres complètes* (Mayer ed.), I:2, 324; Alexis de Tocqueville, *Democracy in America*, ed. Phillips Bradley (New York, 1945), 2:336.
37 Pléiade, III, 51, 339, 438, 466.
38 *Sur le gouvernement de Pologne*, Pléiade, III, 1014–15. Willmoore Kendall, *The Government of Poland* (Indianapolis and New York, 1972), 80–2.
39 *Ibid.*
40 Tocqueville, *Oeuvres* (Mayer ed.), 1:2, ch. XXII.
41 Pléiade, III, 391.
42 *De la Démocratie en Amérique*, in *Oeuvres* (Mayer ed.), 1:2, 74.
43 I have argued this point in my 'Toward a Concept of Political Legitimacy', *Political Theory*, 10 (1982), 185–214.
44 *Oeuvres* (Mayer ed.), I:1, 261.
45 *Ibid.*, I:1, 329.
46 *Ibid.*, I:1, 330.
47 *Oeuvres* (Beaumont ed.), 9, 14.
48 Tocqueville (Mayer ed.), I:1, 413.
49 *Ibid.*
50 *Oeuvres* (Beaumont ed.), IX, 18–19.
51 Tocqueville, *Oeuvres* (Mayer ed.), 2:1, 213.
52 Tocqueville, *Oeuvres* (Mayer ed.), 2:2, 348.

Part II

Interpreting the *Social Contract*

5   Geraint Parry*

Thinking one's own thoughts: autonomy and the citizen

> It is therefore essential, if the general will is to be able to make itself known, that there should be no partial society in the state and that each citizen should think only his own thoughts.

If Rousseau was indeed a man of paradoxes he is remarkable in that his paradoxes are so consistent. It would be an exaggeration to claim that one could open the pages of his works entirely at random to discover the same tensions within his thought, yet it remains the case that again and again the reader encounters passages which appear to pull in the same contrary directions. Occasionally, as puzzled and not always entirely unsympathetic critics of his day were prone to claim, the reason is to be found in Rousseau's dramatic literary style – his desire to surprise the reader with the shock of the new (or perhaps it should be the shock of the old). More significantly, however, the paradoxes arise from his aim of reconciling, in almost dialectical fashion, aspirations each of which makes a powerful appeal to the readers of his own time and ours. In this, as in so many other respects, Rousseau fulfilled another of his paradoxes of being a man unlike any other man and also one whose life and hopes exemplify those of every other man.

One of the most striking of these consistent paradoxes is that in which Rousseau seeks to create a political community in which each citizen will 'think only his own thoughts'.[1] The rival claims of individuality and community are to be combined fruitfully in a polity in which each man will think thoughts which, whilst his own, are appropriate to a participating citizen. In advancing this argument Rousseau raises the contrasting images, or spectres, of individualism and communitarianism, republican liberty and collective authoritarianism, civic education and indoctrination, autonomy and heteronomy.

The autonomous character

The person who 'thinks only his own thoughts' appears to be the epitome of the autonomous individual. He is the person who exercises moral liberty which consists in obeying a law which he has prescribed to himself (*Social Contract*, Book I, ch. 8). There are at least two senses in which such a person can be described as autonomous and both are of some relevance to understanding Rousseau's conception of humanity. One sense is weak, if not however precisely a truism. The other sense is much stronger, even highly demanding.

A first understanding of autonomy is that it entails self-rule. The autonomous agent is one whose actions are chosen, determined by the will (see Lindley 1986: 21). The person's conduct is not determined by the commands of others. Autonomy in this sense indicates a capacity of choice. Such choices are backed by reasons for action. Having a will and being capable of providing reasons for choice is, for some, tantamount to describing a human being. A being lacking these qualities is something else – a brute beast perhaps. Rousseau proclaims that to 'renounce liberty is to renounce being a man, to surrender the rights of humanity and even its duties' (*Social Contract*: 186; Book I, ch. 4). A sour critic might conclude that this is but empty rhetoric for the very reason that Rousseau provides in his next sentence, since 'Such a renunciation is incompatible with man's nature'. If autonomy in this sense is definitional of man, it simply cannot be surrendered.

Clearly, however, Rousseau is pointing to a distinction between, putting it most starkly, *possessing* autonomy and *exercising* autonomy. The truly autonomous person then becomes one who regularly chooses and provides reasons for those choices. It may then be said to follow that the autonomous agent is, ideally at least, one who is able to offer a fully rational account of the choices which have been made. In being able to offer a rational defence of such choices one is taking responsibility for them. Possessing autonomy as a human being implies being responsible. Exercising autonomy involves taking responsibility. The former is inescapable. The latter is not only escapable but is more readily escaped than performed. It is a strenuous duty which many may wish to renounce. Rousseau is asserting, with his customary emphasis, that the failure to take responsibility is a derogation from the idea of man as a being who takes responsibility. The context is Rousseau's attack on forms of social contract theory which he incorporates provocatively and tellingly in a chapter on 'slavery'. Contracts by which either separate individuals or a whole people place themselves under a ruler are precisely comparable to agreements to sell oneself into slavery. The contract of sale involves an exchange of liberty for security. The fact that the rulers seldom truly deliver on their side of the agreement is a powerful point but is secondary to Rousseau's concern. The poor quality of such exchanges had already been remarked upon by Locke, for example, in his famous comment on the threats of polecats and foxes in the state of nature as compared to that from the lion-like absolute state (Locke 1960, para. 93). Rousseau's critique by contrast would comprehend in addition Locke's social contract. The man that sells himself into slavery remains responsible for this act, but is inhumanly declaring that henceforth he will exercise no further responsibility but will rely heteronomously on the will of another. Similarly the parties to the social contract, whilst authorising their own subordination are, at the same time, renouncing the future exercise of their responsibilities and announcing the effective, if not the conceptual, end of their manhood.

The points are well put by Robert Paul Wolff, albeit as a preliminary to his defence of philosophical anarchism:

> Since man's responsibility for his actions is a consequence of his capacity for choice, he cannot give it up or put it aside. He can refuse to acknowledge it, however, either deliberately or by simply failing to recognise his moral condition (Wolff 1976: 14).

Whilst remaining responsible for what one does, one frequently fails to take responsibility. One may shirk responsibility, preferring to allow others to give directions. This may well seem a rational course of action in terms of the allocation of one's time and effort. As Wolff points out, in a modern complex society it becomes ever more difficult to be a genuinely autonomous actor who takes responsibility for the full range of one's conduct. A truly autonomous person would, on this view, need to gather information, think carefully and deliberate fully on a variety of issues. Consequently most of us are content to fall short of a fully autonomous existence.

For this reason Stanley Benn argues that autonomy is 'an ideal, not a normal condition' (Benn 1988: 155). It should be regarded as an excellence of character for which persons may strive. It does not require that a conscious decision be made before every action. 'Someone who did that would be an existentialist gone mad' (Benn 1988: 180). Very often it will be satisfactory to act according to established norms and only in conditions of especial perplexity will it be necessary to articulate underlying principles. In an argument which will be of some relevance to Rousseau's social and political world Benn argues that autonomy is even consistent with the internalisation of the traditional values of the society in which one has grown up, provided that it always remains possible to challenge those traditions and expose any internal contradictions they may contain. As Benn puts it:

> For the autonomous person is not necessarily one who can give reasons for *all* his beliefs; it is required only that he be alive to, and disposed to resolve by rational reflection and decision, incoherences in the complex tradition that he has internalized (Benn 1988: 182, emphasis in the original).

The proviso that the possibility of criticising tradition must be available implies, according to Benn, that 'autonomy is an ideal available only within a plural tradition' (Benn 1988: 182).

In a plural culture there are differences and conflicts which lead to challenges to the various belief systems. The individuals are led, as a result, to reassess their own conceptions of the norms by which they govern their lives. This process is an essential feature of the development of the ideal of the autonomous personality. By contrast, in a total community there would not be the occasions which enable the individuals to perceive alternatives and to choose amongst them and, as a consequence, take responsibility for those decisions.

Education for autonomy

If, as Benn contends, autonomy is to be seen as an excellence of character it becomes pertinent to ask how this quality is to be cultivated. Taking responsibility is a skill to be acquired; it is not merely given. In principle one might examine the production of the autonomous personality in two stages. The first phase would be the education of the self-determining individual. The second would be the incorporation of that individual within a self-determining political community. That second phase might be one which would ensure that the free-thinking person can join with others and together make rules which will leave each as free as before – the problem of the social contract and posed by *Du Contrat social*. If the second phase is the subject matter, or one of the matters, of *The Social Contract*, the first phase, the cultivation of the autonomous individual, is the topic of *Emile*.

It is not the case, however, that the education of Emile should be seen as a preparation for citizenship. The subject matter of the work is not political education, but the education of man (and later the [mis]education of woman). Rousseau is positively eager to insist upon this distinction within the opening pages of *Emile*. For a political education the reader is advised to turn to Plato's *Republic* (*Emile*: 40). Even more one should look at the practices of Sparta.

Not only is Rousseau's concern with private rather than public education but the two are described at the outset as antithetical in their objectives and procedures. The subject matter of private education is natural man and the objectives that the education is to pursue are also natural. This natural man is a complete self. The education he is to receive is intended to develop the whole range of capacities the self contains. It is in this sense that Rousseau can say that the only trade for which this education should prepare the child is life itself (*Emile*: 41). A public education, or any education which takes account of a particular social order, provides a narrower form of training. The child is regarded as playing a role within that order and education may be designed to train a soldier, a priest or a lawyer. It is in this sense that John Dewey was a true disciple of Rousseau in his attack on education as 'preparation' (Dewey 1966: 54–68). That view regards the child as a candidate undergoing preparation for a preconceived social order. Rewards and sanctions become the instruments by which the pupil is reshaped to fit in with the requirements of the society. In Rousseau's terms such education denatures the individual.

This denaturing process occurs not merely in training for a vocation but in the education of a citizen. Although citizenship might be regarded as involving wide responsibilities and hence being less restrictive of the development of human capacities, for Rousseau its essential feature lay in its particularism. The worth of a citizen is in relation to the whole of which he is a part. A good citizen merges himself with the group (*Emile*: 39–40). Accordingly public education should be aimed at creating this readiness to replace the natural man with public man. A citizen of Rome, according to Rousseau, was 'neither Caius nor Lucius, he was a Roman; he even loved the country exclusive of himself'. Rousseau's prime concern in *Emile* is with educating a Caius or Lucius, not a Roman. It is not possible, he states, to train both. Does that mean that one must abandon the age-old hope of combining the good man and the good citizen?

Certainly one can readily see that the way in which Emile is encouraged to develop his autonomy and to take responsibility for his conduct could make him an uncomfortable fellow citizen in certain kinds of civil society. He is in the first formative years to receive an anti-social education. It is, after all, as the opening words of the book have stated, man who has meddled with nature and corrupted it. Rousseau's declaration that Emile is an orphan is intended to abstract the child even from the malign influence of parents who have themselves been shaped by their society and their forefathers. Conservatives may resign themselves to what Philip Larkin thought Mum and Dad did to their children, as had been done unto them; a new start requires the elimination (or re-education) of parents and their replacement by the tutor as the representative of nature.

Rousseau is the great protagonist of 'discovery learning', as it came to be called: 'true education consists less in precept than in practice. We begin to instruct ourselves when we begin to live; our education begins with us' (*Emile*: 42). The major discovery that the pupil must make is of the necessity of nature. To find that one is dependent on things is no injury to one's autonomy, as it would be to find that one was dependent on the will of other men. Thus the child is to discover for himself the rigours of cold or the dangers of falls. He is allowed to run 'freely' and barefoot. As he does so he is brought face to face with 'things', with nature. It is when Emile is confronted with a problem posed by nature that he is ready to learn. It is the need to measure that prompts an interest in geometry and it is the necessity of finding his way home in time for lunch that forces him to resort to navigation by reference to the sun and to recognise the use of astronomy.

In all this, learning is not to be mediated through the authority of books. Here Rousseau is pursuing the Enlightenment's systematic critique of authority to its logical conclusion (or to a *reductio ad absurdum*). Only one's autonomous discoveries are to be trusted. This is a technique which will give Emile self-mastery and also make him a truer scientist. The books of geography will never instruct the child in how to get from Paris to Saint-Denis. If this is thought to be the teaching of science, as an accumulation of knowledge, Rousseau is fashioning the necessary tools for its acquisition (*Emile*: 126). Emile has 'learned to think' (*Emile*: 316).

Taught self-government by nature, Emile is then, with the greatest of caution, to be eased into the company of men. It follows that to limit the corruption which this might entail Emile should be introduced to men who are closest to nature. That means living in the country, not the city. It also involves living amongst artisans and learning one of their trades. The artisan depends on his labour which is part of nature and whose exertions are bounded only by necessity. The artisan is self-sufficient and independent, unlike the labourer who works the fields of a landlord. Agriculture can create dependence which in turn creates the illusion of the smiling fields of pastoral poetry whereas in reality they are watered with the sweat of the brows of the slaves working them (*Discourse on Inequality*: 92). Only the small proprietor can farm and at the same time retain autonomy. A trade, however, will guarantee one the status of a man at any time (*Emile*: 195).

It is this curious youth, and only he, who can reliably be launched into polite society. Even then he will need some further education in history and religion. In each instance a minimalist understanding is to be the aim. Thucydides is the model for historians because he relates 'facts' without offering judgements (*Emile*: 238). The natural religion of the Savoyard vicar is similarly unmediated. Authorities are suspect. The individual thinks his own thoughts, not those of others. Thus equipped, Emile can face the social whirl and cope with Paris. In polite society:

> The man of the world is whole in his mask. Almost never being in himself, he is always alien and ill at ease when forced to go back there. What he is, is nothing; what he appears to be is everything for him (*Emile*: 230).

A concern for appearances ensures that the law of fashion and opinion prevails over such a man whether in matters of dress or intellect. But Emile is prepared. He is a combination of Cato and Alceste. He has learned to think for himself and by now has also been warned of the dangers from those not similarly educated. He knows how to behave with integrity even in the *salon*. Like Rousseau himself, he is an outsider but, whilst plain-speaking, he is to maintain some sense of civility:

> although I want to form the man of nature, the object is not, for all that, to make him a savage and to relegate him to the depths of the woods. It suffices that, enclosed in a social whirlpool, he not let himself get carried away by either the passions or the opinions of men (*Emile*: 255).

With such an armour there is no one in the whole world 'less of an imitator than Emile' (*Emile*: 331). He is not to be mocked out of his views because they are unfashionable. Emile will only be convinced by arguments. He will not care about social esteem. He will be impervious to the women Laclos was later to portray and, Rousseau implies, they will not find him attractive. In the face of all the seductions and temptations of society Emile will remain authentic and autonomous; he will be his own man.

He is, however, scarcely a self-made man. The paradox of autonomous man being shaped by his tutor has been repeatedly remarked upon. As one eminent student of educational theory has put it, 'Rousseau, the prime enemy of the "artificial", produces at least as synthetic a youngster as those he criticises' (Bantock 1980: 272). For Bantock, Rousseau runs up against the limits of a negative theory of education. Emile learns not 'from any environment, but from an *arranged* environment . . .' (Bantock 1980: 273). When a child, Emile was allowed to run barefoot – but his tutor had already removed the broken glass. As an adult he possesses liberty because he has been so well formed that he can be trusted.

> It is true that I leave him the appearance of independence, but he was never better subjected to me; for now he is subjected because he wants to be. As long as I was unable to make myself master of his will, I remained master of his person; I was never a step away from him. Now I sometimes leave him to himself, because I govern him always (*Emile*: 332).

By this stage Emile has fully internalised the lessons of his educator. There is no sense of being inauthentic. He does what he does as if it were, indeed, natural to him. Emile would have no doubts that the thoughts he was thinking were truly his own. In one of the most celebrated (or notorious) passages, Rousseau has Emile choose 'to remain what you have made me and voluntarily to add no other chain to the one with which nature and the laws burden me' (*Emile*: 471).

Emile in political society?

What sort of citizen could Emile be? Is this the sort of man who will think his own thoughts and express them in the assembly in its endeavours to discover the general will?

It has already been noted that at the outset of his treatise on education Rousseau had insisted that the creation of the man and the creation of the citizen were totally different enterprises. The citizen was to be the unit in the group, the part of the whole. To make a citizen was to exchange independence for dependence. The point is made with equal emphasis in *The Government of Poland* where Rousseau explicitly addresses public education. There the citizen is described as 'a mere cipher' when he is alone and as having imbibed a love of his fatherland and of political liberty with his mother's milk (*The Government of Poland*: 19). Nothing, it seems, could be in greater contrast. *Emile* would be the text for those who think of Rousseau as the liberal; *Poland*, along with the chapter on civil religion in *The Social Contract*, the text which raises the most qualms for the liberal.

It is certainly possible to leave the matter there – the two Rousseaus or, rather, one Rousseau but with alternative visions of the ideal life. On this view Rousseau is presenting us with contrasting ideal types of the education appropriate to these ways of life. The idyll portrayed in *Emile* of rustic life is one in which the free man can live without being encumbered with the duties of citizenship. Rousseau would be a 'man of the people', living in his white cottage with green shutters, provided with kitchen garden and orchard, eating out of doors, joining the rustics in their feasts and wedding celebrations. Self-determination extends even to the household for 'we would be our own valets, in order to be our own masters' (*Emile*: 352).

It is true that at the end of the book Emile is introduced to the rudiments of politics by means of the *précis* of *The Social Contract* (*Emile*: 458–67). Yet this passage sits uneasily in the text and Rousseau appears unusually tentative in describing how Emile might properly respond to its lessons. After a passionate passage in which the worth of a fatherland is apostrophised Rousseau reverts to situating Emile and Sophie in the countryside of a nation in which the social contract has not been observed but in which a form of security has been ensured by the public authorities (*Emile*: 473). Here the couple set a moral example to the less fortunate by the simplicity of their lives, doing their best to revive the golden age. This may not be the life of a hermit but it is not that of the citizen.

Peter Gay has suggested that the society of the *Social Contract* which will make 'obedience lawful, and lawful obedience practicable, is a society of Emiles' (Gay 1970: 549). Yet it is more plausible to argue that Emile would have to be denatured, deconstructed and reconstructed to fit into any political community. The private, reclusive vision once again seems opposed to the public and participatory. At the same time it has to be acknowledged that Rousseau declared that 'Society must be studied by means of men, and men by means of society. Those who want to treat politics and morals separately will never understand anything of either of the two' (*Emile*: 235).

Could it be therefore that Gay's interpretation is in part correct – that the citizen of the *Social Contract* will require less in the way of denaturalisation than would the inhabitant of any other state from Sparta to the present? Such a citizen could not be Emile in his purest manifestation (and it hardly needs stating, certainly could not be Sophie). But this might be the political world which Emile would feel least alien to him. It is the polity which Rousseau hoped for in *Emile* in which dependence on men is replaced by dependence on law. In such a political association the 'general wills' of individual citizens are armed 'with a real strength superior to the action of every particular will' (*Emile*: 85). If the laws resulting from the endeavours of such citizens could possess the inflexibility of the laws of nature 'in the republic all of the advantages of the natural state would be united with those of the civil state'. Such a citizen's dependence on law would be comparable to Emile's dependence on things and he would be comparably free. The political education which would bring him to see his dependence on the laws has parallels to the guidance which ended when Emile had imbibed his tutor's instruction so fully that his thoughts could appear authentically his own. In like fashion the citizen of the *Social Contract* will think his own thoughts which are in accordance with the public good. The laws may never attain to the inevitability of a law of nature but they are able to set a standard of conduct which a man might wish to regard as his own. They give him 'the courage to be just even among wicked men'. The good man and the good citizen remain distinct conceptions, as they were for Aristotle. They have been educated in distinctive ways. Yet, if there is to be any country in which the approximations to the two ideals could intersect it would have to be the country of the *Social Contract*.

The public good is for a man such as Emile alone a real motive and not a mere pretext as it is for others (*Emile*: 473). This is the civic attitude that is presupposed if the social contract is to achieve its purpose. Within each man is a general will which may only emerge, but in strengthened form in a person of virtue, after a struggle with private interest. The general will of the community is embodied in law when the public good has been uncovered by men who have voted in the assembly with the public good genuinely in mind. The generality of the public good consists not only in the generality of its objectives but also in the generality of its making, in the sense both that all citizens are equally involved in its discovery and that all are moved by the general will within each of them. If that motivation is absent and the public good is a mere pretext for private or factional interest, the outcome is merely the will of all. Any compatibility with the general will is coincidental. Even without that coincidence such a simulacrum of law (*Emile*: 473) might ensure sufficient tranquillity to deserve respect. But it could not attain the full legitimacy of a law which truly incorporated the general will. It would not be a law which corresponded with the thinking of a good man or a good citizen.

There remains, of course, the problem of how the general will is to be discovered and in what circumstances the discovery is to be made. Rousseau's answers to these questions turn crucially on the formation of an individual citizen who will, in thinking his own thoughts, think of the public good. Rousseau declares that the general will can be found by counting votes (*Social Contract*, Book IV, ch. 2). This assertion is highly troubling. Its apparent inconsistency with Rousseau's fundamental objectives can, it seems, only be rescued by reducing the passage to a tautology. The explanation is ultimately to be found in the public education of the citizen.

The initial formulation appears to equate the general will with the will of the majority. The person who is in a minority should come to a realisation that, by virtue of its minority status, his opinion concerning the general will was mistaken. Indeed if his opinion had been victorious it would have achieved the opposite of his will, i.e. of his general will (of course if majoritarianism were the only criterion a victory would have demonstrated that his opinion *was* the general will). Clearly Rousseau cannot merely accept *any* majority outcome as constituting the general will since the majority could be constructed from any combination of partial wills and general wills. This might be closer to Robert Dahl's pluralist notion of 'minorities' rule' where outcomes in a democracy are constructed from coalitions of minority group preferences. Hence Rousseau can only consider any equation of majority will and general will where the majority is composed of individuals each of whom is acting on the basis of his own general will. The general will is constructed from individual general wills (plural) which have sufficient strength to overcome every particular will (*Emile*: 85).

The danger here is that the argument appears to result in the tautology that the majority will can be the general will so long as the majority is in conformity with the general will: 'This presupposes, indeed, that the qualities of the general will still reside in the majority: when they cease to do so, whatever side a man may take, liberty is no longer possible' (*Social Contract*: 278; Book IV, ch. 2).

A number of commentators have pointed out, however, that Rousseau's arguments can profitably be explicated by comparison with Condorcet's jury theorem.[2] Condorcet demonstrated that if each member of a jury has an equal and above fifty-fifty chance of coming up with the 'right' answer (according to some agreed criterion), then (so long as each votes independently of the others and is seeking the right answer) the majority will be more likely to be correct than will any single voter. The larger the majority, the greater the chance of its being correct.

One response to Condorcet's theorem would be to dismiss its relevance to politics as we know it on the grounds that the conditions required by the theorem are missing. It could, first, be contended that in politics we are not faced, as in mathematics, with problems to which there is a 'right' answer but, rather, with issues over which judgements as to the better, or least bad, policy will differ. Secondly, the theorem requires politically informed voters with a better than fifty-fifty chance of being correct. Finally, it presupposes that these voters are indeed concerned to discover the 'right' answer and will not seek to pursue private advantage or attempt to manipulate the vote.

To require such political conditions is certainly a very tall order, but they are not far removed from what Rousseau envisaged (Grofman and Feld 1988). First, the general will tends always to the right and the task set the citizen when voting in the assembly is stated precisely to be not that of 'approving' or rejecting a proposal but of declaring whether or not the proposal is, in fact, in conformity with the general will. It is comparable to declaring whether an answer is 'correct' or as inevitable as a mathematical law. Secondly, each citizen is required to be informed about his community so that he is a reliable judge of the general will. Finally each is motivated by the public good, and is, hence, pursuing his general will. If, indeed, all these conditions were in place it would, following Condorcet, be possible for the individual who finds himself in the minority to conclude, as Rousseau suggests, that he is mistaken about the general will. The majority is more likely to be right than he is. Moreover, Rousseau's proposal that the more significant laws should require larger majorities would ensure that the decision would be emphatically more 'correct' on these crucial occasions. In these conditions the citizen would accept the legitimacy of the majority vote. He would not continue his dissent but would revise his own ideas. He would regard the majority's rulings as his own and as respecting his autonomy.

Accordingly, a major objective of Rousseau is to set out the social and political prerequisites for achieving this congruence of majority rule and general will. One requirement of Condorcet's theorem was that voters chose independently of one another. Each is supposed to be a competent voter in deciding on the best outcome. No voter is supposed to choose one proposal simply because others intend to do so. This clearly could have implications for the conduct of political deliberations. Rousseau is certainly intent on minimising any possibility that the voter's public motivation might be corrupted by pressure of a partial or factional nature. But his manner of dealing with the problem is open to differing interpretations (see Waldron 1989 and the response by Grofman and Feld 1989). Rousseau in the very passage in which he leads up to his requirement that the individual must think only his own thoughts states that for the general will to emerge in the assembly each citizen must be furnished with adequate information and must vote having 'had no communication one with another'.

The immediate context of this remark provides one interpretation of its meaning. Partial associations and factions can distract the citizen in his single-minded pursuit of the general will, displacing his own thoughts with theirs. For this reason they should ideally be banned. Whilst one can, as Waldron argues, see this as purely an insistence that politics should be conducted in a high-minded political dialogue rather than in terms of the push and pull of sectional interests (Waldron 1989: 1326–7), this limit on communication raises more difficulties than he implies. Instead of the pluralist view that it is through the interplay of interests that one can come to a deeper understanding of the goals of fellow citizens, Rousseau's wish to isolate the individual voter from potential contamination seems to require that forms of campaigning which are overtly sectional in character are to be restrained in favour of others which are more civically oriented.

There is, however, a more far-reaching interpretation of Rousseau which would attribute to him a deeper suspicion of political communication. On this account he would envisage the citizen, who would indeed have more than a touch of Emile about him, coming to the assembly, having thought about the public good in his household, where he would express his opinion in his vote. Political debate would be scarcely necessary and might even serve as an opportunity for the expression of factional interests and the employment of the rhetorical arts of persuasion which Plato had despised. Ideally the citizenry will be so well prepared in advance of the vote that the necessity of any new laws will be self-evident: 'The first man to propose them merely says what all have already felt' (*Social Contract*: 274; Book IV, ch. 1). No eloquence will be needed. Unanimity will be a signal that the general will dominates the society; contradictory views and debates are a sign of decline.

On this reading Rousseau is less an advocate of a deliberative, participatory democracy than of a plebiscitary democracy. In such a state, as in the early years of the Roman Republic before corruption set in, the citizen voted in public. One would imagine that if Emile could be a citizen he would certainly never consider a public affirmation of a vote which was contrary to the public good (*Social Contract*: 290; Book IV, ch. 4). It is here that public and private education combine to create the best reconciliation of the good man and the good citizen, the person whose own thoughts will not be at variance with the community's goals.

The culture of the citizen

Everything in the life of the citizen is designed to bring him to this state of voluntary communitarianism. Rousseau's idyllic description of Neuchâtel in *The Letter to M. d'Alembert on the Theatre* indicates a life which would be a preparation for the independent, self-confident man who could give his vote without fear or favour. Each is a small proprietor living at a certain distance from his neighbours. In winter this separation is reinforced by the snows which 'prevent easy communication' (*Letter to M. d'Alembert*: 61). Within his small holding he is self-sufficient – not being dependent even on the services of such specialists as the carpenter, blacksmith or glazier. Closeted in the privacy of the household he reads and teaches himself enough for his purposes. He knows music. He lives a simple, peaceful life but one in which he can use his technical facility to create artifacts and mechanical contrivances. (One can almost hear Harry Lime responding with his remark about cuckoo clocks.) His occupations are his amusements.

Such a man has sufficient time to think about the way in which the life of his community should be regulated. This will not in many respects be a hard task. The laws will be few. Just as most of his learning will have been handed down by tradition so will most of the customs by which his life is conducted, much of which will in any event be shaped by the rhythms of nature. As with their knowledge of music, many will suppose that they had always known the manners which prevailed in the country. Since all live a virtually identical, self-sufficient life there is little reason to expect the cleavages which are typical of a modern pluralist, differentiated society. The economic base of Rousseau's society is one which is unlikely to generate great inequality and where, ideally, no man is so rich that he can buy another's thoughts and will and none so poor that he feels necessitated to sell. Despite living alone, therefore, each citizen when coming to the assembly is likely to have reached broadly similar, even if not identical, conclusions as to what the community requires. Consensus, if not total unanimity, is to be expected (*Social Contract*: 276; Book IV, ch. 2). Certainly a majority vote, if it comes to that, is more likely to be accepted as corresponding to the public good which each has been brought up to comprehend as inextricably bound up with his own way of living. The passage of a proposal into law is merely the implementation of what every one has already decided to do (*Social Contract*: 274; Book IV, ch. 1).

Is such spontaneity and unanimity a guarantee that each is genuinely thinking his own thoughts and that the individual has preserved his autonomy? The answer may depend, as Stanley Benn argued, on the extent to which the tradition within which the individual citizen acts is sufficiently plural to permit him to assess its value and to contribute his own modifications. Benn argues that autonomy cannot suppose that the individual is so radically desocialised that he lacks any resources out of which to construct the principles which he will live (Benn 1988: 175). These resources can only be acquired by learning from others in society:

> Someone who had escaped such a socialization process would not be free, unconstrained, able to make *anything* of himself that he chose; he would be able to make nothing of himself, being hardly a person at all (Benn 1988: 179, emphasis in original).

On the other hand Benn stresses that the autonomous person cannot be like a soldier who derives his rules from others. A person who relies on unexamined tradition is not autonomous but heteronomous. Into which category does Rousseau's citizen fall?

The evidence for the view that, despite any claims to the contrary, Rousseau's citizen is heteronomous can be readily produced. The main sources are probably *The Government of Poland*, the *Letter to M. d'Alembert on the Theatre* and the chapter on civil religion in *The Social Contract*. Of all these texts it might be said, as Willmoore Kendall says of the Poland essay, that Rousseau 'founds his political regime on a people who have been made more or less homogeneous through the inculcation of a national ethos' (Introduction to *The Government of Poland*: xxxviii). The proposals for public education in Poland represent the extreme instance of instruction designed to make a citizen a unit of the whole and are most obviously at variance with the education offered to Emile. The Pole should ideally never travel beyond his own borders. Taught entirely by Poles, the topics of literature, history and law should be entirely Polish. The lessons should be accompanied by physical exercise and games which will be played in public and in which the contests are judged by the spectators so as to combine competition with fraternity. Ceremonies and festivals and the wearing of distinctive national dress should also cultivate the national spirit otherwise lacking in the modern era of standardisation and Europeanisation. Certainly there is relatively little in this to encourage the emergence of a plural tradition. It may, however, be argued that this may be explained, or explained away, by Rousseau's problem which lay in suggesting means by which a large state, much corrupted and disorganised, and subject to the pressures of Russia and its other neighbours, could attain to some degree of independence and identity.

It may be thought that fewer excuses could be found for the chapter on civil religion in *The Social Contract*. Rousseau is dealing here with citizens of a state which approximates as much to the ideal as human institutions are capable of doing. But, as an heir of the ancients, Rousseau is constantly alluding to the degeneration of polities, primarily arising from lapses in civic virtue. Civil religion is intended to bolster the lessons taught by the legislator through the constitutional laws. Whilst it rightly causes anxiety to a liberal, the clauses of the civil religion are themselves minimal. Admittedly the clauses include an affirmation that 'in God we trust'. Beyond that the clauses are what Rousseau insists on terming *sentiments de sociabilité* rather than religious dogma – a point which he reinforces by his footnote concerning the purely civil, and not theological considerations, which should determine one's obligations to uphold the law. Thus the civil religion comes down to the duty, accepted in the social contract, to respect the laws which one has been an equal partner in determining. It must be acknowledged that such a requirement is far from being without its difficulties (which the attendant death penalty renders more severe). Yet its fundamental intention is one which most democrats would have to acknowledge as possessing considerable legitimacy. Moreover the clauses of this religion are not severely restrictive of the emergence of the plural tradition (apart from the significant prohibition of atheism). Rousseau insists that acknowledgement of this civil religion, or system of social sentiments, is entirely consistent with a citizen's devotion to any other religion so long as that creed does not itself demand the betrayal of one's republican oath. It is the civil religion which is tolerant, but even it cannot tolerate the intolerant.

The *Letter to M. d'Alembert* remains the text which should give rise to the most ambivalent responses from defenders of autonomy. Whilst the ostensible topic is the theatre, the fundamental concern is with the politicisation of culture, and the context is a state, Geneva, which, whilst still falling short of the ideal, has some semblance of being a true republic. Hence Rousseau's revival of ancient, Platonist views of the need to censor the arts because of their politically corrupting effects is understandably a matter of deep concern to those who would dearly love to attach him to one of the liberal camps.

The crux of Rousseau's case is that the modern (Parisian) theatre is an affront to the self-image of Genevan citizens. The refusal to permit a theatre should be interpreted not as an illiberal move but as an affirmation of the general will of this particular collectivity. It is a spontaneous, free expression of a public good which all properly brought up Genevans would recognise. By contrast, the values which the theatre represents are in flagrant contradiction to the harmony of private and public good.

Some of Rousseau's criticisms of the atmosphere of immorality surrounding the theatre merely echo the conventional comments of the age concerning the behaviour of audiences and, especially, of actors, but others take the matter to a different, very specifically political dimension. The central issue is the contrast between the representational nature of the theatre, mirroring contemporaneous politics, and the life of action which should characterise republican politics. The theatre may positively encourage or endorse vice, as in Molière's satire on the severe Alceste – which might be a satire on the austere Genevan or, indeed, on Emile himself. More significantly perhaps the theatre distances people from the active life of virtue. By representing virtue and vice on stage, especially in tragedies peopled by heroes, the effect is to 'relegate them forever to the stage, and to present virtue to us as a theatrical game, good for amusing the public but which it would be folly seriously to attempt introducing into society' (*Letter to M. d'Alembert*: 26).

Just as in representative democracy the representatives pretend to will on our behalf without our exercising responsibility ourselves, so in the theatre the players counterfeit the emotions which we would genuinely feel if we were facing real life dilemmas. We can pretend to have an understanding of vice and virtue, of duty and love whereas we have only experienced a surrogate: 'Thus the most advantageous impression of the best tragedies is to reduce all the duties of man to some passing and sterile emotions that have no consequences, to make us applaud our courage in praising that of others, our humanity in pitying the ills that we could have cured.' (*Letter to M. d'Alembert*: 26).

The physical construction of the theatre reinforces this divorce of art from life. People go to a building in order to obtain together this substitute experience. Yet despite the numbers in the audience this is not a genuinely collective endeavour. 'People think they come together in the theatre, and it is there that they are isolated' (*Letter to M. d'Alembert*: 16–17). Each sitting in his own seat observes the performance of the actors himself but does not share with others in a common enterprise – rather like the electorate in a representative democracy who vote in isolation and are spectators rather than participants.

Such a theatre has nothing to offer the citizens of a true republic. In its place Rousseau offers community theatre and audience participation – a drama congruent with the life of action of a direct democracy. The people should gather in festivals in the open air. The essence of a festival is that it is participatory and collective. It is not an occasion in which specialists perform to others.

> What will be shown in them? Nothing, if you please . . . let the spectators become an entertainment to themselves; make them actors themselves; do it so that each sees and loves himself in the others so that all will be better united (*Letter to M. d'Alembert*: 126).

The actor-spectators are one and the same with the citizen-subjects of direct democracy – at least the men amongst them (Starobinski

1988: 96). Their dances will be as spontaneous and as genuinely an expression of their own feelings about the community, as their votes in the assembly will be an expression of their own thoughts about the general will. The festival in Geneva prompted by the return of the regiment of Saint-Gervais from its exercises provides Rousseau with his most memorable illustration of this spontaneous outburst of civic commitment (*Letter to M. d'Alembert*: 135–6). The citizen-soldiers dance and the rest of the population cannot remain mere spectators but rush to the square to become participants in an event which celebrates the public realm without ever appearing to be consciously planned.

The ideal which Rousseau is holding up for us is a world in which 'the only pure joy is public joy' (*Letter to M. d'Alembert*: 136). There is no sense of alienation from the community. The individual citizen senses no loss of autonomy either in deliberating with the rest of the community or in finding his entertainment only in their company. The thoughts he is thinking are theirs. The pleasures he discovers arise precisely from participating with others. Both in their overtly political lives and their social, but also less overtly political, existences the individual and the public will are merged. Going along with the majority presents no problems – indeed will be accepted as right. Even the independent Emile would find satisfaction.

But will this convince the sceptic? Rousseau knew that it would not. Most readers suffered from what would later be described as false consciousness. Significantly he says of the festival of Saint-Gervais, 'I am well aware that this entertainment, which moved me so, would be without appeal for countless others; one must have eyes made for seeing it and a heart made for feeling it' (*Letter to M. d'Alembert*: 136). With that we return to the original dilemma. How far, indeed, are these eyes *made* for seeing and this heart *made* for feeling?

Whilst one aspect of the festivals which Rousseau emphasises is their spontaneous overflow of powerful feelings, another is their role as instruments of communal order.[3] Needless to say, these festivals share nothing in common with the carnivals of modern cities in which men and women concealed their true selves behind masks (*persona*). Everything is open – as with voting in public. Everyone is on show (see Starobinski 1988: 92–7). Private meetings engender vice just as do partial associations. Reinforcing this transparency, however, is surveillance. A lord commissioner presides over the ceremonies. The elderly, and particularly the married women, are observers and censors.

A queen of the ball is elected as an example to the community of modest conduct. Through these censors the community acts as a partial spectator of individual behaviour. The citizen is taught by the community, just as Emile was taught by his tutor. The outcome should correspond, but cannot now be identical. The citizen should decide to be what the community has made him.

In the final resort would such a community permit the plurality of traditions which Benn argued was a condition of genuine autonomy, of thinking for oneself? Many liberals have long felt that it would not, that it would confirm the negative, conformist tendencies of the face-to-face society. Ultimately Emile might not be able always to choose to obey the laws of a society which approximated to a total community. Yet even a liberal such as Sir Isaiah Berlin has to acknowledge that 'integrity, love of truth, and fiery individualism grow at least as often in severely disciplined communities among, for example, the puritan Calvinists of Scotland or New England . . . as in more tolerant or indifferent societies' (Berlin 1969: 128).

Amy Gutmann has neatly said that modern communitarian critics of liberalism 'want us to live in Salem, but not to believe in witches' (Gutmann 1992: 133). Rousseau wanted this too. Rousseau, it will be recalled, emphasised the inventiveness of the citizens of Neuchâtel (although not of course their political inventiveness of which there was no need). He claimed, too, that there were more original spirits in the obscurity of a traditional-minded provincial town than in great cities such as Paris. He did not believe that his ideal community would lack for reflective, critical individuals. To the degree that Athens was Rousseau's inspiration it would be difficult to deny that a community could occur (if one supposes the elements of slavery and male hegemony to be removed) in which a positive acknowledgement of the collective contribution to the self might coexist with creativeness and originality of an exceptional order. If, by contrast, Sparta were Rousseau's model a modern reader, accustomed to multiple and competing influences on the formation of one's choices, might fear that thinking one's own thoughts would be scarcely feasible. Strong communitarians see the self as a narrative largely 'written' by one's community. Liberals look to a society in which there are many stories which can be told and read. Rousseau, as one of the greatest autobiographers as well as political thinkers, was sensitive to the necessity of writing one's own story which was at the same time also in part the story of others who shared in a common experience. That Rousseau would be far from the last, whether communitarian or individualist, to address this issue is to be inferred from Stanley Benn's statement of the continuing dilemma:

> The problem is to find a sense more direct than Rousseau's, less metaphysical than Hegel's, Kierkegaard's, or Nietzsche's, and less paradoxical than any of them, in which autonomy can be accepted as a personality ideal, without so desocializing independence of mind that the autonomous person is endowed with a capacity to live according to a law he prescribes to himself but bereft of any resources with which to fabricate such a law (Benn 1988: 175).

Notes

* The author gratefully acknowledges the support of the Economic and Social Research Council under Grant No. R000235410.

1 In order to emphasise the paradox I have chosen here to adopt G. D. H. Cole's Everyman edition of 1913 (and many subsequent reprintings), of the original 'que chaque citoyen n'opine que d'après lui'. This is translated in the current Everyman edition by the more accurate but duller 'that each citizen should express only his own opinion' (*Social Contract*, Book II, ch. 3: London, Dent 1986, p. 204). Subsequent references will be to this latter edition. The continuing use of male pronouns will, for reasons apparent to any Rousseau reader, be appropriate in this context.

2 The first to point out the relevance of Condorcet's theorem to Rousseau's general will would seem to be Brian Barry (1965, pp. 292–3). The discussion has been taken forward by Grofman and Feld (1988) and in responses to their article by Estlund (1989) and Waldron (1989) with a reply by Grofman and Feld (1989). It was Black (1958) who revived interest in Condorcet's work. Whilst Runciman and Sen (1965) also interpreted Rousseau's general will in terms of rational choice theory their approach differed in regarding the issue as one of reconciling individual preferences.

3 An interesting discussion of the ambivalence within Rousseau's view of the festival can be found in Vernes (1978).

References

Rousseau texts

The Social Contract and Discourses, trans. by G. D. H. Cole, revised by J. H. Brumfitt and John C. Hall, London, Dent, Everyman Classics, 1986.
Emile or On Education, trans. by Allan Bloom, Harmondsworth, Penguin, 1991.

Letter to M. d'Alembert on the Theatre, trans. by Allan Bloom, Ithaca, Cornell University Press, 1968.
The Government of Poland, trans. by Willmoore Kendall, Indianapolis, Hackett, 1985.

Other works cited

Bantock, G. H. (1980), *Studies in the History of Educational Theory, Vol I: Artifice and Nature, 1350–1765*, London, Allen and Unwin.
Barry, B. (1965), *Political Argument*, London Routledge & Kegan Paul.
Benn, S. (1988), *A Theory of Freedom*, Cambridge, Cambridge University Press.
Berlin, I. (1969), Two Concepts of Liberty, in I. Berlin, *Four Essays on Liberty*, Oxford, Oxford University Press.
Black, D. (1958), *The Theory of Committees and Elections*, Cambridge, Cambridge University Press.
Dewey, J. (1966), *Democracy and Education*, New York, The Free Press.
Estlund, D., J. Waldron, B. Grofman and S. L. Feld (1989), Democratic Theory and the Public Interest: Condorcet and Rousseau Revisited, *American Political Science Review*, 83, 4, pp. 1317–40.
Gay, P. (1970), *The Enlightenment: An Interpretation. Vol II: The Science of Freedom*, London, Weidenfeld and Nicolson.
Grofman B. and S. L. Feld (1988), Rousseau's General Will: A Condorcetian Perspective, *American Political Science Review*, 82, 2, pp. 567–76.
Gutmann, A. (1992), Communitarian Critics of Liberalism in S. Avineri and A. de-Shalit, eds, *Communitarianism and Individualism*, Oxford, Oxford University Press.
Lindley, R. (1986), *Autonomy*, Basingstoke, Macmillan.
Locke, J. (1960), *Two Treatises of Government*, ed. P. Laslett, Cambridge, Cambridge University Press.
Runciman, W. G. and A. K. Sen (1965), Games, Justice and the General Will, *Mind*, 74, pp. 554–62.
Starobinski, J. (1988), *Jean-Jacques Rousseau: Transparency and Obstruction*, trans. by A. Goldhammer, Chicago, University of Chicago Press.
Vernes, P.-M. (1978), *La ville, la fête, la démocratie: Rousseau et les illusions de la communauté*, Paris, Payot.
Wolff, R. P. (1976), *In Defense of Anarchism*, New York, Harper and Row.

6 John Hope Mason

'Forced to be free'

If the most famous sentence Rousseau ever wrote began with the words 'man is born free . . .', his most infamous sentence has surely come to be that which ended with the words '. . . he will be forced to be free'. Like Marx's 'dictatorship of the proletariat', or Nietzsche's 'blond beasts', this sentence has come to be seen as revealing the true character of his thought, showing an otherwise hidden despotic intent. These are the words which launched a thousand crimes committed in the name of liberty, whether in fact (the Jacobin Terror) or in theory (Fichte's *Zwingherr*), and they remain a sinister warning to all who might suppose that political power can be used to enhance freedom. First there was the alarm of Cold War liberals, traumatised by the events of the 1930s and 1940s, restlessly searching through the past for traces of incipient totalitarianism. Then came the children of prosperous Western democracies, seeing liberalism itself as another kind of totalitarianism, all power as oppression, and all (actually existing) toleration as a means of exclusion.

If we return to Rousseau's writings, however, and the problems which he was addressing, this sentence ceases to be alarming. Of course, no amount of explication or analysis will deprive it of its rhetorical flourish, the paradoxical formulation, so characteristic of Rousseau. (And for those to whom language can never surprise or shock or amuse without arousing an inquisitorial suspicion, the account which follows will mean little.) But the apparent paradox can be unpicked.

I

In the Geneva Manuscript, Rousseau's discussion of the founding contract leads him to consider how individuals may act after this initial commitment to form themselves into a single body; they have a collective need to ensure that each person's commitment continues. An individual may wish to benefit from the formation of the political association without acknowledging the limits it imposes; if that were so, he would enjoy the rights of the citizen without wishing to fulfil the duties of a subject. This would be, Rousseau observes, 'an injustice, the spread of which would soon bring about the collapse of the body politic' (291).[1] He continues:

> In order that the social contract may not be an empty formula, it is necessary that, independent of the consent of individuals, the sovereign has some guarantees of their commitment to the common cause. Usually, the oath [of allegiance] is the first of such guarantees. But as it is drawn from an entirely different order of things, and each person, according to his inner ideas, modifies to his liking the obligation which it imposes on him, it is rarely relied on in political institutions. More effective assurances, drawn from the thing itself, are with reason preferred. The fundamental pact therefore tacitly includes this commitment, which alone can give *force* to all the others:[2] that whoever will refuse to obey the general will, will be constrained to do so by the whole body (292).

In *The Social Contract* this passage is reduced to the following: 'In order therefore that the social pact may not be an empty formula, it tacitly includes this commitment which alone can give *force* to the others, that whoever will refuse to obey the general will, will be constrained to do so by the whole body: which means nothing other than that he will be forced to be free'. And Rousseau adds: 'for such is the condition which, giving each citizen to *la patrie*, guarantees him from all personal dependence' (364).

The problem under discussion is that of securing individual obedience to the general rules which the association has been set up to establish. Obviously, the association will not survive unless there is common agreement to abide by these rules, some 'guarantees of . . . commitment to the common cause'. It is unrealistic to expect that a verbal commitment, even if sworn in public, will be enough to achieve this. What is needed is a general recognition or understanding (a tacit commitment) that there is some form of sanction, that people disobeying the rules will be penalised, in other words, that the rules can be enforced.

As we know, Rousseau had an acute sense of the need for individual freedom, and the central issue of politics for him was that of reconciling this with the need for some overall authority. Mutual needs lead people to form themselves into a body politic, 'to assure the liberty of each by means of the protection of all'. But how is it possible 'to force men to defend the freedom of any single person without [at the same time] infringing the liberty of others? . . . to find the means to subject men in order to make them free? . . . How can it be that they obey and no one commands?' (248). Finding 'the harmony (*accord*) of obedience and liberty', he wrote in *The Social Contract*, is 'the essence of the body politic' (427).

This harmony is achieved by means of law: 'it is to law alone that people owe justice and liberty' (249). Law can achieve this because all are subject to it and it applies equally to all. In the panegyric of Geneva which precedes the *Discourse on Inequality*, Rousseau states: 'I would like to live and die free, that is to say, subject to laws in such a way that neither I nor anyone else could shake off their worthy yoke . . . I would therefore have wished that no one in the State could have claimed to be above the law . . . For whatever the constitution of a government, if there is a single person who is not subject to law, all the others are necessarily at his discretion' (112).

Either there is the impersonal rule of law, or there will be the rule of certain powerful individuals. The fear of the latter constantly recurs in Rousseau's writings. 'Dependence on men, being disorderly, gives rise to every vice, and leads to the mutual depravity of both master and slave. If there is any way of remedying this evil in society, it is to substitute the law for the [individual] man'.[3] When a 'prince no longer administers the state according to the laws', then the state is dissolved, 'the social pact is broken' and political life has been destroyed (422–3). 'When the law comes to be subject to [individual] men, there remain only masters and slaves' (808).

'Liberty', he wrote in the *Letters from the Mountain*, 'consists less in doing what you want than in not being subject to the will of another; it consists further in not subjecting another's will to our own. Whoever is master cannot be free'. He continues:

> There is no liberty without laws, nor where anyone is above the law; even in the state of nature man is only free through the favour of the natural law which commands us all. A free people obeys, but it does not serve; it has leaders but not masters; it obeys the laws but it only obeys the laws, and it is through the *force* of the laws that it does not obey men . . . A people is free, whatever form its government takes, when it sees in him who governs it not a man but the organ of the law. In a word, liberty always follows the fate of the laws, it reigns or perishes with them; I know nothing more certain (842).

The connection Rousseau makes in this passage between law and force (in the phrase 'the *force* of the laws') is one which is as old as political theory itself, for the obvious reason that laws are effective precisely by virtue of being able to be enforced. An act of sovereignty, i.e. a declaration of law, has substance because it can be armed 'with real *force*, greater than that of any individual will'.[4] The fact that disobedience to law results in punishments, specified in the form of criminal laws, is 'the sanction to all other kinds of law' (394) (which is why in Genoa the word *Libertas* is written over the entrance to the prisons (440 n)). The sovereign makes law, the government enforces it; the relation between them is the same as that between moral 'will' and physical '*force*' (395). The government is charged with 'the execution of the laws and the maintenance of civil as well as political liberty' (808); it can therefore be described concisely as '*force* applied to the law' (430). The power which the prince has is only 'public *force* concentrated in him'; if he should use this to compel obedience to 'his own individual will', then the body politic is dissolved (399). In the former instance people obey because they are obliged to obey, the force being only an application of law; in the latter case they are 'forced – but not obliged – to obey' (423).

We can therefore see how Rousseau could maintain that the rule of law in principle means that 'each citizen is entirely independent of all the other citizens, and extremely dependent on the city', and that the effective rule of law means that it is 'the *force* of the state which establishes the liberty of its members' (394). Or, as he put it elsewhere, 'a people ceases to be free when the law has lost its *force*'.[5] And only the freedom achieved by law makes possible that continuing free commitment – in Rousseau's words, 'only through laws does liberty exist which gives *force* to the commitment' (807) – which makes the republic legitimate. So we can unpick his infamous sentence to read: 'Whoever will refuse to obey the general will, will be constrained to do so by the whole body; which means nothing other than that he will be forced to [pay the penalty for violating that rule of law which alone enables everyone (including him) to] be free'.[6]

II

There is little or nothing in the foregoing account which could not have applied to a number of Rousseau's predecessors, either ancient, republican or modern. What is distinctive to Rousseau is less his treatment of the need for, and application of, the rule of law than his attention to the making of law. The reconciliation of liberty and obedience is only possible if we are free to participate in determining what should be obeyed. Law must not only apply to all, it must also come from all. The conditions which Rousseau specifies for law-making – the assembly of citizens voting on matters of common interest – are those which ensure that when they obey the laws 'they are not obeying any person, but only their own will' (375). 'We are free and subject to laws because the laws are only the registers of our wills' (379). This notion gives rise to many problems, as Rousseau was aware, but there is space here to deal with only a few of them.

In Book IV of *The Social Contract* he addresses one such difficulty: 'how can a man be free and forced to conform to wills which are not his own?', as is the case when someone has argued against and voted against a proposed law but has been outvoted. Rousseau answers: 'the citizen consents to all the laws, even those passed in spite of him, and even those which punish him when he dares to break any one of them' (440). In other words, participation in the assembly endorses the rule of law, not the terms of any specific law. Since we benefit from the existence of laws in general, we should obey those laws we have opposed; if we break them, we should recognise the punishment as just.

In *The Spirit of the Laws* Montesquieu makes a similar observation: 'the law which punishes a criminal was made for his benefit. A murderer, for example, has prospered from the law which condemns him; it has preserved his life at every moment; therefore he cannot protest against it'.[7] Rousseau, however, goes further than this. In discussing the death penalty he writes: 'it is because a criminal has not been the victim of an assassin, that he consents to die if he himself becomes an assassin' (376). This difference – consenting rather than not protesting – occurs elsewhere in his description of punishment. A prosecutor in a trial must convince the accused person that he has committed a crime: 'in order to be treated as a wrongdoer I must be convinced that I am one' (693). In the passage on liberty and obedience in *Political Economy* (quoted above, pp. 122–3), he asks how it is possible 'to bind people's will by their own agreement; to make their consent prevail over their refusal and force them to punish themselves when they do something they did not wish?' (248, 310).

The use of 'force' in this sentence has led to its being connected with 'forced to be free', in order to read the latter as implying obedience as a matter of psychological constraint, or conscience.[8] The sentence would then read: 'he will be forced to [recognise the justice of the punishment inflicted on him so that the city as a whole (including him) can] be free'. I think that this interpretation is to some extent justified, but that it is misleading to talk in terms of conscience, if that is understood in the way it is described in *Emile*. What is involved is an inner sense of obligation, but it stems not from a personal conviction of right and wrong – 'an innate principle of justice and virtue by which . . . we judge . . . actions . . . to be good or evil'[9] – but rather from a feeling of dependence and belonging.

A vivid illustration of what this means occurs in the most celebrated case of someone consenting to his own punishment – Socrates' refusal to escape from Athens after he has been condemned to death. Crito visits him in his cell to inform him that escape can easily be arranged and to argue that Socrates would do right to escape, for the sake of his sons, if not for himself. Socrates disagrees. He envisages 'the laws and constitution of Athens' confronting him, as he was about to run away, and demanding:

> 'Now, Socrates, what are you proposing to do? Can you deny that by this act . . . you intend . . . to destroy us, the laws, and the whole state as well? Do you imagine that a city can continue to exist . . . if the legal judgements which are pronounced in it have no force but are nullified and destroyed by private persons? . . . Was there provision for this in the agreement between you and us, Socrates? Or did you undertake to abide by whatever judgements the state pronounced? . . . What charge do you bring against us and the state, that you are trying to destroy us? Did we not give you life in the first place? Was it not through us that your father married your mother and begot you? . . . Have you any complaint . . . against the laws which deal with children's upbringing and education, such as you had yourself? . . . Are you so wise as to have forgotten that compared with your mother and father . . . your country is something far more precious, venerable and sacred? . . . Do you not realise . . . that if you cannot persuade your country, you must do whatever it orders . . . both in war and in the law courts?'[10]

They point out that any Athenian, once he has attained maturity, is free to leave if he is not satisfied with the institutions, laws and practices of the city. If he stays, he is deemed to 'have undertaken, in deed if not in word, to live [his] life as a citizen in obedience to us?'[11]

Socrates hears the laws speaking to him 'just as a mystic seems to hear the strains of music';[12] he recognises an inner conviction which is in part intellectual but also emotional, deriving from all that Rousseau referred to in the phrase *l'amour de la patrie*. As a result of that conviction Socrates consented to his own death.

III

The Greek city-state had to vindicate itself against two strong rival claims on people's obedience or loyalty – the claim of the powerful ruler and the claim of kinship and family. Rousseau likewise had to vindicate his political principles against two strong rival claims: the first, that of absolutist rule, was similar, but the second, that of individual right, was very different. The distance between the two standpoints can be seen in the way the city-state, in the *Crito*, is set above the family, while for Rousseau it is usually identified with the family. In both cases it was recognised that the city-state was not a natural development, but in the first the political was achieved by weakening the bonds of kinship while in the second it involved overcoming the limits of the individual self. In Rousseau's account each person has a naturally independent existence, which is not just a question of being naturally free but of seeing oneself as an 'entirely solitary whole' (381). The process of becoming political is therefore one of denaturation: 'good social institutions are those that know best how to denature man, to take from him his absolute existence in order to give him a relative one', no longer as a single whole but as one part of a greater whole.[13]

The establishment of a just political order will not, however, produce deformed or stunted individuals. Good institutions will indeed so alter people's lives that they will find themselves 'forced to act on different principles' (364),[14] from those which obtained in natural conditions. But instead of experiencing this as frustration or restriction they will be enriched with broader ideas, more expansive feelings, a more elevated spirit (364). Institutions of this kind are formed according to the political laws which found a new order, and these laws will succeed the more that they approximate to, or are seen as necessary as, the laws of nature (135, 269, 383 and 842, cited above (p. 123)). In this respect, we could say that the process is one in which denaturation is complemented by renaturation. As nature sets limits to our actions, so do our institutions. The critical question is: can we feel equally content within the artificial limits?

Part of the answer to this lay in Rousseau's concept of law and the rule of law (outlined above), and part lay in his account of *l'amour de la patrie* or *fraternité*. The first is a matter of justice, obtained in ways which are set out in considerable detail, the second a matter of feeling, to which Rousseau never gave comparable attention. He specified three conditions necessary for its existence: geographically, the state must be limited in size, so that everyone can be known to everyone else; socio-economically, a degree of equality must prevail, with no extremes of rich or poor; politically, there must be opportunities to participate in political life, 'so that the citizens feel they are at home (*chez eux*) and that the laws are in their eyes only the guarantees of their common freedom' (258). He also indicated certain forms of education, athletic contests and public festivals which would nurture and sustain *fraternité*. But as a whole the subject is only sketched out in his writings.

The inadequacy of this treatment is all the more surprising given Rousseau's continual stress on the affective aspect of experience. His doctrine of natural goodness is not merely an assertion of the benign character, health and innocence of our instincts in a state of nature, but also an affirmation of 'the feeling of existence' (142), the fact that life naturally feels good. The contractual act generates not merely institutions which satisfy our self-interest and the demands of justice, but also a 'reciprocal sensibility' (245). In the final chapter of Book II of *The Social Contract*, after delineating the features of the different types of law – political, civil, criminal – Rousseau adds: 'to these three kinds of law is connected a fourth, the most important of them all; which is not engraved on marble or brass but on the hearts of the citizens. This forms the real constitution of the state . . . I am referring to *moeurs*, customs and above all public opinion'. The feelings in our hearts, and the values and attitudes expressed in our practices and judgements (to which they correspond), are the most important kind of law, on which all the others depend. Like the other laws these also exert force, namely, 'the *force* of habit', which can make unnecessary 'the *force* of authority' (394).

Socrates consented to die not only because he recognised the need for the rule of law, but also because he loved his city. This love had developed out of a sense of belonging, i.e. of feeling 'at home', and also out of the fact of dependence. As an Athenian citizen he had political rights which he would not have had elsewhere. The freedoms which he (being Athenian-born) enjoyed were distinct to this city-state; individual rights as such did not exist. What he had enjoyed in times of peace he had had to fight to protect in times of war. Success in both peace and war was seen to owe much to the deities who watched over Athens. In these ways political practices, military activity and religious rituals sustained the city-state and made possible the life in which Socrates had been able to flourish. This dependence gave rise to a love of the city and a sense of obligation. The latter was not primarily a matter of either choice, or of duty, or of being morally right, or of providing the most desirable outcome, all of which are views advanced in the *Crito* and contribute (together with the recognition of benefits received) to Socrates' decision. But his sense of obligation is more comprehensive and profound than any or all of these, as the closing remarks in the dialogue indicate.[15] It is the counterpart to Rousseau's fourth kind of law.

The difficulties which Rousseau faces (in describing this kind of obligation) derive to a great extent from the different historical conditions of eighteenth-century Europe. A city-state no longer met the same needs, either in terms of personal freedom, or military survival, or religious identity. The notion of natural rights, the facts of modern warfare, and the universal claims of Christianity, had together transformed people's expectations and experiences. Most important of all, the idea of the person as a distinct individual – as being an 'entirely solitary whole' – was being taken as true in ever more numerous aspects of life. As we know, Rousseau is a significant figure in the emergence of this idea, but his political thought aimed to counter it. The opposing directions in which he was pulled are evident from the way in which *The Social Contract* attempts an impossible task: using the voluntarist terms of contractarian theory to generate the kind of obligation which derives from what is given.[16]

Apart from ancient history, and the particular instance of Geneva, Rousseau has only one resource on which he can draw to describe this obligation – the family. He writes of *la patrie* as 'the common mother' (258) (i.e. both parents in one), whom we love, and of fellow-citizens 'cherishing one another mutually as brothers' (261). Like family life, that of *la patrie* is sustained by its regular festivals and shared events; when Rousseau writes of the citizens running joyfully to the assembly (429) it is this kind of celebration which he has in mind. Without such occasions to be *en corps*, the family, like *la patrie*, will cease to exist, either in terms of knowing what it wants as a family or of providing a reciprocal sense of obligation and belonging.

For the purpose of the discussion here, the most important aspect of this comparison is the way it helps us to understand Rousseau's phrase 'the *force* of habit'. Regular events and shared attitudes give rise to willing participation; the family gathers because of a sense of mutual pleasure and obligation, not because anyone commands it to gather. Should that pleasure and obligation vanish, then family life peters out. It cannot be revived by order or authority. While habit may at times be invoked to override some temporary reluctance, it can never be hardened into any kind of coercion. To admit that only force could be effective would be to admit the extinction of everything which had made family life worthwhile. For exactly the same reasons, Rousseau states that to be kept in the social union 'by *force* alone, produces the dissolution of the civil state' (256). In contrast to this, habits which we find agreeable (because they correspond to our emotional needs) are no more of a burden than the laws of nature; they are merely the conditions which make life in society (as in nature) possible.

IV

In the opening chapters of *The Social Contract* Rousseau argues against any legitimacy deriving from strength or force: '*force* does not produce right' (355). This does not mean, however, that legitimate rule – legitimate if established and continued by the free consent of the citizens – will not itself need to use force to be effective. The crucial point is that such force must never go beyond applying the law.

Rousseau's concern about this matter, which merits more attention than it has received, leads him to put forward a doctrine of separation of powers. In his view there must always be a clear distinction between the making of laws and their execution, between political 'will' and executive '*force*'; the latter, being essentially different from the former (since it deals with particular issues or cases, not general rules) 'is naturally separated from it' (432). Accordingly, the government must be distinct from, and subordinate to, the sovereign legislature. If it usurps the latter, the state is dissolved. Faced with the despotism which then exists, the citizens return to a state of nature, regain their natural freedom, and are absolved from any obligation to obey (422–3).

It is equally important that this separation of functions is observed by the sovereign. Were it the case that the legislature had executive power, 'right and fact would be so confused that it would no longer be possible to know what was law and what was not; and the body politic ... would soon fall prey to the violence which it was set up to prevent' (432). For this reason Rousseau argues against direct democracy: 'it is not good that the person who makes the laws [also] carries them out' (404). The same distinction occupies a prominent place in his description of the Legislator.

The few pages devoted to this figure have probably contributed more than any others to the misreading of Rousseau's statement about 'forced to be free'. His remarks about a 'blind multitude . . . not knowing what it wants', the need for the people 'to be made to see objects as they are, . . . to be shown the good road it is looking for', and the need 'to oblige [individuals] to bring their wills into conformity with their reason, . . . to teach [the public] to know what it wants' (380), have been taken as justifying the use of force to bring about freedom.

The difficulties critics have had with the Legislator arise from reading Rousseau in the light of the actions or theories of later readers of his works, like Robespierre or Saint-Just or Fichte.[17] If we analyse his text in his own words and in the light of his predecessors, these pages present no such problem. On the contrary, they set clear boundaries to the Legislator's power and contain an admission of the limits of Rousseau's own theory, the inappropriateness of the terms in which up to this point he has set out his case.

Laws, he writes, are only 'the conditions of civil association', 'the condition of the society' (380). The laws he is referring to, as he makes clear at the end of this book, are the political laws (394), those which are laid down at the birth of societies (381), the origin of nations (384), in other words those which create the institutional framework which will make possible a fair society. Before an association comes into existence there is only an aggregation of individuals; before there is a society there is only a multitude (359). Rousseau is using the terminology of Sallust or Hobbes or Natural Law writers,[18] juxtaposing the pre-political condition of many individuals (*multitudo*), linked by no common bonds of either values or practices, with what ensues from the adoption of a common framework, the establishing of a society (*civitas*). He is concerned with how this transition can be effected. How can the multitude know how a society might operate, i.e. what a good system of legislation would be? They are blind, lacking judgement or enlightenment, in the same way that anyone would be who has never known political institutions.[19]

The solution Rousseau puts forward – the Legislator – is as traditional as the problem, and no one familiar with Plutarch's biographies of Lycurgus, Solon or Numa, or who has read Machiavelli or Sidney or Montesquieu, would have difficulty knowing what he meant. Since

Rousseau does not rely on his readers being familiar with these writings, he spells out the central features of this figure's role. He is 'the mechanic who invents the machine', not the person who operates it (381); his function, not belonging to the working of the republic, has nothing in common with human rule (382). Since legislation cannot be entrusted to anyone who exercises power, he has no command over men (382). Nor does he actually make law, since only the free vote of the people can do that (383). In the Geneva Manuscript, which devotes more space in this discussion to attacking the kind of absolute ruler advocated by Grotius or Hobbes, this latter point receives more emphasis. The Legislator can act only by persuasion and prescribe only by general consent, for if he did otherwise he would 'destroy at the outset the essence of the very thing which people wanted to form' (316), namely, a just and free society. In these ways Rousseau defines the Legislator's task, following ancient examples, and his account allows no possibility of this figure becoming any kind of despot.

Yet a major problem remains. Not only must the Legislator not use force (383), he cannot use arguments either. Since the people have no experience of what he is talking about, he is faced with the difficulty of 'the effect becoming the cause'; the understanding which will result from living under beneficial institutions is itself needed to preside over the initial establishment of them (383). Here Rousseau confronts the impossibility of reconciling voluntarist assumptions – legitimacy from individual consent – with the major insight of his social theory – that what we are is to a large degree shaped by circumstances. The imperative which the latter generates to construct a just society, since that alone can enable us to live a good life, cannot be fulfilled by the rational choice of free agents, since such agents are not as free as they think, nor is their thinking likely to determine how they act. (This is what he means by 'individuals see the good which they reject' (380).) Only the experience of appropriate institutions – benign circumstances – can enable us to understand how to live together freely.

The Legislator must therefore 'persuade without convincing' (383). He must captivate us by his 'great soul', enchant us by his 'great and powerful genius' (384). In this respect he does exert power of a kind. But it is not political or social power, both because of the limits that have already been spelt out and because what constitutes his happiness is quite independent from us (381). It could be likened, rather, to the power we may attribute to the works of a great composer, the power of Orpheus, the poet who was also a legislator.[20]

V

The Legislator holds no political power and is not a despot of any kind, yet the power he exerts has a decisive and lasting influence on the people who adopt his proposals; because he is not only offering an institutional framework, he is also 'secretly' affecting their thoughts and feelings, their inner disposition and inclinations (394). He uses his charismatic authority, and the religious sanction which he invokes, to undermine the individuals' sense of their own self-sufficiency and release or stimulate in them a new sense of interdependence. He is not only a guide, he is also a guru.

This aspect of the Legislator's task relates closely to the ideas about civic education put forward in *Political Economy*. The latter are not restricted in the manner of the former (which is a once-and-for-all event, and is detached from political life); on the contrary, the government itself is advised to 'form citizens' (259), by making people amenable to civic life. It is desirable, that is to say, 'to make men what they need to be. The most absolute authority is that which penetrates to a person's inmost being and affects his will no less than his actions. It is certain that in the long run people are whatever the government makes them' (251). A civic or public education, of the kind used in ancient Sparta, will achieve this. Although the article *Political Economy* contains a number of ideas which Rousseau later discarded, these suggestions continued to remain valid; he makes similar proposals in his last political text, on Poland. These passages are often taken as evidence of a 'collectivist' or 'totalitarian' aim, forcing people to be 'free'.[21]

This issue is confused because in his political writings Rousseau approaches the question of freedom from different directions, and emphasises different aspects of what freedom involves. On the one hand he writes of the need for the closest possible identification with others, on the other hand of the importance of individuals detaching themselves from any wider group, to avoid sectional or factional interest clouding their own perception of the common good (371–2). On the one hand he speaks of the Legislator or civic education making citizens feel as dependent as possible on the body politic, on the other hand the civil condition is described as one which produces in each person a sense of justice, morality, duty and right, all of which are matters of reason, and therefore opposed to impulses or feelings (364).

As I have already indicated, these differences arise from the contrary directions in which Rousseau was pulled, acutely aware of the individual self as a distinct entity, and at the same time no less conscious of the sociological perspective, the fact that what we are is decisively shaped by the circumstances in which we live. The impossibility of resolving this difficulty is reflected in *The Social Contract* and constitutes its splendours and its misery.

The passages in his political writings which cause alarm do not arise out of any desire to diminish individual freedom. They are, rather, addressing the problem of socialisation. Once we have left the state of nature we are all socialised in one form or another and no modern political theory can adequately ignore that. Liberal writers, of course, do ignore it. They imagine that their educational schemes, as much as their economic arrangements or political structures, exert no harmful influence but merely develop natural abilities and maximise individual freedom. But their education is, in most instances, as manipulative and doctrinaire, as ideologically biased, as education in non-liberal societies. Individual liberty does indeed occupy a central place in liberal ideology, and liberal democracies, more than other regimes now in existence, do allow individuals considerable freedom of expression and action; but that is not the same thing as living in a free society.

Rousseau aims to set out the conditions for a free society, one in which all its citizens could feel and be equally free, and therefore enjoy true human happiness. He describes such a society as one 'where the people love their country, respect the laws, and live simply' (262). These three features are mutually reinforcing: it is a love of our common identity that enables us to perceive, and abide by, good laws; and only a simple life (in which an aggravated self-interest has not yet developed) will make that possible. Neither enlightenment (in the form of clearer thinking) nor 'civilisation' (as it was coming to be called) would bring this about; the first was based on an overly simplistic view of how people behaved, the second on a failure to see the negative effects of commerce and economic growth. A society which followed the precepts of Mandeville could only end up adopting the politics of Hobbes.

The weakness of Rousseau's political thought lies neither in his remarks about force, nor in the unresolved problem of how to combine individual freedom with the fact of socialisation (since that is a failure shared by many others). It lies instead in his desire for homogeneity. He never aspires to a uniformity of attitudes or behaviour – it is only the difference between particular interests which makes us aware of the common interest (371 n) – any more than he wants to stifle individuality as such. But he wants each citizen to see and love another not as an other but as himself,[22] and this is one reason for his excluding from citizenship certain sections of the population (361–2 n). Such exclusion, it is true, is no more than a reflection of the laws of Geneva, and earlier city-states; but desire for homogeneity is an indication of a disabling narcissism. Together, they reduce the scope of that generality on which he otherwise insists. They do not, however, undermine the cogency of his political principles as such, since neither is a necessary part of those principles. Indeed, they can be shown to be inconsistent with them.[23]

In his darkest moments Rousseau saw no alternative to the central political issue – of putting law above individuals – except choosing between 'the most austere democracy or the most complete Hobbism'.[24] The need for austerity, like his emphasis on submission (to just laws), has led some commentators to see a masochistic streak in his thought. Such a view, however, overlooks the vital place occupied by limits in his understanding of what constitutes happiness. To look on, and feel about, positive laws in the same way that we regard natural laws is the mark of a good political order. This means that we accept the limits they impose on us without resentment or frustration. To feel like this about such limits is to recapture in society the happiness which natural man had in nature.

Such an experience is so alien to modern life that it is difficult to convey what Rousseau meant. Perhaps the clearest indication can be obtained by means of an analogy, from Goethe's comments about art. In his poem 'Nature and Art' he depicts constraints as not restricting but enhancing achievement: '*In der Beschränkung zeigt sich erst der Meister,/Und das Gesetz nur kann uns Freiheit geben.* (In limitation is mastery most displayed,/And law alone can give us freedom)'. In his poem 'The Sonnet' he writes of such limitation as something which, for these reasons, we can love.[25] For most of the period since his death Rousseau's insistence on the beneficial aspects of limits made him seem hopelessly unrealistic and out of touch. Today we can see that this was perhaps his most profound insight.

Notes

1 Page references in the text refer to Pléiade, volume III: *Du Contrat social, Ecrits politiques*.

2 While the English 'to force' is an adequate translation of the French *forcer*, the noun 'force' does not always convey the broader sense of strength,

energy and power of *la force*. Where Rousseau uses this noun, therefore, I have left it untranslated.

3 Pléiade, IV, 311. The difficulty which readers nowadays have in grasping the importance of this point stems largely from ignorance about how privilege (*privi leges*) operated under the *ancien régime*, a society in which there were natural inequalities and institutionalised hierarchy, and in which therefore many people were in a state of individual and/or legal subordination. Nowadays, by contrast, exceptions to the rule of law tend to be discussed in terms of 'free rider' problems; these are quite different because they refer to cases in which there is usually no immediate or direct effect of another person's freedom being denied.

4 Pléiade, IV, 311.

5 Leigh, XXIV, 87; letter to J.-F. Deluc, 24 February 1765.

6 The link of 'force' and 'freedom' in this sentence has dramatic impact, but in the previous chapter Rousseau had already shown them as interconnected. He writes there of 'the *force* and freedom of each man being the primary instruments of his self-preservation', of a perceived need to 'unite and direct [their] existing *forces*, . . . to make them act in concert', in order to enable individuals to survive, and how the basic problem they faced could therefore be described as 'finding a form of association which defends the person and goods of each associate with all the common *force*, in such a way that each, uniting with all, nevertheless only obeys himself and remains as free as before' (360).

7 *De l'Esprit des lois*, Book XV, ch. 2; *Oeuvres complètes*, ed. R. Caillois (Paris, 1951), II, 492.

8 See, for example, R. G. Master's edition of *The Social Contract* (New York, 1978), p. 138 (n. 37); N. J. Dent, *A Rousseau Dictionary* (Oxford, 1992), p. 121; or, the most perceptive treatment of this view, J. Plamenatz, 'Ce qui ne signifie autre chose sinon qu'on le forcera d'être libre', *Hobbes & Rousseau*, ed. M. Cranston and R. S. Peters (Garden City, 1972), pp. 318–32.

9 Pléiade, IV, 598. Plamenatz (in the article cited in note 8, pp. 324 and 331–2) sees 'forced to be free' as relating to moral liberty, that is, freedom according to internal rules of what is permissible, in contrast to what Rousseau calls 'civil liberty', which is determined by external rules, being that freedom which is 'limited by the general will' (365). I believe that the emphasis should be on the latter rather than the former, although the two are not wholly distinct, as Plamenatz himself recognises. Rousseau's fullest account of moral freedom (in *Emile*) uses similar language to that used about civil freedom in *The Social Contract*, namely, of law emanating from *volonté* and implying *force*: 'There is no happiness without courage, nor virtue without struggle. The word "virtue" comes from *force* [i.e. strength]; *la force* is the foundation of all virtue. Virtue only belongs to a creature who is weak by nature and strong by its *volonté*' (Pléiade, IV, 817).

10 Plato, *Crito*, 50a–51e, tr. H. Tredennick, *Collected Dialogues* (Princeton, 1963), pp. 35–7.
11 *Ibid.*, 52d; p. 37.
12 *Ibid.*, 54d; p. 39.
13 Pléiade, IV, 249.
14 In the *Confessions* Rousseau's description of his unwritten work *La Morale sensitive* shows another application of the same approach, in terms of our physical rather than institutional environment. The aim of this project was to suggest ways in which we could direct those physical things over which we had some control 'in order to make ourselves better and more certain of ourselves', to establish 'an external regime which, varying according to circumstances, could put or keep the soul in the condition most favourable to virtue . . . How many vices could be prevented from arising if we could force the animal economy to favour the moral order which it so often disturbs!' (Pléiade, I, 408–9, and see E. Gilson's comments on this passage, p. 1469).
15 'Let us follow this course, since God points out the way', *Crito*, 54e, p. 39.
16 For a recent account of this sort of obligation see J. Horton, *Political Obligation* (London, 1992), pp. 146ff.
17 See, for example, N. Hampson, *Will and Circumstance* (London, 1983), pp. 30ff, 226ff and 253ff; and I. Berlin, *Four Essays on Liberty* (Oxford, 1969), pp. 145ff.
18 Sallust, *De conjuratione Catilinae*, para. 6; Hobbes, *De Cive*, II, vi, 1, note.
19 In Book II, ch. 3 of *The Social Contract* Rousseau also writes of how people always want (*veut*) the good but do not always see (*voit*) it (371). But this distinction has an equally precise purpose to that made in introducing the Legislator, namely, to indicate the difference between the general will and the will of all. His discussion of this may in some respects be confused, and it does give rise to serious problems; but no more than is the case with the Legislator does it allow for any use of force in asserting or determining what the general will is.
20 On this subject, as also on the significance of Rousseau's sense of *association*, his concern for individual freedom, and the relation of his social theory to his political thought, see my article, 'Individuals in society: Rousseau's republican vision', *History of Political Thought* 10 (1989), pp. 89–112.
21 L. G. Crocker, *Rousseau's Social Contract* (Cleveland, 1968), pp. 11ff; A. M. Melzer, *The Natural Goodness of Man* (Chicago, 1990), pp. 94ff.
22 *Lettre à d'Alembert*, ed. M. Fuchs (Geneva, 1948), pp. 168–9. For an analysis of the way in which this text relates to *The Social Contract*, see my article, 'The *Lettre à d'Alembert* and its place in Rousseau's thought', in *Rousseau and the 18th Century: Essays in Memory of R. A. Leigh*, ed. M. Hobson *et al.* (Oxford, 1992), pp. 251–69.

23 Neither the kind of identification nor the sense of belonging generated by families require the degree of homogeneity to which Rousseau aspires. To 'cherish one another mutually as brothers' does not mean either that we are all alike, nor that we like all the others; rather, we value them as others within our common bond and through our common heritage. A family upbringing, it has been said, provides socialisation with love; that is what Rousseau wanted to achieve, and in that process seeing others as oneself has no necessary place.

24 Leigh, XXXIII, 240; letter to Mirabeau, 26 July 1767.

25 *Natur und Kunst*, closing lines; *Das Sonett* – 'Eben die Beschränkung lässt sich lieben; *Gedichte* (Berlin, 1988), pp. 259 and 243. In similar vein see Stravinsky's assertion: 'the more art is limited, the more it is free', *Poetics of Music*, tr. A. Knodel and I. Dahl (New York, 1947), p. 67.

7   John Charvet

Rousseau, the problem of sovereignty and the limits of political obligation

In one of his well-known utterances Rousseau says that the problem of the social contract is to show how a subject of communal law can nevertheless be said to obey only himself and remain as free as he was before.[1] The latter freedom consisted in his being his own master in a state of nature. Rousseau's answer to the problem is, of course, that the individual obeys only himself if he is ruled in the community by its general will, which is his own will. But as we know the general will is not necessarily the actual will of the community. Since the general will legitimized constitution specifies a supreme popular legislative assembly operating a majority decision procedure, we can say that the constitutional sovereign – the final decision-making will – is the majority will of the people's legislative assembly.[2] This majority will may not, on occasion, will the general will. Since the general will is said to be sovereign, and indeed to possess absolute sovereignty, it must be sovereignty in a different sense from that in which the majority will is constitutional sovereign. Rousseau says that when the majority is not willing in accordance with the general will, freedom no longer exists.[3] This follows from his claim that the freedom of the subject of communal law depends on his subjection only to the general will.

Since the general will must be a 'superior' sovereign to that of the majority will, whatever that could mean, it would seem that a citizen should be able to appeal from a decision of the majority to the general will. However, his account of the contract includes the standard contractarian argument, to be found in Hobbes and Locke and others, that a necessary condition of political society is the surrender by each contractor of the right of private judgement that he possessed in the state of nature.[4] Leviathan, or the community, or the general will substitutes for the multiplicity of private judgements on the good a binding public judgement. Rousseau endorses the absolute sovereignty of this public reason in common with Hobbes, and in effect Locke *malgré lui*,[5] precisely because he accepts their view that the maintenance of an authoritative public judgement is incompatible with the retention by the individual of the right to judge the justice of the laws. Of course, what they must mean by the right of private judgement here is the right of the individual to make a moral judgement that is authoritative for him in determining how he is morally permitted or required to act. The theory of absolute sovereignty holds that political association is possible only on condition that the 'state' decides these matters for all. So if the envisaged appeal of the individual citizen from the majority will to the general will involves the reclaiming of his right of private judgement, it should not be permissible.

Yet, the surrender of private judgement on Rousseau's account is to the general will, not to the majority will. However, the general will is defined for the most part as the ideal will of the community for its common good – what each person would will as his good when he thinks, together with the others, of his good as community member, and not as separate individual. In this sense the sovereign 'has no need to give guarantees to the subjects, because it is impossible for a body to wish to hurt all of its members ... The Sovereign by the mere fact that it is, is always all that it ought to be'.[6] But as such an ideal will the general will cannot be the actual will of a constitutional sovereign. For such a sovereign is necessarily a particular person or body of persons whose will may not be in conformity with the ideal. Rousseau's constitutional sovereign, as he is fully aware, may be corrupted. So it would seem that Rousseau ought to say that a citizen who believes that the majority will is corrupt may appeal to the general will. But what would such an appeal amount to? Since the general will is essentially ideal, there is, and can be no official body in the community that can declare it. If the majority will cannot, neither could any other. Yet if the appeal of the aggrieved citizen is to the general will as the ideal will of the community, he would appear to be claiming the right of private judgement against duly constituted public authority.

That Rousseau does not see the difficulty must be because he systematically identifies the sovereign general will as the ideal will of persons as community members with the actual constitutional sovereign. For example, in describing the limits of Sovereign power he states that each contractor alienates to the community only that part of his liberty and possessions which the community needs, but that it is for the sovereign to make this judgement.[7] Presumably such a sovereign will cannot be morally criticized by the subject without his claiming an unacceptable right of private judgement. Yet this sovereign must be an actual constitutional sovereign, since his decision must produce a definite law. At the same time it is clear that Rousseau believes that the sovereign he is describing as making this judgement is the general will, and hence necessarily all that it ought to be. Furthermore, it would appear obvious that no one could seriously hold that the solution to the problem of private judgement in a state of nature involves the surrender of that judgement to a purely ideal will, since each person would still have to interpret the ideal for himself, and no move from the state of nature would have been achieved. The only possible solution is the creation of an actual constitutional sovereign with authority to bind everyone, thereby substituting his public judgement for the separate private judgements of the subjects. So Rousseau must believe that his ideal general will is at the same time actualized in the will of the constitutional sovereign. Yet *this* sovereign, as we know, may be corrupted.

We should perhaps attend to the fact that Rousseau is very much concerned in his political theory with the social and political conditions under which a majority decision of the legislative assembly can be expected to coincide with what the ideal general will would legislate. These conditions involve, on the one hand, the independence of each citizen of all the others in respect of his private life and interests, so that each is dependent on the others only politically in his public life as citizen, and on the other hand their equality (more or less). These stipulations are designed to ensure that when each citizen votes for a *general* law in the legislature, and so must express his particular interest in a general form, the interest that he generalizes will be one he shares with his equal and independent fellow citizens. It will be a common interest, and so will satisfy the requirements for a general will. We could, therefore, understand Rousseau to be saying that, provided my constitution is followed, the actual sovereign will be the same as the ideal sovereign, and so there will be no problem of private judgement. If the actual sovereign is corrupted, then freedom is impossible, and legitimate rule and political obligation disappear, so there is no point in raising the question of a subject's appeal from an unjust majority will. The problem is, nevertheless, that the subject must have exercised his private judgement in judging that the majority will is corrupt and hence illegitimate, and this is incompatible with the supposed conditions of political association, which Rousseau accepts.

I now want to consider this problem from a broader contractarian perspective. The problem of sovereignty for Hobbes and Locke, as I said, is also to substitute a unified public reason for the multiplicity of private reasons that exist in the state of nature. This problem does not arise, even for Hobbes, from the lack of common and knowable rules for preserving men in multitudes. Such rules exist; they are the laws of nature, and everyone can see that he has an interest in interacting with others on their basis. The difficulty is that, while everyone has good reason to follow the natural laws, which are both in each person's interest (if generally followed) *and* commanded by God; in fact each also has good reason to distrust the others' willingness to adhere in a state of nature, and under such insecure conditions the laws of nature permit, or indeed command, a person to give priority to his self-preservation over that of others. Hence in pursuing his self-preservation at the expense of others, he will not be acting contrary to the law of nature; he will be following its first law to preserve himself, and Hobbes's famous phrase regarding each person's right to everything is merely the most extreme expression of that situation.[8]

The solution to the predicament of the state of nature obviously involves the creation of a system of collective security through which persons can come to trust each other to follow the secondary laws of nature which enjoin equal respect for each other's liberty, and thus to act in ways which permit of everyone's preservation. But the achievement of this solution requires the surrender of each person's private judgement to the collective authority of the state. This authority unifies the multiplicity of private wills in one public will. In Hobbes's formula the sovereign represents the will of each subject, whose will is thus contained in the sovereign's will,[9] but I take the basic idea of this formula to be present also in Locke's and Rousseau's theories. It is the idea of the subject's commitment through the contract to pursue his self-preservation collectively, together with the others, through a common will designated as the sovereign who speaks for them all. The surrender of private judgement involves the contractor's undertaking no longer to pursue his self-preservation as an *individual* enterprise on the basis of which he has a right to put his self-preservation first in any conflict with another. Instead he commits himself to adopt a common standpoint on each person's self-preservation, including his own, which requires the non-prioritizing of anyone's right, and hence the acknowledgement of their equal rights. The sovereign's will must express this common standpoint, and hence be directed at the common good.

What, then, if the sovereign monarch or assembly fails to act from the common standpoint in pursuit of the subjects' common good? The sovereign is supposed to pursue the common good by following the laws of nature, or rather by giving the general principles of the natural law a determinate content appropriate to the particular situation of the collection of persons whose common will the sovereign expresses. The relation between the natural law and the common will is this: the secondary rules of natural law, which enjoin equal liberty and so on, if they are generally accepted and followed constitute the conditions under which *all* can be preserved, or rather under which each stands the best chance of being preserved. So the secondary rules express the standpoint of community or collective self-preservation. The primary rule, which commands everyone to preserve himself and to give himself the priority if he judges his preservation to be under threat, expresses the standpoint on the good of separate individuality.[10] Contractarian political theory, then, holds that persons cannot successfully follow the secondary rules of the law of nature and adopt the common standpoint on their good without creating a concrete sovereign, who will take decisions binding on everyone, and hence unify their wills in his will. The reason for this is primarily that if an individual acts on his own in adopting the common standpoint, he can have no security that others will reciprocate, and hence there will be a good chance that he will not be preserved. So the problem is not that the secondary laws of nature do not constitute a common standpoint on the good, for they are essentially rules for preserving men in multitudes. It is rather that in the absence of an effective coercive power persons cannot trust each other to pursue their good from that standpoint. There is, however, an additional theme to be found in that contractarian theory which emphasizes the indeterminacy of persons' rights in the state of nature, so that, even with good will and mutual trust, there would still be a need for a concrete collective authority to give determinacy to the general principles of equal liberty.[11]

The common standpoint on the good that is inherent in the secondary rules of natural law is essentially an ideal one. It is the standpoint of morally motivated persons who commit themselves to pursue their self-preservation only in so far as it is compatible with the equal rights of others. If an individual in the state of nature is directing himself by such a law, then he will be acting from a *general* standpoint on the good, yet he will be doing so by exercising his *individual* judgement in determining what the law requires of him and others. Since he has good reason to distrust others in a state of nature, he cannot reasonably act from the common standpoint in such a state. If he does so act, and the others do not reciprocate, he will not be preserved. Hence by the first law of nature he should not commit himself to act from the common standpoint outside a political society. The latter acting through the coercive power of its concrete sovereign brings about the conditions in which each can reasonably undertake to govern himself by a moral general will. However, political society involves a further act of surrender of individual judgement. The contractor must give up his individual self-direction by the natural law for the sake of a collective self-determination in accordance with that law through the judgement and will of the sovereign. The first act of surrender consists in the abandonment of the individual standpoint on the good, that is characteristic of the first law of nature, for the common standpoint of the secondary rules of natural law, while the second surrender is that of individual interpretation of the latter for the collective interpretation expressed through the sovereign. Although one can and must distinguish the two surrenders, the standard 'Hobbesian' argument for the necessity of political society holds that they must be made simultaneously, for according to that argument it is reasonable to commit oneself to act from the moral standpoint only as a member of a political society possessing sovereign power.

We can now return to the question of what is to be done should the sovereign act contrary to the common standpoint on the good which constitutes the rational core of his sovereignty? What if he acts contrary to the natural law basis of his authority? According to the Hobbesian theory of absolute sovereignty, *nothing* can be done. For if we are morally allowed to appeal against the sovereign's will to the natural law principles which should be its foundation, then we would be claiming back the right of individual interpretation of the law of nature which has to be surrendered as the condition of political association. Furthermore, we cannot simply place ourselves in an individually determined moral position, for by reconstituting the state of nature relations between persons we immediately destroy the circumstances in which it is reasonable for us to commit ourselves to act from a moral will. We would be back with the first law of nature and the state of war.

It would seem that Hobbes must be right on this issue. We cannot claim a *moral* right to disobey the sovereign, not because the sovereign cannot be immoral, but because the existence of sovereign power is a necessary condition for the reasonableness of our adoption of the moral standpoint. Since there is no viable moral position outside the political community, we could have nowhere to stand from which we could be morally entitled to reject the sovereign's commands. The apparent ability of one or a few individuals to take up such a stance to the sovereign will depend on the willingness of the great majority to continue to obey. The supposedly moral few will in effect be moral free riders on the law abidingness of the remainder, and may be thought to deserve thoroughly the punishment the sovereign hands out to them.

Can we learn anything on this matter from Rousseau's conception of the sovereignty of the general will? If we understand the general will to involve the sovereignty of the common standpoint on the good, and hence the first surrender of the individual standpoint, then it expresses only the supremacy of the moral point of view over that of private interest or in other words the abandonment of the right of the individual to give priority to his self-preservation over that of others – the move, in Rousseau's terms, from the maxim of natural goodness, which tells us to pursue our good with the least possible harm to others, to the sublime maxim of rational justice which affirms the principle of equality.[12] However, in this sense the general will would be nothing other than the will to live with others from the standpoint of natural law, and Rousseau clearly adopts the 'Hobbesian' argument on our obligations under natural law. He believes that there is a natural law, that it is ultimately derived from God and discoverable by our reason and to which we are obliged in conscience. But we are not required to follow it in a state of nature because to do so would expose the just to exploitation and destruction by the unjust, and everyone is entitled to preserve himself.[13] So the moral life for Rousseau as it is for Hobbes, is dependent on our forming a political community which can solve the security problem and give specificity to our duties. In other words we have to make the first and second surrenders of the individual standpoint at the same time, and the sovereignty of the general will understood as that of the moral standpoint is worthless unless it is actualized in the concrete will of a sovereign power.

Perhaps then the much maligned 'Hobbesian' position on absolute sovereignty must be accepted after all. It seems clear at any rate that Rousseau must accept it. Nevertheless, we should recall what I claimed earlier regarding Rousseau's strategy for securing the conformity of the will of the actual sovereign to the underlying moral structure or ideal general will of the communal personality. We need arrangements which ensure the independence and equality of the citizens from a private point of view and their mutual dependence only at a public-political level, for then a majority will, having to be expressed in the general form of law, will be likely to satisfy the requirements of moral equality and so be a valid utterance of the general will. These arrangements can be understood as the constitution of the political community. They form a basic structure of laws and institutions that are just because they are ones which everyone would agree to in the founding contract made from a position of freedom and equality. So long as this constitution is preserved, then the decisions of the constitutional authorities will be good because the actual conditions in which the decisions are made by a majority, even though they give the majority power over the minority, will approximate to the ideal conditions of just association as defined through the founding contract. Yet, once again, nothing can guarantee that the popular assembly will not be corrupted, and the majority vote for a partial interest rather than the common interest.

However, once we have the idea of a just constitutional structure as providing the basic lineaments of the moral personality of political community, then the members can surely appeal from a decision of the sovereign to the constitution. But they must be able to appeal to someone – to a court that has responsibility to act as guardian of the constitution. Otherwise, a person in rejecting the authority of a particular law will be reasserting his right to interpret the moral standpoint for himself, and as we have seen there can be no actual moral space for such a right to occupy. Of course, Rousseau does not make any provisions for a constitutional court, and in any case one may say that the introduction of such a body would involve only the postponement of the moral crisis that the community faces when the sovereign is believed to be acting contrary to the constitution. For the court itself may be corrupted or be subject to unjust political power, and surely the individual citizen will be capable of making that moral judgement, if he is in a position in the first place to bring a case before the constitutional court.

We need to examine more carefully the nature of the judgement by a citizen of the injustice, and hence moral invalidity, of a constitutionally legitimate decision. Undoubtedly, the citizen can, as a matter of fact, correctly or incorrectly judge that such and such a decision was corrupt. The issue is whether that judgement is a *moral* one in the sense in which the moral nature of the judgement involves the acknowledgement of a duty on persons to act on its basis. In that sense, if the citizen judges a law to be unjust he, *ipso facto*, claims that he is not morally obliged to obey it, and indeed is morally obliged to disobey. The moral nature of the judgement makes the judgement authoritative for him with regard to his actions, and thereby supersedes the authority of the sovereign over them. However, since there cannot be from the 'Hobbesian' position, to which Rousseau subscribes, a duty to disobey the sovereign power, for that would suppose one had a duty to follow the secondary rules of natural law in a state of nature, the individual's critical judgement of the moral quality of the sovereign's will cannot be a moral one. It must be understood as a non-moral, objective judgement that the sovereign's actions are not in accordance with the moral standpoint and are morally worthless. The possibility of such a judgement presupposes that the moral standpoint possesses an objective, structural content, so that anyone can ascertain whether an action conforms to it or not without necessarily taking up the moral standpoint itself. The latter would involve the commitment to interact with others from its perspective, and no one has reason to do that except through the moral personality of the state and its sovereign power.

Let us suppose, then, that we are faced with an unjust sovereign who acts contrary to the constitutional basis of his authority, and we have no constitutional means of redress. What is our morally uncorrupted citizen to do? He can, of course, correctly judge that the sovereign is unjust from a moral point of view. But in doing so he will be taking up a standpoint independent of sovereign power, and hence independent of the moral point of view itself. In effect, he will have placed himself in a state of nature again in relation to the unjust sovereign, but also in relation to his fellow citizens. In a state of nature he can perfectly well see that the commands of the unjust 'sovereign' are not conducive to civil peace, and hence to the possibility of moral life, and this fact relieves him of all *moral* obligation to obey them. But it does not mean that he has any moral obligation *not* to obey them, or to do what he can to defeat them. In the state of nature the first law of nature reasserts itself, and entitles a person to give priority to his own self-preservation over that of others. Hence he may be well advised from a prudential point of view to obey the unjust 'sovereign', since this will not be a state of nature in which all have equal power. The freedom and equality that is necessarily characteristic of any state of nature is in the first place the equal freedom of all from any moral authority, so that no one is *morally* obliged to obey another. It is a morally free world. Yet the uncorrupt person, while morally free to do whatever is necessary to preserve himself knows also that his best chance of self-preservation in the long run, and that of his descendants, is to re-create a morally based state power. Hence he should (prudentially) seek to join himself with any others, whose judgements have likewise remained uncorrupted, in such an enterprise. This may involve him in withdrawing from his unjust state to throw in his lot with its enemies, should these exist. In that case he would be joining himself to a morally constituted state in an undertaking, that aims to create or preserve an international society of states, which itself conforms to the moral point of view.

The 'Hobbesian' argument tells us that it is in our interest to endeavour to unite with others in a political association based on the secondary laws of nature. This must be seen as a prudential, and not a moral, interest. Hence it cannot explain how our prudential obligation to associate on the basis of the moral standpoint can be transformed into a moral obligation. For if the sole motivational support for political association is self-interest, and the adoption of the moral point of view necessarily requires the individual to subordinate his pursuit of his self-preservation to the constraints of equal laws, then he will never have abandoned the individual standpoint in the first place. Whenever the moral requirements conflict with self-interest, the individual cannot but by nature of his non-moral motivation pursue his individual self-preservation at the expense of the moral laws.

Now both Hobbes and Rousseau acknowledge the inadequacy of the purely prudential point of view on the reasons for following the natural law. They recognize that there is something called justice, and both think of justice as stemming from God and obliging us on a basis other than that of our natural self-interest.[14] So perhaps we should see them as saying that once the security problem of the state of nature is solved through the creation of a state structure in accordance with our prudential interest, then we are morally obliged to follow just laws by virtue of our obligation in conscience to observe God's laws. However, this appeal to a moral obligation to obey the secondary laws of nature, that is owed ultimately to God, would appear to make the moral obligation independent of our self-interested reasons for forming a political association on moral terms. If so, it would be fatal to the Hobbesian–Rousseauan position. For then we would have a moral obligation to follow the secondary laws of nature in a state of nature. This is what Locke asserts to be the case. But one obviously cannot say that a person has an unconditional obligation to obey the secondary laws of nature, and at the same time that under conditions of insecurity a person is entitled to give his own preservation priority over that of others. For the latter entitlement makes the moral obligation conditional on the settlement of the security problem, and thus on political association. One cannot be both unconditionally and only conditionally under moral obligation.

Is it, then, that God has made us in such a way that we naturally seek our own preservation and, having made us intelligent, has enabled us to see that we can best preserve ourselves through political association based on the secondary laws of nature; while at the same time God has *commanded* us to preserve ourselves and hence to create political association on moral terms? Although our prudential interest in moral community cannot make us moral enough to support what we nevertheless recognize to be in our interests, our obligation to obey God's commands does the trick by giving us a reason distinct from that of our natural self-interest to commit ourselves to the moral life, but only conditionally on the solution of the security problem. In other words we would have to treat God as commanding us to be moral only conditionally. We would have an unconditional obligation to God to make ourselves conditionally just. This may be Hobbes's view of the matter, but it is hardly Rousseau's. For Rousseau it is our conscience which reveals the obligatory nature of justice to us, and I cannot see that he is aware that justice, to be compatible with his political theory, should command us only conditionally.[15]

Is not the position attributed above to Hobbes similar to the one that Kant adopts in his political theory? On Kant's view there is only one obligation of justice in the state of nature, and that is to join with others in leaving that state and entering a political society.[16] This would be an unconditional obligation to bring about the political conditions under which we can fulfil our other obligations under natural law. However, a moral obligation to leave the state of nature would be different from a purely prudential obligation to the same effect, only if the former obliged us to seek to bring about a political union even at risk to our self-preservation. Since the general spirit of this proposal is to make our obligations of justice conditional on political union, it is surely unacceptable to retain an obligation that binds us unconditionally to acts which may be detrimental to our self-preservation. But if we interpret the obligation as requiring nothing more than what our prudential reason prescribes, then it is difficult to see that it adds anything to that reason, and thus to the solution of the motivational problem that arises from it.

It is the appeal to a moral or natural law which obliges independently of self-interest, whether the law is God-based or not, that destroys the coherence of the classical seventeenth- and eighteenth-century contractarian theories of political sovereignty and obligation. Such an independent moral obligation would, of course, provide the moral space for a citizen's morally inspired disobedience to an unjust sovereign that is lacking in the 'Hobbesian' position. But the appeal undermines the contractarian theory of political association. Contemporary contractarianism in the manner of Rawls and Scanlon would seem to provide an answer to this difficulty.[17] For the principles of justice are purportedly derived from the contract itself through the idea of an agreement on terms of social cooperation under ideal conditions. Yet it is doubtful whether they do avoid a commitment to the equivalent of an independently valid and obliging moral law. Certainly Rawls fails to do this. For although the principles of justice are supposed to be derived from the contract, in fact the original position is structured so as to satisfy our prior moral intuitions as to what is fair. In effect we stipulate that there is an equal bargaining power between the parties represented by the veil of ignorance, and thus ensure that they will agree on the foundational principle of equality. But if we know that equal rights over the social primary good is what is fair independently of the contract, we are back with a natural law which would appear to be binding on us whether or not we have settled the security problem. As for Scanlon, his account of the contract depends on the notion of the 'reasonable' in the formula 'what no-one can reasonably reject' in an initial position in which the contracting parties are committed to cooperating on terms which they can justify to others. However, we are not told enough about the meaning of the reasonable to know how to interpret the Scanlonian contract. Despite the inadequacies of Rawls's and Scanlon's own theories, I still believe that their project to derive the principles of justice through the notion of a contract, subject to certain appropriate changes, is viable.[18]

Notes

1 J. J. Rousseau, *The Social Contract*, translated by M. Cranston, Penguin Books, Harmondsworth, 1968, p. 60.

2 Rousseau, however, requires qualified majority voting on more important decisions. Rousseau, *The Social Contract*, p. 154.

3 *Ibid.*, p. 154.

4 *Ibid.*, pp. 60–1; T. Hobbes, *Leviathan*, Basil Blackwell, Oxford, 1955, p. 112; J. Locke, *Two Treatises of Government*, Cambridge University Press, Cambridge, 1964, p. 342.

5 Locke is standardly supposed to permit a subject to appeal against his government to God, or in other words to Natural Law. He does in fact make a famous statement to this effect. But this would be to permit the *individual* to retain his state of nature right of private judgement of that law, and is incompatible with the passage quoted in note 4 which refers to the necessary surrender of his private judgement in the creation of political society. Locke for the most part refers not to the individual's right against the government, but the *people's* right, and his conclusion emphatically states that the 'power that every individual gave the society, when he entered into it, can never revert to the individuals again, as long as society lasts, but will always remain in the community; because without this, there can be no Community'. *Two Treatises of Government*, pp. 445–6.

6 *The Social Contract*, p. 63.

7 *Ibid.*, pp. 74–5.

8 Actually the first branch of the first law says seek peace, and only the second branch tells us 'by all means we can to defend ourselves'. *Leviathan*, p. 85.

9 *Ibid.*, p. 107.

10 It may be questioned whether Locke embraces such a primary rule. Indeed he does in the following passage: 'Everyone as he is bound to preserve himself, and not to quit his station wilfully; so by the like reason when his own preservation comes not in competition ought he, as much as he can, preserve the rest of mankind . . .'. *Two Treatises of Government*, p. 289.

11 *Leviathan*, p. 110; *The Social Contract*, p. 66. See also I. Kant, *The Metaphysical Elements of Justice*, Library of Liberal Arts, Bobbs-Merrill, Indianapolis, 1965, p. 76.

12 J. J. Rousseau, *A Discourse on Inequality*, translated by M. Cranston, Penguin Books, Harmondsworth, 1984, p. 101.

13 *The Social Contract*, pp. 80–1.

14 *Leviathan*, p. 94; see also pp. 104–5. *The Social Contract*, pp. 80–1. See also J. J. Rousseau, *Emile or On Education*, translated by Allan Bloom, Basic Books, New York, 1979, pp. 289–94.

15 *Ibid.*, p. 289.

16 *The Metaphysical Elements of Justice*, pp. 71–2.

17 J. Rawls, *A Theory of Justice*, Clarendon Press, Oxford, 1972; T. Scanlon, 'Contractualism and Utilitarianism', in A. Sen and B. Williams (eds), *Utilitarianism and Beyond*, Cambridge University Press, Cambridge, 1982.

18 For a discussion of these changes, see J. Charvet, 'Contractarianism and International Relations', in D. Boucher and P. Kelly (eds), *The Social Contract from Hobbes to Rawls*, Routledge, London, 1994.

8   Felicity Baker

Eternal vigilance: Rousseau's death penalty

How may the state be liberated from a tyrant, and its freedom preserved from the danger of tyranny? If readers do not baulk at the shocking words spelling out the death penalty in the 'articles of faith' of the civil religion, but delve into the rhetorical and logical associations which link the violent sanction to the rest of the *Social Contract*, they can grasp this strand of Rousseau's reflection on political evil. The complementary question of how to contain the violence of such a leader's fanatical followers is mentioned in the *Letter to M. d'Alembert on the Theatre*. It is no good trying to make people understand what fanaticism is in the hope that they will then refrain from it; it may even be dangerous to spread such understanding.

> Fanaticism is not an error but a blind, mindless passion which can never be restrained by reason. The only way to prevent its occurrence is to hold in check the people who incite others to it. It is no use showing fools that their leaders are deceiving them; they remain their ardent followers nonetheless. Once fanaticism comes into being, I can see only one way of checking its progress, and that is to use its own weapons against it. Reasoning and persuading are out of the question. Forget philosophy, close your books, take up the sword and punish the imposters.[1]

Persecutory violence, once it occurs, must be met with violence, and those responsible must be punished. Far better, however, if it did not happen at all, which means restraining the would-be instigators before they achieve their desired effect. These remarks put in a nutshell the very practical attitudes leading to Rousseau's extraordinary insertion of capital punishment among the 'articles of faith' to which all citizens must conform, in the final chapter of the *Social Contract*. They are far removed from the optimistic Enlightenment belief in the power of reason to dispel the dark forces which are at times unleashed in human societies. Rousseau's remark in the *Letter to d'Alembert* places some faith in the power of violence to stem violence, while not yet entering into the question of how to restrain the instigators of persecutions. Enlightened reason should not attempt to confront violence directly; instead, Rousseau's writing explores how a different kind of mental process, 'public opinion', might evolve in an original way, away from superstition and prejudice, to become a power against violence. In the *Social Contract*, the religious sensibility must work towards the same end.

Religious passions and public opinion together constitute a field, therefore, which includes fanaticism and prejudice, and in which Rousseau hopes that transformations might take place in the imaginary dimension which are capable of orienting passionate belief towards 'feelings of sociability', as he calls the articles of the civil faith. The reference to religion in the *Social Contract* can be linked in this way to the dimension of collective fantasy which is the social raw material of theatre in the *Letter to d'Alembert*, because Rousseau is dealing not with the symbolic dimension of the sacred but only with the 'social utility' of religion, the imaginary level on which groups and individuals form a passionate link with the sacred law. In both these works, the will to social transformation and integration focuses on the imaginary.

That fact helps to ensure the continuing relevance of Rousseau's political analysis to the post-Revolutionary era, where the political and religious dimensions are held apart so that the centre of democratic power is unappropriated, emptied of all sacred value, not embodied symbolically in any person or place. This condition of democracy, this form of power, is *purely* symbolic; unrepresentable, unfigurable, because the political had never been non-religious, the religious never non-political. The immediate 'return' of the category of the religious *in the imaginary mode* is thus a kind of ghost, occurring wherever a political interpretation structures enquiry into the generative principles of a society. This imaginary reactivation of the religious is thought to attest the fact that democracy cannot easily make itself intelligible in its own eyes, while the tragic character of the modern condition is hard for political and philosophical thinking not to falsify or disguise, in their attempts to come to terms with it.[2] The *Social Contract* appeared in 1762, before that transformation of our political institutions. Yet we can find in it the separation of the political and religious categories, while at the same time the founding lawgiver must of necessity foster an illusory belief in the divine origin of the laws, to ensure that passionate intensity of devotion to the articles of faith which anathematise persecutory violence.

Our central question, that of the death penalty laid down for the persecution of fellow-citizens, opens up two practical paths: violence must be stopped violently, as reasoning will never stop it; preferably, however, it should be prevented before it happens, through working upon the imaginary level of social reality where the subject's passions attach him to the law. Before proceeding to read through the articles of the civil religion and to explore the ways in which Rousseau works out these questions, it makes sense to bring forward the contemporary analogies which must unfailingly come to our minds as we read; not to force today's problems into the *Social Contract* or the converse, but rather to recognise common features so that they need not magnetise our reading in a subterranean way. Only the most practical modern analogies do justice to the radically non-theoretical nature of this strand of thinking in the *Social Contract*; instances of informal discourse in which we can see individuals attempting both to grasp and to modify their social reality: new interpretations of prejudice, for example, or current practical attempts to thwart the activity of the European neo-Nazi movements, or our societies' procedures for restraining demagogic figures who exploit such movements to encourage violence against other individuals or groups.

Rousseau's warning that it may even be dangerous for the people to understand how fanaticism works has a counterpart in the anxiety often expressed today about the exposition of the content of racist doctrines and about the fictional representation of discrimination or persecution. Recent studies show that racist discourse now even expressly incorporates the discourse of anti-racism, rendering the former much harder for the public to recognise and criticise.[3] The assertions in the *Letter to d'Alembert* that violence must be met by violence, and that one does not reason with the fanatical followers of dangerous leaders, are repeated today in some of the active anti-Nazi organisations. An urban myth holds that the energetic enactment of such a policy by anti-Nazis in Britain has kept the National Front subdued there since the 1970s, while the French National Front, unresisted in this way, rose to some prominence during the same period. French anti-Nazis are said to be more disposed to attempt discussion, and to avoid violent confrontations, preferring to stage a counter-demonstration rather than to break up a National Front march.[4] For such freedom movements, Rousseau's practical maxims may confer through myth a group identity on disparate individuals who share the common purpose of stopping the escalation of systematic violence perpetrated by some against others. It is easy to imagine that the French anti-Nazis may circulate a similar local myth, giving due value to their own tactics and successes, the more complex for their national collective memory and very different experience of twentieth-century history. We may observe that apart from the content of Rousseau's maxims, a further common feature resides in the imaginary use to which that content is put. Notwithstanding the informality of the story and the unstructured nature of the organisation of which it is the expression, this story responds to the deeply social impulse to differentiate and to assert a hierarchy, as if to say: '*we* are society'. But it simultaneously opposes the larger society within which it arises, by expressing the ethical conviction of these social activists, individuals who run risks to safeguard for the present and the future a basic value of their societies which the laws do little to protect. The story only tacitly implies a question about that dimension of the law and of the legitimacy of a political power so inattentive to the fate of its defining values. Rather like Rousseau's articles of the civil faith, this story functions not symbolically, but as an *imaginary* social identity, and in fact a repository of the social contract in unjust times, for individual subjects who commit themselves *in reality* to action for the liberty and equality of unprotected others. As for the third of our modern analogies, we can only recognise the frightening dearth of procedures, in our own day, for restraining demagogues from inciting violence, and address forthwith Rousseau's reflections on this grave problem.

Caligula

In the first book of the *Social Contract* some of the most spectacular references to political evil occur in the form of poetic figures embedded in the logical argument; far from merely ornamental, they are subjected to the same analytical rigour as the argument itself. They dynamise the argument and partially determine its course, at the same time involving the reader's emotion through their impact on the senses. The figure of a creature, human or not, holding others captive in order to devour them, evolves into a repeated reference to Caligula at important moments of Rousseau's argumentation. Our enquiry could hardly enter more directly into the question of political evil in this work than through this complex figure of despotic power.

In the chapter 'Slavery' (Book I, chapter 4), Rousseau refutes the theory that a people can voluntarily enslave itself to a despot, by arguing that they would have nothing to gain in so doing, or even to conserve once they had thus given themselves wholly away. Civil peace, perhaps? But hardly in a desirable form. 'You can live peacefully in dungeons; is that enough to make you like them? The Greeks imprisoned in the Cyclops' cave lived peacefully while awaiting their turn to be devoured.' The quiet state of waiting to be devoured: this figure, placed in the fourth chapter, unexpectedly condenses two seemingly opposed figures of political leadership: the man-eating monster, and the shepherd tending his flock. The new figure is critical of our mental images of pastoral safekeeping and civil tranquillity, which must henceforth be redefined in terms of the destiny of the sheep, and the quality of the lives and deaths of the subjects; the criterion of quality, in the latter case, being liberty.

The figure of the shepherd has already been analysed in chapter 2, entitled 'The first societies'. Discussing the questions of how humanity came to live not in natural freedom but in a state of political subordination, and what can render a political structure legitimate, Rousseau protests that Grotius and Hobbes seem to suggest that government is for the benefit not of the ruled, but of those who rule. They thereby portray the human race

> divided into herds of cattle, each with a master who preserves the cattle only in order to devour them. Just as a shepherd possesses a nature superior to that of his flock, so do those shepherds of men, their rulers, have a nature superior to that of their people. According to Philo, that was how Caligula argued, concluding, reasonably enough on that analogy, that kings were gods or else that the people were animals (p. 51).[5]

After establishing that Grotius and Hobbes have that theory in common with Caligula, Rousseau also links Aristotle to the notorious emperor, for having argued that men were not all equal by nature.

Through his work on the figure, both analysing it and making it his instrument for analysing the theories of his predecessors, Rousseau makes the question of human government depend on the larger question of the definition of the human. In a footnote to the *Discourse on Inequality* he had wondered whether the orang-utangs observed by voyagers to the New World might not be men in the state of nature: just as he then exemplified the intellectual duty of modesty, the obligation to desist from differentiating the human species (which is animal) from the animal at what might well be an imaginary border, so in the *Social Contract* he insists on the political need to desist from imposing imaginary hierarchies within the species marked out as human. Rousseau's implied criticism of the myth of the superiority of human nature, whereby humans treat the rest of the living as objects for humanity, extends to the tendency in some humans to treat other humans as objects on some pretext of 'inferiority'.[6] The *Discourse on Inequality* shows that without socialisation, humans are animals among other animals, their only differences being their then imperceptible, latent perfectibility: their potential for freedom of choice, judgement, and thence language and society. Rousseau's philosophy of liberty thus makes him a humanist, but a highly critical one; their liberty only just marks humans off from other animals, and any claim to superiority depends on their using their liberty well; for socialised humans amongst themselves, political equality becomes the condition of liberty. These considerations underpin Rousseau's responding to his predecessor's figurative reduction of subjects to cattle with his own figurative amplification of the ruler to a man-eating monster like the Cyclops. Forming a link between the political theorists and the Cyclops, the figure of Caligula reasons in his own interests.

Caligula appears three times in the *Social Contract* (I, 2; II, 7; IV, 8). He is no afterthought (his reasoning is present in the Geneva and Neuchâtel manuscripts), and the repetition is no accident. In all three passages, we find the selfsame 'reasoning of Caligula' serving a somewhat similar rhetorical function: that of introducing Rousseau's discussion of, first, the leaders of peoples (as we have seen); second, the relative functions of the lawgiver and the prince;[7] third, the political function of men's belief in the gods. The prince, the lawgiver, the god: a trinity making up a figure of legitimate authority. The shadow of Caligula slips in alongside all three. The chapter 'The lawgiver' (II, 7), after describing the rare gifts needed for creating good laws, concludes: 'It would take gods to give laws to men'. This superiority marks the lawgiver off from the ruler:

> The same reasoning which Caligula used to explain a state of fact, Plato used to formulate what should be, in order to define the civil or kingly man in his dialogue *The Statesman*, but if it is true that great princes are rare, how much more so must a great lawgiver be? A prince has only to follow a model which it is the lawgiver's task to provide. The lawgiver is the engineer who invents the machine; the prince is merely the mechanic who sets it up and operates it.

Here the reference to Caligula may strike us as far-fetched; it takes Rousseau's skills to make it fit the case in point. The ideal lawgiver's intellectual and moral superiority is that of a disinterested observer of genius, altruistically serving the happiness of those whom he observes, his only rewards coming long after his labours. Rousseau uses Plato's sense that great princes are rare to reiterate the link made earlier between theorists and Caligula, in order to set a real human difference (the rare, authentic superiority of wise lawgiving) against a difference imagined merely to justify the existing political inequality.

The third and last appearance of Caligula opens the final chapter of the work, 'The civil religion':

> At first men had no kings but the gods, and their only government was theocratic. They reasoned like Caligula, and that time their reasoning was right. It takes a long debasement of feelings and ideas to make a man resolve to take as master one of his own kind, and to flatter himself that he will be the better for having done so.

Whereas Caligula's conclusion (either kings were gods or the people were animals) was only 'right' as a consequence of his chosen analogy with shepherds and their flocks, the earliest men were absolutely right to obey only their gods, and not other men. His reasoning is finally turned on its head. But throughout these three passages, Rousseau has in mind the self-interested *goal* of Caligula's reasoning, which is no less than a will to self-deification. His source text makes this perfectly clear. Philo of Alexandria tells the story in his *Embassy to Gaius*:[8]

> He then believed that, with no one left who dared oppose his will, he ought not to be satisfied with the greatest honours that can be rendered to men; but that he could aspire to those owed only to God; and it is said that in order to convince himself of such a great extravagance he reasoned in the following way. Since those who have charge of herds of cattle, flocks of sheep or herds of goats, are not themselves oxen, nor rams, nor goats, but are men, of an infinitely more excellent nature than that of animals, likewise those who command all the human creatures who live in the world deserve to be considered as being far more than men, and must be held to be gods (Pléiade, III, 1435).

What matters most in all Rousseau's references to Caligula is his legendary name, signifying cruelty identified with imperial power, and with the man who would even confer divine status on himself, the better to crush his people. Through his very name he bespeaks the abuse of community. Certainly his historical existence counts also, in a work closely grafted on to reality, but historical documentation about him was scarce in Rousseau's time and still is today; his negative value as a despot is rooted in fable, the permanent location of Caligula in reality. The figure of the Cyclops can stand for Caligula, but he is himself a figure. Not only can he stand for the Enlightenment's nightmare vision of the absolutely evil despot; a real political discourse is attributed to him, in which Rousseau finds the structure of inequality that he wishes to denounce in the political thinking of the classical and recent past. Caligula's reasoning perfectly serves the logic of Rousseau's argumentation because his discourse, as Philo reports it, manifestly denounces itself as a self-interested lie. The utter familiarity of Caligula to the imagination of readers suddenly makes Aristotle, Grotius and Hobbes less familiar to us, as we see that their thinking has a bit of Caligula in it.

Readers must see as well that Rousseau's own thinking has a bit of Caligula in it. His own procedure consists of reasoning with Caligula at the point of entry of each major incarnation of political authority. That part of his discourse which is not different from that of the great political thinkers, or even from Rousseau's own discourse, becomes integrated into the text of the *Social Contract* with a certain degree of endorsement before we encounter the qualification. There is a momentary identification, recognised as such and thrice reiterated. His presence serves to undermine the grounding of political legitimacy in inequality.

The fleeting identification of the writer and the monster is a formal device of great emotional force, a figure of the unity of the human species, the subject and the object; thus the writing subject internalises evil with good, and allows a place for everybody's unfittedness to judge others. But then a second phase takes the place of the first, in which good and evil are after all differentiated from each other, and recognition is accorded to everybody's capacity to denounce, condemn and stop a great criminal when he is speaking openly of his 'godly' power, when there is death on his lips and in his gaze, and before he has started to persecute others. A certain acquiescence to perversity, even in the writer's own formal procedures which connive repeatedly, if only momentarily, with evil, imposes the urgency of finding a remedy in the disease itself. Readers are drawn into the serious exercise of admitting and undoing the historical perversity of our own political thinking.

The articles of faith

Readers do not usually reach the passage describing the civil religion, however, fully alerted to the possibility of Caligula. On the contrary, the emotional impact of the death penalty comes not from the violence it might avert or punish, but from the violence of the penalty itself, for which the reader feels totally unprepared. The figure of the Cyclops was only an image, but Rousseau means the death penalty literally. He also means to repel readers by the brutal insertion of death into the religious dimension of social reality, where we might rather expect to find gentleness. Today we see the mark of 'fascism' where the death drive surfaces in language in a legitimised form. But the death drive is always there, united with the life drive, its destructiveness only unleashed when it breaks away on its own. The question is what kind of legitimation we witness in the civil religion; whether, in Rousseau's social contract, death or life would prevail. As we re-read the paragraphs setting out the principles of the civil religion, we must bear in mind that Rousseau's thinking is normally opposed to violence.

> The right which the social pact gives the sovereign over the subjects does not . . . go beyond the boundaries of public utility. The subjects have no duty to account to the sovereign for their opinions except when those opinions are important to the community. It is certainly important to the State that each citizen should have a religion which makes him love his duty, but the dogmas of that religion are of interest neither to the State nor to its members, except in so far as those dogmas are relevant to morality and to the duties which everyone who professes that religion is bound to perform towards others. Moreover, everyone may hold whatever opinions he pleases, without the sovereign's having any business knowing any of them. For the sovereign has no competence in the other world; whatever may be the fate of the subjects in the life to come, it is nothing to do with the sovereign, so long as they are good citizens in this life.
>
> There is, therefore, a purely civil profession of faith of which it is the sovereign's function to determine the articles, not exactly as dogmas of religion, but as feelings of sociability, without which it is impossible to be either a good citizen or a loyal subject. Without being able to oblige anyone to believe these articles, the sovereign can banish from the State anyone who does not believe them; banish him not for impiety but as an antisocial being, as one unable sincerely to love law and justice, or to sacrifice, if need be, his life to his duty. If anyone, after having publicly acknowledged these same dogmas, behaves as if he did not believe in them, then let him be put to death; he has committed the greatest crime, that of lying before the law.
>
> The [positive] dogmas of the civil religion must be simple and few in number . . . The existence of a powerful, intelligent, beneficent divinity that foresees and provides; the life to come; the happiness of the just,

the punishment of offenders; the sanctity of the social contract and the law . . . As for the negative dogmas, I limit these to a single one: no intolerance. Intolerance belongs to the religions we have excluded (Book IV, chapter 8).

A quite widespread misreading can be discounted forthwith. Rousseau does not propose that the society of the social contract condemn those who are normally called atheists. Banishment would not be for unbelief but for having been judged anti-social. Not lack of faith, but *behaviour* concordant with lack of faith in the fundamental articles, is unpardonable.

Since any religion is only relevant to the state in so far as it enjoins all who profess it to perform certain duties towards others, the reader's task is to isolate the *moral* content of the third paragraph. Rousseau insists on this procedure. In the first paragraph he differentiates the 'civil religion' from religion as such; clearly this text probes towards a new signification not adequately represented by existing terminology. 'Everyone may hold whatever opinions he pleases, without the sovereign's having any business knowing of them.' The fate of the subjects in the life to come is not the sovereign's affair. After such clear warnings, and having read that the sovereign will 'determine the articles, not exactly as dogmas of religion', the reader really is not free to interpret literally the religious terminology of the 'feelings of sociability'. Rousseau authorises us to interpret the articles of faith otherwise than as religious dogmas. That is not to say that we may project on to the text just any meanings we like, but it is appropriate to read the passage setting aside, momentarily, those elements of the textual surface which the writer has told us do not entirely belong to his argumentation. The terms denoting religious belief are not thereby rendered superfluous, but we should consider their function separately from our analysis of the passage's logical sequence.

Without the element of literal belief in God and eternal life, the articles of faith come down to the fostering of the citizens' subjectivity in a manner propitious to an 'ethics of conviction' (to use a modern expression) and to a disposition to beneficence and associated moral qualities (foresight, good providing). The desired outcome would be an impassioned commitment to do good to others, charged with the hope that virtue will be recognised and with the fear of falling short and reaping the consequences. The individual subject's goodwill to others would feel as important to him as if his life depended on it. This nurturing of beneficence in the city of the social contract might be seen today as a step towards the recognition of human rights, but neither the political nor the moral category as such is treated as sacred. The focus of religious sensibility would be certain feelings which predispose us to believe our happiness is not independent of other people's. We are not far from the 'object relation'; according to one school of psychoanalytical thinking, the relationship to a 'good object' constitutes the sacred for the individual subject. The articles of faith formulated by the sovereign might be thought of as encouraging the development, in the social space, of a sensibility and will to action metaphorically expressive of that subjective matrix of the sacred. In Rousseau's terms we could say that it is beneficence itself which the individual would hold sacred – the good object relation translated into practical actions. In a note to the first paragraph quoted above, Rousseau quotes the formulation of the Marquis d'Argenson: 'Everyone is free to do what does not injure others'. Whereas political justice imposes only the obligation not to harm others, religious sensibility reveres the positive will to do good unto others. That enables us to glimpse an aspect of the link between religion and political justice: social relations are never neutral; they are always either beneficial or harmful; the state only concerns itself explicitly with the latter, leaving the former in the care of religion.

The sanctity of the contract and the law – of the political relationships – makes up the last 'positive dogma' of the civil religion. As our reading omits theological references, we easily recognise the double movement of 'desacralisation' of the traditional institution (in this case, the monarch) and a new 'sacralisation', that of justice and the egalitarian pact. 'The social order', as we read in Book I, chapter 1, 'is a sacred right': the idea of political legitimacy arises out of the image of its lack, the figure of humanity everywhere in chains. At that imaginary level, political right is nothing other than our release from the rule of violence. Physical force and its effects can only create relationships of constraint and obedience, never an association of equals; in such a situation, justice requires that the people shake off the yoke as soon as possible, to recover their 'original liberty'. The sacred right of the social order 'serves as a basis for all other rights'; it is thus a second *origin*, but a human work of art, not a consequence of human nature. Set alongside that inaugural picture of the birth of the social contract, the civil religion cannot be confused with a religion which symbolises a natural plenitude. On the contrary, it has to be called upon to supplement a void – the absence of a sociable human nature. The social space, conversely, must be defined by the absence of violence. The 'feelings of sociability', founded on the passions of hope and fear, generate love and reverence for the contract and the law, because it is these which maintain that empty space.

The feelings of sociability include a threat of being condemned to death. The *Social Contract* is a positive construction, but not an idealising one; the historical pessimism of the *Discourse on Inequality* underlies the later work also, from beginning to end. True, evil is a social creation. But so is right, and so is the sacred as Rousseau understands it, on that level of potential nobility of soul represented by the figure of a work of art, the statue of the god Glaucus (Pléiade, III, 122). Unfortunately the statue's beauty has become disfigured. Even though evil occupies the foreground of the *Discourse on Inequality*, an ambivalent representation of humanity prevails throughout the work, thanks to the Glaucus simile in the preface; the reader cannot lose sight of the anthropological hope invested in that figure. The selfsame ambivalence gives the *Social Contract* its unique form, but the stress is reversed; a filigree of figures of evil – Caligula, instead of Glaucus – runs through the positively-oriented work, and only emerges for one brief moment in the foreground of the argument, when the death penalty suddenly breaks into the midst of the civil religion.

The reader and the crime

The negative side of the ambivalent message appears to target the reader directly. Even if Rousseau attributes to the sovereign the task of enunciating the articles of the civil religion, it is he himself who then proceeds to enumerate them; we can easily find ourselves forgetting that between writer and reader there lies a layer of representation, the imaginary level of the narrative of the first constitution. On close inspection we can remark that this is a deliberate rhetorical effect. Rousseau skilfully carries out the shift from the initial statement ('it is the sovereign's function to determine the articles' of the profession of faith) to the injunction that the citizen who 'behaves as if he did not believe in them' be 'put to death', and thence to the conclusion: 'As for the negative dogmas, I limit these to a single one: no intolerance'. In the space of a mere twenty lines, we are imperceptibly led from the narrative of the sovereign addressing his subjects to a first-person discourse in which the writer addresses the reader directly. Our reading of the civil religion is not quite far enough ahead, yet, for us to interpret that strange manœuvre.

Everything combines to shock the reader, thus drawn into the argument, at this point in the text: the violent negativity of an inflicted death for which nothing that came before seemed to prepare us; the announcement of this death penalty before we even know what crime it exists to punish, and even the total absence, in the passage, of manifest persuasive procedures. The *Social Contract* never comes closer than this to spelling out a specific law. Is this a written law destined to take its place in the penal code of a real legal system? We already know the sovereign gives no specific laws; even the legislator creates only general ones. So Rousseau has resorted to an extraordinary solution, a fact which indicates his assessment of the difficulty of the problem to which capital punishment provides some kind of answer. This penalty does not have the status of a law within a penal code which, after all, does not exist. In the treatise on 'the principles of political right', it can only be a law 'in principle'. Yet advance confirmation of its literal force certainly exists in Book II, chapter 5, 'The right of life and death', where Rousseau agrees to capital punishment, for certain murderers, for example. We are obliged to conclude that a principle so explicitly advanced in the treatise could not but be corroborated by the real penal code of a city faithful to the social contract, since a state must not tolerate major contradictions between the different categories of law contained within it; that is fundamental to Enlightenment teaching. In any case this punishment certainly constitutes for Rousseau a principle of political right of the highest importance, for in the very place where the political and religious dimensions must coexist *dissociated*, the death penalty stands out as the sole exception, where the two dimensions coincide. In this one case, human justice must inaugurate eternal sorrow.

The reader's difficulty in establishing what kind of penalty we are dealing with is likewise over-determined. Among many causes we can mention the brutal reversal of the emotional charge of the reading; up to this point the text carries us along in hope, but here, suddenly, fear or rather (since we do not yet know the crime) anxiety takes hold of us. What ensues scarcely reassures us; judging by the articles of faith, the malefactor could be anyone at all: you or I or the whole human race. Above all, the death penalty awakens in us, as well as anxiety, the sense of the uncanny which indicates the closeness to consciousness of certain unconscious representations.

Applying the sanction to the articles of faith or feelings of sociability, we can define the guilty party incurring the danger of death as being any person who behaved as if beneficence counted for nothing, as if there were no consequence to be expected from our succouring or injurious actions, as if the contract and the law were not sacred. Intolerant behaviour would be specifically proscribed, separately from maleficence in general, because it is a mode of religious action.

On the level of signification, the civil religion with its penalty now clearly epitomises, in moral terms, the egalitarian tenor of the political treatise.[9] But that is where the religious terminology makes a significant difference. The repetition of content involves an increase in intensity; the civil religion emotionally deepens the bonds of attachment linking the citizens to the pact and the law. The penalty is tautological too, 'the same thing' as the pact, but reversed into the negative to mark major transgression. We noted earlier that Rousseau presents the civil religion without noticeable persuasive procedures, but now we see that the very insertion of a reference to the passionate, imaginary function of religion in political reality is entirely a matter of figure; tautology, intensification, reversal into the negative. These are both at once linguistic figures and imaginary processes, which do not change unconscious symbolic structures, and yet they constitute an essential stage in the thought-process, and a necessary condition of our reflection on political legitimacy. These figures are recognisably essential, not ornamental, by virtue of their explosive referential pressure which produces the suddenly *literal* statement (for even while it takes form as a figure, it is meant literally) of the death penalty.

The very consistency of the civil religion with the social contract makes the death penalty shocking. Could such a misdemeanour as behaving as if beneficence counted for nothing warrant being put to death? Here the chapter 'The right of life and death' seems to offer assistance by citing the case of murder; would not maleficent and intolerant conduct be unpardonable, then, only when a life was suppressed? But if that were the case, what should we think of the long note about the marriage of protestants, which Rousseau attached belatedly to his chapter 'The civil religion'? (He later removed it, along with a second note on the subject; we find them at the end of the Geneva manuscript.) There he expresses outrage at the intolerance of the French authorities who had made it impossible for the protestants remaining in France to marry, thanks to a perverse interplay of laws and edicts. Certainly, Rousseau intended the note as an example of the civil effects of religious intolerance, having written it following the execution of four protestant men trapped by the laws in question. But the note is not so much about the injustice of those executions, and does not so much analyse the civil effects of intolerance, as cry out 'I accuse!' in the face of the perverse cruelty of a seemingly impersonal authority.

> Those unfortunates, reduced to the most horrible situation known to any people since the birth of the world, can neither stay nor flee. They are permitted neither to be foreigners, nor citizens, nor humans. Their most natural rights are denied them . . . Thus the protestant people are both at once tolerated and proscribed; it is intended both that they live and that they die (Pléiade, III, 343–4).

The question of the unatonable crime deepens on contact with the above passage. Today's readers cannot fail to recognise in it a perception of the persecutory structure of the 'double bind', here destroying any kind of community life for a particular religious group.

Rousseau's modernity

The crime targeted by the death penalty becomes more clearly defined. Claude Lévi-Strauss saw as much, when he interpreted Rousseau's thinking for our era in the following words: 'In a political society, there could be no excuse for the one inexpiable human crime, which consists of believing oneself lastingly or temporarily superior, and of treating men as objects; whether in the name of race, culture, conquest, mission, or simply expediency'.[10]

Rousseau's argumentation now begins to look very like the perception of evil in modern societies. On the one hand, Lévi-Strauss links Rousseauian unatonability to Christian proselytism, colonialism, racism and any conduct which reduces men – or women – to objects or means to an end. On the other hand, Rousseau brings out the systematic character of a social situation which is doubly inhuman, first because persecutory, and second because it seems to arise out of the mechanical operation of laws in combination with religious rules; persecution without a persecutor.

Modernity sometimes consists in saying that while an evil act or situation can be enormous, in many cases no individual is personally responsible; punitive procedures would have to deal with such a vast number of persons that it would cease to be possible to isolate a definable offence. Others assert that what is inhuman is the social system as such, or language itself. The reflection on social justice launched by Rousseau thanks to his rejection of the doctrine of original sin can be summarily dispatched by either of those postulations. That is what they have in common, and because of that, also, they can curiously resemble the doctrine of original sin itself. If they were fully representative of modernity, we would have to conclude that we have wrongly imposed on Rousseau's death penalty the criterion of 'modernity', for any *rapprochement* with those modern views takes us far from his thinking. After all, his viewpoint, as it emerges from all the foregoing comments, does not strike us so much for its modernity or its antiquity, as on account of its difference from the ideas of both his own times and ours.

If, in some modern states, the modern move towards abolishing the death penalty can seem to us today to be a necessary progress, Rousseau's thinking is bound to appear dated. Admittedly the move towards abolition is far from universal, and even some American liberals at the present time favour capital punishment for certain crimes. However, the diversity of present-day perspectives still does not embrace the Rousseauian formulation. For it is precisely where Rousseau identifies the *impersonal*, modern form of social evil that he proposes the most archaic punishment. Those responsible for the execution of the four protestant men would certainly be, to his mind, 'atheists fit for burning'. In an 'editor's footnote' to *The New Héloïse*, we read: 'If I were a magistrate and the law imposed pain of death on atheists, I would start by burning as such anyone who came to denounce someone else as one' (Pléiade, II, 589). Through his fictional 'editor', Rousseau the novelist here offers support to his character Wolmar, a virtuous atheist; what he writes applies equally to protestants. It has been claimed that Rousseau was 'contradicting himself' in that footnote: the 'moralist' opposing the death penalty for those who, like Wolmar, are normally called atheists, while the 'political thinker' proposes it.[11] But the latter reading is incorrect, and the footnote in the novel is entirely consistent with the civil religion. The words 'as such' clarify the signifying force of Rousseau's play on the word 'atheist', which, in his not literally theological context, can *only* designate the intolerant individual who acts as if it were a matter of indifference whether his actions had beneficent or hurtful effects on others.

At the same time, however, Rousseau shares the modern rejection of the death penalty. 'In my view, the blood of a single man is of greater price than the freedom of the whole human race', he writes in a letter to the Comtesse de Wartensleben.[12] And in *Emile*, on the same page as his warning that 'we are approaching the state of crisis, and the century of revolutions', he writes: 'If there is any State in this world so wretched that no one can live in it without doing wrong, and where the citizens are rogues out of necessity, it is not the offender who is to be punished, but the one who forces him to become an offender' (Pléiade, IV, 468). In these passages, morality and political thought work together to abhor the infliction of death on victims forcibly reduced to criminality. We might infer from this that Rousseau would abhor the very concept of the irrevocable punishment. Yet when he reflects on the possibility of a just state, he brings political and religious thinking together precisely in order to introduce the death penalty, in the chapter 'The civil religion'.

Responsibility for persecution

'All my ideas hold together, but I cannot elaborate them all at once' (Book II, chapter 5, 79). Our survey of Rousseau's relevant statements serves mainly to demonstrate how difficult it would be to find this writer wanting, whether in an enlightened perspective where the goal was religious tolerance, or from a democratic viewpoint which favoured a lesser authoritarianism and harshness of the state; nevertheless, exactly where those two points of view meet, we find the death penalty. We can advance our discussion by reading once more the chapter 'The right of life and death', which contains the warning just quoted. This chapter speaks less favourably for capital punishment than it appears to do on first reading. The opening passage merely states that the philosophical argument against it does not hold up to rigorous scrutiny. Thereafter, the assassin is mentioned as the most logical case for execution. Here, as in the chapter on the civil religion, expulsion from the city is proposed as an alternative. Then Rousseau describes the contractual community's relation to the assassin, using the right of war as both metaphor and comparison;[13] the point being to legitimise the death penalty in the dimension of the principles of political right. But thereafter, Rousseau proceeds to relativise the right of life and death, and the tone of the chapter gradually changes. 'No man should be put to death, even as an example, unless his life cannot be preserved without danger'; a government which resorted frequently to that extreme measure would thereby reveal itself defective. The sovereign may not condemn anyone to death, but only the sovereign (that is, the citizenry as a whole) may confer a pardon. The end of the chapter deals with the question of pardons, which if too frequent, signal, as do very harsh punishments, the deterioration of the state. So in practice, if not on the level of the principles of right, the death penalty should only be risked in extremely rare cases.

The last sentence of the same chapter shifts the angle of vision once more: 'But I feel my heart protesting and restraining my pen; let us leave the discussion of these questions to the just man who has never erred, and has never had need of pardon for himself' (p. 80). That concluding note echoes the end of the suppressed footnote about the persecution of protestants: 'This situation is unique and I hasten to lay down my pen, for fear of giving way to the cry of nature'. These personal authorial interventions do not abandon the problem, but transfer it expressly from the rational and legal level to a passionate and moral level; that is precisely the dimension of the civil religion, which is why the properly political discussion stops there. The cry of nature, the protesting heart, denotes the place of pity – recognition of our common humanity, our shared weakness and mortality – in our reasoning about social facts; we have entered the realm of the morality of beneficence. Rousseau may have suppressed the footnote about the protestants, but his moral indignation remains strong. He had the idea of writing at greater length on that subject, in another context; it is probable that he feared the footnote would be so 'uniquely' dramatic as to pull 'The civil religion' over to itself entirely, whereas the chapter was meant to remain general.[14] On the other hand, if 'The right of life and death' can end on the intervention of the heart's protest against the harshness of capital punishment, that is not a silencing of the heart; rather it is because the heart has spoken, to say that our moral duty requires us to soften that law in practice. Cesare Beccaria, one of the first and most admiring readers of the *Social Contract*, evidently takes his cue from that shift in Rousseau's angle of vision; he rejects capital punishment entirely on moral grounds. Similarly, when the elected representatives of a modern nation vote to abolish it, they may not believe they have found a more effective or more civilised means of preventing or punishing the gravest crimes: they perhaps do so only in order that the scene of official justice might not itself repeat the acting-out of humanity's destructive impulses. In this way, Rousseau shows himself as reluctant as many people are today to retain the death penalty, and for the same reasons. And yet that chapter, 'The right of life and death', founds mercy on the *principle* that the death penalty can be legitimate. He holds absolutely to that principle.

Since there is no reason to assume Rousseau guilty of a flagrant contradiction in the context of such carefully refined distinctions, we are obliged to reconsider our reading. The notion of modernity led us off course, induced us to read the footnote about the protestants too simply. Noting in Rousseau's accusation that impersonal character of modern forms of evil which no longer need the presence of a persecutor, we omitted to remark that his terms closely correspond to the language he uses to describe 'dependency on men', that is, the oppressive experience of anti-egalitarian political power, which he always defines as a *personal* power.[15] That may even be one of the most striking contributions of the political analysis inaugurated by Rousseau: while sweeping aside any metaphysical explanation for servitude, and while affirming that man, having been born free, is everywhere 'in chains', he never ceases to denounce persons. In the footnote about the protestants, therefore, the guilty parties are the priests, although it is very clearly implied that the political authorities are guilty too, for having conceded so much effective power to the clergy. The rhetorical force of the passage dramatically evokes a perverse situation set up by malefactors who are anything but anonymous, even if they are referred to by the impersonal pronouns 'they' or 'one' – a procedure familiar to the reader of Rousseau's autobiographical writings, as indicating the perpetrators of a persecutory action.

The footnote delineates persecution as the worst case of that dependency on men against which the *Social Contract* would seek to guarantee us. 'In relations between one man and another, the worst that can happen to the one', we read in the *Discourse on Inequality*, is 'to find himself at the other's discretion'. The *Social Contract* hopes to found political legitimacy on a truly impersonal dependency on the *law*, the same for one and all, similar in that respect to the 'dependency on things' which, far from breaching human liberty, is even the condition of it. All the aspects of the *Social Contract* which designate the sacred characterise the experience of dependency on the law by *love of the pact*, of the law itself, of beneficent relations. Theory can hardly be expected to take into account the role played by love in the founding of political legitimacy; we all know as well as Rousseau does, however, that where love of the community is missing, dependency on the law is not worth much: in civil life, we need to be 'better than free' in order to be free. In that sense the object of love is the guarantee that no person has power over another; loving the law means loving its impersonal quality. That fact constitutes an essential pivot in the Rousseauian representation of affectivity, liberty and political reality. It touches the essence of the *Social Contract*'s enquiry, and the tenor of certain formulations which are sometimes misunderstood, starting with the passage in Book I, chapter 9, 'Of estate', where property is redefined as safekeeping. Throughout Rousseau's writings, the relation of safekeeping signifies dependency without 'alienation', without loss of self-possession, without enslavement. In the *Social Contract*, where the presence of this stable structure is not sufficiently appreciated, it serves as a foundation for beneficence not only by mitigating property rights, but also by transforming the meaning of political authority; it structures concretely the proscription on any appropriation of sovereign power, by defining the governing person or group as *depositary* of that power.

The safekeeping structure (*le dépôt*) contains the one chance, on Rousseau's reckoning, that the state might be the citizens' object of love.[16] The unbalanced French laws of the eighteenth century which make victims of the protestants entail a perversion of community relations. Only the concern for justice, the love of all people, could undo that perverse system. 'Concern' is not systematic, quite the contrary; it is a matter for the citizens, primarily as individuals. It is each individual's liberty which creates the social contract, the new system, in order that each person remain free. Therefore when Rousseau sees something systematic in the persecuting of the protestants, he certainly does not mean that the *contractual* system could be condemned as a persecutory machine. This is consistent with his opposition, in *Emile*, to the death penalty in the perverted system where people are not free but 'rogues out of necessity'. And if he declares that those who abuse their power to force others to become rogues *should* be hanged, he is merely affirming a death penalty which might be efficacious in the city of the social pact, but would certainly be useless in such an oppressive milieu; he knows well enough that a political system constructed to guarantee a personal mode of power will never countenance the death penalty for the holders of power. Now the profound coherence of Rousseau's diverse reflections on the death penalty is coming to light. In the perverse social system, all the people live dependent on one another, or as Rousseau puts it, they all devour one another. Relations of possessiveness, enslavement, destruction. In that setting, the person who forces another individual to become criminal, and not the latter, ought to be hanged. The movement of Rousseau's whole thought-process on the utility of the threat of the death penalty is fundamentally oriented in the direction of *ultimate responsibility*. This movement consists in making the threat of death *climb up the hierarchy* of political power, liberating the class of victims to oppress the oppressors instead, or to abolish through terror the very desire to oppress. Yet the hierarchy is not merely reversed; a deep transformation of the perception of political relations is at stake.

What we recognised as the modern perception of persecution is for Rousseau himself just a particular, new form (unique and without precedent, he felt) of the phenomenon of the 'absent master', a characteristic mode of despotism, the extreme form of political violence for the eighteenth-century mind. Captivity, enslavement, murder: oppression is never impersonal. Montesquieu's eunuchs, in the *Lettres persanes*, figures of the violence of the absent master, may be said to prefigure the anonymity of violence which marks our own century, and yet they are human figures, whose wound denounces the crime of him who commanded it. For Rousseau justice does not exist unless it undoes the perversion of social relations, not a natural or 'essential' perversion, yet an integral part of social reality, living in and off it; not even the quest for legitimacy which constitutes the *Social Contract* leaves this perversion out of account. In our own day, we are told that racism is part and parcel of Western rationality, inseparable from the mental structures constitutive of our societies, going back to our Greek myths.[17] This train of thought in no way changes individual or collective responsibility; quite the contrary: it leads us to the Rousseauian perception of a form of persecution which is both at once a crime attributable to someone and a function of the social machine.

Whereas some have felt it necessary to read the *Social Contract* as a confusion of liberty and despotism, and as heralding the modern totalitarian systems, this work in fact defines the necessity of a dependency on the law which will never be a dependency on men, and does so precisely against the background of oppressive structures, where the impersonal violence of the system cannot exonerate individuals, even large numbers of individuals, for the acts of violence committed – committed by someone, therefore inexorably personal. The political system whose principles he spells out would guarantee the liberty of every subject in his relations with others. The attenuation and diminution of partial associations and personal relations stand in opposition to the manœuvres of captivation which bind together the subjects in unjust regimes. Political relations, thus mitigated, come closer to the model of safekeeping than to that of dispossession or alienation. When Rousseau rejects all metaphysical definitions of the law, when he places the civil religion at the conclusion of his treatise, far away from his description of the inauguration of the city through a pact among individuals, and well after Book II, chapter 5 where the legislator must make people believe in the divine origin of the law, he is working towards an 'ethics of conviction' and a conception of the *faith* of the (rational) pact as founded in those affective ties which are the site of the sacred. That is an inescapable consequence of a political system founded by, and for, the liberty of the citizens. In the *Essay on the Origin of Languages*, we learn that political liberty and the free expression of the passions go together, which is not to say they are the same thing. In the *Social Contract*, the citizen 'will be forced to be free': instead of trying to force upon those words the causality of the Terror and of twentieth-century violence, we might recognise in them a major intuition of Rousseau's about the links between political reality and the subjective dimension. For the structure of the relation thus defined between the sovereign's authority ('on le forcera': 'one', here, designates the people) and the freedom of the individual subject can be found repeated in the description of the writer's youthful happiness when living with Madame de Warens: 'I was perfectly free, and better than free, for, subjected solely by my ties of attachment, I did only what I wished to do'.[18] Even the miscreant, in the city of the pact, experiences that freedom which only ties of attachment make possible. If we insist on misunderstanding Rousseau's paradox of force and freedom in the *Social Contract*, we lose the whole sense of his vision of our chance of liberty and his defensive construction against persecution.[19] Nothing is gained, either, by regretting that Rousseau indulges in such violent rhetorical figures even while we acknowledge that his thought is basically anti-violent. Through the violence of the figure he leads us to the literal violence of the death penalty, partly because the non-violent writer and reader countenance only the literary forms of violence; he sees danger in that reliance on the poetic figure. The *Social Contract*, as can now be seen, removes us far from the problem mentioned in the *Letter to d'Alembert*, that of the popular leader's fanatical followers whose violence must be met by violence and not by reasoning. Instead, we have now moved deeply into a very different field of problems, created by the possibility of a powerful, intelligent and even enlightened personality, but politically ambitious and disposed to violence. For this situation, Rousseau follows and transforms lessons learned from Montesquieu, according to whom such a personality, who does not fear the law, is only likely to be held in check by religious dread. The violence in question, in other words, cannot be arrested by either violence or reason. Something which includes both, but is more complex than both, is required, and our reading of the civil religion has already taken us right into the midst of it.

Rousseau acknowledges a problem associated with the anchoring of contractual theory in reality, a form of the problem of power, at the level where the principles of right are actualised: it is possible to lie when one pronounces the words of the social pact. Of course any individual citizen's transgression might put his own fidelity in question, but this need not raise any grave problem for contractual theory; the whole social body is there to constrain the individual, in case of need, to obey the general will, to 'force him to be free', so that he lives like all the other citizens within the constraints of the responsibility of free men. Nor is the problem of the sovereign's fidelity to the pact an irreducible one in Rousseau's estimation, because, however complex the modalities of expression of the general will may be, the sovereign 'can have no interest contrary' to the interest of the individuals who compose it. 'Owing its being to the sanctity of the contract alone', the sovereign would destroy itself by any act of contempt for the feelings of sociability expressed by the civil religion. 'To violate the act which has given it existence would be to annihilate itself; and what is nothing can produce nothing' (Book I, chapter 7). From the moment that a sovereign people had thus abolished its sovereignty, the 'society' in question would fall outside the framework of the *Social Contract*.

However, between the individual and the sovereign, there is the government; as indicated by the derisory contract described in the *Discourse on Inequality*, the lying words 'Let us unite together', pronounced by an oppressor, would create no contractual association, but merely mask the enslavement of a people (Pléiade, III, 177). The same preoccupations underlie the *Social Contract*, and the death penalty finally makes them explicit. Rousseau's entire intellectual production is at stake in the possibility of lying when enunciating the pact, and would founder if his thinking were simplistically systematic, but he is always willing to complicate the process further in order to take account of problems on many levels. What happens when the mysterious powers of rhetoric are deployed in the service of evil?

Shakespeare illustrates that classical dilemma in the character of Iago, who by brilliantly misusing the art of persuasion, makes himself the master of Othello's sensibility and annihilates reason and political obligation.[20] A government might well *dissolve* the very mediation or 'correspondence' which it exists to ensure between the citizens in their capacity as sovereign and the same citizens as individual subjects; in so doing it would deliver itself over to the death drive. Such a reading is called for by the paragraphs describing the civil religion and the death penalty, whose terms would not, of course, correspond to Rousseau's thinking if they were rigorously applied to just any intolerant individual, or even to just any murderer. But the logic of the passage becomes clear once we tell ourselves that its target is the criminal head of state, the prince who murders the citizens, or any powerful leader who sets some of the people against others.

The death penalty refers primarily to the prince, 'the man or the body' charged with 'the legitimate exercise of executive power' (Book III, chapter 1), defined as a simple officer of the sovereign and as the depositary or custodian of power: that is, the government elected by the people. It has been argued that the implied reader whom Rousseau addresses in the *Social Contract* is, in fact, a prince.[21] A prince eminently capable of following the complexity of the argument, for Rousseau displays here none of the anxiety about being misunderstood by his reader, so easily perceptible in his other writings. Much of the time, therefore, the identity or status of the text's addressee might appear irrelevant. It is when the writer attends most studiedly to his own persuasive effects that the question of the addressee imposes itself upon us; for instance, in the passages dealing with the law and the civil religion. If we provisionally admit the hypothesis of the princely reader, would he be a virtuous man? The positive, confident tone of the work would lead us to believe so. However, once the writer resolves to address his treatise on political right to a prince, no doubt he finds himself obliged to suppose that prince virtuous; otherwise his appeal for justice would have little hold over the privileged reader. That makes it difficult to embark on the vices of government (not to mention the practical risks of censorship and condemnation). Rousseau uses indirect procedures which enable him to imply, under his breath as it were, another possible prince, as intelligent as the first one, just as capable of grasping the tenor of the principles of right, but intending to deflect them towards a goal of criminal exploitation. The force of the death penalty would be that where the sovereign, in acting contrary to the pact, cannot but annihilate itself, an equally objective situation brings about the annihilation of a prince who destroys the lives of the citizens.

Precisely on the level of the text's relation to its readers, therefore, the *Social Contract* includes what is absolutely other than itself: destruction. Hence the force of our reaction, which perhaps resembles in fact the reaction sought by the writer: our minds filled with the principles of the *Social Contract*, we hold the idea of this death penalty in absolute horror. Finding ourselves faced with that very harsh law at the moment when the text placed us in the presence of our best possibilities gives us that feeling of the uncanny which signals the proximity to our conscious thoughts of the unconscious scene most radically opposed to our virtuous aspirations – the scene of tormentor and victim. Then we might linger in that sense of *Unheimlichkeit* (deriving a certain pleasure, perhaps, from not understanding it), or else denial might take over, in the guise of moral rectitude and projection of blame, and finally the accusation of inhumanity laid at the door of the writer himself.

The possibility, in any state, of a criminal ruler constitutes the most violent conflict within the *Social Contract*: what if the pact were made to work in the service of death? This work does not remotely proffer a utopian construct, if by that we mean a space characterised by the exclusion of evil. If it gives absolute priority to the positive possibility, it none the less does not hide its reflection on the other possibility, which preoccupies the discussions of the tension between general will and particular will on the level of the government, or of the tendency of governments to degenerate. Readers need to follow this reflection on evil right to its conclusion precisely because the potentially criminal leader may well be masked among them. That presence in the work of a different target, another addressee, may after all have provoked an even stronger reaction in readers than the one Rousseau worked for, because it touches a universal depth of whose existence he could know nothing – the unconscious ambivalence which makes all of us feel ourselves to be potential tormentors. It is true that Rousseau was able to admit that nothing human was foreign to him, and that in the chapter 'The right of life and death' he admits he is in need of grace. It is also true that his theory of self-love and *amour propre* already contains all the elements of a fundamental affective ambivalence. In his writing, however, the extremes of love and hate remain distributed along different planes in the history of the human species and of the individual life; in the history of civilisation as Rousseau describes it, hatred is a perversion of self-love, the source of the 'secondary passions' which, although less strong, can eventually dominate the loving 'primary passions'.[22] Freud was the first to give us a conception of primary processes in which linking and unlinking operate perpetually within the psychical makeup of the individual, and Klein even made us conceive a sort of priority of the destructive drive, necessitating the elaboration of reparative love without which psychical survival would not be possible. The surreptitious character of that strange appeal, which is obscurely heard by the reader of 'The civil religion', addressing a virtual and yet already unatonable criminality, must certainly coincide with our unconscious knowledge of the instincts lurking beneath the most banal impulses of everyday intolerance.

In the eighteenth century, Rousseau was not able to take those facts into account; yet he had his reasons for excluding no one, for sending out to all of us his threatening message. He must undermine, through fear, the potential for destruction, and do so from the point of entry into the pact or from the moment of reading the treatise, before it is too late. The passage on the civil religion would seem to exclude the death penalty by virtue of that appeal to absolutely everybody. But Rousseau obviously sees some gain in all his readers' being shocked by the presence of the death penalty in the civil religion, in everybody's applying the moral judgement momentarily to themselves, and in experiencing the anxiety awakened by the reference to violent death. The intellectual labour triggered by that openness of a principle which ultimately targets only very rare individuals, and which is the very effort of our own reading, becomes a reflection on the fact that differences of degree are sometimes differences in kind. The principle arising out of that reflection at once abolishes severe penalties at the level of forced criminality which is the level of the victims of evil – and which should scarcely exist in the city of the just pact. Only in a context thus transformed, and only by virtue of that transformation, should the principle of the death penalty be established for the maleficence and intolerance which always designate victims. This principle would function in accordance with the total openness of a founding moral teaching addressed to a newly-formed people, who would thereby conceive a metaphysical dread of such feelings as might develop into persecutory tendencies. The object of dread would have the name of the death penalty but would not take its objective form except in the extreme case where an individual or group were in a position to pervert the pact and to impose a violent system in place of the law. That final outcome of the principle (which includes in its sights all the points on a continuous scale of modes of behaviour which negatively affect the bonds of community) need not culminate in literal condemnation to death. Essentially, this is a principle which would make all of us assume the responsibility for recognising a difference in the continuity, a drift towards harmful acts and towards the disintegration of the sense of community.

Always bearing in mind that the civil religion, and the death penalty for maleficent, intolerant actions, take shape in people's consciousness at the time of the founding of the new society, we may say that the penalty reiterates tautologically, but in the negative, the very desire for community. Nothing could be more fundamental than the prohibition of intolerance by the community, since the community is the object of desire for individuals and groups by virtue of their very diversity. If the law did not establish at least *in principle* the death penalty for a great persecutor, the state would stand in contradiction of everything which makes it exist and subsist; that is, according to Rousseau, with the citizens' love for the community. Persecutory intolerance is not just any form of violence to be repressed in civilised societies. It is not anti-social; it exploits the fundamental social impulse to differentiation and hierarchy; it is an always-possible perversion of that impulse.

The death penalty comes like a *coup de théâtre* in the final pages of the enquiry into the question of legitimacy, not as part of any penal code but as a sanction finalising the principles of right, a law to associate fear with any thought of behaviour tending to the eventual destruction of the community itself. Whereas the transfer to the moral dimension of pity replaces and concludes the considerations of political justice in the chapter 'The right of life and death' and the footnote about the protestants, the death penalty, constituting the one and only intersection of the principles of political right with religion, concludes the political treatise: not on the note of pity this time, but of terror. The political function of religion consists in investing the citizen's relation to the law with the passions of love, hope and fear. Rousseau seems inspired by Montesquieu, who writes in the *Spirit of the laws* (XXXIV, chapter 2):

> A prince who loves his religion and fears it is a lion yielding to the hand caressing it or to the voice appeasing it; a prince who fears his religion and hates it is like those wild beasts who bite the chain that restrains them from leaping upon those who pass by; a prince who has

no religion at all is the terrible animal which cannot feel its liberty except when it tears and devours.'

Only such considerations can explain this sanction and its abrupt fusion of the political and religious dimensions. Only a government – or a tyrant, or a demagogic leader – can render the law futile. Montesquieu's remark (XXXIV, chapter 16) that 'religion can sustain the political State when the law is reduced to impotence' makes us think of a government needing to contain a people in revolt. But in the context of the *Social Contract*, we are rather called upon to think that the sovereign people might need to contain a prince if the latter found a way of treating as his own the fiduciary power entrusted to him; a prince who grew impatient with the status of 'simple officer' of the sovereign and who meant to subject the people to his will. If leaders traditionally induce fear in the people by referring to divine power, would not Rousseau think it fair for the sovereign people, true to the legislator's inspiration, to remind the prince that he ought to fear the outcome if he were to forget the modesty of his function and the fidelity he owes, as a citizen, to the code of beneficence and the prohibition of intolerance?

If we now bring together Rousseau's death penalty and our earlier exploration of the figure of Caligula in the *Social Contract*, we can grasp the fact that this work contains Rousseau's contribution to, and radical transformation of, the classical tradition of tyrannicide. We have stressed that Rousseau intends the death penalty to work as a deterrent, on the imaginary level and through religious dread, and that its potential realisability would mainly serve that goal of fear. The *Social Contract* says nothing about legitimate ways and means for carrying into practical effect the condemnation of a prince or other leader who could not be banished. It would not be out of the question, in the last analysis, for the reflection on the death penalty in this work to assist the deliberations of a just citizen deciding for or against recourse to tyrannicide in a desperate political situation. Rousseau's total silence on this matter does not preclude that reading; we may even infer that his silence has exactly that semiotic function.[23] It is a silence partially structured by explicit information constituting its borders such as the fact that the citizenry as sovereign cannot pass sentence of death or execute anyone. In a time of tyranny, the government would be either powerless or implicated in the crime. That would leave only the citizen as individual subject to reach the decision and attempt to carry out the death penalty on some new Caligula. All we can say about this potential reading is that a reader who needed to elicit it would have had to reflect deeply, already, on the difference between tyrannicide and self-interested political assassination, and would have to be already resolved on his or her course of action before turning to Rousseau's analysis of the principles of political right, since these contain no encouragement to violence; only the civil religion's moral endorsement of a death penalty which there would be no other way to carry out.[24]

How could we claim, in the face of that implication of the death penalty, that this work constructs a totalitarian utopia founded on the illusory exclusion of evil? If our vision of the work is passably faithful, the only person condemned to death would be someone it was not even possible to banish, who wished to put himself above the law and render it powerless. The criminal who would not let go of the pact but bound himself up in it to pervert it from within, using it to harm others. It would seem, then, that the *Social Contract* does include the violence of humanity, 'men as they are'. The civil religion, located with the ritual of the pact at the founding of the state, would first confront the potential persecutor when he was in the state of 'nascent monster', allowing at least the hope that he might be trapped then and there by his very fanaticism, long before he could pass from thoughts to deeds. The persecutor might be destroyed within him, his tragic itinerary annihilated in the bud; he might restore within himself the union of the erotic and destructive drives, giving himself the possibility of passing to the other side of humanity, no longer below the wild beasts but above them. The pact is Eros bound, integrated, evolved; it includes death. Violence is not 'essential' to humanity, but the effect of a 'long debasement', a perverse product of reflective thinking. Another, different kind of reflection is needed, one which would be equally cunning, capable of confronting this perversion and wrecking it, a new, anti-violent mode of thinking which, however, would have to admit the possibility of an equally violent force of opposition and interruption, if the need arose.

We have had to describe Rousseau's procedures in this discussion as almost surreptitious, because he does not pass immediately from his positive political construction to the literal insertion of the death penalty, but integrates the question of evil principally through that formal, indirect dimension of writing which is the poetic figure. On the level not of logic but of rhetoric, where the readers' passions are solicited, the *Social Contract* confronts and deals with a possible, perverse over-investment of its content. Rousseau does not thereby give passion the victory over reason. Reason itself requires such recourse to detailed work on the emotional level, since reason alone does not suffice to defend the cause of reason. When he writes in the first person to say '*I* exclude intolerance', every intolerant reader (every one of us) must hear the call, from one subject to another, to exclude intolerance. His poetic figures call our passion and imagination to action in combination with a complex but rigorous argumentation into which we are required to throw ourselves completely, because there is no freedom without paying that price. The complexity of the *Social Contract* exemplifies that psycho-social labour of eternal vigilance. At the end of our reading of this work's contribution to freedom from persecutory leadership, it would be difficult to maintain that Rousseau believed a purely political solution could be found for the problem of civilisation. The instance of the death penalty shows that the force of the fundamental laws lies much less in their external enforcement – although that is crucial – than in the passionately critical and imaginative activity which they generate in individual subjects.

Love and death in the *Social Contract*

If the *Social Contract* has a utopian dimension, it consists neither in an illusory exclusion of evil, nor in the projection of a false promise or an incitement to impossible attempts – impossible, that is, inexorably destructive of hope – to realise a dream. Its utopian function would rather reside in that faculty which it nourishes, to imagine the founding principles of the legitimate institution, something which has no resemblance to anything that could be seen in the universe of the eighteenth century. Enlightenment thinking analysed in its own secular way that tension between the political and the religious dimensions which is productive of legitimacy, always interpreting it as an intensification of the passions of love, hope and fear. The contribution of Rousseau to that analysis consisted in adding that that fear must be the fear of death.

The *Social Contract* founds the right of life and death on an argument about our right to risk our own life (Book II, chapter 5). Rousseau dismantles Locke's argument against the death penalty (having no right to kill ourselves, we may not grant that right to the sovereign), by saying that suicide is not the only case in point and that, on the contrary, we are perfectly entitled to risk our life in order to try to save it – to throw ourselves out of a window in order to escape from a fire, for instance. This opening passage of 'The right of life and death' clarifies the following comparison of the assassin with the enemy waging war against the state, or does so as soon as we note that Rousseau is thinking about the prince. For a question underpins this whole discussion: how is it conceivable that a powerful individual could wreak destruction on his fellow-citizens, incite some of his neighbours to persecute others, without his ever having to believe that he thus risks losing his own life at the hands of those who represent justice? How can we allow that such an individual need never fear losing his life by acting in such a way; how can we allow that, on the contrary, he can rest assured that whatever happens, the state will preserve his life? Rousseau therefore envisages power over others in terms of its most concrete logical consequence: if illegitimate power destroys lives, legitimate power likewise will link the exercise of power to the idea of death; not just death as that which may befall those ordinary criminals under my power, but as *my* possible death.

All the complexity of the civil religion and the right of life and death become obligatory to prevent that imbalance which is catastrophic for the community, whereby only those officials who became supremely powerful could feel themselves above danger, immortal, divine, like Caligula, while all the other component members of the state must know themselves to be perpetually subject to constraint (the citizens, as subjects) if not possible annihilation (the sovereign, if it contravened the pact). The community is constantly subject to interruptions; if it were not, that would be fusion, and then we could speak of 'totalitarianism'. But there are many beneficial breaks in the continuity, the first being that created by the limits on sovereign power which leave intact that part of each individual where the 'citizen' is silent and the 'man' takes over as subject of his own inner life. The community contains gaps of many kinds, not only those produced by the tendency of governments to deteriorate. If death is the supreme figure of the interruption of community, the existence of a death penalty for the persecutory prince or leader may be conceived as a necessary factor of equilibrium. Supposing the community does exist, it is therefore intimately linked to the consciousness of death, and if ever that reality saw one single powerful exception, disaster would ensue. The community is more than prone to breaks in its own fabric, nothing could be more 'natural' to it, and it is fully capable of abolishing itself entirely.

Rousseau therefore channels towards the preservation of the community the tragic passions of pity and terror, which the theatre of his time deflects away from society into unlifelike situations – a dangerously futile catharsis, as he argues in the *Letter to d'Alembert*. These tragic passions are none other than the originary passions of man in the state of nature: fear or terror expressing self-love, preservation of the self and of the species; pity expressing the transfer to others of the love of self, in recognition of our universal humanity, frailty and mortality. The imaginary channelling of the passions is the same for the nascent monster as for the rest of us, for the anti-Nazi activists and for the tyrant's future killer, because there is no fundamental difference, beyond the uniting or disuniting of the life and death drives. On the level of the principles of right, the right of life and death must yield to pity, while the civil religion fostering feelings of sociability culminates in the death penalty. To contain the violence of the state, the slow birth of a morality of human rights; to contain our own and others' potential violence against other people, or for the dark day when tyrannicide becomes a need, a momentary religious politics of death.

The difference which marks out Rousseau's death penalty is above all that of a new departure, the legitimate inauguration of a new society. If we were to consent, today, to designating as a fundamental 'utopian thinking' just that one power of imagining something *other* than our liberal system, we would have to admit that we have lost that power, and that our loss impoverished us. Whether or not we agree with the *principle* of the death penalty as it is worked out in the *Social Contract*, we will at least acknowledge that it offers us a chance of imagining a society in which everyone knew they were obliged to resist the ascension of a modern Caligula.[25]

Notes

1 *Lettre à d'Alembert* (Paris, Gallimard, 1987), 176–7.

2 This point is made by Claude Lefort. For the relation of chiasmatic tension between the political and the theological dimensions in modern societies, see Lefort, 'Permanence du théologico-politique?', in *Essais sur le politique* (Paris, Editions du Seuil, 1986), 251–300.

3 See Pierre-André Taguieff, *La force du préjugé: essai sur le racisme et ses doubles* (Paris, Gallimard, 1987).

4 The British Anti-Nazi League's story was related to me by my colleague George Paizis.

5 The *Social Contract* is cited from the translation by Maurice Cranston (Harmondsworth, Penguin, 1968). I have occasionally altered the translation slightly. Chapter or page references are inserted in the text.

6 *Discours de l'inégalité*, in Pléiade, III, 208–14.

7 'The prince' here designates the governing body, 'an intermediary body established between the subjects and the sovereign for their mutual communication', which is 'charged with the execution of the laws'; this administration may be one man or a group of men (Book III, chapter 1).

8 Philo of Alexandria, *Embassy to Gaius [Caligula]*, 76ff. The passage cited in Pléiade, III (1435) comes from the version Rousseau must have known, an adaptation of Philo's text by Arnault d'Andilly, included in the latter's French translation (1687) of the *History of the Jews* of Flavius Josephus.

9 Ralph Leigh remarks that the relation of the civil religion to the social contract is tautological, in the discussion following the communication of Robert Derathé, 'La religion civile de Rousseau', *Annales de la Société J.-J. Rousseau* (Geneva, Julliard, 1963), vol. 35, 161–80.

10 Claude Lévi-Strauss, 'J.-J. Rousseau fondateur des sciences de l'homme', in Samuel Baud-Bovy *et al.*, *Jean-Jacques Rousseau* (Neuchâtel, A la Baconnière, 1962), 239–48.

11 For example, Jean-Louis Lecercle, introduction to the *Contrat Social* (Paris, Editions sociales, 1968), 38–41.

12 Leigh, 5450 (27 September 1766).

13 Robert Derathé considers that the death penalty has nothing to do with the right of war (Pléiade, 1460, note 377). But Rousseau's very free, figurative *rapprochement* indicates that he seeks here to carve out a new path for political thought. Cesare Beccaria saw fit to imitate Rousseau's procedure, in his passage on the death penalty in *On crimes and punishments* (1764).

14 Rousseau mentions the possibility of such a project in his letter to Marc-Michel Rey of 18 March 1762 (Leigh, 1715).

15 See *Emile* (Pléiade, IV, 311), where Rousseau distinguishes between 'two sorts of dependency, that of things, which pertains to nature; that of men, which pertains to society'.

16 See Felicity Baker, 'Remarques sur la notion de dépôt', in *Annales de la Société J.-J. Rousseau*, vol. 37 (1971), 57–93.

17 See Christian Delacampagne, *L'invention du racisme: Antiquité et Moyen Age* (Paris, Fayard, 1983).

18 *Rêveries du promeneur solitaire*, 10e Promenade.

19 On the paradox 'forced to be free', see Felicity Baker, 'La route contraire', in Simon Harvey, Marian Hobson, D. J. Kelley and S. B. B. Taylor (eds), *Reappraisals of Rousseau: studies in honour of R. A. Leigh* (Manchester, Manchester University Press, 1980), 132–62.

20 For Iago's abuse of the rhetorical art, see Marion Trousdale, *Shakespeare and the rhetoricians* (Chapel Hill, University of North Carolina Press, 1982), 162–8.

21 See Roger Masters, *The Political Philosophy of Rousseau* (Princeton, Princeton University Press, 1968), 306–12. In affirming that the principal teaching of the *Social Contract* is that the prince is, or should be, subject to the laws (311), Masters remarks that the princely addressee would not necessarily be a virtuous man. On the question of the implied reader's intellectual gifts, see Robert Ellrich, *Rousseau and his Reader: the rhetorical situation in the major works* (Chapel Hill, University of North Carolina Press, 1969).

22 The distinction between primary and secondary passions does not appear in Rousseau's works until the *Dialogues de Rousseau juge de Jean-Jacques* (Pléiade, I, 668–72).

23 See Izydora Dambska, 'Sur les fonctions sémiotiques du silence', in *Revue de métaphysique et de morale*, 75e année, no. 3 (July–September 1970), 309–15.

24 Rousseau cites Xenophon's classical text on tyranny, which became a subject of new interest after World War II. See Leo Strauss, *On Tyranny: an interpretation of Xenophon's Hiero* (Glencoe, The Free Press, 1948). It seems likely that Rousseau's unusual rhetorical procedure of partially identifying himself as writer with Caligula is a modern transformation of Xenophon's procedure. The latter represents the tyrant Hiero in dialogue with Simonides, known for his greed: a far cry from the virtuous Socrates. However, Xenophon is not explicitly present as narrator; he is thus twice distanced, both from Hiero and from the dialogist's compromising task of negotiating intellectually with him. Rousseau, unlike Xenophon, compromises his illustrious predecessors as well as himself. A valuable study is that of Oszkár Jászi and John Donald Lewis, *Against the Tyrant: the tradition and theory of tyrannicide* (Glencoe, The Free Press and The Falcon's Wing Press, 1957). Among Rousseau's contemporaries, tyrannicide receives respectful attention from the Chevalier de Jaucourt in the article 'Tyran, tyrannicide, tyrannie' of the *Encyclopédie*; most influential was the defence of tyrannicide in the Abbé Raynal's *Histoire philosophique et politique du commerce et des établissements des Européens dans les Deux-Indes* (1770). The theory of tyrannicide (of which Jean Marat's death at the hands of Charlotte Corday was an application) became obscured by the Terror and the modern revolutionary movements, until the post-war period.

25 This article reworks, with many additions, material published in my earlier article, 'La peine de mort dans le *Contrat social*', in Marian Hobson, J. T. A. Leigh and Robert Wokler (eds), *Rousseau and the Eighteenth Century: essays in memory of R. A. Leigh* (Oxford, Voltaire Foundation at the Taylor Institution, 1992), 163–88.

Part III
Locating Rousseau's meanings and significance

9 Robert Wokler

Rousseau and his critics on the fanciful liberties we have lost

I

Rousseau's critics have often complained that his love of humanity embraced few individuals apart from himself. In passing from the cravings of his own nature to the common interests of mankind, he has appeared inattentive to the needs of other persons. Instead of recognising the differences between men and women in their pursuit of disparate goals, he is said to have imagined a world in which the people act as one, prompted by the solidarity of their shared general will. Nowhere is his neglect of individual aspirations and behaviour more conspicuous and sinister, according to his detractors, than with regard to his conception of freedom. To speak of liberty as obedience to a law which we prescribe to ourselves, as Rousseau defines it in the *Social Contract*,[1] is to confuse true freedom with a collective obligation that restricts it. His conception of liberty under the rule of an absolute sovereign not only submerges the fundamental distinctions between free individuals which he ought to have been anxious to preserve; it also ascribes liberty to those very powers of the state which interfere with it most gravely. To the extent that freedom is the central principle of his philosophy, it seems that Rousseau was determined to destroy the very ideal for which he stands.

His misinterpretation of the meaning of liberty has been traced by his critics to at least four main sources. The first and most important has to do with his confusion of our private and public domains and his focus upon freedom through state control. No other major political thinker has ever been so foolish as to suppose that a sovereign citizen assembly was the instrument of each individual's personal freedom. Contrary to Adam Smith and other liberal writers of his day, Rousseau was convinced that everything depends upon politics[2] and that a properly constituted state, in promoting the virtue of its subjects, secured their liberty as well. In this belief, it is alleged, he failed to grasp that actual states, however constituted, always threaten freedom, which can only be protected by keeping state powers in check.

Second, it is complained that he lacked any notion of individual rights. In extolling the merits of state control over human affairs in general he not only failed to distinguish our private from our public activities; he equally overlooked the fundamental demarcations between separate persons. He had no conception of natural property rights, such as Locke or Diderot had espoused, which every state was bound to respect. Nor, like John Stuart Mill in the next century, did he believe that the liberty of individuals in society required their protection from the tyranny of public opinion as well as from state powers. Social solidarity stemming from shared beliefs was, in principle, as congenial to Rousseau as the spirit of fraternity engendered by participation in the making of law, and in both cases he appears to have defined liberty in terms of collective action rather than individual choice.

Third, he has been assailed by his liberal critics for adopting the idea of the infinite malleability of human nature, which they correlate with his belief in the limitless powers of the state. To such readers his view of moral perfectibility raises the terrible spectre of mass political indoctrination, in accordance with ideals which violate our ordinary sense of personal freedom. Unlike Montesquieu or Hume, among his contemporaries, Rousseau claimed that it is better to make men what they must be than to deal with them as they are.[3] If, as he supposed, our moral nature is shaped by our governments,[4] then good governments may be deemed to manufacture human virtue no less than bad governments produce vice. Yet nothing could be more injurious to freedom than the refabrication of men's characters in accordance with a state's scheme for the enhancement of virtue, especially since the liberty Rousseau conceived in his *Social Contract* involved the transformation of each individual from a solitary being into part of a greater whole.[5] Modern totalitarian regimes, it is alleged, have aspired to reshape human nature in a strikingly similar way.

Fourth, the agents of such authoritarian manipulation – whether lawgivers that create new states, or sovereign assemblies presiding in them, or tutors entrusted with the care of children – are deemed, in Rousseau's phrase, to force men to be free.[6] Citizens and pupils alike imagine themselves masters of their own will, and yet all their wishes accord with those of the persons who have framed the world they inhabit. The more completely our natural independence is annihilated by our lawgivers, Rousseau suggests in the *Social Contract*, the more perfect are our shared institutions.[7] Kant, who upheld a similarly dualist view of human nature, could not have subscribed to such an authoritarian approach to the manufacture of freedom. How perverse of Rousseau to elaborate an idea of liberty which infiltrates the recesses of our mind, and permeates all the activities of which we suppose ourselves the agents, just when we have been subjected to the will of others who have altered our constitution as they see fit.

These, roughly, are the principal charges against Rousseau that can be distilled, at least in part, from the writings of De Maistre or Constant in the early nineteenth century, and from Jacob Talmon or Lester Crocker today. I take it that the contemporary libertarian response to his political philosophy, moreover, incorporates all such allegations and, no doubt, many others as well. To my mind, they are serious charges, levelled against an author whose professed love of freedom rings out from almost every page of his works. How could Rousseau have so strangely misconceived the meaning of a principle he held so dear? His admirers certainly have a case to answer, and they should take little comfort from the fact that other detractors of a more collectivist persuasion – Hegel, Proudhon and Marx, for instance – have complained instead of his narrowly individualist idea of freedom and the lack, as they see it, of an overarching political or underlying social dimension within which true liberty can be fulfilled. Such dimensions have, of course, already been uncovered by his libertarian critics, to his cost, at almost every turn, but Rousseau is not alone among major thinkers in having garnered together utterly contradictory objections.

Some friendly commentators of a liberal disposition have in recent years attempted to blunt the challenge of his critics by closer examination of those safeguards for individual liberty which he introduced to curtail the abuse of sovereign power. Robert Derathé, for instance, perhaps the most distinguished contemporary interpreter of his political philosophy, has focused upon the supremacy of natural law in Rousseau's doctrine and upon the illegitimacy of any popular assembly's transgression of this precept of reason and God. Somewhat like Howard Warrender in his reading of Hobbes, Derathé has stressed the importance for Rousseau of a divine framework which circumscribes our obligations in society and which sets limits to the powers that may be rightfully exercised by the sovereign of any state.[8] John Plamenatz has instead addressed himself to the reflexive nature of Rousseau's conception of duty, according to which persons who are mutually dependent upon one another accept in law a discipline they find necessary as morally responsible agents. In so far as our individual appetites are often stronger than our shared desire to abide by the rule of law, our sense of political obligation may be seen, he argues, as constraining and liberating us at the same time.[9] Ralph Leigh, by contrast, has placed special emphasis on Rousseau's conception of religious toleration, which, unlike that of Locke, for instance, could admit atheists to membership of the state.[10] Other, predominantly liberal, defenders of Rousseau's politics have responded to critics who accuse him of advocating totalitarian democracy by reminding their readers of how inimical to freedom he judged any continuous assembly of the people, and by emphasising his strictures on the need for multifarious particular wills within every state, without whose tensions and opposition the formation of a true general will was impossible.

There is much to commend in these readings of Rousseau, each of which, to my mind, is immeasurably better informed as to his meaning than are the charges to which they respond. Yet they nevertheless strike me as rather too tame in his defence. In deflecting the blows of crude attacks they seem to me to lose some of the force of Rousseau's own pronouncements on liberty, which fired the imagination of so many followers in the course of the French Revolution and were judged no less incendiary by such contemporary critics as Voltaire and Burke. I propose therefore to address Rousseau's views on freedom here in a manner somewhat different from Derathé, Plamenatz and Leigh and mean to respond to some of the charges against him by suggesting certain ways in which he may himself have anticipated the complaints of his critics. Of course, as a political thinker who always counselled restraint, Rousseau could scarcely imagine that he might one day be accused of having inspired the worst excesses of totalitarian despotism. Even the liberation of the whole of humanity, he once remarked, did not justify shedding the blood of a single man.[11] But he formulated his ideas of freedom in response to other doctrines which he believed had misdescribed it and against a political background from which he thought it had been wiped away. I believe Rousseau would have found such absence of real freedom and similar misconceptions about its meaning to be no less characteristic of our own epoch than of the regimes of his day. And if such baleful continuities would have prompted him to seek solitude and refuge from the tribulations of our world too, I hope they may at least provide some justification for my pursuit here of an otherwise anachronistic reading of his thought.

II

Perhaps the most serious censure of his political philosophy has turned upon his assimilation of liberty to popular sovereignty, a link commonly perceived as discredited in both theory and practice under the Jacobin dictatorship of the French Revolution. There is no doubt that this conjunction of liberty with sovereignty forms an original theme in his writings, setting Rousseau apart from such precursors as Plato, Machiavelli and Montesquieu, who like him were concerned with political and not just personal liberty. Before he imbued it with a new meaning, the concept of sovereignty had been connected by its interpreters with the idea of force, power or empire, and it generally pertained to the dominion of kings or other governors over their subjects rather than to citizens' freedom. But in identifying the supreme authority of the state as the subjects themselves, Rousseau ascribed sovereignty to the ruled as well as to the ruling element, and he connected it with the concepts of will or right rather than force of power – that is, with *le moral* of politics and not *le physique*, a fundamental distinction in his philosophy to which I shall return presently. Yet is it not just because of his innovative association of an altogether unlikely pair of terms – in effect, *liberty*, as drawn from an ancient republican tradition with its emphasis upon self-rule, and *sovereignty*, from a modern absolutist ideology addressed to the need for a predominating power – that liberal critics have found Rousseau's doctrine to be so remarkably sinister in design? How can absolute force and perfect liberty possibly go hand in hand? The suggestion that citizens may be 'forced to be free' seems one of the vilest deceptions imaginable from an author claiming to be liberty's truest friend.

Rousseau, however, attempted to meet the charge that his conception of absolute popular sovereignty threatened our freedom by defining it in such a way as to exclude precisely that infliction of harm upon persons which his theory is alleged to justify. The authority of the sovereign, he insisted, must come from all and apply to all.[12] The voice of the general will which it enacts cannot pronounce on individuals without forfeiting its own legitimacy, since it articulates in laws the common interest of every citizen, whereas the exercise of force over disparate persons is reserved exclusively for a nation's government. Rousseau's sovereign never implements its own laws and never punishes transgressors against it,[13] nor, indeed, forces anyone to be free.

More than any other major political theorist before or after him Rousseau distinguished 'right' from 'power', the formulation of principle from its application, or, in this context, the moral will which determines laws from the physical force that administers them, by placing each in different hands – here, respectively, the legislative power and the executive power. Critics misread the meaning of this unique passage of his works in which he describes force as the agent of liberty when they attribute to Rousseau the view that the punishment we suffer for flouting the law renders us truly free. For such force as only governments may apply to recalcitrants was designed, he maintained, to protect them from personal dependence, which invariably *does* deprive individuals of their freedom, and to legitimate their own civil undertakings, without which the social contract would be 'absurd, tyrannical and liable to the gravest abuse'.[14] Rousseau believed that according to the terms of their association, all subjects undertook to obey the laws and that without exception they were then required to take part in the laws' formulation as members of their state's sovereign assembly. His point about force and freedom means scarcely more than that citizens must always be bound by their own agreements, even if they are occasionally inclined to break or overlook them. No force is exercised except over persons who have reneged on their decision to abide by laws they enact themselves, and no force at all is exercised in the state by the sovereign, or by unarmed lawgivers or powerless tutors.

The tyrannical abuse of authority which liberal critics impute to Rousseau's sovereign was actually perceived by him to be a misappropriation of the powers of government, against which the absolute sovereignty of citizens was the only real safeguard. In their periodic election of parliamentary representatives the people of England perversely entrusted their legislative authority to what should have been merely an executive power, and thereby showed themselves unfit for the liberty it was their duty to exercise directly themselves.[15] In Geneva, somewhat differently, the executive power (that is, the *Petit Conseil*) had made itself progressively more dominant by arrogating responsibilities that properly belonged to the assembly of citizens (the *Conseil Général*), even obstructing that sovereign body from meeting. With the executive force of Rousseau's native state substituted for its popular will, absolute right was corrupted into unfettered power. 'Where force alone reigns', Rousseau remarked in his *Lettres from the Mountain*, 'the state is dissolved. That . . . is how all democratic states finally perish'.[16]

In the light of such claims it is worth bearing in mind that Rousseau's conception of civil liberty in the *Social Contract* was drawn as much from an idealised model of Geneva as from Spartan and Roman sources, and that his political self-identification as 'Citizen of Geneva' thus referred to a republic whose constitutional liberties, in his view, had already been undermined. The modern citizens of Geneva, no less than our primitive forebears which he portrayed in his *Discourse on Inequality*, had been deprived of their liberty as they passed under the sway of political tutelage, but in the case of his compatriots that was because they had allowed their sovereign will to be stilled and the executive power of government to rise up despotically in its stead. Paradoxically, it seems, Rousseau's conception of an absolute sovereign ensured civil liberty not so much by virtue of an overarching natural law (to which there is anyway no reference in the final version of his *Social Contract*) as on account of an infrastructural separation of powers. As is so often the case, Hobbes, for whom absolute sovereignty entailed the undivided concentration of all powers, appears to be his foremost adversary. Rousseau, no less than Locke, was determined that governments must not exercise 'force beyond right'. Unlike Locke, however, he found protection from such despotism only in a vigilant sovereign of the whole people. Liberty was thus made secure, in his view, by the very institution which, his liberal critics have since alleged, can only destroy it. So long as the general will of a community remained general, citizens kept their freedom under the rule of its laws.

I take this novel association of the ideas of sovereignty and freedom to have informed the meaning of what Rousseau termed *civil liberty*, but it must be remembered that the *Social Contract* also introduces a second positive concept of freedom, which I have mentioned already, that is *moral liberty*, or obedience to a law we prescribe over ourselves. So considered, the concept may seem to mean little more than the ancient Greek notion of autonomy, although in Rousseau's doctrine, especially in its affinities with his idea of the general will, it has distinctive connotations somewhat different from the sense of autonomy as political self-rule or independence. Both in his definition of moral liberty and in his novel use of the expression *general will*, Rousseau articulated classical principles of freedom in a modern vocabulary which may, at first glance, seem as alien to those principles as his invocation of ancient liberty in justification of modern sovereignty. Indeed, some of Rousseau's most striking images derive their force from just such attempts to illuminate the values of old cultures in a new language commonly thought to have dispensed with them, and much may be learnt about his meaning if we regard him, to use his own words (although not about himself) as one of those 'moderns who had an ancient soul'.[17]

The most distinctive feature of his concept of moral liberty, as Plamenatz has noted, is its element of self-prescription. For Rousseau, every morally free agent was required to determine the rules that would guide him by looking inward into the depths of his own conscience in a self-reliant manner, free from the influence of all other persons. The most absolute authority, he observed in his *Discourse on Political Economy*, 'is that which penetrates into man's innermost being', incorporating him in the common identity of the state, as he adds in the *Social Contract*.[18] Liberal critics recoil in horror from these claims, in so far as they take them to imply the complete submergence of our separate wills under the collective (perhaps even organic) will of the body politic which envelops and moulds us. Yet what Rousseau meant by his conjunction of moral liberty with the general will has no such significance, and it was designed to avert rather than achieve the social indoctrination of individuals. Not only did he insist upon the fact, which Leigh has underscored, that a nation's general will could only be realised through opposition to the particular wills of each of its members, so that the constant tension between two kinds of will, and not the suppression of one by the other, proved indispensable to the achievement of the common good.[19] He also stressed that the same opposition was present in the minds of all citizens, so that every person was motivated by both a particular and a general will, dividing his judgement of what was beneficial to himself from what was right for the community.[20] Especially in the modern world, Rousseau believed, our general will was much weaker than our particular will, and it was to be strengthened and animated, not by our imbibing the collective opinions of our neighbours in a public assembly, but just the reverse – by all men expressing their own opinions alone, 'having no communication amongst themselves', which might render their separate judgements partial to this or that group interest.[21] To ensure that in the assembly there were as many votes as individuals, every member must act without regard to the rest, consulting his own general will as a citizen, thereby still obeying himself alone. Our personal identity was only lost when in legislation we echoed the opinions of an unreflective, undiscriminating, multitude. For Rousseau, the more perfect our independence from others – the more profoundly we turned into ourselves for guidance – the more likely were our deliberations to yield the common good.

In the social contract state which he envisaged, deep introspection was therefore the corollary of the outward pursuit of that common good or public interest. As has been frequently noted before, the idea of 'will', in this context, expresses the voluntarist, contractarian, strain of modern political thought, whereas what is general encapsulates the ancient idea of a public good towards which each person's will should be aimed. It follows that, according to Rousseau's philosophy, in order to be a citizen of a *res publica* one must look deep within oneself for a personal commitment to a collective goal. Of course, in promoting the general will, it is our dedication to the shared good of all which renders our moral liberty, as he conceived it, so much grander and more noble than the natural freedom he claimed men forfeit when they enter into civil society. But that belief in an uplifting form of liberty, so often decried by his critics, requires for its fulfilment no great leap forward into the modern world of totalitarian democracy. It is, rather, an expression of a wholly familiar ancient idea of liberty that Rousseau drew from his reading of Cicero, Seneca, Plutarch and other classical sources, and then more latterly from Machiavelli, Montaigne and Montesquieu. Already in his writings he contrasted that conception of liberty with what he took to be the ill-considered modern notion of personal freedom which had been introduced by Hobbes, whereas after the French Revolution Constant and other liberals were to reverse his preferences by associating true liberty with privacy and individual rights as against the ancient ideal which he had upheld, but which in their judgement had given rise to the worst excesses of Jacobin tyranny.

We have only to turn to Rousseau's *Considerations on the Government of Poland* to note how passionate was his commitment to ancient political liberty as against the modern, individualist, notion. In a chapter of that work entitled 'The spirit of ancient institutions' Rousseau grieved over the civil and moral liberty we had lost in passing from antiquity into the modern world, much as in other contexts he lamented our forsaken natural liberty, destroyed in the abandonment of our primeval state. 'Modern men', he wrote, 'no longer find in themselves any of that spiritual vigour which inspired the ancients in everything that they did'.[22] Ancient legislators sought to forge links that would attach citizens to their fatherland and to one another, in religious ceremonies, games and spectacles. The laws that rule modern men, by contrast, are solely designed to teach them to obey their masters.

In his *Letter to d'Alembert* on the theatre he pursued a similar theme, complaining that we have lost all the strength of the men of antiquity. Whereas the festive citizens of Sparta assembled in the open air and consecrated their lives to great matters of state, the shady inhabitants of modern republics only come together for private meetings and intrigue.[23] Ancient liberty had been lost, according to Rousseau, largely because of its displacement from the public arena into the world of private affairs. Where today, he asked, is 'the concord of citizens'? 'Where is public fraternity . . . liberty . . . innocence?'[24] The term *fraternity* cited here in conjunction with liberty does not figure often in Rousseau's works, however much its meaning resonates so clearly in his conception of the general will and indeed throughout his political writings as a whole. But it does figure again in his *Considerations on the Government of Poland*, where he proclaimed the need for Polish youth to become accustomed to 'equality' and 'fraternity', 'living under the eyes of their compatriots, seeking public approbation'.[25]

By so linking the ideas of liberty, equality and fraternity, Rousseau – in this as in so much else – heralded an incoming French Revolution with his gaze fixed upon a bygone ancient world. Without equality, he observed in the *Social Contract*, 'freedom cannot subsist', for between the estate of the rich man and the pauper, public liberty is always traded; the one buys, and the other sells. 'Each is equally fatal to the common good'.[26] For that common good to be promoted, he added in his *Project for a Constitution for Corsica*, it was necessary that 'no one should enrich himself'.[27] In the feast of the grape harvesters which he portrayed in his *New Héloïse*, moreover, all three principles were drawn together. 'Everyone lives under the most intimate familiarity', he wrote; 'all the world is equal'. At dinner each gaily joins with all the rest, in 'sweet equality' but without luxury, in the enjoyment of liberty limited only by perfect candour.[28]

That exultant feast in which all partake freely, equally and fraternally was of course purely imaginary; and no doubt similarly fanciful was Rousseau's belief that it reflected, or even surpassed in joy, the saturnalian banquets of the ancient Romans. But there is no doubting the fact that the concept of liberty which his image evokes is altogether different from the modern idea of personal freedom. For in the contemporary world, as he perceived it, liberty had come to be shorn of its associations with equality and fraternity. Rousseau observed in his

Essay on the Origin of Languages that whereas our ancestors had once sung *aimez-moi* and cried out *aidez-moi* to one another, we now only mutter *donnez de l'argent*.[29] The same expression, repeated in the *Social Contract*, is described there as the harbinger of a society in chains, ruled by the slavish institution of finance, unknown to the men of antiquity.[30] We moderns have been transformed into mute auditors of declamations from the pulpit and proclamations from the throne, our collective voice stilled. Where once our interests were openly shared and inscribed in our hearts, now they are in conflict, secreted away in the linings of our purses. Have we forgotten that once we aspire to serve the state with our purses rather than our person, it is on the edge of ruin? Have we forgotten that in a well-ordered city everyone flies to the assemblies?[31] Modern liberty, stripped of fraternity, on the one side, and of equality, on the other, stands exposed as nothing more than private gain. But so far from it embracing the only proper use of the term *liberty*, the contemporary ethos of private gain was for Rousseau just ancient slavery in a modern form, all the more psychologically insidious for our pursuing it as if it were real freedom. Turned inward on himself and outward against his neighbours, modern man in fact, like primeval man in fiction, had run headlong into chains which he supposed had made him free.

III

I have so far addressed myself only to Rousseau's conceptions of civil and moral liberty, as they figure in the *Social Contract* and are elaborated in his other political writings. Both of these notions are linked with his view of sovereignty, and, in the terminology of Isaiah Berlin, they may be deemed *positive* concepts of liberty, directed as they are towards an ideal of self-determination by citizens in their conduct of public affairs.[32] Yet they scarcely embrace all of Rousseau's reflections on freedom. On the contrary, his most fundamental principle was not that of liberty within the state, but rather of freedom outside it, and whereas his political conceptions may have been inspired by republican images of antiquity, his more general idea revolved around the liberty we had lost in subjecting ourselves to the trappings of culture and civil society as a whole.

In his first *Discourse on the Arts and Sciences* Rousseau charged that civilisation had been the bane of humanity and that men in society had forsaken, as he put it, 'that original liberty for which they seem to have been born'.[33] It is this deprivation of the freedom for which we had been born that in Rousseau's philosophy marked our passage from nature to culture and our enslavement in the stultifying social world we had constructed. In his *Discourse on Inequality* he developed that proposition largely in terms of the subjugation of our freedom attributable to private property and all the morally pernicious institutions and forms of government built upon such a miserable base. Liberty, he exclaimed there, was an essential gift of Nature, which men possessed by virtue of their humanity alone[34] – an attribute which thus could only be impaired and not fulfilled through our political undertakings. In his *Essay on the Origin of Languages* he put forward much the same thesis in terms of the corruption of our speech that had occurred in the course of our social history, as modern languages, increasingly devoid of their original musical inflection, had rendered those who spoke them progressively more passive, servile and unfree. These themes occur throughout Rousseau's works and lie at or very near the heart of most of them. However sharp was the contrast between his own account of the state of nature and that of Hobbes, he certainly agreed with Hobbes that our fundamental liberty was to be found there, and not under the political hegemony of any sovereign's rule.

As distinct from Hobbes, however, Rousseau is alleged by his liberal critics to have believed in an illusory form of freedom, which was realised when men were bound by civil laws, or 'artificial chains', as Hobbes described them. That illusion of freedom can indeed be found in Rousseau's doctrine, but only because it is explicit in his argument, in his claim that civil society was fabricated from it. Throughout the course of our history, he contended, we have made ourselves slaves just because we have been credulous, 'running headlong into our chains', he remarked, 'supposing that [we] had ensured our freedom'.[35] How else could we have accepted the yoke of despotism but because it had been wrapped around us like a mantle of justice? No sphere of our social life, he believed, had escaped the ravages of such self-delusion. In his conception of private property as the crucial institution marking our passage from the natural to the civil state, he of course raised an economic dimension of striking significance in his political thought, addressed as it was to the class origins of different constitutions and to the perpetual conflict, at least of interest, between rich and poor. So strong was the link he perceived between inequalities of wealth and deprivations of freedom (in effect between poverty and slavery) that we might even with some justice ascribe to Rousseau an economic theory of history, indeed a theory of economic determinism, according to which our political systems were shaped by forces of a still more fundamental kind. But we must bear in mind that in his account of private property Rousseau placed greatest emphasis upon the cunning eloquence of those who claimed that right, and on the foolishness of persons so readily beguiled. Rhetoric, persuasion and deception were as central to his account of how we had ensnared ourselves as was the institution of private property, established through the manipulation and abuse of language. Property, as Rousseau conceived it, was thus more than the economic mainspring of human bondage; it was also an emblematic expression of the fixation of social man in an abstract world of his own making.

Rousseau's whole theory of culture, moreover, reinforces, elaborates and embellishes this conception of the illusory bonds under which political slavery masquerades as freedom. Our arts, letters and sciences, he remarked in his first *Discourse*, are but 'garlands of flowers round the iron chains by which [men] are weighed down'.[36] Contemporary theatre, he complained in his *Letter to d'Alembert*, not only makes an adornment of the most terrible vices but also promotes and increases the inequalities of fortunes, which is incompatible with the preservation of liberty. Music, displaced from its springs of poetry and melody, he lamented in his *Essay on the Origin of Languages*, has become a collection of artificial scales and listless harmonies, echoed in speech by the prosaic rhetoric of mountebank kings and charlatan priests.[37] Just as in society we have come to be enmeshed within hierarchical moral relations, so in music we have become enthralled by the calculation of harmonic intervals, each measuring the loss of our independence under artificial chains more insidious than any imagined by Hobbes, each a proof of the strength of our illusions and the captivating power of the instruments of our captivity. When liberals decry Rousseau's commitment to an uplifting form of positive liberty that threatens our true freedom, they forget how profoundly negative was his philosophy of history, according to which our liberty had been lost already. Others might suppose that individuals gained their freedom as society developed and its arts and sciences were perfected. For Rousseau, every stride in the apparent advance of civilisation had in reality been a step towards the decrepitude of our species and the alienation of our fundamental liberty.[38]

Of course it must be remembered that his idea of natural liberty was in an important sense illusory as well, in so far as mankind never actually inhabited the innocent pristine state in which such liberty could be enjoyed. According to Rousseau's philosophy, as he remarked himself, in order to get at the truth it was often necessary to lay the facts aside, and although we must not exaggerate this distinction, since he drew much of the evidence for his portrait of primitive man from the available historical record of our origins, it remains the case that the state of nature he conceived was a fiction. There could therefore be no point in our attempting to return to it, he noted in a long discussion on the subject in his *Discourse on Inequality*;[39] there was no sense in our trying to recover the merely hypothetical freedom he had ascribed to mankind in that state. Critics who believe that in his political doctrine Rousseau sought to re-establish the independence from one another which we had lost rather neglect this feature of his thought, and they also overlook his repeated claims that in political society man's nature is transformed.[40] With duty substituted for instinct as our guide, Rousseau observed, our constitution is altered, and our lives are reshaped. Good social institutions do not fulfil human nature but instead *denature* man, depriving him of the wholeness of his physical existence in exchange for a moral existence that is relative and partial. For these very reasons, Rousseau's liberal critics have been wrong to locate his fundamental account of freedom in the state. The liberty that was most expressive of human nature in his philosophy could not be gained or restored in a new form under the institutions he described in the *Social Contract*. Nowhere did he map out a programme for the political redemption of our freedom, made progressively more remote from our grasp as civilisation and society advanced relentlessly towards our subjection.

Indeed, it is almost everywhere else apart from in his political writings that we find Rousseau longing for and attempting to preserve that fragile independence of the human spirit that in the modern world was at least akin to natural liberty. A passionate desire to find freedom informed his botanical communion with Nature in his later years, when the company of other men had become so burdensome to him. Earlier it had inspired his disenchantment with much of the Enlightenment establishment, from whose dark and oppressive influence he had sought refuge in his escape from Paris. Rousseau's uncompromising, if eventually unsuccessful, determination to refuse the pensions that were offered to him, his contempt for urban artifice and culture and his love of the open sky outside the closed city – indeed, much of his life, and most of its crises – were inspired by this essentially solitary dreamer's rapturous attachment to uncultivated Nature. 'I was never really fit for civil society', he wrote with weary resignation in his *Reveries*, his last major work. 'My natural independence always left me incapable of the thraldom necessary for anyone who wishes to live among men'.[41] The isolationist lines of Defoe's *Robinson Crusoe* formed a better guide to his deepest affections even than the consolidating paths of Plato's *Republic*.

In their neglect of these central features of his philosophy of history, perhaps the most striking of his critics' omissions is the very definition of our fundamental liberty which Rousseau put forward. For the freedom we had suppressed, he believed, was no uplifting principle of public virtue but only a faint distinction between savage man and beast. All other creatures, he remarked in the *Discourse on Inequality*, behaved as their instincts impelled them to do, while we alone, even in our original state, must have been the authors of our actions, as we came to terms with each situation in a manner free from Nature's control. It was therefore because we lacked a set of prescribed responses to our natural drives rather than because we were endowed with any positive traits unique to our species that, according to Rousseau, we must always have enjoyed a prospect of development – in due course out of the state of nature and into another of our own making – which animals did not share.[42]

This idea of liberty as a merely inchoate trait distinguishing man from beast is perhaps the most remarkably negative conception of freedom in Western social and political thought. In Rousseau's philosophy it was linked to no substantive goal or desirable end of any sort, being without a determinant moral content such as his critics have judged to be the principal illiberal characteristic of his doctrine in general. Quite the contrary, Rousseau's conception of our natural liberty was at least partly designed to show how other accounts of freedom were inadequate just because they were not negative enough, a thesis which he developed above all in response to Hobbes, whose reflections on this subject he found wanting for two reasons.

First, Hobbes had failed to grasp the fact, so central to our plight, as Rousseau understood it, that persons may render themselves subject to internal impediments, which in their operation upon the human spirit were no less a constraint upon their freedom than shackles round their wrists or threats to box their ears. Any suggestion that we might be or become slaves to our passions was as absurd for Hobbes as the correlative idea of a disembodied freedom of the will, but freedom of the will and the absence of human slavery to innate passions were for Rousseau crucial to that otherwise scarcely perceptible *differentia* between man and beast. If we were not at least capable of being the agents of what we did, if it was only our appetites and aversions that moved us, then our lives were just a succession of events that happened to us, lacking all merit, vice or perfectibility, with each member of our species trapped in the same changeless world as all the others. Without free will, he supposed, both morality and human history were impossible. In his opposition to Hobbes on this point, Rousseau's view that our distinctive qualities were not wholly explicable with reference to natural causes or impulsions comes to much the same verdict as Isaiah Berlin's contention in his essay on 'Historical inevitability' that if determinism were true then we would not be free to act in a morally responsible way.[43] No less than for Berlin in his understanding of moral agency, for Rousseau the language of free will lay at the heart of our ordinary perception of social relations – with this difference, of course, that according to Rousseau our history bore witness to our becoming slaves to new passions, that is, to the fundamental and ever worsening abuse of our liberty, rather than, as for Berlin, to diverse cases of its exercise for better or worse.

Rousseau's second reason for regarding Hobbes's conception of liberty as insufficiently negative has to do with the fact that Hobbes had, in his view, drawn too complex a picture of human nature in support of his belief that the freedom of each person was imperilled by that of all his neighbours. In ascribing certain socially developed characteristics of our lives, such as the pursuit of power and glory, to humanity in general, Hobbes had wrongly supposed that masterless men were naturally in need of a commonwealth for protection. This is to say that he found fault with human nature mainly because, in Rousseau's terminology, he mistook *amour propre* for *amour de soi*, imagining that we cared for ourselves at the expense of others rather than without regard to them. Much the same error, moreover, was held by Rousseau to be a common failing of most philosophies of natural law and the social contract, including those of Grotius, Locke and Pufendorf, who attributed rather more benign qualities or principles, such as a sense of justice or community or a right of property, to mankind in the state of nature. All such thinkers had failed to strip away our social traits from their postulates about the essence of the human race as a whole; according to Rousseau, they had confused our acquired attributes with what was fundamental to our constitution.

Yet in their focus upon his unduly collectivist conception of liberty, critics of Rousseau's illiberalism forget that he claimed time and again that it was just because we had already made ourselves social that we had forsaken our freedom. While savage man lives within himself, Rousseau remarked, 'sociable man, always outside himself, only knows how to live in the opinions of others'.[44] Our natural integrity, and with it our freedom from one another, had been lost just because we had come to value ourselves in the light of qualities that we imagined others judged worthy of esteem. Rousseau agreed with Hobbes that the natural life of man must have been solitary, but it could only have become poor, nasty, brutish and short when subject to the fears and aspirations of a social world he did not at first inhabit. The more negative our approach to an understanding of human nature, the less negative, or, at any rate, the less defective, appears the state of nature we uncover.

As is well known, Rousseau believed that civil society must originally have been founded when men, already socialised by vice, attempted to obtain Locke's political warrant for the morally pernicious institution of private property, which in turn must have occasioned Hobbes's vile state of war, fought over the distribution of property. Rather like the debauched protagonists of the Marquis de Sade's *The New Justine*, the so-called natural men portrayed first by Locke and then Hobbes might well have said of themselves, 'No sooner did we commit a horror than we sought to legitimate it'.[45] These two thinkers and others had inadvertently drawn an accurate picture of the state of civil society, supposing it to be a description of the state of nature, for the vices in need of remedy which they depicted were not those of our original constitution but rather those that stemmed from the very social systems they commended to us. According to Rousseau, in short, Hobbes, Locke and other jurisprudential defenders of civil society had conceived their ideas as solutions to some problems of which those solutions were in fact the cause.[46]

Liberal thinkers since the end of the eighteenth century, and libertarians more recently, have apparently inherited Hobbes's and Locke's concern with inviolable frontiers, safeguards and barriers between persons; but Rousseau would have been the first to remark that this was because their philosophies are imbued with many of the assumptions about our essential motives, fears and desires that his social contract precursors had confused for natural traits. To that extent their views of human nature seem overburdened with the weight of attributes they believe universally characteristic of mankind; and, tied to these encumbrances, they stand apart from Rousseau's emptier, more formal, more strictly negative, conception of our distinguishing behavioural traits – unique only because, in his judgement, they are uncontrolled by instincts. Paradoxically, it is at least some of the doctrines of negative liberty so often contrasted with his positive idea which in contemporary political thought constitute the prevailing forms of 'the retreat to the inner citadel', as Berlin has termed it. In the light of the argument Rousseau himself presents, we could only retreat to citadels we had already taken the trouble to construct, and we were only prompted to seek sanctuary there because we had contrived to make enemies outside.

IV

This account of Rousseau's conceptions of liberty may not be exhaustive, although I confess that it was meant to be, partly because I believe that it embraces most specific applications of the word *liberté* in his philosophy, and partly because I know of no other expressions of the term which he employed beyond *liberté civile*, *liberté morale* and *liberté naturelle*. Conversely, I think that it would be a mistake to dwell on the absence from his writings of such ideas as freedom of conscience, or of speech, or of the press, on the grounds that these individualist notions are excluded by his collectivist approach. Leaving aside some complexities of translation and contextual problems raised by principles addressed to different issues from those he broached himself, there seems to me no reason to regard those freedoms as alien to or irreconcilable with his ideals. Indeed, Rousseau argued passionately that each individual's conscience was the sole guide to religious faith, and it may be said, with some justice, that he perceived his own life as an outspoken expression of the freedom of conscience of a man who at every turn confronted forces seeking to deny him freedom of the press.

It does not follow from this that Rousseau approved of liberty in all human activities. He judged free love to be an abuse of the proper relations between men and women in civilised societies, and he supposed that, at least in small republics, freedom of the stage only undermined the integrity of onlookers, transfixed by a spectacle in which they played no part. To the extent that he associated liberty with the virtue of citizens, he showed no sympathy for either sexual licentiousness or theatrical licence, which he deemed incompatible with self-restraint, on the one hand, and with public engagement, on the other. With regard to these matters, no less than the idea of personal freedom, the contrasts between his political theory and the doctrines of liberals and libertarians remain sharp.

More difficult to explain, perhaps, if only because Marxists and libertarians alike have held it against him, is his apparent lack of any idea of economic freedom. Yet in that charge, too, I believe that his critics are mistaken. Not only did Rousseau anticipate a Marxian conception of slavery built round the institution of private property; as we have seen, he also stressed the need for economic equality as a condition of civil and moral liberty. Of course Rousseau differed from Marx in denying that the abolition of slavery required the abolition of property as well. According to his social doctrine, that would have shifted responsibility for human subjection from the rich in society to a state that was no less oppressive, thereby bringing the principle of equality into conflict with that of liberty. But the fact that Rousseau rejected any socialist notion of the expropriation of private property scarcely warrants the criticism that he lacked an idea of economic freedom.[47]

Neither is that complaint warranted by his difference from libertarians. If we may regard Smith's idea of the link between economic freedom and the public interest as a principle approved by libertarians which had already been enunciated in his own lifetime, I think we can ascribe this difference to three sources. First, Rousseau denied that the public interest of a state could be achieved by each citizen's pursuit of private gain. In his terminology, that would be to confuse the general will with the will of all, which was no more than the aggregated particular wills of individuals and was always distinct from the interest of the community as a whole. Second, he was opposed to the inegalitarian distribution of wealth, which he believed invariably puts liberty up for auction. To discourage relations of personal dependence which were fatal to the common good, Rousseau contended that states should ensure that no citizen was so wealthy as to purchase another's freedom, nor so indigent as to be obliged to give his freedom away. Third, he held that the accumulation of wealth, however distributed, was itself inimical to the public good. Commerce, luxury, opulence and all the trappings of advanced civilisation bore witness, in his view, to moral corruption rather than economic freedom, and he believed that persons who acquired great fortunes were as much ensnared by their unnatural avarice as were the poor by their envy. Smith and Marx together might both have been persuaded that freedom and prosperity went hand in hand, but for Rousseau these were incompatible objectives.

It may be said that the positive and negative conceptions of liberty which I have ascribed to him share a common frame of reference, since each excludes any idea of personal dependence, either to the will of other individuals, or indeed to one's own passions in society. But in discriminating between the civil and natural states in which they largely figure, and which Rousseau continually distinguished in his political theory, I have tried, rather, to emphasise the contrasts between them. Civil and moral liberty were associated by him with the notion of *l'homme moral*, whereas natural liberty was ascribed instead to *l'homme physique*. The same dichotomy generally sets apart love from sex, in his writings, as well as authority from power, right from force, even legislation from government. And just as in his *Discourse on Inequality* he maintained that our moral distinctions could not be attributed to any natural differences between us, so likewise he attempted to disengage two fundamentally opposed ideas of freedom. As he observes in the *Social Contract*, civil and moral liberty require for their achievement the alienation of our original freedom.[48] In political society we do not make our natural liberty secure, but renounce it in exchange for liberty of another sort. 'Give man entirely to the state or leave him entirely to himself', Rousseau concluded in a fragment 'On public happiness',[49] for the contradiction between our desires and our duties renders our condition miserable. Men could not possibly enjoy both forms of liberty together.

Neither form of liberty, it is as well to remember, had ever been enjoyed by individuals at all, for Rousseau identified both his positive and negative conceptions with a fictitious past, one ancient, and the other antediluvian. Each was drawn from a different imaginary world which mankind had lost, and each illuminated the world he inhabited himself only in the sense that the governments of his day had betrayed them. It is true that, towards the end of his life, when he agreed to draft constitutions for Corsica and Poland, he conceived plans to enshrine his principles in the institutions of actual states. But judging from the experience of Corsica, which was invaded, and Poland, which was partitioned, each soon after he set out his programme for the achievement of their freedom, the impact of his ideas upon those few specific political causes which he advanced should have been more a matter of concern to his friends than alarm to his enemies.

If Rousseau largely despaired of men's achievement of civil and moral liberty in the modern world, still less did he suppose that they might be won in the future. In *Emile* he anticipated the demise of European monarchies in a century of revolutions,[50] but that was not a prospect which he welcomed. Nowhere did he propose any revolutionary transformations of corrupt society into new republics of virtue, and it cannot be stressed too strongly that he wished to avert rather than promote revolution and spurned the idea of overthrow, through violence, of any of the governments of his day. The uplifting enhancement of our social relations which he envisaged was all entirely in his dreams and reveries, inspired by what in his *Moral Letters* he called the 'devouring strength' and 'noble distraction' of 'sublime delirium'.[51] While 'the world of reality has its limits', he exclaimed, 'the world of imagination is infinite'.[52] Transported into the domain of reverie, like his own fictitious pupil Emile, Rousseau could drink from the waters of oblivion, the past effacing itself from his memory, with a new horizon opening up before him.[53] There, in savouring the solitary enjoyment of undisturbed natural liberty, he could contemplate a social world of perfect civil and moral liberty as well.

It is perhaps such flights of fancy which offend Rousseau's liberal critics most of all. In his dreams he appears to raise what they perceive as the nightmare prospect of reshaping human nature in accordance with ideals that violate their sense of personal freedom. How else, they ask, are we to understand his account of lawgivers – those persons who occupy an extraordinary position in the state, attempting to 'change . . . human nature' and 'transform each individual' from a solitary person into a fragment of a whole community?[54] Does this idea not suggest the complete indoctrination of our minds under governments more despotic than any ever previously experienced? Have we not finally witnessed, in the totalitarian world of Hitler and Stalin, how Rousseau's monstrous ideal of the lawgiver may be given real substance?

In reply to his detractors, it is perhaps pointless to recollect his insistence that the lawgiver was the father of a nation and not its ruler, that he had no subjects but instead inspired individuals to form their own new state, and that, if he miraculously succeeded in transforming human nature, this was because his divine eloquence had persuaded others to establish a sovereign for themselves. Never mind the fact that Rousseau's lawgivers – principally Moses, Lycurgus and Numa – were for the most part ancient prophets and guides who had pointed the way to men's achievement of civil and moral liberty such as had been unknown to them before. In probing the metamorphoses of human nature which Rousseau conceived in his dreams on the model of ancient myths, his liberal critics resolutely uncover a vision of an alternative world that they judge dangerously abhorrent. Yet where else but in his dreams could Rousseau find escape from the social and political tyrannies under which liberals believe their true freedom is enjoyed already? Where else but in reverie could Rousseau's imagination have come to legislate for all mankind? Why is it that his critics find his fanciful ideals more intolerable than all the weight of the social systems of the world that he described and they inhabit? So long as liberal principles prevail, individuals in society who are anxious to learn why their liberty seems so oppressive will find in Rousseau's works the resonant voice of a solitary prophet of the brotherhood of man.[55]

Notes

1 In Book I, ch. 8 (Pléiade III.365).
2 See Rousseau's *Confessions*, Book IX (Pléiade I.404).
3 See his *Discours sur l'économie politique* (Pléiade III.251).
4 See his preface to *Narcisse* (Pléiade II.969).
5 See the *Contrat social*, Book II, ch. 7 (Pléiade III.381).
6 In the *Contrat social*, Book I, ch. 7 (Pléiade, III.364).
7 See the *Contrat social*, Book II, ch. 7 (Pléiade, III.382).
8 See Robert Derathé, *Rousseau et la science politique de son temps*, 2nd ed. (Paris 1970), especially pp. 151–71. Cf. Howard Warrender, *The Political Philosophy of Hobbes* (Oxford 1957), pp. 97–102 and 302–11. I have addressed the subject of natural law in Rousseau's political thought elsewhere on several occasions, most recently in my 'Rousseau's Pufendorf: Natural Law and the Foundations of Commercial Society', in *History of Political Thought*, 15 (1994).
9 See John Plamenatz, '"Ce qui ne signifie autre chose qu'on le forcera d'être libre"' (originally published in vol. V of the *Annales de philosophie politique* in 1965), in *Hobbes and Rousseau*, ed. M. Cranston and R. S. Peters (New York 1972), pp. 318–32.
10 See especially Leigh's Taylorian Lecture of 26 October 1978, 'Rousseau and the Problem of Tolerance in the Eighteenth Century' (Oxford 1979).

11 See Rousseau to the comtesse de Wartensleben, letter 5450 in Leigh XXX.384–8.
12 See the *Contrat social*, Book II, ch. 4 (Pléiade III.373).
13 See the *Contrat social*, Book II, ch. 5 and Book III, ch. 1 (Pléiade III.377 and 397).
14 *Contrat social*, Book I, ch. 7 (Pléiade III.364).
15 *Contrat social*, Book III, ch. 15 (Pléiade III.430).
16 *Lettres de la montagne*, Eighth Letter (Pléiade III.815).
17 *Jugement sur la Polysynodie* (Pléiade III.643). The terms refer to the abbé de Saint-Pierre.
18 See the *Discours sur l'économie politique* and *Contrat social*, Book I, ch. 6 (Pléiade III.251 and 361).
19 See especially Rousseau's comment in a note addressed to the marquis d'Argenson's *Considérations sur le gouvernement ancien et présent de la France*, in the *Contrat social*, Book II, ch. 3 (Pléiade III.371).
20 See the *Contrat social*, Book I, ch. 7 (Pléiade III.363).
21 *Contrat social*, Book II, ch. 3 (Pléiade III.371). In the same chapter (p. 372), Rousseau insists that in a properly constituted state 'chaque Citoyen n'opine que d'après lui'. Geraint Parry's contribution to this volume is centrally addressed to the possible meanings of that passage in Rousseau's political thought.
22 *Considérations sur le gouvernement de Pologne*, ch. 2 (Pléiade III.959).
23 See the *Lettre à d'Alembert sur les spectacles*, ed. M. Fuchs (Bordeaux 1968), pp. 172–3.
24 *Ibid.*, pp. 178–9.
25 *Considérations sur le gouvernement de Pologne*, ch. 4 (Pléiade III.968).
26 *Contrat social*, Book II, ch. 11 (Pléiade III.391–2).
27 *Project de Constitution pour la Corse* (Pléiade III.924).
28 See *La Nouvelle Héloïse*, Part V, Letter 7 (Pléiade II.607–9).
29 See the *Essai sur l'origine des langues*, ed. Charles Porset, 2nd ed. (Bordeaux 1970), chs 10 and 20, pp. 131 and 197–9.
30 See the *Contrat social*, Book III, ch. 15 (Pléiade III.429). Cf. the *Projet de Constitution pour la Corse* and the *Considérations sur le gouvernement de Pologne* (Pléiade III.929 and 1004).
31 See the *Contrat social*, Book III, ch. 15 (Pléiade III.428–9).
32 See especially Isaiah Berlin's 'Two Concepts of Liberty', in his *Four Essays on Liberty* (Oxford 1969), pp. 131–41.
33 *Discours sur les sciences et les arts*, Part I (Pléiade III.7).
34 See the *Discours sur l'inégalité*, Part II (Pléiade III.184).
35 *Ibid.* (Pléiade III.177).
36 *Discours sur les sciences et les arts*, Part I (Pléiade III.7).
37 See the *Essai sur l'origine des langues*, ch. 20. pp. 197–201.
38 See the *Discours sur l'inégalité*, Part II (Pléiade III.171).
39 See the *Discours sur l'inégalité*, n. 9 (Pléiade III.202–8).

40 See the *Contrat social*, Book I, ch. 8 and Book II, ch. 7, and *Emile*, Book I (Pléiade III.364–5 and 381–2, and IV.249).
41 *Rêveries du promeneur solitaire*, Sixth Promenade (Pléiade I.1059).
42 See the *Discours sur l'inégalité*, Part I (Pléiade III.134–5 and 141–2).
43 See Berlin's 'Historical inevitability', in *Four Essays on Liberty*, especially pp. 63–6 and 73–5. Of course for Berlin, as Lester Crocker intimates in his contribution to this volume, the most appropriate place in which to identify Rousseau's main conceptions of freedom is in the tradition of positive liberty, not least because of Rousseau's conjunction of liberty with sovereignty. But it is striking how much more like Berlin Rousseau appears with regard to the subject of determinism, on which Berlin parts company from the foremost philosopher of negative liberty, Hobbes. This theme is addressed in my 'Rousseau's Perfectibilian Libertarianism', in *The Idea of Freedom: Essays in Honour of Isaiah Berlin*, ed. Alan Ryan (Oxford 1979), pp. 233–52.
44 *Discours sur l'inégalité*, Part II (Pléiade III.193).
45 *La Nouvelle Justine, ou Les Malheurs de la vertu*, in Sade's *Oeuvres complètes* (Paris 1966–7), VII.37.
46 See the *Discours sur l'inégalité*, Part II; the *Manuscrit de Genève*, Book I, ch. 2; the 'Etat de guerre'; and *Emile*, Book IV (Pléiade III.184, 288 and 610; Pléiade IV.524).
47 With respect to Rousseau's anticipations of, and differences from, Marxism, see especially John Plamenatz, *Karl Marx's Philosophy of Man* (Oxford 1975) and my 'Rousseau and Marx', in *The Nature of Political Theory*, eds David Miller and Larry Siedentop (Oxford 1983), pp. 219–46.
48 See the *Contrat social*, Book I, ch. 8 (Pléiade III.364–5).
49 'Du bonheur public' (Pléiade III.510).
50 See *Emile*, Book III (Pléiade IV.468).
51 *Lettres morales*, Letter 4 (Pléiade IV.1101).
52 *Emile*, Book II (Pléiade IV.305).
53 See *Emile et Sophie*, Letter 2 (Pléiade IV.912).
54 See the passage from *Contrat social*, Book II, ch. 7 cited for n. 5 above.
55 In a different order, and with a new first section, this essay at once compresses and recasts much material from my 'Rousseau's Two Concepts of Liberty', in *Lives, Liberties and the Public Good: New Essays in Political Theory for Maurice Cranston*, eds George Feaver and Frederick Rosen (London 1987).

10 Ursula Vogel

'But in a republic, men are needed': guarding the boundaries of liberty

Sexual difference, order and the vulnerability of liberty

To approach the theme of this collection with the question of what Rousseau has to say about 'women and liberty' would be a thankless task. It matters little in this respect whether we recall his notorious misogynist utterances or those, equal in weight and number, that celebrate women's unique capabilities, virtues and magic powers over men's hearts. On neither side does liberty come into play. Thus, the virtuous wives and mothers of Rousseau's ancient *polis* live a life of strict domestic seclusion away from the public arenas that constitute the freedom of citizens (the same entrenched boundaries between political and domestic worlds render women altogether invisible in the egalitarian republic of the *Social Contract*). The corrupt counterpart of ancient virtue in modern times – the women of *le monde* – are, like men, agents and victims of the process of civilisation. But their depravity, i.e. the distance that separates them from nature, is measured by the loss not of liberty but of shame (*pudeur*) and chastity. The same divide between incommensurable values structures the story of Emile's and Sophie's education. Not for her the journey of exploration and self-discovery that will enable him to be a natural man and his own master in the midst of civilised society. She is to be prepared for a life of unremitting submission to the dictates of propriety: 'do not allow' – thus the educator's quintessential advice to the parents of daughters – 'for a single instant in their lives that they no longer know any restraint' (*Emile*: 370). Even Julie's world, remote as it is from the placid domesticity that will be Sophie's fate, lies within clearly demarcated boundaries. Her virtue is the fruit of renunciation and self-constraint and conditional upon the unquestioning acceptance of her husband's patriarchal rule. Her freedom – if we want to call it that – resides in the inner realm of feeling and spiritual exploration. It is no accident that her miraculous garden, the mirror image of a beautiful soul in the outside world, should be a secret place hidden from view to all but her most intimate companions. Images, like these, that cast women's nature and the essential features of femininity into closed, walled-in spaces are the most characteristic and revealing rhetorical device in Rousseau's reflections on the relationship between the two sexes.

Why did Rousseau assume that liberty was the preserve of men rather than a good to be shared by all human beings irrespective of sexual difference? Given that the author of the *Second Discourse* and the *Social Contract* emphatically denied the moral and political significance of natural, merely physical distinctions among 'men', why should he have looked at the differences associated with the sexual body as if they belonged to an altogether different normative order? There is no simple answer which would successfully eliminate dissonances of this kind and magnitude. They cannot be resolved, as some of Rousseau's interpreters seem to claim, by attributing to his 'sexual politics' a deeper coherence, and a more subtle understanding of complex human relationships than is available to us today (influenced, that is, by the distorting perspectives of modern feminism) (Bloom 1991: 19; Schwartz 1984: 142–54). Nor can those dissonances be reduced to the pervasive effects of personal bias without losing sight of the important problems that Rousseau attempted to address.

Rousseau has often been singled out as the Enlightenment's most eloquent defender of women's subjection to men. Judged merely by the force and ferocity with which he denounced any quest for sexual equality as the incontrovertible sign of modern corruption, there is some truth to this claim. But he was, of course, not the only writer in his time to insist on the absolute boundaries of sexual difference (Rendall 1985: 8–24). Although his arguments are set out in a distinct and original framework they cannot be divorced from the concerns and the languages that he shared with, or had inherited from, other modes of discourse. Firstly, he shared those aspirations of eighteenth-century scientific reasoning which, as Laqueur has argued, heralded the 'invention of sex', i.e. of the sexual body as the sole determinant of male and female identity (Laqueur 1990: 198). Secondly, he drew upon a different, juridical language derived from the tradition of natural law and its emphasis on the normative structures of marriage as an hierarchical order based upon principles of rule and subordination. Thirdly and most importantly, Rousseau's perception of the different place of men and women in the moral and political order owed much to the ideal of the ancient republics. It was this legacy more than any other that led him to postulate the demarcation and, indeed, separation of male and female worlds as a necessary guarantee of public liberty. Finally, Rousseau also spoke as the representative of a new cult of sensibility and as a precursor of romanticism. In this respect, the differences between the sexes appeared less as marks of division and inequality than as complementary and equally valuable elements in the relations of mutual love.

Set out in different frameworks and often in contradictory terms, Rousseau's attempt to define and order the relation between men and women was intimately connected with his understanding of, and fear for, liberty. Gender was as central to the endeavour to chart the loss of liberty in the modern world as it was to the hope of ascertaining those exceptional circumstances under which it might still be maintained. To put it differently, Rousseau searched for principles of order which would harness sexual difference to the purposes of both personal happiness and the common good and which would, at the same time, protect the vulnerable domain of men's liberty.

Rousseau's distinctive emphasis, and the originality of his approach, derived from the endeavour to secure the conditions of liberty in an order founded on *both* the essential difference and the complementarity of men's and women's natural dispositions. He pursued this aim – and that will be the main focus of this chapter – by assigning to each sex its own and separate space: 'Such is, I said to myself, the plan of nature which gives different tastes to the two sexes so that they live apart and each in his own way' (*Letter to M. d'Alembert*: 107). This principle of demarcation 'on which all good morals depend' (*ibid.*: 107 fn.) applies to the inner world of reason and feeling as much as to the tangible political arenas of the republic. While the *Letter to M. d'Alembert* is mainly concerned to ensure the physical segregation of the sexes as the indispensable condition of political freedom, *Emile* builds the defences that are to protect a man's personal independence and self-sufficiency upon the separate education of male and female children. Postulated as each possessing its unique worth, male and female worlds are meant to complement each other. But this intention to establish the genuine equivalence of capabilities and virtues is time and again undercut by a fundamental asymmetry. It manifests itself in a rhetorical posture of recrimination which blames the fateful transgression of boundaries upon women's intrusion of a terrain that is not theirs. Men are never portrayed as the transgressors. The dualism of moral principle is equally revealed in a language of power and subjugation, dependence and constraint which tells of a need to force women into a sphere which allegedly accords with their 'nature'. And this may be one reason why Rousseau's experiment of reconciling liberty with a non-hierarchical conception of sexual difference did not succeed. He assumed both women's natural dependence on men and, equally unwarranted, their superior power of corrupting them.

Liberty and public fraternity (*Letter to M. d'Alembert*)

> Whether a monarch governs men or women ought to be rather indifferent to him, provided that he be obeyed; but in a republic, men are needed (*Letter to M. d'Alembert*: 100f.).

Reflections on the nature of women and men and on the moral principles that should govern their relationships intervene at strategic points in this impassioned speech as it moves back and forth between the two poles of modern corruption and ancient virtue. To defend the last enclave of ancient liberty in the modern world – Geneva – against the corrosive forces of modern civilisation, this is the overriding concern of Rousseau's argument in the *Letter to M. d'Alembert on the Theatre*. Because the particular circumstances and the urgency of the moment force him to take up arms against the theatre he does not, on this occasion, identify republican freedom with the principles and mechanisms of legitimate government. Rather, he seeks to ascertain the conditions of public liberty in the customs, habits and practices of everyday life which form the character of citizens. And it is from this dominant perspective upon morals (*moeurs*) that gender relations come to be of crucial importance to the constitution of liberty.

That the decadent culture of the moderns invariably leads to the ascendancy of women, on the stage as well as in the world at large, and that this subversion of the natural order of the sexes must in turn erode the foundations of republican morals, is one of the main charges that Rousseau brings against the theatre. The polemical intensity of an argument which casts the female sex, together with the ill-reputed profession of actors, the plays of Molière and the philosophy of the Enlightenment as instigators of moral corruption is bound to take most readers by surprise. Moreover, the writer who in the *Second Discourse* had exposed the hypocrisy and self-deception at the heart of social conventions and who, most importantly, had torn the mask of moral legitimacy from all forms of inequality seems in this instance to invert the status of prejudice and truth. Thus, women's claims to knowledge are derided as but the fraudulent parading of men's learning (*Letter to M. d'Alembert*: 49), their artistic talents as resulting in works 'cold and pretty like they are' (*Letter*: 103 fn.); as for female virtue, it has all but disappeared from the globe. Although the actress and the *salonnière* are made to bear most of the blame for the depravity of modern morals the focus of recrimination shifts continually between these special cases and women in general. Just as the actress in presenting herself to the eyes of all thereby incurs the stigma of the prostitute, so 'any woman who shows herself off disgraces herself' (*Letter*: 83). This is the central point on which the argument turns. And it is further reinforced by the few examples of uncorrupted female nature – by the chaste wives and mothers of the ancient republics who never appeared in public and 'kept out of men's ways' (*Letter*: 86); by simple peasant women in the Swiss mountains who 'dare not raise their eyes to men, and keep silence before them' (*Letter*: 86); by the rare case of a modest woman framed in the idyllic picture of bourgeois domesticity. In short, women can be called virtuous only to the extent that they are invisible, do not partake in speech, and keep within the strictest confines of social propriety. Chastity, exalted as the female virtue par excellence, is in Rousseau's rendering the product above all of the closed space which tangibly constrains any potential for agency. The question quoted as the voice of 'enlightenment', namely whether the common nature of women and men would not imply the same freedom, is posed only to be dismissed as empty speculation spun by 'this philosophy of the day which is born and dies in a corner of the big city' (*Letter*: 83).

It would be futile to vindicate Rousseau by defending the impartiality of such claims. They are meant to be offensive. They all revolve around the same grievance which motivates his critique and serves as its central premise. He speaks as the aggrieved citizen of a community who warns his fellow-citizens of fateful developments 'threatening from afar the public liberty' (*Letter*: 96). The political liberty that flourished amongst the ancients has been lost in the modern world due to the progress of refined sociability which has drawn the sexes into a terrain no longer divided by natural difference, whether it be the theatre, the salon in the big city or, on a different level of concern, the illusory claims of abstract philosophical reasoning. It is the 'scandalous mixture of men and women which has made of our theatres so many schools of bad manners.' (*Letter*: 78).

As Rousseau understood it, the shared sociability and 'mixture' of the sexes in the same spaces would have only disastrous effects on men's character and, thus, on their capacity for liberty. In the company of women and through 'a commerce that is too intimate' (*Letter*: 100) men are lured into the empire of love and gallantry which they can conquer only 'at the expense of their liberty' (*Letter*: 49). Women's speech and manners, their vanity, frivolity and insincerity pose a threat, it seems, to those masculine qualities, of body as well as mind, from which citizen virtue derives:

> Men are affected as much as, and more than, women by a commerce that is too intimate; they lose only their morals, but we lose our morals and our constitution; for this weaker sex, not in the position to take on our way of life, which is too hard for it, forces us to take on its way, too soft for us; and, no longer wishing to tolerate separation, *unable to make themselves into men, the women make us into women* (*Letter*: 100; my emphasis).

The underlying assumption or, rather, apprehension to which this curious view of the dynamic of sexual relationships seems to be owed remains largely unexplained. Why, in the first instance, should shared company turn each sex into the counterfeit of the other, making men effeminate and women masculine, rather than fostering more open and less constrained forms of social intercourse? A second question that perhaps comes closer to reveal Rousseau's concerns must refer to the asymmetrical pattern in this web of sexual disorder. Women are unable to 'make themselves into men'. Men, on the other hand, appear powerless to prevent being turned into women. What is stated here is a belief – which we will encounter again in *Emile* – that women, although the weaker sex, have yet the power to corrupt men. Men, it is true, are 'voluntary prisoners' (*Letter*: 101) in an empire of delusion and degenerate morals. But it is women who are the empire-builders and the main agents in a process which has broken down the boundaries between separate spheres and, as a consequence, undermined the conditions of republican liberty.

To the extent that Rousseau's understanding of liberty was inspired by his love and admiration for the ancients he was bound to see in the separation of male and female worlds, of household and polis, an indispensable condition of political freedom. The spell that this ideal held over him might go some way to explain why he drew those boundaries as rigidly as he did and why he judged any move towards their relaxation in modern times as but a further stage of decline. The *Letter to d'Alembert* does not offer a philosophical argument to define and demarcate public and private spheres. Rather, it conveys the meaning of public liberty in the difference between masculine and feminine virtue and by charting the physical spaces that pertain to this moral distinction. The seclusion of women in the inner domain of the house and the prohibitions against their public visibility are the necessary guarantee of chastity. But this seclusion also guarantees the conditions of public liberty. For the latter needs to be embedded in practices of 'public fraternity', i.e. in the possibilities of civic friendship and fraternal love among men. These civic bonds require open terrains beyond the confines of the house – terrains suited for the manly exertions of body and mind and, above all, free from the presence of women:

> The ancients spent almost their whole lives in the open air, either dispatching their business or taking care of the state's in the public place, or walking in the country, in gardens, on the seashore, in the rain or under the sun, and almost always bareheaded. *In all of this, no women* (*Letter*: 101; my emphasis).

Compare the vision of open spaces free from the presence of women with the image that immediately follows upon it and which encapsulates, in a single focus, the lifestyle of the moderns – 'every woman at Paris gathers in her apartment a harem of men more womanish than she' (*Letter*: 101). The inversion of the common connotations of 'harem' (here a place where men are held in subjection) vividly portrays modern men's loss of their natural liberty in terms of enclosed rooms and their stifling atmosphere.

Rousseau uses the contrasting images of Greek liberty and modern slavery as a means of reminding his fellow citizens that they still possess, in their all-male civic circles, the vestiges of 'ancient morals'. His nostalgic depiction of the vigorous fraternal sociability once common in his city recreates Geneva in the image of Sparta. Here as there, unbounded space in the open air to exercise the body – gardens, spacious courts, lakes, the whole country open to the hunt. Moreover, freed from the fetters of gallantry and from the need of tailoring ideas 'to the range of women' the men can engage in grave and serious discourse:

> In a word, these decent and innocent institutions combine everything which can contribute to making friends, citizens and soldiers out of the same men and in consequence everything which is most appropriate to a free people (*Letter*: 101).

Rousseau does, of course, not suggest that a 'free people' could do without women. The account of the ancients hardly gives any hint about the quality of their domestic relations. But the vision of a public festival recalled from childhood memories indicates how modern antagonisms might be overcome. Joining the simplicity and innocence of 'public joy' to the tranquillity of conjugal affection the utopian image both confirms and connects the distinct spaces that nature has allocated to the sexes (*Letter*: 135–7).

However, this vision offers an escape route rather than a solution to the divisions which Rousseau recognised as the irreversible effects of modern civilisation. The hope of arresting the process of decline in the recreation of 'antique simplicity' leaves the most intractable problems unresolved. And the latter are owed not least to Rousseau's own, distinctly 'modern', understanding of sexuality and love which does not easily accord with the ideal of liberty and citizen virtue that he borrowed from the ancients. Based as they were on the distance between men and women, republican morals admitted of love only in the form of rather bland conjugal affection. Modern sentimental love could not be contained within these confines; nor could the liberty of modern men be protected against the disorder of women by the clear, external divides of physical segregation. Those boundaries had to be drawn from within.

Male and female nature:
the difference of freedom and dependence (*Emile*)

> There is no parity between the sexes in regard to the consequences of sex. The male is male only at certain moments. The female is female her whole life or at least during her whole youth. Everything constantly recalls her sex to her . . . The strictness of the relative duties of the two sexes is not and cannot be the same. When woman complains on this score about unjust man-made inequality, she is wrong. This inequality is not a human institution . . . (*Emile*: 361).

The question of how to reconcile liberty with those forms of dependence that arise from the intimate relationships between the sexes appears in *Emile* in a radically changed context of intentions. Not Geneva or Sparta but modern society with its corrupt institutions and distorted values is the terrain in which an enclave of freedom is to be established. In the world of *Emile* public liberty, the collective good shared by men as citizens, has been irretrievably lost. Instead of searching for conditions that would mould men into 'friends, citizens and soldiers', the philosopher of liberty has to focus on those exceptional and precarious circumstances that might enable a man to live a life of personal independence and self-sufficiency. In this setting, sexuality and love, marriage and domestic life are more directly and centrally related to the fate of liberty than they were in the domain of austere republican morals. In the education of the natural man sexual love marks that crucial stage of transition which transforms the solitary, asocial human being into a character who will be both independent of the repressive conventions of civilised society and capable of emotional and moral commitments to other individuals. These two imperatives are to be met in the making of the natural woman. Sophie must be what Emile needs her to be if he is to experience personal intimacy, mutual dependence and the fulfilment of sexual desire without becoming alienated from himself through the subversive powers which, as Rousseau understood it, reside in the 'terrible passion' of a man's love for a woman. In other words, Sophie must be Emile's equal as lover and companion and, at the same time, his willing dependant whose submissiveness and strict adherence to the rules of female propriety will safeguard his freedom of will and confidence in himself.

'After having tried to form the natural man, let us also see how the woman who suits him needs to be formed so that our work will not be left imperfect' (*Emile*: 363). Sophie enters the novel only in the last book, i.e. at the point when she is needed to complete Emile's development into mature adulthood. And this asymmetrical structure will be replicated in all important aspects of an education which construes the natural woman wholly in relation to the purposes that are to be realised by man.

> Thus the whole education of women ought to relate to men. To please men, to be useful to them, to make herself loved and honoured by them, to raise them when young, to care for them when grown, to counsel them, to console them, to make their lives agreeable and sweet – these are the duties of women at all times, and they ought to be taught from childhood (*Emile*: 365).

Statements like these are profoundly ambivalent. On the one hand, they imply women's but auxiliary function in a world centred upon men. But this implication is qualified by the claim that men's 'morals, their passions, their tastes, their pleasures, their very happiness also depends on women' (*Emile*: 365). Moreover, as far as Rousseau's intentions are concerned, there can be no doubt that the different educational designs for women and men are meant to serve but a single and undivided purpose, namely, to form two individuals capable of finding self-fulfilment and personal happiness in love (which, in turn, is to be the basis of a secure marriage and stable family). The aim of Sophie's as of Emile's education is to lay the grounds for a relationship in which harmony is guaranteed in the mutual dependence as well as in the mutual enrichment of two complementary characters. Such harmony, that is the pivotal claim, can only be achieved where the personality traits of man and woman have been formed in such a way as to express the physical and moral qualities specific to each sex. Rousseau takes issue with the egalitarian vision of Plato's *Republic* on precisely this point. As a consequence of having abolished marriage and the family, he argues, Plato no longer knew 'what to do with women' other than making them equal with men. By calling both sexes to the same tasks and pursuits he deprived his state of those ties of affection and those 'sweetest sentiments of nature' which, although not political relations in themselves, must provide the natural basis for the artificial bond of citizenship: 'as if it were not the good son, the good husband and the good father who make the good citizen' (*Emile*: 363).

But why does Rousseau convey the essential differences between man and woman in the moral distinction between freedom and dependence? How can a natural disposition to submit to the will of another be seen as a genuine equivalent for a natural potential aimed at autonomy? The whole point of Emile's unconventional upbringing is to enable him to learn from discovery rather than from pre-established rules. All he knows about nature and about the world of men must be owed to experience resulting from unconstrained exploration. In his case, education proceeds in the manner of a journey which develops the self by continuously expanding the horizons of the familiar world. The formation of Sophie's character, by contrast, lies enclosed within the walls of the home. She will leave the sheltered abode of her parents' house only to enter the equally bounded space of the matrimonial home. And these spatial boundaries are but the tangible expression of the educator's main principle that woman 'have – or ought to have – little freedom' (*Emile*: 370). In Sophie's case, then, successful education will produce a person for whom obedience has become habitual and self-restraint effortless. Whereas the young boy must never confront other wills as merely an external force superior in strength to his natural powers the educators of the young girl, Rousseau contends, must take great care to rein in any sign of wilfulness before it might give rise to the dangerous illusion of independence: 'What is commanded them is good; what is forbidden them is bad. They ought not to know more' (*Emile*: 382). Whether it be the demand of modest speech and demeanour in the company of men, the insistence on female chastity as a virtue to be proven above all 'to the eyes of others' or, most disconcertingly, the duty to accept the religious faith decreed by fathers and husbands, the principal aim of a woman's education is to make her adopt the opinion and will of others as the unfailing guide of her conduct (*Emile*: 361, 377, 384).

Paradoxically, however, there is one situation of momentous consequence where the woman trained for 'docility' is expected to submit to no authority other than her own conscience: the choice of her marriage partner must be hers alone (*Emile*: 400ff.). In radical opposition to the still common practice of arranged marriages, especially in the higher echelons of society, Rousseau always insisted that neither paternal authority nor interests of family prestige and property but only the authentic voice of mutual love could establish the legitimacy of the conjugal bond. Yet even here, a woman's freedom resembles the kind of choice made by individuals upon entry into, and submission to, a pre-established hierarchical order. She is free, that is, to renounce liberty – in the choice of 'a master for the whole of life' (*Emile*: 404). Once married, Rousseau insists, she 'will be hardly less of a recluse in her home than a nun is in the cloister' (*Emile*: 387).

This last quotation praises 'the true mother of a family' in contrast with the woman of *le monde* who has abandoned the 'cloister' of domestic duties for the open world of frivolous amusement and public self-display. Rousseau's purpose is twofold. He sees women's seclusion as the indispensable guarantor of domestic harmony and of that happiness of which human life might be capable under the most favourable conditions. And he is, at the same time, concerned to fortify the borders of an enclosed domain against the threat of disorder that women's predatory freedom – their usurpation of men's rights – would wreak upon men's liberty. In the context of the novel the task of affirming this principle of sexual order is more difficult because a man's independence can no longer be secured in a sphere separated from domestic life. Liberty has to be reconciled with the bonds arising from close intimacy and from the coexistence of man and woman in the same space; their relationship has to be based upon mutuality of affections and needs and, yet, has to be framed by an order of indisputable authority.

That the problem does not admit of a conclusive resolution is manifest in the conflicting accounts that aim to anchor the moral and political meanings of sexual difference in the dictates of 'nature'. Rousseau's argument oscillates between three perspectives on sexual nature. One establishes difference as an unequal relation of natural strength and weakness; another accords priority to the complementarity and equivalence of natural dispositions; and the third entails a curious inversion of the first, stressing men's vulnerability in the face of women's superior sexual power. The first and most assertively argued claim focuses on the physiological constitution of the male and female body. Men's and women's sexual natures and reproductive functions, Rousseau insists, are not only different – they are incommensurable. And so are the moral characteristics embedded in those physical distinctions: 'Where they differ, they are not comparable' (*Emile*: 358). The salient point here lies in the assertion, stated as the indisputable conclusion of scientific enquiry, that men are less subject to biological determination than women. To put it the other way round (which is Rousseau's main emphasis), women are prisoners of their sexual body in a way that men are not. Inferior bodily strength together with the burdens of pregnancy, childbirth and care of the young tie them into bonds of lifelong dependence on men and, similarly, into a closely circumscribed circle of all-absorbing domestic duties. While each sex is dependent upon the other for the satisfaction of sexual desire, women in addition are reliant on men in virtue of their most basic needs: 'We would more easily survive without them than they would without us' (*Emile*: 364).

From this line of reasoning it would seem to follow that, as a matter of empirical fact, only men's nature contains an original potential for freedom and that all efforts on the part of women to imitate such freedom must indeed, as Rousseau held, be doomed to failure. However, his insistence that the very claim to such equality is not merely absurd but constitutes a usurpation of men's rights (*Emile*: 408) can be vindicated only if the physical demarcations of men's and women's nature coincide with moral boundaries. And that is, indeed, Rousseau's view: 'These relations and these differences must have a moral influence'. Man's merit and primacy of right are owed to the fact of his strength; by the same token, 'woman is made to please and to be subjugated' (*Emile*: 358).

From Mary Wollstonecraft onwards feminist critics have argued that in deriving the normative difference between freedom and subjection from biological nature Rousseau betrayed the basic premises of his moral and political philosophy – collapsing the distinction between natural and moral inequalities, turning might into right, closing the gap between the original attributes of human nature and those imposed upon it by history and convention (Wollstonecraft 1975 (1792): chs 2–4; Okin 1980: ch. 6; Canovan 1987: 80–5; Coole 1988: ch. 5; Gatens 1991: ch. 1). It is difficult to reconstruct the coherent pattern of an argument in which these contradictions would somehow fall into place because Rousseau seemed to consider the special moral status of sexual difference as self-evidently given in our basic experiences and moral intuitions alike. The Cartesian principle that the mind is not subject to the distinctions of sex – the principle mainly invoked to legitimate demands for sexual equality in this time – would have been anathema to him. He would have considered it absurd, certainly in the context of education, to treat man and woman as 'individuals' whose capacities for moral development stand in no relevant relation to the constitution of the sexual body. His anti-egalitarian stance which typically aligned itself with a wholesale attack upon the philosophical foundations of the 'progress of the enlightenment' appeared in the first instance to target philosophy in the guise of the superficial intellectual fashions of the day. Behind that, however, his critique aimed at the very procedure of abstract moral reasoning which led to the conclusion 'that the two sexes are equal and that their duties are the same' (*Emile*: 362).

To state that the natural dispositions of men and women are not the same is one thing. To express the differences of sexual nature in the contrast between open potentialities and closed, pre-determined functions is quite another. The point here is not that Rousseau saw the well-being of the family as of society at large dependent upon women's willing and competent performance of their duties as wives and mothers. So did Mary Wollstonecraft, his most emphatic critic, and many advocates of 'republican motherhood' in this time (Rendall 1985: ch. 2; Landes 1988: part 2). In contrast with these latter demands for improved female education Rousseau's educational scheme offers to women no path of self-development because it rests ultimately on the assumption that there is no malleable self open to uncharted possibilities. What a woman can and should become is already exhaustively determined from the very beginning. They 'seem in many respects never to be anything' but 'big children' (*Emile*: 211).

However, in the narration of Emile's and Sophie's romantic love Rousseau offers a second perspective upon the meanings of sexual difference. Here, the rigid divides between male and female nature cede to an emphasis on difference as felicitous complementarity. Genuine love is possible only between two individuals who, each incomplete as a human being, find in the other what they lack themselves. Man's capacity for abstract reasoning has its counterpart and complement in woman's proclivity for practical knowledge. His judgement based upon experience of the world is balanced by her intuitive grasp of reality derived from the unfailing guide of inner sentiment (*Emile*: 377; 387). The moral asymmetry between dominance and subordination becomes submerged in an equilibrium of countervailing powers in which man's formal right of command is balanced by woman's effective practical authority and influence. A false education aimed at sameness of character traits would make each sex independent of the other and produce a situation of permanent discord. If their natural differences have been developed they will allow for a partnership where 'each obeys, and both are masters' (*Emile*: 377; 408). Considered from the perspective of mutual love, woman's difference poses no threat to man's independence and sense of self. On the contrary, her capacity to sustain the sentimental bonds of conjugal and familial relations upholds the conditions under which alone autonomy can be maintained.

But this model of natural harmony constituted by the spontaneous interplay of male and female character dispositions is inherently fragile. It does not accord with, and cannot possibly result from, an education in which the dominant emphasis lies on the inculcation of self-constraint, the assertion of authority, the acquiescence in men's injustice, the scaling down of talents to the measure of pleasing mediocrity. One of the most striking features of Rousseau's account of Sophie's education is a language that consistently and overtly speaks in an idiom of political subjugation and enslavement. And this language points to what is perhaps the most powerful, if subterranean, thrust in Rousseau's reflections on the relation between the sexes. Propelled by a sense of apprehension more than by rational analysis this perspective closes in on women's power to corrupt men and, in its most extreme implications, on their responsibility for the ills of modernity. This charge in which the natural hierarchy of male strength and female weakness is turned upside down is intimately bound up with Rousseau's understanding of sexuality. He considered women's capacity to arouse men's desires as exceeding men's ability to satisfy them

(*Emile*: 360). In the troubled realm of sexual passion, that is, the naturally stronger sex proves in fact the weaker; it is here that man's hard-won capacity 'to be free and in command of himself' is most threatened by dependence, if not annihilation. Mankind, Rousseau warns, would perish by the very means that nature intended for its preservation unless women are taught to hide their 'unlimited desires' (*Emile*: 359) behind a screen of trained resistance and duplicity so as to leave men the illusion of superior strength and the success of conquest. This paradoxical inversion of the meaning of sexual difference, and the underlying resentment which seems to drive it, come to life in a vision that implicates women, together with the perverse philosophy of the modern age, in a debacle of apocalyptic dimensions:

> If there were some unfortunate region on earth where philosophy had introduced this practice [i.e. of granting to women the same freedom of expressing their sexual desires, UV] – especially in hot countries where more women are born than men – men would be tyrannised by women. For given the ease with which women arouse men's senses ... men would finally be their victims, and would see themselves dragged to death without ever being able to defend themselves (*Emile*: 359).

It would be misguided to dismiss this perspective as only marginal to Rousseau's argument. It is, in fact, the missing link that connects otherwise incompatible claims. That he saw women at one and the same time as naturally incapable of independent agency and, yet, as agents of superior power and instigators of moral corruption goes some way to explain why the natural foundations of sexual difference could not be left to assert themselves spontaneously but had to be as rigidly enforced as they were in Sophie's education. As in the *Letter to d'Alembert*, there remains in the end a fundamental ambiguity as regards the order of cause and effect and the respective role of men's and women's agency in the process of moral degeneration. Is the depravity of modern women and the need to force back their illicit freedom just the effect of society's corrupt institutions? Or is, on the contrary, women's subversive nature itself one of the root causes to which present ills must be attributed? Rousseau seemed to hold both views:

> They ought to be constrained very early. This misfortune, if it is one for them, is inseparable from their sex ... Amidst our senseless arrangements a decent woman's life is a perpetual combat against herself. It is just that this sex share the pain of the evils it has caused us (*Emile*: 369).

Conclusion

It has not been the purpose of this paper to interpret Rousseau as merely the exemplary exponent of eighteenth-century patriarchal thought. True, he shared in many respects the perceptions and values as well as the prejudices of his time. That his formulation of the nature of sexual difference and of the moral and educational principles entailed in it struck a chord among his contemporaries is attested by the extraordinary popularity of *Emile*. Most commentators today will devote attention above all to the ideas that pertain to Emile's development which, moreover, is frequently misunderstood as that of a representative human being. In the nineteenth century, by contrast, Rousseau's proposals for female education had an equally profound impact and provided, for a long time to come, the authoritative statement on the place of women in modern society. Portalis, the leading draftsman of the *Code Napoléon*, quoted copiously from Rousseau to justify the strict hierarchical order of marriage in an otherwise liberal civil law as the work not of arbitrary political will but of benevolent nature (Portalis 1988: 107–8). Tocqueville attributed the success of the American experiment in democracy to the healthy state of domestic morals rooted securely in women's virtue and secluded lifestyle (Tocqueville 1968: 763–81). All over Europe Rousseau seemed to speak to those, liberals and conservatives alike, who saw in the confusion of traditional gender roles the ominous portent of social disorder (Honegger 1991: chs 2–3).

But although his ideas might have been used in the ideological defence of the existing patriarchal order Rousseau himself was, of course, not a conventional writer. While he did take sides with some of the most restrictive and inequitable traditions he endowed them with new meanings by linking them to ideas and apprehensions that were distinctly his own. He understood the loss of freedom in the modern world not merely as a matter of defective legal and constitutional arrangements but, more seriously, as following upon the erosion of the concrete circumstances of liberty. He feared the egalitarian tendencies that would collapse the boundaries between distinctly male and female spheres precisely because he saw liberty embedded in, and dependent upon, a natural order of sexual and familial relationships. In this he was not, in the vein of conservative ideologists, lamenting the decline of the family as a structure of male authority. Rather, he defended the family as the site of those affective bonds without which neither political liberty nor personal autonomy could flourish.

His attempt to safeguard the conditions of liberty by strengthening the boundaries of sexual differences, however, contains no open spaces in which a case for women's emancipation could be made. The very premises of Rousseau's argument exclude the possibility that women could share with men in the good of liberty. For the latter is understood in such a way that it can only be the property of men – a kind of property, furthermore, that has to be defended against women. He did much to compensate women for what he saw as their natural and socially necessary dependence on men by assigning them a place at the centre of the moral order of the family. But, then, no writer argued more compellingly than Rousseau that there was no substitute for the good of liberty.

References

Rousseau texts

Emile or On Education, trans. by Allan Bloom, Harmondsworth, Penguin, 1991.
Letter to M. d'Alembert on the Theatre, trans. by Allan Bloom, Ithaca, Cornell University Press, 1968.

Other works cited

Bloom, A. (1991), Introduction to *Emile or On Education*, Harmondsworth, Penguin.
Canovan, M. (1987), 'Rousseau's Two Concepts of Citizenship', in E. Kennedy and S. Mendus, eds, *Women in Western Political Philosophy*, Brighton, Wheatsheaf Books, pp. 78–105.
Coole, D. H. (1988), *Women in Political Theory*, Brighton, Wheatsheaf Books.
Gatens, M. (1991), *Feminism and Philosophy. Perspectives on Difference and Equality*, Cambridge, Polity Press.
Honegger, C. (1991), *Die Ordnung der Geschlechter*, Frankfurt/New York, Campus Verlag.
Landes, J. B. (1988), *Women and the Public Sphere in the Age of the French Revolution*, Ithaca and London, Cornell University Press.
Laqueur, T. (1990), *Making Sex. Body and Gender from the Greeks to Freud*, Cambridge, Mass. and London, Harvard University Press.
Okin, S. M. (1980), *Women in Western Political Thought*, London, Virago.

Portalis, J. E. M. (1988), *Ecrits et Discours Juridiques et Politiques*, Marseilles, Presses Universitaires d'Aix-Marseilles.
Rendall, J. (1985), *The Origins of Modern Feminism*, London, Macmillan.
Schwartz, J. (1984), *The Sexual Politics of Jean-Jacques Rousseau*, Chicago and London, University of Chicago Press.
Tocqueville, A. de (1968), *Democracy in America*, ed. J. P. Mayer and M. Lerner, London and Glasgow, Collins.
Wollstonecraft, M. (1975), *A Vindication of the Rights of Woman*, Harmondsworth, Penguin.

11 *Maurice Cranston*

Rousseau's theory of liberty

Freedoms lost

In the state of nature, Rousseau says, man is free in several senses of the word 'freedom'. First he has free will. This is a crucial form of freedom for Rousseau. Most of Rousseau's friends in the circle of the *Encyclopaedia* were determinists,[1] believing that man was a 'machine', albeit more complex than any other machine in nature, but subject to the same laws of cause and effect. Rousseau was willing enough to use the metaphor of a machine, but he claimed that whereas among the beasts nature alone 'operates the machine', in the case of human beings the individual contributes to his own operations in his capacity as an autonomous agent: 'The beast chooses or rejects by instinct; man by an act of free will'.[2]

This metaphysical freedom, or freedom of the will, is for Rousseau a defining characteristic of man, and as such is possessed by all men in all conditions, whether of nature or society. But there are other forms of freedom which he sees men as enjoying in the state of nature, and losing in society. One of these freedoms man could not possibly possess in civil society, and this is anarchic freedom – freedom from any kind of political rule or positive law. This would, of course, be absolute in the state of nature since that state is by definition a condition in which there is no government and no law. The third freedom enjoyed by man in Rousseau's state of nature is personal autonomy, the independence of a man who has no master, no employer, no superior, no one on whom he is in any way dependent. While Rousseau's remarks on anarchic freedom are ambiguous, there is no uncertainty about the value and importance he attaches to personal freedom or independence. This is the great advantage the savage has over the civilized man. In the civilized world, men are enslaved; in the state of nature no one can enslave anyone else:

> Is there a man who is so much stronger than me, and who is, moreover, lazy enough and fierce enough to compel me to provide for his

sustenance while he remains idle? He must resolve not to lose sight of me for a single moment . . . for fear I should escape or kill him.³

Besides having free will, Rousseau's natural man differs from the beasts in possessing *perfectibilité*. Now this word must not be translated, as it often is, as 'perfectibility'; because Rousseau does not assert that man can become perfect; all he claims is that man can better himself by his own efforts. The capacity for *perfectibilité* which Rousseau attributes to human beings is nothing more than a *capacity for self-improvement*.⁴

The story of human evolution as Rousseau unfolds it in the *Discourse on Inequality* is in many ways a melancholy one, marked, in the first place, by man's loss of much of the freedom he enjoyed in the state of nature and then by his misuse of his capacity for self-improvement to do things which have made him worse instead of better.

In the state of nature man is also free in a sense in which President Franklin Roosevelt chose to speak of freedom: he was free from want. In Rousseau's state of nature abundance prevails. 'The savage man', he says, 'desires only the things he knows and knows only things that are within his reach, or easy to acquire, so that nothing ought to be so tranquil as his soul and nothing so limited as his mind'.⁵

This fourth type of freedom is the first, in time, to be diminished, as men move from the true state of nature to what Rousseau calls 'nascent society'.⁶ This evolves as man starts to live in huts, acquire settled mates, and make the acquaintance of neighbours. Simultaneously the increase of population means that there is less easy abundance for everyone. 'To the extent that the human race spread, men's difficulties multiplied with their numbers. Differences between soils, climates and seasons would have forced men to adopt different ways of life. Barren years, long hard winters, scorching summers consuming everything, demanded new industry from men.'⁷ As the supplies of vegetation to eat became scarcer, primitive man became carnivorous and formed hunting groups with his neighbours to catch game. With a mate and children living with him in his hut, man in nascent society had more than one mouth to feed. He was no longer free from want.

Man's effort to overcome want prompted the introduction of agriculture and metallurgy. This leads to the division of labour, and the emergence of the concept of property. As a result of these developments, many men (not all) lose their autonomy; they become dependent on other men. So two more kinds of freedom have been lost: freedom from want, and freedom as independence. The need for the rich to establish rightful ownership of their possessions, and the need for everyone to end the state of war which disputes over possessions generate, prompts universal acceptance of government and law, and this marks the end of another kind of natural freedom: anarchic freedom. Thus, as Rousseau puts it, 'all ran towards their chains believing that they were securing their liberty.'

In his *Discourse on Inequality* Rousseau describes this social contract which 'must have happened' as a distant moment in human evolution, after 'nascent society' relapsed into 'a horrible condition of war of each against all.'[8] At this point Rousseau's argument recalls that of Hobbes. The great difference between Rousseau and Hobbes is that Rousseau argues in the *Discourse on Inequality* that a social condition, and not a state of nature, immediately preceded the introduction of government. Rousseau, as we have seen, claims that the state of nature was peaceful and innocent, and that it was only after the experience of living in society that men were led to introduce government – led to do so because conflicts over possessions arose with the division of labour.

This state of war in pre-political society is seen by Rousseau as having different causes from the state of war depicted by Hobbes. Hobbes speaks of a war between equals; Rousseau sees a war provoked by inequality, by what he calls 'the usurpations of the rich and the brigandage of the poor.'[9] War begins when the idea of property is born and one man claims as his own what another man's hunger prompts him to seize, when one man has to fight to get what he needs while another man must fight to keep what he has. For Hobbes war sprang from natural aggressiveness; for Rousseau war first began with the unequal division of possessions in the context of scarcity, coupled with the corruption of human passions which was the work of culture rather than of nature.

Both Hobbes and Rousseau envisage men finding the same remedy for the state of war between each and all; namely, by the institution, through common agreement, of a system of positive law which all must obey. But whereas Hobbes's social contract is a rational and just solution equally advantageous to all, Rousseau's social contract, as it is described in the *Discourse on Inequality*, is a fraudulent contract imposed on the poor by the rich. In his later book, *The Social Contract*, Rousseau describes an altogether different sort of social contract – a just covenant which would ensure liberty under the law for everyone. But that is something men must enter in full knowledge of what they are doing. In the *Discourse on Inequality*, Rousseau is describing a contract taking place in the remote past, when men first emerge, most of them without much intelligence, from anarchic communities to political society.[10]

Types of servitude

Man's history of servitude begins as soon as he enters nascent society, even though Rousseau speaks of nascent society as an ideal moment in man's life on earth: 'the golden mean' between the 'indolence of the original state of nature and the petulant activity of modern pride, the best period the human race has ever known' and 'the true youth of the world.'[11]

An early form of servitude human beings experience is sexual servitude. Once females started to live in huts with a mate, they began to bear more children, and so became less capable of providing for their nourishment and protection. The female became dependent on her mate and the father of her children; and she became sedentary and weaker as she remained in the house; while the man became stronger as he roamed through the forest, with male companions, seeking food. Rousseau rejects the idea that the family is natural or that males and females are naturally different; in his state of nature, males and females are equal and almost identical in their powers and their independence. The differences develop in society, even as the family itself first emerges in society.

In society, the females are the first to lose their independence in servitude to the family; but then males lose their autonomy in servitude to the females. Sex, a trivial thing in the state of nature, becomes a powerful force in human life as it is transformed into love. 'Love', Rousseau claims, 'is cultivated by women with much skill and care in order to establish their empire over men, and so make dominant the sex that ought to obey.'[12]

Rousseau's argument is that women, weakened as they are domesticated, and grown to be dependent on men to an extent that men are not dependent on women, have to use cunning to make a man stay attached to them. Each woman must make some man love her enough to shelter, feed and protect her, to choose her as his cherished mate. In order for women to make men as dependent on them as they are dependent on men, they must dominate men, and dominate them by devious manœuvres and manipulations, since they cannot dominate them by force. These skills increase as society progresses, so that it is in the most sophisticated communities that women are most dominant, and men most sexually enslaved.

The second form of servitude which man experiences in society is servitude to others, or social servitude. This again originated in nascent society when men began to make frequent contacts with their neighbours, and each to compare himself with the others. Individuals looked at one another, and each was certain that others looked at him or her. Each wanted to excel in his neighbours' eyes: 'He who sang or danced the best, he who was the most handsome, the strongest, the most adroit or the most eloquent became the most highly regarded; and this was the first step towards inequality, and at the same time towards vice.'[13]

Men began to base their conception of themselves on what other people thought of them. The idea of 'consideration' entered their minds; each wanted respect, and soon demanded respect as a right. The duties of civility emerged even among savages; a man who was wounded in his pride was even more offended than a man who was wounded in his body, and each 'punished the contempt another showed him in proportion to the esteem he accorded himself'.[14]

In society, says Rousseau, man becomes 'denatured'. His *amour de soi-même*, or self-love, an instinctive self-protective, self-regarding disposition derived from nature, is transformed in society into *amour propre*, or pride, the desire to be superior to others and to be esteemed by them. In this way, a man loses an important part of his autonomy: he becomes enslaved to the opinion of others, almost owing his identity to his existence in the judgement of others.

Another type of servitude which men experience in society is moral servitude: this takes two forms, servitude to passions and servitude to desires. In the state of nature, Rousseau argues, men's passions are weak. Having no prolonged contact with other human beings, and no experience of shortage, men's lives are calm. Nothing happens to inflame their passions. Even in their sexual relations, 'everyone waits peaceably for the impulse of nature, yields to it involuntarily with more pleasure than frenzy'.[15] But once they acquire mates, human beings develop the passion of love and this in turn leads to the destructive passion of jealousy. And once they associate with neighbours, individuals all develop *amour de soi-même*, vanity, pride, selfishness, envy and greed. As society progresses these passions become so strong that people's conduct is dominated by them, instead of being governed, as social man's conduct ought to be, by reason and conscience, together with compassion.

This enslavement by the passions goes together with enslavement to desires. In the state of nature man only desires what he can easily acquire: 'Savage man, when he has eaten, is at peace with the whole of nature . . . But for man in society, it is a question of providing first what is necessary, next what is superfluous, then afterwards come luxuries, then immense riches, then subjects, then slaves; man in society does not have a moment of respite. What is more singular is that the less natural the desire and the less urgent the needs, the more the desires increase.'[16]

Besides social servitude, sexual servitude and moral servitude, social man also experiences economic servitude – but this is rather less evenly distributed than the other forms of servitude. As a result of the division of labour, which has produced the two categories of rich and poor, the poor become slaves of the rich. The rich are not free – since they are more enslaved than are the poor to desires, passions, and the opinion of others; but the institutionalization of property separates those who have from those who have not, and forces the latter to become dependent on the former. As Rousseau wrote to Mme de Francueil, in the famous letter explaining why he had put his children in an orphanage: 'The earth produces enough to feed everybody; it is the life-style of the rich; it is your life-style which robs my children of bread.'[17] In robbing the poor of a fair share of the earth's wealth, the rich also enslave them, for without servitude to the rich, the poor cannot even acquire an unfair share.

Next, there is political servitude. From the historical perspective, Rousseau argues that the establishment of law and the right of property was the first step in the evolution of political institutions; then came the institution of magistrates, and then the transformation of legitimate into arbitrary power. In the first stage there are rich and poor; in the second, strong and weak; in the third, masters and slaves. Again, political servitude is not universally experienced. Most governments in the modern world are arbitrary governments; but there are a few exceptions.

Freedoms acquired

Political servitude, we have noted, is not universal; and when Rousseau turns to the problem of attaining freedom in the social state it is political freedom to which he gives most attention. He makes it clear that he does not entertain any thought of men recovering the anarchic freedom they enjoyed in the state of nature. There can be no going back to an early stage of evolution, however idyllic it might seem to be. Political freedom for civil man must be a form of civil freedom. The development of this thought is Rousseau's purpose in writing *The Social Contract*. Hobbes was in Rousseau's mind when he wrote this book, just as he had been when he wrote the *Discourse on Inequality*.

Hobbes, as Rousseau understood him, argued that men had to choose between law and liberty, between being governed and being free. For Hobbes freedom meant the absence of opposition: 'the liberties of subjects depend on the silence of the law'.[18] Freedom went with anarchy: law to be effective meant the rule of an absolute sovereign. Men loved freedom, but the consequences of anarchy were so appalling that any sort of government was better than no government at all. Under Hobbes's social contract men surrendered collectively their natural right to freedom to a sovereign in return for the peace and security of a civil order which that sovereign could secure by holding all men in awe; what liberty remained was what the sovereign did not forbid.

Rousseau did not agree that freedom was antithetical to the constraints of government. Freedom was not the absence of opposition, but the exercise of ruling oneself. He believed it was possible to combine liberty and law, by instituting a regime which would enable men to rule themselves. Such an arrangement would entail, as Hobbes's system did, a covenant being made between individuals to surrender their natural rights to a sovereign: but that sovereign should be none other than the people themselves, united in one legislative corps.

Rousseau not only rejects Hobbes's idea that men must choose between being free and being ruled; he asserts that it is only through ruling themselves that men can experience freedom. In the *Discourse on Inequality* Rousseau speaks of the several kinds of freedom men lose on entering society. In *The Social Contract* he speaks of a kind of freedom which they can experience only in society: civil freedom.[19] And this is something he suggests is altogether superior to anarchy.

In *The Social Contract*, Rousseau has less to say about the innocence of savage man, and more of his brutishness. Man in the state of nature is described as a 'stupid and unimaginative animal' who becomes 'an intelligent being and a man' only as a result of entering civil society. Assuredly, as a result of the development of passions and desires which society breeds, men have generally grown worse with the passage of time; but there is still a way of salvation – or liberation.

In the state of nature, a man cannot, by definition, be a citizen. But once he has quit the state of nature and entered society, man's nature can only be realised if he becomes a citizen.

In a way, Rousseau's response to the challenge of Hobbes is wonderfully simple. Clearly, men can be at the same time ruled and free if they rule themselves. For then the obligation to obey will be combined with the desire to obey; everyone in obeying the law will be acting only in obedience to his own will. In saying this, Rousseau was going a good deal further than liberal theorists such as John Locke, who associated freedom with the people's consent to obey a constitutional monarch in whom they invested sovereignty. For Rousseau there is no investment or transfer of sovereignty: sovereignty not only originates in the people; it stays there.

Rousseau's solution to the problem of being at the same time ruled and free might plausibly be expressed as 'democracy'. But this is a word he seldom uses, and even then his use of it looks paradoxical. In the dedication of the *Discourse on Inequality* he praises the republic of Geneva as a 'democracy well tempered' but in *The Social Contract*, he writes: 'If there were a nation of Gods, it would govern itself democratically. A government so perfect is not suited to men'.[20] There is in fact no contradiction here, in view of the particular use Rousseau makes of the word 'government'. He carefully separates government, as administration, from sovereignty, as legislation. He maintains that legislation must be democratic, in the sense that every citizen should participate in it, and participate in person. This is the democratic element in the constitution of Geneva which Rousseau has in mind when he speaks of that state as a 'democracy well tempered'. At the same time, Rousseau rejects – as unsuited to men – democratic administration. The participation by all the citizens in the executive government of the state he considers altogether too utopian an arrangement to be desirable in practice. Executive government, he argues, must be entrusted to duly elected authorities. He sees no abridgement of liberty entailed by the institution of magistrates.

In the dedication to his *Discourse on Inequality*, Rousseau declares 'I would have fled from a republic, as necessarily ill-governed, where the people . . . foolishly kept in their own hands the administration of civil affairs and the execution of their laws'.[21] He stresses the need for a state to have 'chiefs' (*'chefs'*). 'I would have chosen a republic where the individuals, content with sanctioning the laws and making decisions in assemblies on proposals from the chiefs on the most important public business . . . elected year by year the most capable and upright of their fellow citizens to administer justice and govern the state'.[22]

The point Rousseau dwells on is that superiority in public office must correspond to superiority of capability and rectitude or 'virtue'. Such a system he can call 'aristocratic' in the true classical sense of that word: government by the best. This is clearly the sense he has in mind when he speaks in *The Social Contract* of an elective aristocracy as 'the best form of government';[23] and in doing so he does not contradict the preference expressed in the *Discourse on Inequality* for 'democratic government, well tempered' – for what he means there is democratic legislation, well tempered by an aristocratic administration, democratically elected. He contrasts this sort of aristocracy with an aristocracy based on heredity, which is characteristic of feudal regimes: 'the worst form of government'.[24]

Rousseau was anxious that his *Social Contract* should not be read as a piece of utopian literature. As he explained in his *Letters from the Mountains*,[25] he had based his blueprint for a free republic on the original model of Geneva, and he believed that other nations in the real world could attain political freedom by adopting the methods and institutions he had outlined in the pages of his book. He did not believe that civil freedom was an idle dream. He argued that the citizens of Sparta had known it; that the city-state of Geneva, before the eighteenth-century regime had corrupted it, had enjoyed freedom; and that it would not be impossible for other men to attain it.

Moral freedom was another form of freedom which social man could attain. Savages could have no experience of this because they had no moral life: they were good, but they had no occasion to be virtuous, or to know what virtue meant. Moral freedom for social man was largely a matter of overcoming his servitude to passions and desires. Just as Rousseau's political freedom was achieved by a community obeying only the rules it imposed on itself, so moral freedom for the individual was achieved by his obeying only the rules which he imposed on himself.

Rousseau clearly subscribed to that philosophy which divides man into soul and body. When the soul ruled the body, the man was free; when the body ruled the soul, he was a slave. The metaphysical freedom – or free will – of man was not of real importance to him in the state of nature, but in the social state it is crucial. The soul has a voice, as Rousseau explains in the 'Profession de foi' in *Emile*, a divine instinct, an immortal celestial voice, which is conscience. A man who acts in obedience to conscience acts in obedience to the voice of his own soul; if he acts in obedience to the passions and desires which have their seat in his body, he is acting in obedience to something which is alien to him. This conception of moral freedom was, of course, developed in a more elaborate way by Kant, who nevertheless acknowledged the inspiration of Rousseau.

Unlike political freedom, which could only be enjoyed under a well-ordered republic, moral freedom was something that could be attained anywhere. Rousseau believed he had attained it himself; although he did not think that many people had done so. He hoped with his books – and the examples of his life – to encourage others to try.

Personal freedom was also something that Rousseau believed could be achieved. This would go beyond moral freedom to include liberation from servitude to the opinion of others as well as servitude to passions and desires. He believed he had found that himself in quitting the social life of Paris to live in what he called 'solitude' in the country. In a letter to Malesherbes he wrote

> I went . . . in search of some wild or deserted place in the forest, where there would be no trace of the hand of man to proclaim servitude and domination, some refuge that I might think I was the first to reach, and where no unwelcome visitor would come between nature and me.[26]

In his *Lettres morales* he tried to persuade Sophie D'Houdetot that the way to free herself from bondage to *le monde* was to arrange to be more continuously alone. But he did not have high hopes of success.

In *Emile* he confronts the difficulty of learning to be a free man in a society characterized by servitude, and he there outlines the programme – the really extraordinary programme – which a tutor must follow to bring up a boy who really will achieve personal freedom. The one book he allows the boy to read is *Robinson Crusoe*; Emile hardly sees his parents or other children; he never goes to school; he is either alone or *en tête-à-tête* with his tutor. It is almost as if Rousseau accepts the impossibility[27] of his own enterprise: the only way to avoid servitude to other people is to avoid the presence of other people.

Rousseau offers no prospect of human beings acquiring sexual freedom in civil society. One formula he proposes is that men should rule in public and women rule in private: in the home, man should accept the domination of women, but in the state, women should be silent and allow the men to legislate and govern. In the dedication of the *Discourse on Inequality* to the Genevan citizens Rousseau says to the women of the city: 'The destiny of your sex will always be to govern ours. Happy are we so long as your chaste power is exercised solely within the marriage bond . . . makes itself felt only for the glory of the state and the well-being of the people.'[28] But in the text of the same *Discourse* he protests that the development of love between the sexes has 'made dominant the sex that ought to obey.'[29]

In *La Nouvelle Héloïse*, where Rousseau depicts Clarens as an ideal little domestic community, Wolmar dominates the family, and Julie dominates Wolmar[30] – so it would seem that neither is free from sexual servitude; nor does Rousseau seem to think such freedom available to anyone else.

Rousseau has relatively little to say about economic freedom – a form of freedom that has occupied the forefront of much subsequent speculation. Although he believed that the introduction of private property marked a decisive step in man's march towards slavery, Rousseau did not propose to abolish it. Instead, he advocated frugality. In his own style of life – which was undoubtedly meant to be exemplary – he resisted all forms of employment or patronage which would make him economically dependent on other persons and institutions. In his advice to the Corsicans he wrote: 'Commerce produces riches, but agriculture assures men of liberty.'[31] He suggested that the state should be rich and each person have a share in the wealth in proportion to his services. 'It is not my intention to destroy private property because that is impossible, but to confine it within narrow limits, to give it a measure, a rule, a control that will restrain it, and hold it subordinate to the public good. In a word, I want the property of the state to be as great and powerful, and that of the citizens as small and weak, as possible.'[32]

In a note he wrote while preparing his *Constitution for Corsica* Rousseau added: 'With private property being so weak and so dependent, the Government will need to use very little force, and will lead the peoples, so to speak, with a movement of the finger.'[33] These words suggest that the formula for economic freedom Rousseau proposes for the Corsicans would jeopardise their political freedom. But if that thought entered Rousseau's mind, he did not dwell on it.

Notes

1 See N. Hampson, *The Enlightenment*, Harmondsworth, 1968, pp. 73–96.
2 Pléiade, III, p. 141.
3 *Ibid.*, III, p. 161
4 See Robert Wokler, 'Perfectible Apes in Decadent Culture', *Daedalus*, CVII, 1978.
5 Pléiade, III, p. 214.
6 *Ibid.*, pp. 168–9.
7 *Ibid.*, p. 163.
8 *Ibid.*, p. 176.
9 *Ibid.*
10 *Ibid.*, p. 177.
11 *Ibid.*, p. 171.
12 *Ibid.*, p. 158.
13 *Ibid.*, p. 169.
14 *Ibid.*, p. 170.
15 *Ibid.*, p. 158.
16 *Ibid.*, p. 203.
17 Leigh, vol. II, p. 143.
18 *Leviathan*, ch. XIII.
19 This is the kind of freedom which Benjamin Constant calls 'la liberté ancienne' as opposed to 'la liberté moderne'; which Hegel and Berlin call 'positive' as opposed to 'negative' liberty; and which is advocated as 'participatory freedom' by such theorists as Hannah Arendt, Benjamin Barber and Bernard Crick.
20 Pléiade, III, p. 406.
21 *Ibid.*, p. 114.
22 *Ibid.*
23 *Ibid.*, p. 406. See also p. 809: 'The best of governments is aristocratic, the worst of sovereignties is aristocratic'.
24 *Ibid.*, p. 406.
25 *Ibid.*, p. 810. He says of his critics: 'They have been pleased to relegate the *Social Contract* with Plato's *Republic* . . . to the land of chimeras.'
26 Pléiade, I, pp. 1139–40.
27 Wittgenstein, however, seems to have adopted this particular Rousseauesque conception of freedom, and tried to achieve it. One of his biographers writes: '[Wittgenstein] never saw himself through the eyes of others, and he had no other standards than his own. The awe in which he was held by those who knew him was due to this freedom of his and the means he used to become free and assure his freedom. He simply gave up everything in which mental troubles and complexes breed and flourish: wealth, family, community and nation ties.' F. Pascal on 'Wittgenstein's Freedom', in R. Rhees (ed.), *Ludwig Wittgenstein*, Oxford, 1981, pp. 59–60.

28 Pléiade, III, p. 119.
29 Ibid., p. 158.
30 See Joel Schwartz, *The Sexual Politics of J.-J. Rousseau*, Chicago, 1984, pp. 121–41. Schwartz suggests that Rousseau has two different teachings about sexuality. 'In Rousseau's first teaching, he argues that sexuality and freedom are compatible . . . in his second teaching, he contends that they are incompatible, or that true freedom could be achieved only on the basis of freedom from sexuality' (p. 142).
31 Pléiade, III, p. 905.
32 Ibid., p. 931.
33 Ibid., p. 949.

12 Lester G. Crocker

Rousseau's soi-disant *liberty*

In *Four Essays on Liberty* (Oxford, 1969) Isaiah Berlin developed a distinction between 'negative' and 'positive' liberty. 'Negative liberty' refers to an area where an individual can act without interference and to legal protections that establish minimal limits to opportunities for action. 'Positive liberty' refers to the question, 'Who governs me?', with the political implication of self-government. Historically, it developed into a doctrine of 'liberation by reason' (p. 144), leading to the rationalist view of a superior self identified with reason or our 'higher' nature, which is our 'real self' (pp. 132, 144, 162). And from this idea of man, as it grew into 'the desire for positive freedom of collective self-direction', came the authoritarian and totalitarian creeds we all know. Sir Isaiah admits that participation is also desired by liberals for the protection of negative liberty (p. 165). The difference is that they wish to curb authority, whereas the proponents of positive liberty 'want it placed in their own hands'.

One of Berlin's postulates, then, is that participation does not in itself assure the adequate measure of self-direction that can be considered as liberty. It may indeed negate it. Instead of his phrasing of the difference between the two liberties as 'Over what area am I master?' and 'Who is master?', we may see the issue more clearly this way: 'Who is master over what area I am to be master of, and how large is that area?' This is the ultimate question because the ultimate reply lies in the possession and the use of power – a factor Berlin does not deal with but that is at the heart of Rousseau's political devices.

Berlin's distinctions are fragile and in some ways blurred. They have been criticized. The object of this essay is not to explore his theory. Its theme will be that Rousseau excludes 'negative freedom' and utilizes 'positive freedom' only for the 'authoritarian and totalitarian' end Berlin alleges to be its outcome, or one of its potential outcomes, a way that sets a goal to which all else is instrumental.

To define liberty is as hazardous and futile as to define truth, beauty, or Romanticism. Reductionism is the peril in all definitions. Also, words do not have the same meaning for revolutionaries as for upholders of a *status quo*. Thus Rousseau can speak of 'the hard yoke of liberty', rephrased by Saint-Just as 'the despotism of liberty'. We shall do better, then, to describe some characteristics, as viewed by the libertarian. (I use this word instead of the confusing 'liberal'.)

Liberty certainly includes the assurance of an unassailable private realm, the most basic human and civil right. A person belongs to himself, not to others and not to society except in a limited way that preserves a personal sanctuary and the right to try to make a life for oneself, to maximize one's potentials and goals within what is taken to be justifiable external constraints.

Liberty protects adversarial contention, toleration of differing opinions, dissent, debate. It entails participation (in some fashion) in granting power to those who will govern, inasmuch as that power affects the extent to which liberty is available, though in some forms of government participation may result in decrease of liberty. It insists on the right of judgement and its open expression. Liberty, then, presupposes pluralism. Its extreme antithesis is one nation with one mind. This implies orthodoxy, or one right opinion, which is antipodal to freedom of thought about life's complexities. Given human nature and reason as they are, it signifies conformity and control.

Inevitably, the idea of liberty refers ultimately to the individual, though he cannot be loosed from the community, even when he opposes it. A frequent simplistic antithesis is between 'what one wants to do' and 'what one ought to do'. A better statement of difference is between 'what one wants to do' and 'what other sources of authority and power tell us we ought to do'. If 'what we ought to do' is an autonomous decision, it is still freedom. We shall see that Rousseau's method is to *make* it or to make it *seem like* an autonomous decision; then the antithesis disappears.

Popular sovereignty is not of itself a determining character of liberty, because liberty admits of no will that has the power to constrain all wills, opinions and unthreatening behaviour.[1] Totalitarianism demands the surrender of one's judgement to a heteronomous judgemental power, be it church or state, and strives for willing ('free') conformity to it. Liberty presupposes that the individual is the only living, feeling, thinking and willing component of a society, and that in these respects, he has protections against the power of government and the rule of the majority.

Lists of specific freedoms are useful indications that express certain forms of liberty, but we must go deeper, to a general concept. Liberty stipulates the power of choice. In a polity, liberty is power, of a special kind: the power to exercise rights or choices. The more rights one can claim and exercise, the more liberty one has, and vice versa. The implication is that there are differences of degree. As in other spheres, when such differences are great enough, they become differences in kind: in this case, to point to extremes, anarchy, which does not respect mutuality of rights, or tyranny, whose apogee is the Nazi death camps, where all power and rights and the very status as human beings are wiped out and liberty reduced to absolute zero.

The relation between liberty and equality – two important ideas in Rousseau's writings – is a variable. The greater the inequality, the more liberty for some and the less for others. On the other hand, total equality would entail the annihilation of liberty in all spheres where equality obtains. This is so because of the facts of human nature (which Rousseau so eloquently described in the *Discourse on Inequality*) and the consequent repression necessary to create, enforce and maintain that equality. Let history be the judge. There is a paradox here. Liberty cannot be dissociated from the degree of equality and especially the kinds of equality that obtain. On the other hand, absolute equality would be the death-knell of liberty. Rousseau never advocates it.

To put the matter in a different mode, pluralism (the antithesis of orthodoxy and unanimity) implies different identities with their incongruous proclivities. Decisions where choice is involved, when not prompted by reflexive emotion, are determined by a choice of priority of value. Values may be societal or individual. The two often coincide, as the former introjects its values into the latter. Or they may clash. In this case the individual may be condemned for antinomian placement of the self as its own judge. Or else his conflict and refusal may be seen to be in the name of something he considers to be a higher value and which even society pretends to hold as a higher value. This human privilege is another kind of equality, a kind that is consonant with liberty.

After these initial *prises de position*, and in their light, let us turn to Rousseau. Too many commentaries concentrate on his institutional scheme, especially in the *Social Contract*. It is my view that his institutions can be properly interpreted only as instruments towards an end – the kind of society he envisions – and that that vision must be brought to bear in each instance. We must delve beneath the surface of institutional structures to such matters as their management, the methods of control they exercise, the kind of rigid, organic society they are designed to establish.

I also maintain that one cannot fully appreciate these factors without an understanding of Rousseau's life and personality. I have treated this subject elsewhere, and the limits of this essay enable me only to mention in passing such matters as alienation and distantiation, resentment, a private phantasy life, especially phantasies of uniqueness and power as the prophet and guide who will be revered in the future for having shown men the true path from which history and their vicious potentialities have led them to stray or, with rare exceptions, not even to envisage.

Rousseau's project, like Plato's and Aristotle's, was a moral, not a purely political one. Cassirer calls it his true revolutionary act. Politics, being the necessary means, absorbs but does not replace the moral end. Yet because politics absorbs morality, it becomes the dictator and the test of morality.

The project was to create imaginatively a real society, therefore antithetical in every way to his own. Society had corrupted the natural good in men. But who made society? Who corrupted it? Men – whose evil proclivities spring into action as soon as there is a society. Every man, he asserts, prefers self-love to the love of order. Thus the political problem is also a moral problem, since it is men who have to be changed. The task of the statesman is to 'form citizens', since that is something for which nature has not formed men. There was the great problem, the obstacle Rousseau was trying to overcome in his theorizing, the stumbling-block over which later revolutionaries all have failed. It was human nature, the eternal, invincible enemy of all utopias.

The word 'heart' is important to Rousseau. But the heart must be 'formed', else it says, 'Me first'. That is a theme of *La Nouvelle Héloïse*. The Legislator's work is to 'denature' men, he insists, to 'make them what he needs them to be'. To take men as they naturally are would make the project hopeless. No political institutions, no laws can by themselves accomplish this staggering, hallucinatory conception. We cannot make a better world without making better men.

Rousseau does not deny personal morality; it simply becomes politically irrelevant. Where, in the *Social Contract* or the *Project for Corsica*, does one find reference to a personal conscience? Conscience is a personal decision. In the true society it is superseded by a collective 'conscience', so that one *knows* what to do. From the viewpoint of the polity, conscience is, implicitly, an element fraught with danger to the unity of the body, a decision and a will of its own, potentially destructive to the general will which overrules it as the determinant of right and wrong. Rousseau describes the political body as 'un être moral', with its own distinctive qualities, unrelated to those of its constituent parts.[2] As the criterion of right and wrong, all its laws are legitimate. Its judgement supersedes that of its parts and becomes their 'real' judgement, thus preventing a person from being 'in contradiction with himself' (*EP*, 245). A people, he declares, should be given not necessarily what they want, but what they ought to want, which is what they really want.

Like the facets of a jewel, the parts of Rousseau's utopian vision shine only in coordination. The end-all is to make men happy, despite the ravages caused by nature's conflict with society and in disregard of their subjective individual preferences – a happiness imposed on them, *nolentes volentes*. It is (in Platonic fashion) to create a just order, justice being defined by right laws and order, by everyone being in his proper place. It is also to create a fraternal community, to be crafted by the organic character of society, fostered and enforced by stated mechanisms. It is to create a society of liberty, according to a novel conception of that word. The two main thrusts are absorption of the individual into the whole and the shaping of behaviour into reflexive, predictable responses.

This is Rousseau's principle: only artifice can remedy the evils that artifice began. His use of the word 'nature', as in *Emile*, is a beguiling and deceptive rhetorical stratagem. It is all artifice, supposedly to restore the natural by following it. This is obviously not so, besides being self-contradictory. Rousseau deftly identifies the natural with his own ideas – a common fault in the eighteenth century – in order to give them the magical authoritativeness associated with that word. But the marquis de Sade's 'nature' is just as natural as Rousseau's, so that the word denotes only a subjective preference or decision.

The problematic of nature and artifice (culture) is definitely resolved in Rousseau's scheme in his parable of Julie's garden in *La Nouvelle Héloïse*.[3] I take it as the master key, the symbol encapsulating the whole dream. Nature as given must be rejected and overcome, and a new nature designed and maintained by the 'main cachée' of the 'gardener', to make it accord with his rational scheme of order. It is a new 'nature' fashioned by human rationality. There are no pages more revealing than these about Rousseau's ultimate aim and the character of the methods envisaged to attain it. The symbol appears again in the fourth paragraph of *Emile*.

The political translation of the symbol is the suppression of merely human self – the natural self – and its replacement by a new communitarian self, 'le moi commun' or 'la personne publique'. The hypothesizing of such a non-empirical, intangible entity stipulates its having a will, the equally non-empirical, unfalsifiable 'general will'. It implies the conception of the true society as a living body, a notion Rousseau explicitly develops in *Economie politique* and often returns to.[4]

The notion of the community as a living body has two advantages. It justifies the subservience of the part to the whole, though the whole to survive must take care of its parts.[5] 'As nature grants each man an absolute power over all his limbs, so does the social pact give the body politic an absolute power over all its parts' (*SC*, II, 4, I, 2). And it mends the cleavage, the state of war within each of us between self-centered and socially oriented impulses. 'I look forward to the moment when I shall be myself, without contradiction' (*Emile*, 386). The imposed harmonious interplay (imposed because there is no other way it can come about) among the parts also puts an end to the state of war among men so eloquently described in the early tracts.

The formation of the corporate body and its will is not dissociable from the 'denaturing' of men: 'Good social institutions are those which best denature man and transport the self within the common unity, such that every particular no longer thinks himself complete, but part of a unity which only has feelings within the whole' (*Emile*, 12). And in the *Social Contract*: 'a single body . . . a single will' (IV, 1). This surely puts the individual in his place. Rousseau's political arrangements will carry out his draconian law. Its deep significance is the displacement of identity, thus eliminating what prevents a true society.[6]

According to Roger Masters, the social contract's purpose is to 'generate binding obligations constituting the group's collective self-interest'.[7] This statement is accurate but does not address the essential question: how does Rousseau plan to do this? It can be done only by the submergence of personal self-interest as an actuating motive. It is admittedly the natural motive of action. His scheme, then, is to induce the refractory individual to lose natural identity and acquire a new one, seeing himself only in the body of the organic whole rather than as a quasi-independently functioning body within the larger body. Not surprisingly, Rousseau's Savoyard vicar defines virtue as love of order, rather than of justice or right, for each man naturally prefers self-love to the love of order. Therefore, he tells the reader of *Emile*, he who wants to keep the primacy of nature's feelings in the civil order knows not what he wants. Rousseau's true state, writes Robert Nisbet, is 'the collective will purged of purely individual wills – with their egoisms, avarice and selfishness'.[8] In other words, it is a society in which the private is not distinguished from the public.[9]

Rousseau knows full well that he is 'working' with the most perverse and recalcitrant of materials – human nature. What vast and deep molding is needed to achieve the terminus: to control men with their own free consent! That is the only way, because the appearance of oppression leads surely to resistance and revolt. The entire system reduces itself, then, in its most elementary terms, to one of total control that is not perceived as control. *Emile* is only one application of a universal, consistent method. Its plot is a changing but relentless series of steps ensuring the tutor tighter and more total mastery over the *pâte* he is shaping. How often he exults, each time the vise closes its grip more tightly! And never is the boy or youth aware of what is being done to him.

Rousseau proposes effectuating his goal in diverse ways. One is a rigid hierarchization. Hierarchy is necessary to order, and Rousseau's societies, from the first to the last, are elitist. It is specified in *La Nouvelle Héloïse*, in the well-known passage about preventing individuals from developing their inherent potentialities, just as the economic order forbids overexploiting gold mines. Rousseau is insistent. In *Emile*, 'to assign each person to his place and to keep him there ... is all that can be done for the well-being of man' (Pléiade, IV, 303). Emile learns that the 'natural' order forbids men from leaving their pláce. He also affirms that 'le pauvre n'a pas besoin d'éducation'. There is plain logic in all this. The striving for self-realization would reintroduce ambition, a competitive, self-centered society, and throw order into disarray. A clear conclusion also ensues. In the Rousseauian polity, there is little or no respect for persons or personality. The demiurge objectifies the subject, depriving him of part of what is essentially human in him.

A second way is what is now called operant conditioning, self-reinforcement by inevitable punishment or reward which is made to seem necessary, not inflicted; in other words, the inculcation of habitual, reflexive behaviour. Rousseau first develops such procedures in *La Nouvelle Héloïse*, with Wolmar's 'method', applied to the children, the helots of Clarens and the two protagonists. Emile's governor tells the reader that habit puts the boy in his power. The state's control of 'education' serves the purpose of instilling a way of life, an unchallenged moral regimen. Education (so called) is indoctrination, 'formation' in a desired mold.[10] Rousseau has anticipated B. F. Skinner's method of shaping behaviour. The purpose, according to Skinner (and Rousseau) is to design a collective environment in which human beings can be taught to build a society based on cooperation, not competition. This goal requires the elaboration of a detailed code of behaviour that governs community life. Skinner calls this an engineered utopia. Rousseau had already done it – as we shall shortly see.

It is well known that he had conceived this theory early on, as he tells us in the *Confessions*. The 'sensitive morality' he dreamt of was to make desired moral responses reflexive rather than reflective, thus giving them the same necessity that physical laws possess. He never gave up this idea, but rather carried it forward. In *Emile* he tells his pupil: 'extend the law of necessity to the moral domain' (Pléiade, IV, 320); and 'If the laws of nations, like the laws of nature, could have an inflexibility which no human force could overcome, dependency upon men would revert to dependency on things'. And – especially – dependency on things 'causes absolutely no harm to liberty', he assures us, thus expecting the reader to make the transfer from 'things' to human laws (pp. 310–11). To make such a transfer is to expunge distinguishing human factors and to treat men as things.

A third way is the deliberate, persistent use of artifice and trickery to assure willing docility. *La Nouvelle Héloïse* and *Emile* are handbooks on trickery.[11] Deception is necessary. Already in *Economie politique* Rousseau writes: 'the greatest talent of leaders is to disguise their power so as to make it less odious, and to direct the state with such tranquillity that it seems not to need directors' (Vaughan, I, 247). But it *does* need them: and Rousseau reaffirms this strategy in *Emile* where, as already mentioned, the puppet must never know that he is being observed or realize that he is being directed. A maze of tricks is deployed to capture Emile's mind and will and make him think that he is willing freely. In the *Social Contract* Rousseau develops his idea with irrefragable clarity. The most important of all laws is the law of habit, better than authority. 'I am speaking of mores, of customs and above all of public opinion, a power unknown to political thinkers, but on which depends the success of all others, a power with which the Great Legislator deals *in secret*, while he *appears* to restrict himself to particular regulations' (III, 12, italics added). Citizens too, then, must be controlled and directed without their being aware of it. Deception is necessary because the end is illusion, 'the beneficent illusion': that the citizen is not sacrificing himself, that his self is not his self, that his loss of autonomy is not a loss, that renunciation is not renunciation. This requires all the ruses of power and the lofty explanation by which Rousseau justifies them. So it is with Emile, who is 'most completely subjugated when he has the appearance of independence' – an idea Rousseau repeats several times.[12] One must not rely on logical argument. He calls the people 'children' and his theory treats them as such.

A constant theme is that everything depends on 'opinion'. 'Opinion', to put it in plain language, is what people *think*. Control of opinion is thought control. And it is the method's target. Wolmar uses it on Saint-Preux and Julie. Emile's governor uses it on him. The legislator keeps it constantly in mind. 'Whoever undertakes to form a people must know how to shape public opinion, and through it to govern the passions of men' (*CGP*, Vaughan, II, 437).[13]

In the *Social Contract* the censors are the controllers: 'Public opinion is the form of law which the censor administers' (IV, 7). Rousseau never has scruples about deluding his reader any more than his fictional subjects.[14] He would have us believe that his censors only *express* public opinion and that their decisions, if they violate it, are void. But how will public opinion be determined? How will decisions be made 'null and void'? In the next paragraph Rousseau gives the game away. 'Correct men's opinions and their mores will purge themselves. Men always love what is good, or what they find so, but it is in making this judgement that they go wrong. This judgement, therefore, is what must be regulated.' And he goes on, leaving no doubt: 'Censorship upholds men's mores in preventing opinions from becoming corrupt, in conserving their rectitude by wise applications, sometimes in giving them substance when they are still uncertain'. Obviously, the censor does not merely reflect opinion; he has an active role. However, constraint must never be visible, Rousseau warns again. As in Geneva, as in the *Lettre à d'Alembert*, censorship drapes itself over everything – morals, the arts and literature, behaviour, speech and thought.

Beliefs are subject to punishment, and not only in regard to the civil religion, to which commentators often think it confined. 'Why does a man', he asks in the *Lettre à M. de Beaumont*, 'take notice of the faith of another, and why does the state scrutinize the faith of its members? It is because the faith by which persons live is assumed to determine their morality'. But religion is only one instance. Thought control is enthroned in Rousseau's imaginary worlds. Mutual spying is twinned with informing. Rousseau justifies it as an act of patriotism and merit. It is an inviolable law in La Nouvelle Héloïse, bringing expulsion or reward. How far does it extend? Rousseau is not precise. History shows it has no limit. In countries we speak of as 'free' it is abhorred. What many would consider to be perverted morality, Rousseau praises as moral. More exactly, moral considerations are irrelevant when it is a matter of 'the cause'. 'Who wills the end wills the means' (SC, II, 5). Reliance on such methods says much about Rousseau's mind-set and the kind of regime his true society would be. The accompaniment of surveillance is repression, eventually terror, and a collection of people who fear one another.

Manifestly, the inner space we call privacy is shrunk as far as possible in Rousseau's plans for denaturing men and forming them into social units or 'citizens'. He says so. In a properly run state, 'there is less private business' (SC, III, 15). Eulogizing Lycurgus for imposing 'an iron yoke' and making his people identify with that yoke, he ecstasizes: 'He would show it the fatherland in its laws, in its games, at home, in its loves, in its feasts; not even for a minute would he leave the people to themselves alone. And from this constraint, ennobled by its aim, would be born in the people that ardent love of their country' (CGP, Vaughan, II, 428–9). Privacy implies the exclusion of others, and especially of the state. It nourishes personal and family loyalties outside of its reach. Rousseau, one scholar has written, 'was only one of many who have hoped to dissolve the private into the public'.[15] But Justice Brandeis has called privacy – the right to be left alone – 'the most comprehensive of rights and the right most valued by civilized men'.

One must also take into account Rousseau's intuition, probably unique in his time, of the psychological dynamics of politics as distinct from its rational goals. Zeal stimuli – public games, athletic contests and exercises, nationalistic ceremonies of a semi-religious character, historical spectacles to arouse patriotic emotion and emulation – every possible means must be used to make country the 'largest concern' of people's lives (LM, Vaughan, II, 491–2). This method, he assures us, dissipates any *suspicion* of arbitrary power. The twentieth-century observer will recognize it.

Rousseau was the first to apprehend the power of symbols, the language of 'impressionable things' as a technique of conditioning. In

La Fête révolutionnaire (1976), Mona Ozouf has studied the power of *fêtes*, which were inspired by Rousseau. They 'mobilized symbols and rituals of solidarity in support of a new order and a myth of unanimity and transparency, of sacred, civic values, and a dehistoricized order'.[16] Participation and commitment – these were Rousseau's goals.

The preceding outline of his 'true society' makes it evident how unsound it is to concentrate on the political institutions he sets up in the *Social Contract*. They are essential as means to his end; but the proper method, I have urged, is to interpret them in the light of the ends we have examined.

The limits of this article do not permit a close analysis,[17] but these are the main points: 1) The social contract: renunciation of rights, some of which may be recreated by the state at its discretion, but none of which are reserved or protected against unlimited majority rule – even if it were not manipulated; the unlimited power of the sovereign (*LM*, Vaughan, II, 279); the 'moral and collective body' in place of the individual (*SC*, I, 6); 2) the invention of a supposititious general will which empirically may be no one's, but is known to the managers ('guides') as their real will – an unconditioned will assuring the state through its agencies a direct grip on the individuals (no intervening bodies or 'factions' being allowed to disrupt the monolithic wholeness), a will that being infallible is not criticizable or subject to protest or dissent; 3) the assemblies which vote the laws proposed by the guides, citizens not being allowed to propose, amend or discuss them, or to communicate among themselves (*SC*, IV, 1); assemblies where the citizens are 'guided' (Rousseau says 'informed', but it is not a matter of giving out information – another of Rousseau's word-games), thus achieving participation, the illusion of freedom, the feeling of belonging to a whole, and the solution to Rousseau's paradox, 'libres et dociles';[18] 4) the government.

Before scrutinizing somewhat more extensively the role of government in this scheme, it will be useful to consider the idea of power. Often discussions of Rousseau's thought (such as R. R. Palmer's in his *Age of the Democratic Revolution*) deal only with abstractions about formal aspects of institutions. Among the important dimensions such an approach leaves untreated are the actual location of power and its use. In fact, more fully than any other in his time, Rousseau was aware of the potential uses of power, and we have seen to what ends he thought it should be put. He recognized it as a fundamental element of our being in the world, our *Sitz im Leben* (*PCC*, Vaughan, II, 345–6)

– or, in Dilthey's words, that power relations can never be eliminated from the living together of psycho-physical beings. Finally, he recognized it as the ultimate political reality, and thought deeply about how it might be localized and deployed.

Rousseau knew that the fundamental problem was to control and redirect the uses of power. Power, not liberty, is his pressing concern. The proper use of power, which he always confides to an elite, is to eliminate the blind play of forces in the social relations of men. It is to 'form' the human clay, to orchestrate all social activities, to create and maintain, against original human wishes, one body, one will, one right way; in sum, to forge a unity not found in historical (i.e. haphazard rather than planned) societies. 'The more such natural forces die and are destroyed the more those which are acquired are great and durable, and the more also is the institution solid and persistent' (*SC*, II, 7). It follows that all activities are viewed as ultimately political, hence subject to control.

History, Rousseau realized, was not made solely by institutions, but by the men who made and controlled them. Therefore power had to be given to charismatic leaders. The strategy is to take advantage of people's propensity to follow such leaders. As Robert Nisbet observes, the chapter on the Legislator 'is about nothing else but the relentless and absolute power necessary to remake human nature'.[19] Except at one point (*LM*, Vaughan, II, 285), Rousseau seems unaware that his leaders and guides would be involved in a power struggle among themselves.

Rousseau proclaimed popular sovereignty, whence the common belief that he wanted (what we call) democracy with assured rights – which he did not. Wanting to avoid the exploitation he hated by a king or power group, he imagined leaders, superior beings, who would speak in the name of, and on behalf of the whole civic community. He gave his citizens the power of consent (and theoretically of refusal), but under three conditions: they must have been 'denatured' and 'formed' into citizens who see themselves only in the whole; they must be subjected to unremitting surveillance to prevent their falling back under the natural domination of the 'moi humain'; they must be guided into the correct path. The people is sovereign in the state, but the individuals who compose the people are not the sovereign of themselves, and must not be. The whole could not exist if the parts considered themselves independently of it. In sum, there is no relation between the power of the people as sovereign (theoretically, at least, to approve the laws) and the actual exercise of power, which is located in the government: 'the total force of government always being that of the state' (*SC*, III, 2). Nothing could be clearer, more emphatic, or confirm this point more irrefutably, than the third paragraph of the chapter on the Legislator (*SC*, II, 7), too long to quote here. Mario Reale, in his excellent discussion of the general will, points out that it is necessary to keep working on the original elements of the structure in order to sustain the identity of the singular part with the social whole.[20] To assert its ends, the general will must yield to a more efficient and persuasive energy.

Legislators and guides can exercise control only through government and its agents, such as censors. Rousseau did not distinguish between society and the state, because the good life could be realized only in community. The entire apparatus for 'educating', 'controlling opinion', 'forming citizens', changing *moeurs*, fomenting zeal and patriotism belongs to the government.[21] It issues 'acts', which do not have the generality of laws and may be applied to individuals or groups. The government is not responsible, except for a vote of confidence, to the periodic assemblies, which are also subject to its management (the 'guides'). This will not present difficulties, Rousseau reassures us in *Economie politique*: 'By its deference the people, convinced that its leaders only work to achieve its happiness, dispense them from the task of affirming its power'. And again: 'In the exercise of its power, it is sufficient for it to bend everything to its will, little by little' (*LM*, Vaughan, II, 265).

As Nisbet remarks, 'Rousseau designed, in the *Social Contract*, and even more perhaps in the *Discourse on Political Economy*, the most powerful state to be found anywhere in political philosophy' (p. 52). Power, put to the goal of acquiring control over human life, ultimately signifies compulsion — preferably concealed and indirect but direct when necessary ('forced to be free', the censors). As François Furet has convincingly shown, those who pre-empt the symbol of speaking in the name of the people (or the nation) acquire power over the people.[22] And the natural prey of power is liberty and rights.[23] We may grant that extreme cases of gross oppression and mismanagement which are evident and *felt* as such could result in rebellion in the assemblies against the managers. However, the workings of the system are designed to obviate such situations by skilled management and to prevent *felt* oppression by the thoroughness and deviousness of control.

And so it is that the government, through its 'chefs' and its 'guides', chooses goals which its agents carry out in the manifold ways of achieving them. In theory, power belongs to the sovereign people and cannot be alienated. However, since its actuation is alienated to the government, the effect is to reverse theory as it becomes practice. It is the government that makes the sovereign body a body.

The common opinion is that we best see Rousseau's planned society in the *Social Contract*. I maintain that however important that work is in the realm of theory, the most significant place to grasp his ideal intentions and how he imagines them to work out is not the *Social Contract* but the *Projet de constitution pour la Corse*, which is usually scanted by commentators. Nor is it the *Considérations sur le gouvernement de Pologne*, in which he adheres as far as he can to his unswerving conception, but is constrained by the need to reckon with customs and existing social institutions, and thus can think only of reform and not total revolution. Only in the Corsican project does he outline freely and without restraint the applications of his theory to practice. And the proper approach to Rousseau's thought, remarks J. V. Harari (*Scenarios of the Imagination*, p. 104), is to 'understand the system as a function of its application'.

In the *Projet* we see *en toutes lettres* the inflexible subordination of natural relationships to the state. It lays bare the illusoriness of his assurance that the state will keep only those surrendered rights that it judges to be of social importance. 'The nation must be formed for the government' (Vaughan, II, 303). It confirms the all-invasiveness of power. It reveals how the same methods used in *La Nouvelle Héloïse* and *Emile* are transposed to another level. 'I shall not preach morality; I shall not compel virtues. But I shall put the people in such a position that they will possess such virtues, without recognizing their significance, such that they will be good and just without knowing what *justice* and *goodness* mean . . . the *government* [my italics] needs little force and directs peoples, so to speak, with a flick of the finger.'

While I cannot recapitulate the details of the planned regimentation and intrusion into every aspect of every individual's life by a central authority, they include continuous control and conditioning to inculcate habits 'impossible to uproot', the assignment of permanent jobs and stations, abolition of privacy as far as possible, mobilization of the arts and of labour, maintenance of a retrograde agricultural economy. The way of dressing and lodging, of arranging one's sexual life, of living or not living in groups, are among the items that are resected from the realm of privacy. *Fêtes nationales* will replace religion as far as possible. Fear, hope and vanity are to be used as incentives, aided especially by ignorance. The people will not be able to imagine a better condition. As Restif later wrote, 'To desire something you must know it'. Or as a modern scholar has put it, 'before a government can control production, it must first regulate imagination and delimit desire; it must tyrannize thought' (Richard Vine, 'Walter Benjamin', *New Criteria*, 8 (1990), p. 48).

As to property, Rousseau comes to the logical point he had avoided in the *Social Contract*. He does not propose abolishing it 'absolutely', but limiting it in a way that 'subjugates it and always keeps it subordinate to the public good'. 'I should like, in a word, that the property of the state be as great and as durable, and that of citizens as slight and weakly held, as possible . . . Everyone should live and no one enrich himself from it.' Central control extends to all economic activity.

Although equality is proclaimed, this society is hierarchical, with three orders based on service to the state, each with its privileges. The right to vote is maintained, but now we see clearly how correct was my previous interpretation. This is how it is done. The leader speaks: 'Corsicans, be silent, I wish to speak in the name of all. Let those who do not agree depart, and those who consent raise their hand' (PCC, II, 349).

Rousseau's aim is stated. It is to possess men, and their will, 'Let us refrain from augmenting the treasure of wealth at the expense of the treasure of morality: it is the latter which really puts us in control of men and all their power, while through the former we only obtain their services; the will cannot be bought' (II, 340). And again 'the arbiters of the public opinion of a people are its actions.' This is the job of the government, which must show the people 'what it ought to esteem' and tell them 'what it ought to do' (II, 344–5). Rousseau is only carrying forward what he had written earlier, but just as forcefully (*EP*, Vaughan, I, 248, 257). As Primo Levi has put it, 'In a totalitarian regime, propaganda and information meet with no obstacles.'

There are no individual rights, Vaughan has noted, except those derived from the *prior* right of the state (II, 303). In fact, one searches in vain for a trace of personal liberty in his *Project of a Constitution for Corsica*, for a recognition of the needs and feeling of the individual. Responsibility is transferred to a higher authority, and the visionary end justifies the means. Rousseau has lost touch with human reality. It is all summarized in the sacred and irrevocable oath each must swear: 'I unite my body and worldly goods, my will and all my power, to the Corsican nation, so as to belong to it utterly, I and all that depends on me' (*PCC*, II, 350).

Surely, it is not too much to say that it is only a small step from the project for Corsica to a totally controlled police state, a 'people's democracy', where individuals are indoctrinated and terrorized into submissive conformity, with the show of plebiscitary consent. The unspoken underlying theme harks back to the *Second Discourse*. If you don't have absolute control over people, the evil that is natural to them in any social situation will erupt into unsocial competition.

Rousseau was a humanist, in the sense that he believed that men make their own history and destiny. Utopianism, however, is a perverted form of humanism. It postulates abstractions, the social organic whole or 'body', the general will, Man substituted for men. It is a harmless game when confined to idle fancy. It becomes disastrous when deluded dogmatists try to put it into practice, when enthusiasts become convinced they have discovered the only road to happiness. Let history speak.

Neither of Isaiah Berlin's two categories of liberty applies to Rousseau's state and society. 'Negative liberty', the relative absence of limit, direction, regimentation, repression by the authorities, does not exist, in his thinking, in any measurable degree. 'Positive liberty' is defined as participation in making laws; but laws can be wicked and crushing, and collective oppression can be the most severe when there is no recourse. Rousseau's aim was to produce the feeling of participation, of involvement, a part of the illusion of being free that he constantly proclaims as essential to his technique for forming citizens. In a word, Berlin's distinction disappears, and liberty with it.

Rousseau was the great illusionist. In *La Nouvelle Héloïse* he grafts on to Saint-Preux the illusion of being happy, in *Emile* the illusion that the subject of the process is autonomous and independent, in the *Social Contract* and the *Projet pour la Corse* the illusion that the individual citizen is free. The reproach one might address to many commentators is that they believe him and fall prey to suppositions or phantasies that he pretends to have demonstrated. His superb rhetoric aims at inspiring such faith. They accept his assurances without examining the contradictions and underlying realities, as when he writes, 'By what unimaginable device have we found the means to make men subject so as to render them free' (Pléiade, III, 310). They do not recognize how, as Raymond Polin has explained, the social contract itself is a deceit and a lie, one that carries with it moral and even physical violence as essential structures of the public authority.[24] Elimination of dissent implies persecution of any who resist and escape the net of indoctrination and conformity. Surely, a regimented society is not a society of liberty. Whereas Spinoza had said that a state lacks the power to control freedom to think for oneself, Rousseau wants to show how it can be done. A suffocating orthodoxy is not a society of liberty, even if willing consent to it has been engineered.

When Rousseau speaks of 'the hard yoke of liberty', he means something peculiarly his own. A person, having alienated his liberty, supposedly finds it again because he is no longer himself as he was. If his own opinion should not prevail, he should rejoice: 'I would have done something other than I wished. I would then not have been free' (SC, IV, 2). Since adherence to the one right will, the collective will purged of all marks of individual wills, is liberty, it resides outside the experienced will, on the assumption that it is what one really wills, unknowingly. And so we have the paradox of freedom consisting in a person's not doing what he knows he wants to do, because he knows that his knowing is wrong. Everyone must be made to believe this hoax. The only freedom, then, is the freedom to conform, to participate in a monolithic conformity whose noble aim is to end alienation.

The practical principle is to inculcate belief. Julie says everyone obeys Wolmar submissively and everyone is free. Saint-Preux is made to believe that the frustration of his desires is his liberation. The principle of physical necessity in the moral realm eliminates the need to *choose* virtue. Since human nature is such that spontaneous identification of self with all will not occur, and reason is powerless to defeat the impulses of *amour propre*, we are thrust back into the paradox of being forced to be free.

For Rousseau what counts is society as a whole, *le tout*, with its 'self', its ('general') will, therefore the *liberty* of *that* will. Liberty, its liberty, depends on the possession of power. Contrariwise, what counts, if liberty is to have real meaning, is what happens to individuals in a society and their wills; for a society is not comparable to an organic biological body, but is a conjunction of concrete individuals – of disparate individuals. What Rousseau has done is to transfer the locus of liberty and therewith to transmute its meaning.

To transform the state into an ideal state and men into social units is to harbour an absolutist conception. Infallibility ensures total power. We cannot transform a system of total power, wherever it resides, into a system of liberty. Sidney Hook once said, 'It is the spirit of absolutism that is the greatest enemy of a liberal civilization, and orthodoxy is fatal to honest thinking'. History and utopian literature both show that unanimity is possible (if at all) only with draconian pressures. People do not agree with each other. The character of reason is that of a contention among ideas.[25]

One cannot doubt Rousseau's good intentions. If he submits the words 'liberty' and 'equality' to a radical transformation in a utopian scheme, it was because he wanted happiness for men. He thought that his kind of liberty was the best that could be synthesized within a true society and that his 'true society' was the best, the only solution for human destiny. The resulting paradox is that men are enslaved by liberty.

This was the way he had to think. 'Instead of adapting himself to a society which shuts itself before him, he curses the whole of it and reconstructs it in the image of his delirium . . . The power of man over man is a dreadful stimulant of dark passions, a substitute for personal impotence, the great consolation for failure.'[26] In his own life, as earlier mentioned, Rousseau saw himself as the abused prophet (he once compared himself to Christ). In his prophecies, he was the revolutionary demiurge, doing the work nature did not do. He had all the marks of a classic paranoid: delusions of grandeur ('men should raise statues to me'), the construction of a labyrinthine, internally logical system to account for everything, one that was unquestionably true and, in his case, would remedy everything. For what Rousseau wanted was redemption – a *total* redemption. If this required a conspiracy, since men could not regenerate themselves – not through reason or through will – it was a conspiracy to lead them out of the human predicament. And what is more typical of the paranoid, what greater constant is there in Rousseau's life and personality, than obsession with conspiracy? Conspiracy was his explanation of the origin of society. A maze of conspiracies rules the world of *La Nouvelle Héloïse* and controls Emile. Conspiracy was his element. He saw it everywhere around him. He could not help thinking in those terms. Though he was a loner, he was the first in the line of conspiratorial thinkers, stretching from Babeuf and Buonarroti through nineteenth-century revolutionaries, to Lenin and Trotsky. They were all conspirators for salvation.[27] Not to read Rousseau this way is to suppose another man than the man he was, and to suppose a complete scission between the man and his work.

History and common sense show that there is no more destructive illusion than to think there can be a definitive, absolute solution for the ills of society and human existence. Rousseau had that illusion. His vision was of a reordering of the human condition. He articulates a revolutionary absolute that reaches to its final limit, human nature. Its end-point would be to produce 'mummies rather than citizens . . . by shrivelling and binding the dynamic political and economic processes that freedom releases'.[28] It shows that 'the cruelty of ideas lies in the assumption that human beings can be made to fit them'.[29]

Rousseau's vision was a religious one, as Marx's was to be, a faith in something transcending reality, the secular eschatology of the Kingdom of God, the parousia of a new Moses. Not much later, Saint-Just, Rousseau's devoted disciple, thought for a while that he (or Robespierre) would be the new Moses.[30] But not for long. Brief exaltation faded into the realization that the game was lost. Human nature is too resilient, cannot be snuffed out. The challenge cannot be won. Despite maximal pressure, men are incapable, except in orgasmic spurts, of the kind of 'virtue' Rousseau demanded of them. Fraternal harmony never lasts. There is no ideal city; if there were, it would succumb to the countercurrents of history. Rousseau's conception results in dividing men into two categories, the good and the bad, but the good and the bad are inextricably linked in them.

The libertarian knows that freedom and order are in a delicate balance. There can be no freedom without order. Yet they are in an adversarial relationship and law must determine the limits of each.

The libertarian knows there are no certainties, that there are always several possible answers to problems, that men can rarely, if ever, completely agree, and that each is an autonomous center of decision. 'One right way' may be the wrong way. No procrustean bed is conducive to human welfare. *Emile* and *La Nouvelle Héloïse* testify to the folly of treating human beings according to an abstract and rigid system. Conflict may within limits be more healthful than harmony — more, certainly, than an imposed harmony that leaves little or no room for the free play of individual energies and intellect. To suppress doubt is to cut away a uniquely human capacity.

There are, in fact, two conceptions of liberty running through Rousseau's life and writings. They have often been confused by commentators. In the context of his own society – a false society – that word meant the proud independence of the individual and the refusal to be a slave to 'opinion'. Rousseau considered himself and indeed was the exemplar of this rebellious liberty, which is proclaimed in the *Discourses* and the autobiographical writings. In the pattern of his dreamed-of 'true society', however, into which he projected himself as prophet, lawgiver and guide, heralding the road to happiness, revolutionary new relationships outlaw such independence as anti-social.

The libertarian, finally, holds that each has the right to arrange his own life, as far as he can, according to his preferences, without injuring others. He knows that human lives have their own loyalties and are not entirely shaped to the demands of an overwhelming community. He does not separate his ideals from the limiting conditions of their realization and does not dream of utopias that reality will not allow.

Rousseau, however, believed in the possibility of conceiving, if not realizing, a perfect social order, a rational order, a true society engineered in an historical vacuum. He was convinced that he had found it, and that some day, somewhere, men might possibly make it come true, or at least, that they should. Not for him was the conviction that the destiny of man does not lie in an ideal future, but in a feasible one. Not for him Candide's garden. His formula and his faith were, to use Berlin's phrase, that of a final solution. A final solution abolishes history, the evil history of the past and any significant future history. But history is man's dimension of living in time. It is development through a dialectical counterpoint of opposing aims, interests, ideas and forces. There is no room for this in Rousseau's brave new world.

Notes

1 Who decides what is threatening behaviour brings us back to the question of participation and the limits of such determinations. Some behaviour is absolutely threatening (e.g. murder), others depend on the degree to which power may be exercised (e.g. abortion, dissent, demonstrations).

2 *Economie politique*, in Vaughan, vol. I. This work will be referred to as 'EP', the *Social Contract* as 'SC', *Considérations sur le gouvernement de Pologne* as 'CGP', *Lettres écrites de la montagne* as 'LM', the *Projet de constitution pour la Corse* as 'PCC'. In references to the *Social Contract*, the Roman numeral indicates the Book, the Arabic numeral the chapter.

3 For the meaning of the three gardens in that novel, see my article, 'Order and Disorder in Rousseau's Social Thought', *PMLA*, 94 (1979), 247–60. The frequent references to my publications are motivated not by egotism but by the impossibility of presenting all the textual evidence within the compass of this essay.

4 And in *Emile*, 'au lieu de la personne particulière de chaque contractant, cet acte d'association produit un corps moral et collectif . . . Cette personne publique prend en général le nom de *corps politique*' (Pléiade, IV, 840). As Michèle Duchet has aptly said, 'Il nous paraît difficile de voir dans les expressions "corps social", "corps politique" de simples métaphores . . . la relation des parties au tout devient l'essentiel' (*Anthropologie et histoire au siècle des lumières*, Paris, 1977, 309). See also my 'Burlamaqui et Rousseau', in *Etudes sur Jean-Jacques Rousseau* (Reims, 1990).

5 Rousseau assures us that 'tous ont engagé leurs beins et leurs vies à la défense de chacun d'eux' (*EP*, 253). This is not intended as a valorisation of individualism, but is an extension of the basic idea of a society as an organic body comparable to a biological body, in that work.

6 'Le recours compensatoire à la fusion avec le tout a pour fonction axiologique de réprimer les velléités de sortir des bornes qu'imposent le sort et les hommes, notamment lorsque leur caractère douloureux, voire injuste, semblerait autoriser la rébellion . . . La tendance à la totalisation, pourtant indispensable afin de situer les parties et les ordonner dans un tout, devient source de dénaturation' (L. Marcil-Lacoste, 'Pourquoi faut-il qu'Emile soit borné?', *Dialogue*, XIX, 4, Paris, 1980, 621).

7 R. D. Masters, 'The Biological Nature of the State', *World Politics*, XXXV (1983), 161–93.

8 Robert Nisbet, *The Present Age*, New York, 1988, 52–3.

9 De Maistre, an opponent of Rousseau, borrows the notion when he writes that individual reason must be absorbed into the national reason, and the existence of the individual transformed into 'une commune existence' (*Etude sur la souveraineté*, ch. X).

10 'C'est ici l'article important. C'est l'éducation qui doit donner aux âmes la forme nationale, et diriger tellement leurs opinions et leurs goûts qu'elles soient patriotes par inclination, par passion, par nécessité. Un enfant, en ouvrant les yeux, doit voir la patrie, et jusqu'à la mort ne plus voir qu'elle . . . Cet amour fait toute son existence; il ne voit que la patrie, il ne vit que par elle; sitôt qu'il est seul, il est nul' (*CGP*, Vaughan, II, 437). It is only with respect to such souls that laws can be effective.

11 See my article, 'Docilité et duplicité chez Rousseau', *RHLF*, 68 (1968), 448–69.

12 Julie von Bondéli remarked in a letter on the confusion of artifice and nature in *Emile*, and Grimm wrote, 'What is no less strange is to see this writer preaching the love of truth everywhere and constantly using artifice and lies.'

13 'Construed as rational, universal, impersonal, unitary, "opinion publique", during the Revolution took on many of the attributes of the absolute authority it was displacing'. The men who did this were avowed disciples of Rousseau. (In Keith Baker, Introduction to *The Political Culture of the Old Régime*, Oxford and New York, 1987, xviii.)

14 See my 'Rousseau's Two Discourses: The Philosopher as Rhetorician', in *The Philosopher as Writer*, London and Toronto, 1987, 15–47.

15 Bernard Williams, in a review of Barrington Moore's *Privacy*, *New York Review of Books*, 25 April 1985.

16 In Keith Baker, 'Enlightenment and Revolution in France', *JMH*, 53 (1981), 288–91.

17 See my *Jean-Jacques Rousseau. The Prophetic Voice*, New York and London, 1973, ch. 5 and Norman Hampson, *Will and Circumstance*, University of Oklahoma, 1983, 57–8, 79, 82, 175, 180, 219.

18 A curious point that Rousseau dodges: how is this unqualified 'blind multitude', who all need guides to discern the right way, qualified to decide whether the guides are in fact telling them the right way? How is it possible that individuals who see the good but don't follow it can no longer see it when they are together? For Rousseau's ambivalent attitude toward the people, see my article, 'Rousseau and the Common People', in *Essays in Honor of Otis Fellows*, Geneva, 1974, 89–111. Rousseau's model was doubtless the Roman *comitia* or *comitia curiata*, with which he was familiar (*SC*, IV, 4). At their meetings, the assembly was addressed by the magistrate. 'The magistrate brought his formulated request before the people, who accepted it . . .' The citizens 'individually replied *ut rogas*, "yes" or *antiquo*, "no" . . . Herein is involved the fundamental idea of *lex*, which was not a command addressed by the sovereign to the people or a contract between ruler and ruled, but an obligation which the citizens took upon themselves at the request of the magistrate'. No speaking or discussion was allowed (G. W. Botsford, *The Roman Assemblies*, New York, 1968, 178–9). See also L. R. Tayler, *Roman Voting Assemblies*, Ann Arbor, 1966, 2, 15, 34. Rousseau writes of the comitiae, 'Chacun donnait son suffrage à haute voix' and goes on to condemn the degeneracy of the secret ballot. Oral and public voting are stipulated in *PCC* (Vaughan, II, 349).

19 *Op. cit.*, 115.

20 M. Reale, *Le ragioni della politica*, Roma, 1983, 575–98.

21 For education, see especially *EP*, 256–8 and my 'Diderot and Rousseau: Education as Politics' in *Analecta Romanica*, Heft 48, 1983, 28–46.

22 F. Furet, *Penser la Révolution Française*, Paris, 1978, 51.

23 Bernard Baylin, *The Ideological Origins of the American Revolution*, Cambridge, Mass., 1967, 59.

24 Raymond Polin, 'Principes du mensonge politique', Société de philosophie et de langue française, Actes du XIIIe Congrès, Neuchâtel, 1966, 356–60. In a later work Polin writes that Rousseau pretends to save the individual 'en lui ôtant toute charge de son autonomie'. He adds picturesquement, 'adieu à l'individu authentique, autonome, actif, responsable et bonjour à l'individu content comme peut l'être un animal domestique par le tout dont il dépend absolument' (*La Creation des cultures*, Paris, 1933, 247–8).

25 Forrest Macdonald's observations about classical republicanism apply to Rousseau. See *Novus Ordo Seclorum*, University of Kansas, 1985, 71, 160. Kant's borrowing from Rousseau is obvious. See *Kant's Political Writings*, Cambridge, 1970, 44–6, and especially Huntington Cairns, *Legal Philosophy from Plato to Hegel*, Baltimore, 1949, 448. The enlightening question of Platonic and Aristotelian elements in Rousseau's ideas cannot be gone into here.

26 J.-M. Domenach, *Le Retour du tragique*, Paris, 1967, 162, 143.

27 For Rousseau as revolutionary, see my forthcoming 'Qu'y a-t-il de révolutionnaire dans l'*Emile*?' (Colloque de Montmorency, 1992, 147–52). Several items of particular pertinence can only be mentioned and recommended here. They include Michael Oakeshott's *Rationalism in Politics* on the choice between collectivism and liberty (New York, 1967, 5, 50–4); the concluding chapter of Michèle Ansart-Dourlen's *Dénaturation et violence dans la pensée de J.-J. Rousseau*, Paris, 1975; parts of Claude Polin's superb thesis, *L'Esprit totalitaire* (Paris, 1977, esp. 104–34); and the remarks of Bronislaw Baczko in *Lumières de l'utopie*, Paris, 1978, 8, 30, 51, 95, 247.

28 J. H. Billington, *Fire in the Minds of Men*, New York, 1980, 197.

29 Paul Johnson, *Intellectuals*, New York, 1988, 26.

30 See Saint-Just, *Discours et rapports*, Editions Sociales, *passim*, and, for example, p. 135.

13 Iain Hampsher-Monk

Rousseau and totalitarianism – with hindsight?[1]

At the conference on Rousseau which was to have been hosted by Ralph Leigh, and sponsored by the Liberty Fund in Cambridge in the midst of the upheavals of 1989, Peter Laslett observed that if there was one book to be put in the hands of those then struggling to establish political liberty in Eastern Europe, it was not *The Social Contract* of Rousseau, but the second of Locke's *Two Treatises of Government*. That a Cambridge historian of political thought should then have considered the dissemination of *any* historical text to be an action of contemporary political import might itself have raised an eyebrow or two, but methodological issues aside, Laslett's remark stayed with me, and provides as it were my text: hovering as it does between a comment on Rousseau and a comment on the meaning of 1989 for us in the West.

For the collapse of communist regimes in Eastern Europe has removed an essential point of difference in the self-perceptions of 'Liberal' Western European regimes. Supervening as it did on a period of anti-collectivist, deregulatory, and in some cases triumphalist rejection of social democracy, it was – and indeed still is – unclear whether the ultimate effect of 1989 will be the unopposed and unexamined flourishing of economic individualist presuppositions and their organisational and civic consequences, or whether, on the other hand, the liberation of their defining ideological opponents will in turn liberate those in the West to undertake a less inhibited appraisal of the varieties of political and economic arrangements consistent with some version or dimension of liberty.

Recognising the range of issues connected with liberty has implications for those assessments of Rousseau which were closely tied to one particular view of it, for deprecating Rousseau's version of freedom in favour of Locke's is, of course, the more sensitive end of a scale which ranges to the familiar insinuation of links, historical or conceptual, between Rousseau and totalitarianism. This has, since the middle of our century, been accomplished by reflecting the prevalent ideological divide in a sharp conceptual distinction between individualistic liberalism and state collectivism and locating Rousseau on the wrong side of it. The collapse of that ideological bipolarity should not only remind us of how crude an exercise this was but provide us with a perspective from which to view the construction – and complete the deconstruction – of the totalitarian Rousseau.

Just as in his life Rousseau consummated the role of outsider, so in his posthumous reputation, more often than not, Rousseau has been the 'other'. Yet whilst totalitarianism has, even *avant la lettre*, been for most of our century the liberal individualists' other and Rousseau its expression, Rousseau's identity has historically been more equivocal: for the generation after Rousseau saw unbridled individualism as the threat – and Rousseau as the expression of it. Burke, and later Mackintosh and Coleridge in England, Bonald and de Maistre in France, all saw – from their different perspectives – the danger to be the heightened role that Rousseau gave to the untutored, abstracted, individual will in the establishment of the state. The danger of revolutionary ideology was not conceived – as with modern totalitarian regimes – to arise from its claim to *shape* the minds of its citizens, but from its *destroying* the shape which the discipline of a civilised, religious order had imposed on individuals (whether through reason, socialisation or fear). In this initial perception of Rousseau, the danger his theory was seen to pose is precisely the opposite of that in more recent criticisms. For modern critics of totalitarianism Rousseau threatens freedom because (amongst other things) he justified the enforced socialisation of individuals into a set of beliefs supportive of the state. For first generation critics Rousseau had, at the very least, prepared the way for the revolution because he *destroyed* the hold on individuals of those socialised beliefs and attachments which supported the ancient regime states, or indeed, as some of them claimed, any society at all.[2] This was not a simple issue (as modern relativists might claim) of disagreement as to *what* it is we should be socialised into. As paradoxical, often, as his ideological *alter ego*, Burke was insistent that art was man's nature, and it was Rousseau's attack on artifice itself, indeed on the very grain of conventional life as subjectively experienced and his substitution of an abstract reason, that ingenuously facilitated a return to an individuality so free that only force, or the continual and visible threat of it, was capable of creating order.³

Nineteenth-century liberals – unsurprisingly for descendants of the *philosophes* whom Rousseau had rejected – stressed, by contrast, his dangerous collectivism and – starting famously with Constant's more indulgent judgement – the hostages he had perhaps unwittingly given to collective as well as individual tyranny.⁴ Nevertheless there were even at this time strains sympathetic to Rousseauian themes. Even John Stuart Mill – whose references to Rousseau usually reflect only the 'noble savage' cliché – can be found asserting that obedience and 'even personal slavery . . . may accelerate the transition to a better freedom' than 'savage independence'.⁵ More presciently the interesting and neglected Anglican essayist Mark Pattison in an essay on Calvin published in the *Westminster Review* pursued the idealist distinction between liberalism and mere liberty. Praising Calvin for 'the tyranny of the discipline [which] became the cradle of liberty' he claimed that

> It may easily happen that Liberalism may be found on one side and Liberty on the other. For Liberalism is only the irreflective desire to be quit of constraint; the natural instinct of the free man, but nothing more . . . true liberty is only realized through self control, when 'the weight of chance desire' has been felt, and been shaken off by an effort of will.⁶

Whilst the above examples are perhaps untypical, with the rise of the new social liberalism at the end of the century the polarities were decisively reversed again. T. H. Green, for example, in his influential *Lectures*, rejected Rousseau's contractarianism mainly in order to salvage the latter's conception of sovereignty and his identification of a higher moral and political self, above and distinct from the actual empirical one.⁷ Bernard Bosanquet, with similar enthusiasm, continuously invoked Rousseau in explaining that 'The Conception of a real Will' was necessary to understand 'the conception of Liberty'.⁸

The twentieth-century origins of worries about what metaphysical selves might aspire to – so recently endorsed by Bosanquet and Green – might be traced to the 'Epilogue' to Vaughan's edition of *The Political Writings of Rousseau*, written under the impact of the First World War.⁹ Vaughan candidly emphasized how total war had exposed the delicacy of the relationship between the state and the individual. He stressed the inadequacy of both the individualist account of this and its opposite extreme, the absolutist conception of state. Conceding slight worries about Rousseau's soundness on such matters it was, nevertheless, not Rousseau but Fichte whom Vaughan identified as absolutism's 'most clear sighted exponent'. Whilst deprecating each thinker's characterisation of the political incorporation of the individual as a 'surrender', it was Fichte, he pointed out, who had dismissed as irrelevant those popular or legal-egalitarian safeguards which for Rousseau were the very condition of the legitimacy of such a surrender. On the second pressing issue of the day, the rights of the state against its neighbours, Rousseau too was unequivocal: peace was not only an idea (perpetual peace), it was commanded, wherever possible, under natural law. 'It (was) not lawful to cement the bonds of a single community at the cost of the rest of mankind.'[10] For Vaughan, Rousseau provided an 'ideal of self government and of corporate if not individual freedom within: and of respect for the rights and freedoms of others without.'[11]

By the end of the war L. T. Hobhouse, claiming to see the fruits of the metaphysical theory of the state in the horror of Ypres, aerial bombardment and the Somme, traced it back, via Bosanquet and Hegel to Rousseau's identification of freedom with the real, the real with the general will, and the general will with the state.[12]

The argument was often subsequently fought in terms of this intellectual ancestry. Rousseau's liberal critics stressed the continuity of the line that could be constructed from Rousseau through Kant and Fichte to Hegel and so, supposedly, to twentieth-century Fascism. Defenders of Rousseau by contrast pointed out that whilst Kant did indeed praise Rousseau, both Fichte and Hegel developed detailed critiques of him, each of which focused on the limitations which his individualism posed to the establishment of the nation-state.[13] The line of totalitarian descent contained an important caesura, with, it could be claimed, Rousseau on the far side.

But sympathy for a liberal version of Rousseau was not yet exhausted: even during the Second World War, whilst Popper and Talmon were preparing their indictment of his place in the genealogy of totalitarianism, A. D. Lindsay, whose pluralism set him at odds, was nevertheless concerned to stress how 'important and profound' was Rousseau's claim that the idea of political freedom entailed political obligations; moreover, despite the misuse to which the idea was put it was 'not absurd to say that the general will is each individual's good or real will, and that if he dissents from a vote expressing the general will, he must be not merely mistaken, but bad.'[14] As late as

1956, John Chapman, reviewing assessments of Rousseau as a liberal which drew on earlier conceptions of liberalism, from Derathé, Cassirer, Wright, Cole, Lindsay and others, summed up his liberal defenders' case by claiming that it was: 'Emphasis on his concern for moral creativity [that] makes Rousseau a liberal.'[15]

This would shortly become a perplexing claim to make. Following Berlin's influential distinction between negative liberty – which stressed the absence of human constraint on action – and positive liberty – which focused on the wider conditions for a particular use of it, liberals have come to stress the totalitarian danger inherent in positive liberty and identify Rousseau as the exponent of it. But Chapman's 'concern with moral creativity' was, by contrast, a concern with the use of liberty in a particular way.[16] Considerably more than the absence of constraint, it is what we would call positive liberty. Whilst this might confirm the views of those individualist liberals who wished to sustain a totalitarian Rousseau, they must note that they would be invoking, as proof of his totalitarian tendencies, the very criteria which at least two generations of idealist liberals had used to establish his liberal credentials. A difference within the liberal tradition, when projected on to Rousseau became an ideological antithesis.

The nature of the case against Rousseau is further complicated by the fact that not only, as the above sketch suggests, has Rousseau been held responsible for different – even manifestly contradictory – reasons by critics from different political positions for the excesses of successive revolutions, but this responsibility has been held to operate in different ways and through different mechanisms. At root there are two different claims about the danger Rousseau has posed to liberty.

On the one hand there are a group of essentially philosophical claims to the effect that Rousseau asserts conceptual relationships which in and of themselves misconstrue the character of freedom, that his ideas, taken together, comprise an essentially illiberal vision, which directly licenses the subordination of the individual to the state in a way that free societies do not, that, in the words of Saint-Just – who himself knew a thing or two about the matter – Rousseau 'strangles liberty with his own hands'. On the other hand there is the historical claim that even though Rousseau may not be the perpetrator, so misguided was his thinking that, to complete Saint-Just's argument, 'the more safeguards he established against despotism the more weapons he forged for tyranny.'[17] On this view whatever Rousseau himself may have *intended* or indeed, on any dispassionate view *actually written*, the influence nevertheless exerted by his works, the political consequences drawn from them have, as a matter of historical fact, been malign and illiberal, so that we can say, as Bertrand Russell most baldly put it 'Hitler is an outcome of Rousseau'.[18]

Although one may want to argue a case for their being related, it is important not to confuse the conceptual and the historical claims. Even the most famous – indeed iconic – criticism of Rousseauian liberty, Isaiah Berlin's 'Two Concepts of Liberty', never claimed – as do so many of those who cite it – that there was a *necessary* connection between positive liberty doctrines and oppressive, totalitarian regimes. The connection claimed was, rather, a contingent and historical one.[19]

Of the historical claims connecting Rousseau with totalitarianism I will not have much to say. The more historically sweeping of such charges are so detached from the transmission of actual ideas as either to become essentially philosophic claims, or to require unpacking into a series of more local assertions which turn out to need considerable qualification. Even in the case of Rousseau's supposed influence on the French Revolution for example, scholarship has stressed his symbolic importance, rather than the detailed influence of his doctrines.[20] Moreover, even where his political ideas were directly invoked, they were used, or rather misused, in a highly selective way: the most obvious instance of this being the way Rousseau's doctrine of popular sovereignty was allied to the principle of representation which he so explicitly deprecated.[21]

The rest of this essay focuses on the supposed philosophical identity of Rousseau's political theory and totalitarianism. I shall, I hope, quickly be able to dispose of the more extreme charges. But having done so I shall be less interested in locating Rousseau on one side of a line, than in showing how fuzzy the line is and how provocative Rousseau is in considering issues of which any theory concerned with liberty must take account.

In his synoptic study of totalitarianism, Leonard Schapiro claimed that Rousseau 'became enmeshed in an abstraction, the "general will" and failed to discern that the Utopia which he proposed, and in which he provided no safeguards for the individual against the state (why should a man need safeguards against himself?) could lead to the most complete tyranny.' Rousseau's prohibition of sectional associations, abandonment of representative government, forceful imposition of civil religion, 'these and more can be described as essential aspects of totalitarian thought and practice'.[22] Schapiro draws the criteria for this judgement from the influential analysis of totalitarianism by Carl J. Friedrich in which he identified six elements of the totalitarian 'syndrome': an official ideology directed to a perfectionist 'end', a single mass party led by an individual, subordinating or enmeshed in the state apparatus, a technically assisted monopoly of control of weapons, monopoly of the means of mass communication, the systematic application of terror as a means of police control, to which was added the central direction of the economy.[23]

One wonders at the motives of those who, even in the midst of the cold war, felt happy to link a concern for inequality with state direction of the economy, a concern for civic education with state monopoly of communications, and continually exercised direct democracy with the totalitarian subversion of its representative version.[24] For it is immediately clear that what Rousseau has to say about freedom and the state falls far short of what would admit him to the totalitarian club. Not only does he (unsurprisingly) have little to say about the modern mass party controlling the state, or its monopoly of weapons or communications, the use of terror or central direction of the economy, but even on issues where he might be thought to be sailing close to the wind – the political rather than the individual character of freedom, the importance of a civic religion, the role of censorship, and economic equality – he poses interesting questions which thoughtful liberals ought to, and have, taken seriously. This is particularly so when, as the historical influences on political theory in the last three decades as well as the current liberal–communitarian debate have led us to, we look in detail at the role played by these ideas in the whole of what Rousseau is saying, rather than using them as isolated counters out of context.

Yet, it might be claimed, this dismissal of the more obviously anachronistic elements of the case surely doesn't give the critics a run for their money. We clearly cannot expect Rousseau to have anticipated the modern technological components of totalitarianism. But is it only 'modernist' definitions of totalitarianism – those which focus on specific social and technical features of modern societies – which can so easily be shot down?[25] Amongst the ways of defining totalitarianism are not only those which attempt to identify phenomenologically, objective attributes of such polities, a device which would tend historically to localise the phenomenon, but also essentialist definitions which focus more on less measurable ideological features, imputed goals or properties of the system as a whole, an approach which lends itself more to transhistorical comparisons.[26] If we recast the criticisms and the criteria by which they are made at this higher level of abstraction, does the case against Rousseau look any stronger?

Let us review Friedrich and Schapiro's list of criteria reformulated, where possible, at a higher level of abstraction to see whether this exercise of interpretive charity sustains their applicability to Rousseau, and so illuminates the liberal or illiberal character of his thought.

'An official ideology directed to a perfectionist "end"' might be identified with Rousseau's civil religion. There is some disagreement about how deeply modern totalitarian ideology was meant to pervade the mind of the individual, but on at least some accounts this complete inner penetration is what distinguished it from old-fashioned tyranny, and both the phenomenon of the show trials and some accounts of individuals' responses to them suggest the truth of this. But Rousseau's civil religion was never meant to penetrate private belief and, indeed, like the good protestant he intermittently was, he explicitly denied that it could. The civil religion required a 'purely civil profession of faith . . . not as religious dogma . . . but as social sentiments without which a man cannot be a good citizen or a faithful subject.'[27] It is true that Rousseau's code required public recognition of 'a Deity', but if we are going to extend interpretive charity to Rousseau's totalitarian critics we should extend some to Rousseau. No state tolerated avowed atheism at the time he wrote, indeed, in famously 'liberal' England within a year of the publication of the *Social Contract* the 90-year-old Peter Annet was sentenced to be set twice in the stocks after a month in Newgate, and to a year's hard labour, for publishing supposedly atheistical literature – and unsurprisingly died shortly afterwards.[28] Rousseau's claim that the state needs some minimal declaration of allegiance to its institutions is widely recognised today by unimpeachable liberals – indeed it is acted out every morning in American schools.

As to the 'perfectionist end' it seems to me less clear that Rousseau's political commitment is to a particular view of the good, than that it is to avoiding a particular view of the bad. This is not a trivial distinction, and attention to it might generate some progress in current debates about scepticism and value pluralism. Rousseau is notoriously sketchy on the content of the general will. What he does tell us about it suggests he is concerned not to pre-empt citizens' views about where their good lay but rather to avoid two features which he sees to be objectively against their interests since destructive of their liberty. The first of these is that the general will has 'a constant tendency to equality', for serious economic inequalities destroy liberty.[29] The second stipulates that the general will can only articulate the equal subordination of all to laws which are established by all.[30]

However contentious Rousseau's arguments about material inequality, there is no doubt that this first is an *issue* which liberals can, do, and should debate. Ideals aside, it is an empirical question at what point, not whether, inequalities destroy the viability of the institutions of political liberty. In the euphoria of the collapse of communism a preoccupation with individuals' negative liberty, and the priority of Locke's message over Rousseau's might have occupied the centre stage. Five years on, the dismantling of welfare provision, growth of unemployment and obscene economic inequalities with their attendant growth in the discrepancies of power and related real civil liberty has seen unpredictable yet procedurally unimpeachable electoral revivals of socialist parties in Poland and Hungary (quite apart from more impeachable ones elsewhere), revealing second thoughts by populations with no grounds for naive optimism about collectivist prospectuses.

Secondly, Rousseau's claim to equality of legal condition, and to the operation of the rule of law was not only an extremely radical claim at the time – and one which cannot be taken for granted today – but it clearly identifies him as a liberal constitutionalist.[31]

Without wishing to open up the whole issue of liberal neutrality, it is at the least plausible to argue that if by the 'ideology' Rousseau supports one means the civil religion then it is the minimal one calculated to sustain the state. If by the 'ideology' is meant the content of the general will, then the particular content given to this by Rousseau (as opposed to the content that may be given to it by citizens) is not a totalising one but, again, the minimum necessary to avoid those features leading to the destruction of the state and its liberty. Whilst there may be argument about the point at which this destruction takes place, Rousseau rightly points out to us that a liberal political theory needs to concern itself not only with the identity of liberty, but with identifying the conditions under which that liberty can be sustained. If that necessarily leads political theory into areas which are perceived as illiberal, such as a concern with the social and economic conditions of citizens' lives and with their beliefs and values, this is less a problem in Rousseau than a problem in that particular conception of liberalism, and one which liberals ignore at their peril.

'A single mass party led by an individual, subordinating or enmeshed in the state apparatus, prohibition of sectional associations.' 'Party' of course in the eighteenth century had different connotations from what it has today. But if Rousseau was against party it was because he was against an association which threatened or had the potential to usurp the political identity of the whole. *A fortiori*, then, his position could not provide support for a party which had this aim as its very *raison d'être*, indeed, he notoriously favoured many parties if there had to be any at all.[32] In fact it is in discussing the tendencies of government to degenerate that Rousseau himself virtually identifies one analysis of totalitarianism; for it is the destruction of the rule of law and usurpation of the popular sovereign's powers by a 'government' that creates a relationship between people and rulers which is 'merely master and tyrant'.[33] Much the same defence could be made of Rousseau's attitude with respect to the 'strong leader' charge: with the exception of the legislator-figure Rousseau seemed to prefer collective, rather than individual political agency. The Legislator is a founder, not a participant in the political life of the community; good legislators, he makes clear, depart when their task is done.[34] In discussing the constitutional provision for dictatorship – the modern equivalent would be martial law or special powers – he shows great sensitivity to the potential for dictatorship in the now ordinary sense, stressing the limited term of such offices and the fact that incumbents were subsequently answerable for their conduct.[35]

As regards the charge of abandoning representative government, Rousseau was, of course, concerned that it was the *introduction* of representative government – a modern device – which signalled the loss of liberty.[36] It would take the debates surrounding the American Constitutions to establish the identity of representative institutions with republican liberty, and, even later, democracy – and this is an identity we might do well to dwell on.[37] But Rousseau was in any case writing in a context in which even the King could be considered your representative and where the identification between voting and representation was by no means secure.[38] Ironically, those who charge Rousseau with sanctioning the overriding of one's actual will in the name of a higher – or at least distinctly other – will, seemed oblivious to the fact that the device of representation can be – and particularly in the eighteenth century was – used in the same way.

About the other identifying criteria of totalitarianism less can be said. It is difficult to think of more abstract or less historically specific ways of conceiving of 'the technically assisted monopoly of control of weapons'. Rousseau, in any case, preferred a citizen militia. Central control of the means of mass communications can again hardly be reconceived in more historically abstract terms. Although Rousseau might be thought vulnerable here in defending censorship, his discussion of that office is revealing. Rousseau's Censor did not (unlike the 130 or more operating in the Direction of the Book Trade in Rousseau's time[39]) issue or withhold permissions to publish. For, in the society of the social contract, public opinion was not to be 'subject to any constraint'. What the censor did, rather, was to hold up to public ridicule actions and utterances which, he invited the public to agree, offended the civic integrity of the society. Like the stocks, the censor worked only if the public shared his sense of political vice and virtue.[40] He was ineffectual in a society where individuals did not share his outrage or disgust at the actions they were invited to disdain. It was simply – like public voting – a way of providing a public space in which reflective judgements about public values could be made: it could not itself coerce or enforce those judgements.

Whilst Rousseau was concerned about the political implications of material inequality there is no suggestion that he sanctioned – even had he been able to conceive of – the total central direction of the economy, nor does what he has to say about the importance of individual security and the rule of law lend any credence to the view that he would have supported anything like the systematic application of terror as a means of police control.

There is almost a banality about responding to these particular charges, yet they illustrate a certain point which perhaps helps resolve some of the puzzles in the historical sketch given earlier. Rousseau's *Social Contract* contains both an extremely abstract conceptual argument, and a series of practical institutional specifications of it. Indeed his failure to disentangle these two kinds of statements has been a long-standing criticism of him. Making guesses about how Rousseau's institutional proposals (themselves archaic in his own day) would translate directly into the devices of twentieth-century totalitarianism short-circuits consideration of the conceptual argument of which institutions might or might not be the expression. Because totalitarianism itself is so readily identified with techniques and institutions specific to modernity, discussions of Rousseau's totalitarianism commonly take this form, but once the anachronistic character of this way of proceeding is exposed, if we wish to continue the assessment we must move, as we have done, from the specific, historically particular institutions, to a higher level of abstraction. But the charge of totalitarianism then becomes difficult to sustain, not only because – trivially – the distinguishing features of it disappear from the frame, but because – more substantially – at that level of abstraction Rousseau is clearly dealing with issues central to the viability of liberal politics. The argument then becomes more interesting and more potentially relevant, as I shall hope to show. For the contention here is that Rousseau's political thinking operates not on any one side of a totalitarian–liberal divide but in a vital middle ground of infinite gradation in which thinking about the identity and various conditions of political freedom should proceed unencumbered by the presumption of unified totalitarian or liberal syndrome.

Perhaps the most difficult of the more abstract issues to meet concerns what Rousseau has to say about the denaturing character of political association, and in particular the distinction between natural and political freedom. Interestingly this at once differentiates him from those totalitarian ideologies of the right which invoked 'nature', identifying their claim with blood, visceral feeling, the atavistic, the tribal identity, and opposed to it the decadent, cultivated, reflective sensibility, and the civic identity. Whilst Rousseau's name and *personality* were widely and rightly associated with the cult of nature, and whilst in his view, successful legislation indeed required a people 'already bound by some unity of origin, interest or convention'[41] it is quite clear that he did not regard the social contract as an efflorescence of man's (much less woman's) nature. On this issue Rousseau flirts only with the totalitarianism of the left. The political and the natural are explicitly opposed in his thought. In a political society man's 'natural resources are annihilated', the foundation of a state involves 'changing human nature'.[42]

There are at least two versions in Rousseau of the way this can happen. According to the *Discourse on the Origins of Inequality* the foundation of political society changes human nature in unpremeditated but irrevocable ways, increasing our interdependence, our reflectivity and self-consciousness, and our exploitative capacities and dispositions over others. Although its content is changed, and changed in such a way as to engender slavery and dependence, such 'liberty' is still, as was natural liberty, exercised – where it is capable of being exercised – by individuals.

The *Social Contract* is an exploration of the possibility not of how political society could be constructed in accordance with our natures, but of how our political natures could be constructed in accord with liberty, not natural liberty – for political society is inconsistent with the full exercise of natural liberty – but political liberty.

Once we agree that the full exercise of natural liberty is impossible within political society we must give it up, seek acceptance of its political substitute or allocate natural liberty some residual space (as do thinkers as different as Hobbes and Hegel) but we cannot, consistent with our desire for political society, reject altogether the claims of political liberty. Some of Rousseau's critics accept that natural (or negative) liberty must accommodate itself to political, their charge is that he doesn't allow natural liberty enough residual space. This is a reasonable criticism, there is room for argument – and evidence – about how much can be reserved to the private individual (and under what circumstances) consistent with the maintenance of a liberal state at all. Rousseau's analysis here correctly identifies a conceptual space within which argument about liberty can take place. Whilst Rousseau thought a constitution better 'the more do public affairs encroach on private in the minds of the citizens', this preference for a particular dispositional trait in the citizens is clearly not a stipulation about a necessary or legally enforceable divide; moreover the relative scope of public and private is an issue which he clearly envisages his citizens having to settle amongst themselves.[43]

Whilst there is room for disagreement here, some of those most hostile to Rousseau seem to base their criticisms on an almost wilful misconstrual of his text. Perhaps the most notorious of these is J. L. Talmon. Rousseau, he claimed,

> was unaware that total and highly emotional absorption in the collective political endeavour is calculated to kill all privacy, and that the excitement of the assembled crowd may exercise a most tyrannical pressure, and the extension of the scope of politics to all spheres of human interest and endeavour ... was the shortest way to totalitarianism.[44]

The fact is that Rousseau shows a keen awareness of the dangers of what we might now call crowd psychology, stressing that it is 'impossible to be too careful to observe all ... the formalities necessary to distinguish a regular and legitimate act from a seditious tumult', and requiring each voter not to communicate and to 'think only his own thoughts.'[45] Once again it is an equivocation in modern conceptions of totalitarianism – conceived sometimes as atomistic sometimes as collectivist – that means Rousseau cannot win. When we seek to rebut charges of totalitarianism as herd, or crowd mentality by showing how he tries to isolate the individual's political decision-making Rousseau can then be accused of atomising society, itself a precondition identified by other, opposing conceptions of totalitarianism.

Not only does Rousseau seek to isolate individual decision-making from 'the excitement of the assembled crowd', his conception of the sovereign's scope, and intensity of activity, far from 'extending the scope of politics to all spheres', and provoking a 'highly emotional absorption' seems to suggest the opposite criticism. It seems actually far too limited in scope and low key to generate the degree of politicisation which Rousseau seems otherwise to presuppose in the individual. The 'sole object' of the Sovereign body's meetings is the 'maintenance of the social treaty', and the only two examples of agenda items Rousseau can suggest are whether the present form of the constitution should be kept, and whether the personnel of the government should be kept. This formalised, intermittent meeting, limited to dealing in generalities hardly has the flavour of the Jacobin debates, but is it even enough to generate in the individual whatever degree of identification with the public good is necessary to sustain the society?

Rousseau does observe the need for personal and private space – the social contract is designed to protect 'persons and their goods'. His point, in the famous passage about each giving himself to all, and giving himself absolutely, is not that there are no private possessions or rights, but that whatever there are have the status of being political and not natural – for if they were natural they could always be claimed against society, and could never be withheld from individuals without injustice. The *extent* of private rights – on which it is true, Rousseau expresses views, is quite a different matter from the *grounds* of them.[46]

The extent of private space which Rousseau allows is of course, for many commentators, an index of his totalitarianism. However, like many more abstract indicators, it is in danger of catching too much in its net. The idea of a 'totalising society' in which all aspects of individuals' lives come under collective scrutiny fits the Swiss village and Tocqueville's America as well as it does Stalin's Soviet Union. The issue then turns firstly on whether there is a relevant distinction between the society as a whole and the state or party apparatus doing the scrutinising. Here Rousseau is unequivocal that only the citizens, directly and as a whole may do so. The issue secondly concerns what area is reserved to the individual from the collectivity. Rousseau does not deny that there might be such an area. But how, in practice, is it to be decided where the boundary lies?

We might try to decide the boundary by appeal to objective moral or natural laws, and we know that Rousseau was aware of the possibility of such a move. However, the published version of the *Social Contract* does not refer to them, and in any case, as even Locke acknowledged, natural law has to be interpreted, only human beings or God – if we believe in him and that his history is providential – can interpret that law. Ultimately, therefore, the decisions as to where the boundary lies between public and private, and about what the public can require from us in order to preserve both our private and our public liberty is a political judgement that has to be made – because it can only be made – by the society concerned:

> What is well and in conformity with order is so by the nature of things and independently of human convention. All justice comes from God, who is its sole source; but if we knew how to receive so high an inspiration we should need neither government nor laws. Doubtless, there is a universal justice emanating from reason alone; but this justice, to be admitted amongst us, must be mutual.[47]

The principle of liberty requires that the boundary be the same for all, but it cannot tell us where the boundary is to fall; that must be decided by all, and Rousseau's only comfort is that under equality before the law, 'no-one has any interest in making them [the conditions of association] burdensome to others.'[48]

To liberal societies with well-established traditions about such distinctions, this might have looked like a threatening hostage to collectivist fortune, but without customary agreement on roughly where the boundaries lie, how else are they to be decided except by those comprising the political community? It simply *is* a feature of autonomous, democratic political communities and the evident indeterminacy of natural law and right that there is no other way of settling the issue. That a political community has (which it cannot, practically speaking, fail to have) the right to decide what falls into the public and what into the private does not entail that it will decide that issue in an illiberal way. The two issues are conceptually quite distinct, and whilst Rousseau undoubtedly expresses a preference for enlarging the public sphere, his claim that only the whole community can decide its limits distinguishes him not from defenders of individual freedom, but from divine rightists and deontologists on the one hand and anarchists on the other who deny that communities can so decide.

If the question is not the individual and abstract one – how much liberty should the individual have? – but the much more concrete and politically practical one – how much liberty can the individual have consistent with the maintenance of a state which will sustain that liberty? – then we get, I would suggest, some idea of the complexity of the problem Rousseau was trying to answer. We know that not all degrees of individual liberty, not all degrees of inequality, not all varieties of belief are consistent with political liberty. Our own experience of the rise of totalitarianism provides ample evidence that objective socio-economic factors and the changes in belief associated with them can destroy what had been formally free and liberal democracies.

Rousseau's claim, as I read him, is that if we are to be free – i.e. to be capable of sustaining free political institutions – we must avoid certain political and social states of affairs. Avoiding those outcomes constrains our (natural or individual) freedom, but it guarantees, or at least makes more likely, the maintenance of our political freedom, not to mention a good deal of individual, private freedom too. Since the unconstrained exercise of individual freedom would not guarantee or make likely the continued enjoyment of that private freedom, it seems perverse not to acknowledge that Rousseau's preoccupation with the social and economic conditions of freedom, far from necessarily leading in the direction of totalitarianism, is a preoccupation that those who value free institutions ignore at their peril.

Moreover, analytically, there is all the difference in the world between a political conception of freedom which points out certain preconditions for its realisation, and the conception, so often attributed to Rousseau of 'freedom' as the necessary pursuit of a particular goal. Having free institutions is a condition for pursuing a wide range of goals. Rousseau's conception of freedom, as I've outlined it, although it is clearly a 'positive', even an 'exercise' conception of freedom, does not thereby commit us to pursuing a particular conception of the good, only to maintaining certain institutions by which some range of conceptions of it might be pursued.

In recent debates between so-called Liberals and Communitarians, the extreme positions have been adopted by those who pursue individual rights without much thought for the kind of polity that might be needed to realise or sustain them, and communitarians whose conceptions of rationality and value are so community-bound that there seems little role for politics in resolving value differences. These have been linked to different conceptions of freedom – negative: freedom as the absence of impediments, and positive: freedom as the realisation of certain goods or goals – or opportunity and exercise conceptions of freedom, and these may be further connected in some way to 'liberal' and 'republican' traditions. Yet it is less and less clear that these distinctions or their historical affiliations can be sustained.

Recently both writers concerned with the philosophy of contemporary liberalism and those concerned with the history of conceptions of liberty have urged eirenic positions which would support the plausibility of the view attributed here to Rousseau.

Stephen Macedo, for example, has defended, against communitarian critics, a liberalism which he claims 'stands first and foremost, for individual freedom and rights, the rule of law, limited and accountable government' with the striking (and strikingly Rousseauian) claim that 'Liberal citizens ought to subordinate their personal interests to public moral principles' and again that 'liberalism positively requires that everyone's scheme of values include certain features: respect for the equal rights of others, a willingness to persuade rather than coerce, the subordination of personal plans, projects and desires to impersonal rules of law and a contribution to the provision of public goods . . . Some things are excluded completely and everything is limited and conditioned.'[49] The idea of a thickly textured liberalism with a substantive conception of the general good with some kind of eminent domain over individual private rights seems to be gaining ground.[50]

In the historical field Quentin Skinner has argued in a series of articles over the last decade or so, that far from negative and positive liberty being at odds with each other, a strong commitment to public political duty, as required by certain views of positive liberty, 'constitutes the only means of guaranteeing the very liberty we may seem to be giving up'.[51]

If these are more than straws in the wind, then the sterile opposition between a negative liberty-based liberalism which cannot give an account of the political conditions for its own existence, and a conception of positive liberty which sees the spectre of the Gulag behind every attempt to specify it, is giving way to a more fertile and supple debate in which Rousseau can take his place. Although

Rousseau's specific recommendations are often unacceptably austere, the principles informing them raise unavoidable and vital issues for the health of liberal societies.

Finally, to return very briefly to John Locke. Locke so often fails even to confront those very necessary issues which Rousseau raised, to the evident peril of his reputation as a defender of freedom. Locke notoriously avoids identifying just what rights he would attribute to individuals within political society in order to optimise its chances of survival, what political – i.e. voting – rights his theory entails or for whom, and despite a tantalising paragraph in the *First Treatise* (§43) disqualifying contracts entered out of necessity there is no pervasive recognition of the political effects of economic inequalities, nor does he have any political account of citizens' character formation. Through his defence of prerogative, Locke specifically denies that the executive is or could be ultimately subject to the rule of law, and because he has no continuing conception of Democratic sovereignty, he sees no mechanism for disciplining a delinquent government except revolution. All of these are important issues in liberal political theory, and it is Rousseau who – even if we reject his specific answers – devotes explicit attention to them.

If the horrendous experience of totalitarianism this century has anything to teach us, it is surely that free societies cannot take for granted the social, economic and belief conditions which sustain their political liberty. In a paradox which Rousseau would surely have relished it is precisely where he has appeared to some liberals most totalitarian – in his political characterisation of freedom, his collectivist concern with inequality, and in his promotion of a civic education – that he most challenges present Western polities, and it is to be hoped forces us, if not to be free, then at the very least to reflect on the conditions of our freedom.

Notes

1 I am very grateful to Robert Wokler, for encouraging me to believe (rightly or wrongly the reader will judge) that there was still something worth saying about this issue – and to him, John Hope Mason of the University of Middlesex and Eldon Eisenach of the University of Tulsa for discussions and suggestions.

2 Thus, Coleridge claimed, reason must 'clothe itself in the substance of the individual Understanding and specific inclination in order to become a reality and an object of consciousness and experience.' *The Friend*, ed. B. Rooke, 2 vols, vol. i, p. 201, *Collected Works*, vol. III. Cited in Seamus Deane, *The French Revolution and Politics in England* (Cambridge, Mass., Harvard University Press, 1988), p. 60. Deane has an excellent discussion of this, see ch. 4, 'Coleridge and Rousseau'.

3 Edmund Burke, *Reflections on the Revolution in France* (Harmondsworth, Penguin, 1968), pp. 150ff, 171–2.

4 For Constant's criticisms of Rousseau see *Benjamin Constant Political Writings*, ed. Biancamaria Fontana (Cambridge, Cambridge University Press, 1988), pp. 106 (*Spirit of Conquest and Usurpation*), 177ff (*Principles of Politics*) and 318 (*Liberty of the Ancients*) for the tenderest version: 'this sublime genius, animated by the purest love of liberty, has nevertheless furnished deadly pretexts for more than one kind of tyranny.'

5 J. S. Mill, *Representative government*, in *Utilitarianism, On Liberty and Considerations on Representative Government*, ed. H. B. Acton (London, Dent, 1987 [1861]), p. 213.

6 Mark Pattison, 'Calvin at Geneva' [1858], in *Essays*, ed. Henry Nettleship, 2 vols (Oxford, Clarendon Press, 1889), vol. II, p. 39.

7 T. H. Green, *Lectures on the Principles of Political Obligation* (London, Longman, 1966 [1882]). Rejection of contractarianism (§75–6), to salvage his conception of sovereignty (F esp. §100), identification of a higher moral and political self (§§117–18).

8 Bernard Bosanquet, *The Philosophical Theory of the State* (London, Macmillan, 1965 [1899]), ch. V, 'The Conception of a "Real Will"' and ch. VI, 'The Conception of Liberty as Illustrated by the Foregoing Suggestions'.

9 Vaughan, vol. 2, p. 517ff.

10 Vaughan, vol. 1, p. 501 (*Contrat Social*, Geneva Version).

11 Vaughan, *Epilogue*, vol. 2, p. 526.

12 L. T. Hobhouse, *The Metaphysical Theory of the State* (London, Allen and Unwin, 1926 [1918]), pp. 40–3.

13 Alfred Cobban, *Rousseau and the Modern State* (London, Allen and Unwin, 1964 [1934]), pp. 22–9.

14 A. D. Lindsay, *The Modern Democratic State* (Oxford and New York, Oxford University Press and Galaxy, 1962 [1943]), pp. 131–3.

15 J. W. Chapman, *Rousseau, Totalitarian or Liberal?* (New York, Columbia University Press, 1956), p. 75.

16 Berlin's distinction was first published in his inaugural Lecture as Chichele Professor in 1958; it was republished in *Four Essays on Liberty* in 1969 (Oxford, Oxford University Press).

17 Cited in Norman Hampson, *Will and Circumstance* (London, Duckworth, 1983), p. 250.

18 Bertrand Russell, *A History of Western Philosophy* (London, Allen and Unwin, 1959 [New York, 1945]), p. 660, a judgement which, as Ben Barber pointed out, would have pleased Hitler as little as it would have pleased Rousseau! 'Conceptual Foundations of Totalitarianism', in C. J. Friedrich, M. Curtis and B. Barber, *Totalitarianism in Perspective: Three Views* (New York and London, 1969), p. 50.

19 Isaiah Berlin, 'Two Concepts of Liberty', in D. Miller (ed.), *Liberty* (Oxford, Oxford University Press, 1991), pp. 46–7. Since Berlin's claim is so widely misrepresented as a conceptual rather than an historical one it is perhaps worth quoting it. After characterising the misuse to which the positive idea of freedom can be put he goes on: 'This magical transformation, or sleight of hand . . . can no doubt be perpetrated just as easily with the negative conception of freedom . . . But the positive conception of freedom as self-mastery . . . has, in fact, and as a matter of history, of doctrine and of practice, lent itself more easily to this' (*ibid.*, p. 47).

20 Joan MacDonald, *Rousseau and the French Revolution, 1762–1791* (London, Athlone Press, 1965); and Hampson, *Will and Circumstance*, ch. xi, allows more, but stresses the selective and opportunistic use of Rousseau's theories, for example Robespierre's adoption of the doctrine of the general will, whilst he was allowing it to be located in the representative assembly – indeed, eventually in himself.

21 For a detailed account see Keith Baker, 'Fixing the French Constitution', esp. pp. 286ff, in *Inventing the French Revolution* (Cambridge, Cambridge University Press, 1990).

22 Leonard Schapiro, *Totalitarianism* (London, Macmillan, 1972), p. 79. Schapiro does, however, record and endorse Constant's judgement absolving Rousseau from responsibility for the terror.

23 Carl. J. Friedrich, 'The Unique Character in Totalitarian Society', in *Totalitarianism*, ed. Friedrich (Cambridge, Mass., American Academy of Art and Sciences, 1954); Friedrich and Z. Brzezinski, *Totalitarian Dictatorship and Autocracy* (2nd revised ed., New York, 1966 [1965]).

24 Ben Barber and H. J. Spiro, APSA paper, 1967, 'The Concept of Totalitarianism as the Foundation of American Counter-Ideology in the Cold War', cited in Barber, 'Conceptual Foundations', p. 41.

25 For Friedrich and Brzezinski totalitarianism is an historical innovation characterised by unprecedented social changes and technical facilities, see *Totalitarian Dictatorship*, pp. 15, 24. By contrast for Karl Popper, 'what we call nowadays totalitarianism belongs to a tradition which is just as old or just as young as our civilization itself' (*The Open Society and its Enemies*, 2 vols (London, Routledge & Kegan Paul, 1966 [1945]), vol. 1, p. 1.

26 These distinctions and others are developed in Barber, 'Conceptual Foundations', pp. 10ff.

27 Jean-Jacques Rousseau, *The Social Contract*, trans. and introd. G. D. H. Cole (London, Everyman, 1968 [1913]), p. 114.

28   Ella Twynam, *Peter Annet 1693–1769* (Liverpool, n.d.).
29   *Social Contract*, p. 42.
30   *Ibid.*, pp. 25, 26, 30.
31   Rousseau's insistence on democratic sovereignty might be thought to impugn his commitment to the rule of law, but he insists that 'every assembly of the people not . . . in accordance with the prescribed forms should be regarded as unlawful.' *Social Contract*, p. 75.
32   *Ibid.*, p. 23.
33   *Ibid.*, p. 71.
34   *Ibid.*, p. 33.
35   *Ibid.*, p. 104ff.
36   *Ibid.*, p. 78.
37   See *Conceptual Change and the Constitution*, ed. T. Ball and J. G. A. Pocock (Lawrence, Kansas, Kansas University Press, 1988), esp. essays by Terence Ball, 'A Republic – If You Can Keep It', and Russell Hanson, 'Democratic Republicanism as the new American Hybrid'.
38   See the authorities cited and debates recounted in Baker, *Inventing the French Revolution*, pp. 224ff.
39   For an account see Daniel Roche, 'Censorship and the Publishing Industry' in Robert Darnton and Daniel Roche (eds), *Revolution in Print: the Press in France 1775–1800* (Berkeley and Los Angeles, University of California Press, 1989), pp. 3ff.
40   *Social Contract*, p. 105.
41   *Ibid.*, p. 41.
42   *Ibid.*, p. 32.
43   *Ibid.*, pp. 77, 24ff. See below, p. 281.
44   J. L. Talmon, *The Origins of Totalitarian Democracy* (Harmondsworth, Penguin, 1986 [Secker and Warburg, 1952]), p. 47.
45   *Social Contract*, pp. 83, 23.
46   *Ibid.*, pp. 12–13.
47   *Ibid.*, p. 29.
48   *Ibid.*, p. 12.
49   Stephen Macedo, *Liberal Virtues* (Oxford, Clarendon Press, 1990), pp. 2–3, 256, 259.
50   See, for example, many of the essays in R. Bruce Douglass, Gerald M. Mara and Henry S. Richardson (eds), *Liberalism and the Good* (London and New York, Routledge Chapman and Hall, 1990), especially William M. Sullivan, 'Bringing the Good Back In'.
51   Quentin Skinner, 'The Paradoxes of Political Liberty' (Tanner Lectures on Human Values, 1984) reprinted in *Liberty*, p. 203. See also, 'The Idea of Negative Liberty', in R. Rorty, J. B. Schneewind and Quentin Skinner (eds), *Philosophy in History* (Cambridge, Cambridge University Press, 1984) esp. pp. 217ff: 'Machiavelli has no quarrel with the Hobbesian assumption that the capacity to pursue such (selfish) ends without obstruction is what the term

"liberty" properly signifieth. He merely argues that the performance of public services and the cultivation of the virtues needed to perform them, both prove on examination to be instrumentally necessary to the avoidance of coercion and servitude, and thus to be necessary conditions of assuring any degree of personal liberty in the ordinary Hobbesian sense of the term.'

For a critique of Skinner's position, which nevertheless endorses the interconnectedness of individual and public liberty, see John Charvet, 'Quentin Skinner and the Idea of Freedom', in *Studies in Political Thought*, vol. II, 1 (1993), p. 5ff.

Index

Académie des sciences morales et politiques 75
Académie française 91
Alceste 105, 115
America and United States 74–5, 86–7, 167, 228, 274, 276, 280
amour de soi and self-love 32–3, 37, 177, 182, 204, 235
amour propre, egoism and vanity 2–4, 7–8, 11, 16, 20–1, 32, 35, 37–8, 42, 47, 176, 204, 235
anarchism 46, 282
ancien régime ix, 70–1, 85, 89, 268
ancients and moderns 7–8, 11, 23, 40, 50, 61, 73, 90, 114–15, 124, 135, 166–7, 170, 172, 193, 195–200, 208, 210, 213–14, 216–20, 226, 273, 277
animals 61, 156–8, 203–4, 231
Annet, P. 274
Aquinas, St Thomas 76
Argenson, Marquis d' 162
aristocracy 79, 83, 239
Aristotle 2, 10, 29, 108, 156, 159, 247
  Politics 82
Arnauld, A. 2
arts and sciences ix, 29, 32, 37, 54, 61, 81, 115, 201, 252, 257
atheism 60, 274
Athens 118, 126, 128
Augustine, St, and Augustinianism x, 13
  De Libero Arbitrio 8, 12

authority 3–4, 7–10, 16, 18, 21, 23, 31, 42, 76, 80, 84, 104–5, 122, 128, 130, 133, 140, 143–4, 146–7, 159, 173, 193–4, 196, 208, 223–4, 226, 228, 238, 244–5, 251, 255, 257–60
Babeuf, G. 261
Baczko, B.
  'Moïse, législateur' 1
Baker, F. xi, 152–85
Bantock, G. H. 106
barbarism, savagery and primitivism 17, 82, 105, 202–3, 205, 231–2, 235–7, 239, 269
Barbeyrac, J. 81–3
Barry, N. x, 29–52
Bayle, P.
  Pensées sur le comète 4
Beccaria, C. 169
Benn, S. 101–2, 113, 119
Bentham, J. 30
Berlin, Sir I. xii, 74, 118, 199, 204, 206, 259, 263, 271
  Four Concepts of Liberty 244
  'Two Concepts of Liberty' 272
Berthier, G. F., père 71
Blake, W. 11
Bonald, Vicomte de 268
Bonapartism 71–2, 74, 80, 84, 86–8, 91
Bonnet, C. 55–6, 60–1, 63
  'Letter from Philopolis' 55, 58–60, 65
Bosanquet, B. 269–70
botany 55, 202

Brandeis, Justice L 253
Bruni, L. 82
Buffon, Comte de 55
Buonarroti, P. 261
Burke, E. 76, 192, 268

Caesar, Julius 84, 91
Caligula xii, 155–9, 163, 179, 182–3
Cambridge 267
Calvin and Calvinism 6, 118, 269
Cassirer, E. 247, 271
Castel, L. B.
  L'Homme moral opposé à l'homme physique 66
Catholicism x, 63, 71
Cato (the younger) 105
censorship ix, 115, 117–18, 175, 252, 256, 273, 277
Cessa, M. de 88
Chapman, J. W. 271
Charvet, J. xi, 9, 139–51
childhood and children 103–4, 106, 126, 190, 221, 225, 252
Christ, Jesus 261
Christianity 18, 20, 29, 166
Chronologie universelle 18
Cicero 197
citizen and citizenship x–xi, 4, 9–11, 16–18, 20–2, 24, 29, 35, 45–6, 49–51, 63, 70–1, 86–8, 99, 103–4, 106–11, 114–16, 118, 124, 128–30, 133–4, 139–41, 146, 160, 163, 165–6, 168–9, 173–5, 179, 182, 190, 193–8, 207, 213, 216–17, 219–22, 238–9, 241, 247, 251–6, 258–9, 262, 268, 274–5, 277, 279, 281, 283–4
civilisation and culture ix, xiii, 17, 34–5, 37, 39, 90, 134, 176, 181, 199–202, 208, 213, 216, 220, 231, 233, 248, 253, 261, 268
Code Napoléon 228

Cole, G. D. H. 77, 81, 271
Coleridge, S. T. 268
commerce, luxury and commercial society ix, 29, 31, 35–40, 44, 46, 48, 50, 70, 80–1, 134, 207, 241
common or public good 4, 7, 9, 19–20, 29, 43, 45–7, 49, 196–8, 207, 215, 220, 241, 258, 280, 283
communism 267, 275
community, communitarianism and collectivism x–xiii, 7, 29, 30–4, 38–40, 44–5, 48–50, 63, 73, 99, 102, 107–8, 110, 113, 116–18, 139–40, 143–6, 149, 160, 166, 168, 170–1, 178, 182–3, 195–6, 204, 209, 217, 241, 245, 248–9, 251, 255, 263, 268–70, 273, 275, 279–84
Condorcet, Marquis de 110
Confessions 54, 56–7, 60, 66, 251, 263
conscience 6, 14, 125–6, 145, 148–9, 196, 223, 236, 240, 247
consent 4–5, 7, 22, 77, 81–2, 122, 125, 132, 238, 255, 258
conservatism ix, 43–4, 49, 76, 104, 228
Constant, B. 76, 84, 86–7, 191, 197, 269
constitutionalism 71, 87–8, 123, 126, 139–41, 146–7, 228, 238, 275–6, 279–80
contract, association and obligation xi, 4, 7, 9–10, 13, 15, 20–2, 30–1, 34, 36, 40, 43, 45–6, 48, 78–80, 100–2, 107–8, 121–3, 128–9, 139–51, 160–4, 168, 170–1, 173–4, 180, 182, 192, 194, 197, 204, 206, 233–4, 237, 249, 254, 259, 269–70, 277–8, 280, 284

Index

Conzié, F. J. de 57, 60–1
Corsica 85, 208, 241, 257–9
Cranston, M. xii, 231–43
crime and criminality 125, 159, 166, 168, 171–2, 175–7, 179–80, 182
Crocker, L. xii, 74, 76, 192, 244–66
Cromwell, O. x, 84, 91
custom and convention 16–17, 42, 44, 113, 257

Dahl, R. 109
Darwin, C., and Darwinism 62
death penalty xii, 115, 125–6, 152–85
decadence and corruption 37, 82, 208–9, 216–18, 227, 233, 247, 252, 276, 278
Defoe, D.
  Robinson Crusoe 203, 240
De Maistre, J. 192, 268
democracy x, 70–95, 109, 112, 115–16, 121, 130, 135, 153, 168, 192, 194, 228, 238–9, 255, 259, 267, 273, 276, 281–2, 284
denaturation xiii, 1–3, 7, 10, 16, 20, 22, 103, 107–8, 127, 202, 210, 235, 247, 249, 253, 255, 278
dependence and interdependence x, 35–7, 40, 108, 122–4, 126, 128–9, 133, 141, 170, 172, 192, 194, 208, 215, 220–3, 227, 229, 232, 234, 236, 241, 278–9
Derathé, R. 75, 191–2, 271
Descartes and Cartesianism 225
despotism, tyranny and demagogues ix–xi, 76–8, 80–4, 87, 89–91, 121, 130, 133, 150, 152, 158–9, 172, 179, 183, 190, 192, 195, 197, 200, 209–10, 245–6, 269, 271, 273, 276, 279

Dewey, J. 103
dictatorship 71–2, 74, 84, 88, 276
Diderot, D. 16–20, 190
'Droit naturel' 17
Dilthey, W. 254
Discourse on Arts and Sciences x, 54–5, 64, 199, 201, 263
Discourse on Inequality (Second Discourse) x, xii, 5, 9–10, 13, 19, 33, 37, 40, 53–6, 58–9, 65–6, 72, 76–7, 80–2, 86, 90, 105, 123, 156–7, 163, 170, 174, 195, 200, 202–3, 208, 214, 216, 232–4, 237–9, 241, 246, 259, 263, 278
'Discourse on Political Economy' 2, 7–9, 20–1, 40, 77, 125, 133, 196, 249, 251, 256

economics 47, 70–1, 113, 134, 198–9, 201, 208, 236, 241, 250, 257–8, 262, 273, 275, 277, 282, 284
education x–xi, 2, 6, 8–11, 16, 23, 41, 88, 99, 102–5, 107–8, 112, 126, 128, 134, 190, 213, 215, 221–3, 225–6, 228, 240, 250–1, 256
  civic and political 1, 3–4, 7, 9, 18, 20, 22, 103, 109, 114, 133, 273, 284
Emile xii, 2, 3, 5–10, 14, 20, 23, 66, 75, 77, 102–9, 111–12, 114, 116, 118, 126, 168, 171, 213, 215, 218, 220–8, 240, 248–52, 257, 261–2
'Profession of Faith of Savoyard Vicar' 5, 14, 23, 105, 240, 249
empiricism x, 11, 32–3
Encyclopédie and Encyclopedists ix, 17, 66, 231
Encyclopédie méthodique 88
England and Great Britain xiii, 154, 194

Enlightenment ix, 10, 20, 67, 88, 90–1, 104, 131, 134, 152, 159, 164, 181, 202, 214, 216–17, 225
Epicurus and Epicureanism 57
equality and inequality x, 9, 35, 38–43, 46–7, 49, 54, 70–2, 74, 78, 80–1, 84–91, 113, 128, 143–7, 155, 157, 159, 162, 165, 170, 198–201, 207, 214–15, 217, 220–2, 224–5, 228, 232–6, 246, 258, 261, 270, 273, 275, 277, 281–2, 284
Essay on Origin of Languages 173, 199–201
Europe ix, 54, 70, 72, 85, 114, 129, 154, 209, 228, 267

family 127, 129–30, 222–3, 225–6, 228–9, 234, 241, 253
fanaticism 152–4, 173, 180
Fascism and National Socialism 154, 183, 246, 270
femininity and masculinity 214–20, 226, 228, 234
Fénelon, Archbishop 2, 4, 11, 18
Fichte, J. G. 121, 131, 270
'Final Reply' (to Borde) 54
force x–xi, 2–4, 9–10, 72–3, 75, 77–8, 80, 88, 121–5, 127–9, 131, 134, 162, 173, 190, 193–4, 208, 256–7, 260, 269, 284
France and French x, 23, 61, 70–4, 85, 87–8, 90, 154, 165, 171
Francueil, Mme de 236
fraternity xii, 114, 127–8, 190, 198–9, 210, 219, 248, 262
French Revolution ix, xii, 70–1, 73–5, 84–6, 88–91, 153, 192–3, 197–8, 272
Freud, S. 177
Friedrich, C. J. 273–4
Furet, F. 256

Gay, P. 107–8
Geneva 9, 16–18, 20–1, 55, 79, 115–17, 129, 135, 194–5, 216, 219–20, 238–9, 241, 252
Genoa 124
Germany, Prussia and Teutonic 11, 16, 21
Goethe, J. W. von 135
government x, 40–2, 44, 48, 50, 71–5, 79–81, 83, 87–8, 90, 123–4, 130, 133, 156, 174–6, 179, 190, 193–5, 200, 208–9, 216, 231, 233, 236–9, 241, 244–5, 254, 256–8, 273, 276, 280–1, 283–4
Government of Poland 7, 9, 17, 20, 77, 107, 114, 197–8, 257
Greece and Greeks 83, 126, 156, 172, 195, 219
Green, T. H.
 Lectures on Political Obligation 269
Grotius, H. 75, 81–3, 156, 159, 204
 De iure belli ac pacis 83, 204
Guizot, F. 73, 76, 86
Gutmann, A. 118

Hampsher-Monk, I. xiii, 267–88
happiness and unhappiness 15, 20, 65, 132, 134–5, 162, 173, 208, 215, 221–2, 248, 256, 259, 261, 263
Harari, J. V.
 Scenarios of Imagination 257
Hegel, G. W. F. x, 3–4, 12, 21–2, 119, 191, 270, 279
 Phenomenology of Spirit 6
 Philosophy of Right 21
Hitler, A. 209, 272
Hobbes, T. xi, 4–5, 33, 35, 43–5, 75, 131, 134–5, 139, 141–2, 144–5, 147–9, 156, 159, 191, 195, 197, 200–1, 203–5, 233, 237–8, 279

Hobhouse, L. T. 270
Holbach, Baron d' 60
homogeneity and conformity 134–5, 245, 259–60
Hook, S. 261
Hope Mason, J. xi, 121–38
Houdetot, Mme d' 240
human nature and natural man x, 5, 15, 30, 32–3, 37, 39, 42–4, 56, 58, 100, 128, 157, 190–1, 201, 204–6, 208–10, 217, 220, 224–5, 244–6, 260, 262, 278
Hume, D. x, 29–38, 40–5, 47–50, 190
  'Of Commerce' 30, 50
  'On the Original Contract' 77
  Treatise of Human Nature 32–3
Hungary 275

imagination 153–6, 163, 165, 179, 181–3, 198–9, 208–10, 247, 253, 258, 261
individualism and individuality x–xi, xiii, 1, 4, 7, 29–31, 34, 42–3, 46, 48–9, 71, 88, 90, 99, 118, 129, 134, 191, 206, 260, 267–71, 281
Institutions politiques 76
interest and self-interest 7, 37, 49, 73, 112, 128, 133–4, 141–2, 148–9, 181, 196–7, 199–200, 207, 249, 281

Jackson, A. 71
Jacobinism 193, 197, 280
Jouvenel, B. de 6
justice and injustice 6, 17, 19, 31, 33–4, 40, 42, 44, 46, 48, 59, 121, 123, 126–8, 133, 140, 144, 146–50, 160, 162, 166–9, 171–3, 175, 178, 200, 204, 220, 226, 233, 239, 248–9, 257, 281

Kant, I. x, 3–6, 9, 11–16, 18–22, 50, 149, 191, 240, 270
  Critique of Practical Reason 15
  Critique of Pure Reason 13–15
  Grundlegung zur Metaphysik der Sitten 6, 15
  Religion within Limits of Reason Alone 16
Kelly, C. x, 53–69
Kendall, W. 114
Kergolay, L. de 75
Kierkegaard, S. 119
Klein, M. 177
Königsberg 16

Laclos, C. 106
Laqueur, T. 214
Larkin, P. 104
Laslett, P. 267
law 3–4, 11–12, 15, 17, 30, 32–4, 36, 41, 43–5, 48, 50–1, 80–1, 84, 100, 108, 114–15, 119, 123–32, 134–5, 139–41, 143–4, 146, 148, 150, 153–5, 160, 162–5, 170–6, 178–9, 191, 193–4, 200, 228, 231, 233, 236–7, 239, 247, 249, 251, 254, 256, 262, 275, 281
  natural 19, 31, 41, 61, 82, 108, 127, 130–1, 135, 142–4, 147, 149–50, 195, 204, 214, 251, 270, 281
  rule of xi, 4, 36, 123–5, 127–8, 180, 192, 195, 275–7, 283–4
legislation and participation 29, 36, 44–45, 50–1, 85–8, 90, 99, 112, 116–17, 124–5, 128–32, 139, 141, 189–92, 194, 196, 199, 208, 237–9, 241, 244–5, 248, 254, 259–60, 278
legislator xiii, 2, 8, 14, 19, 42–3, 131–3, 153, 157, 164, 173, 179, 190–1, 194, 197, 209–10, 247, 251, 255–6, 263, 276

legitimacy 70–95, 130, 132, 141, 155, 160, 162, 165, 170, 172, 216, 270, 280
Leibniz, G. W. 2, 4, 55–6, 58–60, 64
Leigh, R. A. 60, 74, 114, 192, 196, 267
Le Roy L. G. x, 55, 61–2
Lenin, V. I. 261
Letters from the Mountain 14, 123, 194, 239
Letter to d'Alembert on the Theatre xii, 71, 112, 114–17, 153–4, 173, 182, 198, 201, 215–20, 227, 252
'Letter to Philopolis' 56, 58–9, 61–2
'Letter to Voltaire' (on optimism) 55, 57, 59–63, 66
Lettre à M. de Beaumont 4, 252
'Lettre à M. de Franquières' 3, 23
Lettres morales 5–6, 14, 209, 240
Levi, P. 258
Lévi-Strauss, C. 166
liberalism ix, xiii, 43, 46, 48–51, 73–4, 76, 80, 86–7, 107, 115, 118, 121, 134, 167, 183, 189, 192–7, 200–3, 205, 209–10, 228, 238, 244–5, 261, 267–76, 278, 281–4
libertarian and libertarianism 191, 205, 207, 245, 262–3
liberty or freedom
  as absence of opposition 237
  absolute 80, 231
  anarchic 231, 233, 237
  ancient ix, 195, 197–8, 216
  of association 88
  as autonomy or self-determination ix, xi, 1, 3, 8–10, 15–16, 21, 37, 73, 99–120, 195, 199, 222, 226, 229, 231–2, 234–5, 245, 252, 281
  of choice 157, 246
  civil xii, 30, 32, 42–3, 45, 79, 124, 195, 197, 199, 206–10, 237, 239, 275
  collectivist 205
  common 128
  of conscience 206
  as control 58
  corporate 270
  economic xii, 30, 207–8, 241
  exchanged 43
  fundamental 200
  hypothetical 201
  illusory 200
  inchoate 203
  as independence 10, 14, 19, 21, 35, 38, 87, 91, 106–7, 127, 141, 190, 196, 201–3, 215, 221, 223, 226–7, 231–2, 234, 252, 262
  individual 30, 45, 49, 134, 171, 197, 245, 262, 270, 273, 282–3
  as innocence 201
  from law 231
  under law 50, 135, 237
  of love 206–7
  metaphysical 231, 239
  modern 197, 199
  moral xii, 100, 195–7, 199, 206–10, 239–40
  natural xii, 30, 32, 40, 42–3, 45, 130, 156, 190, 197, 199–203, 206, 208–9, 219, 231–3, 278, 279
  negative xii–xiii, 13–15, 30, 203, 206, 208, 244, 259, 271, 275, 278–9, 282–3
  as obedience to law 189, 238–9
  original 162, 199, 208
  personal 129, 190, 193, 197–8, 207, 209, 221, 229, 231, 240, 258
  political 29, 59, 72, 79, 124, 173, 193, 197, 215, 217–18, 229, 236–7, 239–41, 267, 270, 273, 275, 278–9, 282, 284

positive xii–xiii, 14, 30, 74, 199, 201, 208, 244, 259, 271–2, 282–3
practical 67
of the press 88, 206
as privacy 197
private 281–2
public 198, 216–17, 281
rational 22
as rebelliousness 263
republican 218, 276
as security 32
as self-control 227, 269
as self-direction 244
as self-government 104, 270
as self-reliance 196
as self-rule 237–9
as self-sufficiency 35–8, 40, 112, 215, 221
sexual xii, 240
as silence of law 237
social 33
as solitude 192, 209, 240
of speech 206
as spontaneity 36, 113, 117
of the stage 206–7
of thought 102
from want 232
of the will 30–1, 53, 58, 65–7, 204, 231–2, 239
Liberty Fund 267
Lindsay, A. D. 270–1
Lisbon 66
Locke, J. 4, 8, 10–11, 22, 41, 43, 45, 101, 139, 141–2, 181, 190, 192, 195, 204–5, 238, 275, 281, 284
First Treatise of Government 284
Second Treatise of Government 19, 267
Louis XIV (king of France) 86
Lycurgus 1–3, 8, 10, 16, 18, 131, 210, 253

Macedo, S. 283
Machiavelli, N. 131, 193, 197
The Prince 71
Mackintosh, Sir J. 268
Malebranche, N. 2, 4, 7–8, 10–11, 18, 63
Malesherbes, C. G. de 8, 240
Mandeville, B. 35, 134
Manuscrit de Genève (Première version du Contrat social) 4–5, 13, 16, 18–20, 72, 82, 121, 132, 157, 165
Marx, K., and Marxism 36, 121, 191, 207–8, 262
Masters, R. x, 53–69, 249
materialism 23, 60, 65, 90
militia 277
Mill, J. S. 30, 190, 269
moeurs and mores 87, 128–9, 216, 252, 256
Molière 115, 216
Le Misanthrope 105, 115
monarch, prince and monarchy xii, 71–2, 79–80, 83, 89, 142, 157, 175–6, 178–9, 182, 209, 216, 238, 276
Montaigne, M. de 197
Montesquieu, baron de 1, 22, 35, 70, 75–6, 82–3, 86, 131, 174, 190, 193, 197
Lettres persanes 172
Spirit of the Laws 125, 178–9
morality and immorality 1–7, 12–14, 16–17, 19–21, 23–4, 29–30, 32, 34–5, 39–40, 42, 45, 56, 58–9, 63–5, 74, 84, 90, 101, 108, 115–16, 124, 126–7, 133, 144, 146–50, 153, 159–61, 168, 178, 180, 189–90, 192, 194, 200–4, 208–9, 213, 215, 217–21, 224–5, 228–9, 239, 247, 251, 253, 257–60, 269, 277, 283
Moses 1–3, 8, 11, 16, 18, 210, 262

music and theatre 57, 112–13, 115–16, 126, 201, 216

Napoleon I xi, 72–5, 79–80, 84–6, 88–9, 91
Napoleon III 72, 74
Nature 16, 31, 56, 60–2, 65, 104–5, 135, 200, 203, 213, 215–16, 233, 236, 240, 248–50, 257, 261, 278
  political 279
Neuchâtel 118, 157
Newgate 274
New Héloïse (Julie) xii, 13–14, 66, 167, 198, 213, 241, 247–8, 250–3, 257, 259–62
Newton, Sir I. 13, 61
Nietzsche, F. 119, 121
Nisbet, R. 76, 250, 255–6
Numa 1, 8, 10, 18, 131, 210

Oeuvres complètes 75
optimism and progress x, 32, 55–9, 61–5, 67, 152, 217, 275
Orpheus 132
Ozouf, M.
  La Fête révolutionnaire 254

Palmer, R. R.
  Age of the Democratic Revolution 254
Paris 57, 60, 72, 104–5, 115–18, 219
Parry, G. xi, 99–120
Pascal, B. 2, 4, 6, 11, 23, 75–6
passions and feelings 5, 17–20, 38, 105, 127, 133, 152–3, 163, 169, 173, 177, 181, 183, 204, 208, 215, 221, 226–7, 233, 235–7, 239–40
patriotism 126–7, 134, 253, 256
Pattison, P. 269
Pelagius 6, 23
perfectibility and perfectionism 33–4, 65, 67, 157, 204, 232, 274

Philo of Alexandria 156, 159
  Embassy to Gaius 158
philosophes ix, 60, 269
philosophy of history xii, 201, 203, 228
pity, compassion and sympathy 33, 35, 37–8, 178, 182
Plamenatz, J. 191–2
Plato and Platonism 1–2, 8, 11, 15, 112, 115, 158, 193, 247–8
  Crito 126–7, 129
  Euthyphro 2
  Meno 16
  Phaedo 2
  Phaedrus 1, 12
  Protagoras 2
  Republic 1–2, 7, 103, 203, 222
  Statesman 157
plebiscite 71–2, 74, 88, 259
pluralism 114–15, 118, 245–6, 270, 274
Plutarch 131, 197
Poland and Poles 114, 133, 198, 208, 275
Polin, R. 259
Pope, A. 55–6, 58–9, 63–4
  Essay on Man 57
Popper, K. 270
Portalis, J. E. M. 228
power xii, 4–5, 7, 13–15, 22, 40, 44, 71–2, 76, 80, 83, 87–91, 121, 130–3, 143–4, 146–8, 150, 153, 155, 159, 171, 174, 179, 182–3, 190–1, 193–5, 204, 208, 218, 221, 226–7, 244–7, 252–60, 275
Project of Constitution for Corsica 77, 85, 198, 241, 247, 257–9
property x, 34, 39–43, 77, 81, 85, 90, 171, 200–1, 204–5, 207, 223, 229, 232–3, 236, 241, 258
Protestants and Protestantism 6, 165–7, 169–71, 274
Proudhon, P. J. 192

Index

providence 55–6, 58–60, 63–4
public and private xii, 7, 10, 19, 21, 29, 36, 44–6, 49–51, 107–9, 112–13, 115, 117, 139–42, 144, 189–90, 198–9, 219–20, 223, 241, 245, 250, 253, 257, 279–82
Pufendorf, S. 75, 81–3, 204
  De iure naturae et gentium 83
  De officio hominis et civis 82

Rawls, J. xi, 150
Reale, M. 256
reason and rationality 3–4, 6, 8, 11, 13–21, 23, 31–2, 41, 49, 146, 152–3, 172–4, 181, 215, 236, 244, 248, 261, 268, 281, 283
religion and theology ix–x, 2, 4–8, 10–12, 14, 16, 21–2, 53–4, 57, 60–2, 65, 73, 105, 128–9, 133, 142, 145, 148–50, 153–4, 158–66, 168, 170, 173–4, 179, 181, 191–2, 199, 201, 206, 209, 223, 253, 257, 262, 268, 281–2
  civil religion xii, 55, 63, 73, 107, 114–15, 152–3, 155, 158–60, 162–5, 168–9, 173–5, 177–8, 180, 182–3, 197, 252, 258, 273–5
representation 70, 72–3, 76, 88, 115–16, 142, 153–4, 163–4, 169, 171, 194, 272–3, 276
republic and republicanism xii, 1, 3–4, 18, 20, 22, 35, 36, 40, 43, 47, 71, 79, 81, 84, 91, 99, 108, 112, 115–16, 124, 132, 193, 195, 198, 206, 213–16, 220–1, 225, 238–40, 283
Restif, N. E. 258
Reveries 203
revolution and revolutionaries 70–2, 74, 80, 85, 168, 209, 247, 257, 261–3, 268, 271, 284

Richter, M. x–xi, 70–95
rights
  civil or political 86–7, 122, 128, 162, 245, 258, 270, 280, 284
  moral 144, 235
  natural, human or individual xiii, 41, 44–5, 71–3, 77, 85, 88, 100, 127–9, 142–4, 150, 162, 166, 190, 197, 223, 237, 245–6, 253–8, 263, 280, 282–3
Riley, P. x, 1–28, 63
Robespierre, M. 22, 131, 262
romanticism ix, 41, 215, 244
Rome and Romans 3–4, 7, 11, 17–18, 20, 84, 103, 112, 195, 198
Roosevelt, F. 232
Rousseauism ix, xi, 22, 172
Royer-Collard, P. P. 86
Russell, B. 272
Russia and Soviet Union 114, 280

Sade, Marquis de 248
  New Justine 205
Saint-Denis 104
Saint-Just, L. A. L. de 131, 245, 271
Sallust 131
Scanlon, T. x, 150
scepticism 60, 62, 65, 274
Schapiro, L. 272, 274
Schleifer, J. 70
Scotland 118
security 82, 101, 107, 142, 149, 277
Seneca 197
sexuality and love xii, 1, 103, 208, 213–18, 220–9, 234–5, 241, 257
Shakespeare, W.
  Hamlet 22
  Henry V 3
  Othello 175
Shklar, J. 1
Sidney, A. 131
Skinner, B. F. 251

Skinner, Q. 283
slavery and servitude xii, 4, 7, 36, 80–3, 89, 100–1, 105, 118, 123, 155, 170–2, 174, 199–201, 204, 207, 226, 231, 234–6, 239–41, 261–2, 269, 279
Smith A. x, 29–32, 34–50, 189, 207–8
  Lectures on Jurisprudence 41
  Theory of Moral Sentiments 38
sociability 34–5, 42, 114, 153, 160, 163–4, 174, 183, 205, 217–19
Social Contract xi–xii, 2, 4, 7, 14, 19, 30, 33, 36, 40, 42, 44, 66, 71–2, 75–83, 86, 90, 97–185, 191, 195–6, 198–9, 202, 208, 213–14, 233, 237–9, 246–7, 249, 251–2, 254, 256–9, 267, 274, 277, 279, 281
socialism 207, 275
society and civil society xii, 19–20, 29, 31, 33–4, 39–42, 44, 46, 48, 55, 65, 78, 84, 101–4, 108, 113, 130–2, 134, 144, 148, 155–6, 166, 174, 183, 197, 199–200, 202–3, 205, 208, 220–1, 225, 227, 231, 234–8, 240, 245–50, 254, 256–7, 259–63, 277, 279–81, 284
  nascent 232–4
Socrates 126, 128–9
Solon 131
Sophocles
  Antigone 22
sovereignty xii, 6, 31, 45, 50, 73, 78–80, 83, 89, 122, 124, 130, 139–51, 160, 162–4, 169, 171, 173–5, 179, 182, 189–91, 193–5, 199–200, 209, 237–8, 254, 269, 280, 284
  popular xi, 40, 71–4, 77, 80, 87, 89, 193, 195, 237–8, 245, 255, 257, 272, 276

Sparta 3–4, 7–8, 11, 16–18, 20, 103, 108, 118, 133, 195, 198, 219–20, 239
Spinoza, B. de 14, 260
Staël, Mme de 86
Stalin, J. 209, 280
Starobinski, J. 72, 116–17
state of nature 32–5, 53, 123, 127–8, 130, 139, 141–5, 147–9, 182, 197, 200–1, 203–5, 208, 231–4, 237–8, 240
Stoicism 14, 18
Switzerland 16, 217, 280

Talmon, J. L. 73–4, 76, 192, 270, 279
Terror 22, 73–4, 76, 86, 121, 173, 178, 182, 253, 259, 273, 277
Thrasymachus 7
Thucydides 105
Tocqueville, A. de x–xi, 70, 72, 74–6, 84–7
  Ancien Régime 91
  Democracy in America 70, 75–6, 84, 89, 228, 280
  Souvenirs 91
toleration 115, 121, 161, 163–8, 175, 177–81
totalitarianism xiii, 43, 73, 121, 133, 172, 180, 182, 192, 244–5, 253, 255, 258, 267–88
Trotsky, L. 261
tyrannicide 179–80, 183

universalism 3, 11, 16–22, 33, 44
utility and utilitarianism 10, 30–1, 34, 40, 48

Vaughan, C. E. 270
  Political Writings of Rousseau (ed.) xiii, 269
Versailles 61
Vincennes 57

Vine, R.
  'Walter Benjamin' 258
violence ix, 2, 6, 44, 73, 152–5, 159–60, 162–3, 172–4, 176, 178, 180, 183, 192, 209, 260
Vogel, U. xii, 213–30
Voltaire x, 55–63, 65–6, 75, 192
  Candide 57, 263
  'Poème sur le Désastre de Lisbonne' 55
  'Poème sur la Loi naturelle' 55
voting and elections 45–7, 49, 73, 79, 108, 110–11, 117, 125, 169, 239, 256, 258, 270, 276–7, 280, 284

Waldron, J. 111
Warens, Mme de 173
Warrender, H. 191
Wartensleben, Comtesse de 168
Westminster Review 269

will, real will and volition 1–18, 21–4, 29–30, 32, 45, 47, 51, 89–90, 100–1, 106, 109, 123–5, 129–30, 132, 140–2, 144–5, 179, 190–1, 194, 196–7, 208, 222, 228, 238, 248–9, 253–6, 258, 260–1, 269–70
  general, particular and majority x–xi, 1–28, 45–9, 63, 72–3, 78–9, 89, 99, 106, 108–11, 115, 117, 122, 124, 139–41, 144–6, 174, 176, 189, 192–3, 195–8, 207, 248–9, 254, 256, 259–60, 270, 272, 274–5
William of Moerberke 82
Wokler, R. xii, 17, 74, 189–212
Wolff, R. P. 101
Wollstonecraft, M. 225
women 213–30, 234–5, 241
Wright, E. H. 271